El Sistema

EL SISTEMA
Orchestrating Venezuela's Youth

Geoffrey Baker

OXFORD
UNIVERSITY PRESS

OXFORD
UNIVERSITY PRESS

Oxford University Press is a department of the
University of Oxford. It furthers the University's objective
of excellence in research, scholarship, and education
by publishing worldwide.

Oxford   New York

Auckland   Cape Town   Dar es Salaam   Hong Kong   Karachi
Kuala Lumpur   Madrid   Melbourne   Mexico City   Nairobi
New Delhi   Shanghai   Taipei   Toronto

With offices in

Argentina   Austria   Brazil   Chile   Czech Republic   France   Greece
Guatemala   Hungary   Italy   Japan   Poland   Portugal   Singapore
South Korea   Switzerland   Thailand   Turkey   Ukraine   Vietnam

Oxford is a registered trade mark of Oxford University Press
in the UK and certain other countries.

Published in the United States of America by
Oxford University Press
198 Madison Avenue, New York, NY 10016

Library of Congress Cataloging-in-Publication Data
Baker, Geoffrey, 1970-
El Sistema : orchestrating Venezuela's youth / Geoffrey Baker.
pages   cm
Includes bibliographical references and index.
ISBN 978-0-19-934155-9 (hardback : alk. paper)
1. Fundación Musical Simón Bolívar—History.   2. Music and youth—Venezuela.
3. Music—Social aspects—Venezuela.
4. Symphony orchestras—Venezuela—History.   I. Title.
ML26.F864   2014
780.71'087—dc23   2014012628

This volume is published with the generous support of the Manfred
Bukofzer Endowment of the American Musicological Society, funded in part by the National
Endowment for the Humanities and the Andrew W. Mellon Foundation.

1 3 5 7 9 8 6 4 2

Printed in the United States of America
on acid-free paper

For L. B. C.

CONTENTS

ACKNOWLEDGMENTS

Due to the nature of this research, I am unable to thank my collaborators in Venezuela by name. Nevertheless, I gratefully acknowledge the help of dozens of musicians, cultural officials, and journalists who gave up hours of their spare time to share their views and concerns about El Sistema. Without them, there would be no book.

In the United Kingdom and the United States, a number of people made valuable comments on written and spoken versions of this material. I am particularly grateful to Sophia Blackwell for her fine editorial work on two drafts of the book, and to Lucy Green, Julia Buxton, Elizabeth Eva Leach, Flávia Narita, and Anna Bull for reading and providing feedback on the complete manuscript, even if I was unable to act on all their excellent suggestions. Responsibility for the final content is entirely mine.

My thanks to all at Oxford University Press, especially Suzanne Ryan, Adam Cohen, and Richard Johnson, and to the reviewers of my manuscript.

LIST OF ACRONYMS

CAP	Carlos Andrés Pérez (twice president of Venezuela)
CASM	Centro de Acción Social por la Música (Center for Social Action through Music)
CONAC	Consejo Nacional de la Cultura (National Council for Culture)
CYO	Caracas Youth Orchestra
EPATU	Escuelas Para las Artes y Tradiciones Urbanas (Schools for Urban Arts and Traditions)
FESNOJIV	Fundación del Estado para el Sistema Nacional de Orquestas Juveniles e Infantiles de Venezuela (Venezuelan State Foundation for the National System of Youth and Children's Orchestras)
IDB	Inter-American Development Bank
IRCAM	Institut de Recherche et Coordination Acoustique/Musique (Paris)
IUDEM	Instituto Universitario de Estudios Musicales (University Institute of Musical Studies)
JAL	José Ángel Lamas Conservatoire
ODILA	Orquesta de Instrumentos Latinoamericanos (Orchestra of Latin American Instruments)
OSV	Orquesta Sinfónica de Venezuela
SBSO	Simón Bolívar Symphony Orchestra
SBYO	Simón Bolívar Youth Orchestra
TCYO	Teresa Carreño Youth Orchestra
TED	Technology, Entertainment, Design
UCAB	Universidad Católica Andrés Bello (Andrés Bello Catholic University)
ULA	Universidad de Los Andes (University of the Andes)
WEDO	West-Eastern Divan Orchestra

LIST OF ILLUSTRATIONS

Introduction

Todos lo comentan, nadie lo delata.
(Everyone talks, no one tells.)
—Héctor Lavoe, *"Juanito Alimaña"*

In August 2007 an audience of thousands crammed into London's Royal Albert Hall for the electrifying Proms debut by Gustavo Dudamel and the Simón Bolívar Youth Orchestra of Venezuela (SBYO). "Was this the greatest Prom of all time?" asked the *Daily Telegraph*'s arts editor (Gent 2007). A turning point in the orchestra's rise to global prominence, this concert's impact stretched back to Venezuela, where President Hugo Chávez read out the rapturous U.K. press reports on his television show *Aló Presidente* and announced an expansion of the music education program known as El Sistema, of which the SBYO forms the summit. As I left the Albert Hall, exhilarated, I decided to study this phenomenon.

*   *   *

Three years later, I was sitting in a car outside Montalbán, El Sistema's model music school in Caracas. With its high walls topped with barbed wire and gates manned by security, it had the air of a correctional facility. The director came out to the car to greet me and show me in. As I walked through the main entrance, I saw a large poster—of me. They had downloaded my photo and biography from the Internet and created a poster to announce my visit.

I barely had time to register this before a brass fanfare sounded off to my left. An ensemble of a dozen French horns launched into "Hymn to Joy," announcing my entrance with perfect precision. I listened, entranced. No sooner had the piece finished than I was ushered off into a nearby classroom, where a choir of sixty children awaited me and burst into song as soon as I walked in. And so the visit proceeded, as I was led to hear the beginners' orchestra and the next-level "Mozart" orchestra. The climax was the 120-strong Montalbán Children's Orchestra, awaiting me in the main hall, which performed Bizet's "March of the Toreadors" and Bernstein's "Mambo." As we left the room, a fifty-strong wind ensemble that had miraculously formed outside in the hallway struck up the "William Tell" Overture. Along the way, the staff bombarded me with friendliness, attention, and positivity. I left overwhelmed by the musical skill of the students, the enthusiasm and attentiveness of the staff, and the organizational capacity of the school, which had orchestrated this musical spectacle for my visit with military precision. Montalbán is El Sistema's "shop window," and it knows how to put on a show.

What is El Sistema? The Venezuelan State Foundation for the National System of Youth and Children's Orchestras (Fundación del Estado para el Sistema Nacional de Orquestas Juveniles e Infantiles de Venezuela, FESNOJIV) describes itself as "a social program of the Venezuelan state devoted to the pedagogical, occupational, and ethical salvation of children and young people, via the instruction and collective practice of music, [and] dedicated to the training, protection, and inclusion of the most vulnerable groups in the coun-

CENTRO ACADÉMICO INFANTIL DE MONTALBÁN
CRONOGRAMA PARA LA DEMOSTRACIÓN
VIERNES 12 DE NOVIEMBRE DE 2010
HORA: 04:00 PM
DEMOSTRACIÓN PARA EL DOCTOR GEOFREY BAKER PROFESOR DE LA UNIVERSIDAD DE LONDRES ROYAL HOLLOWAY

ORQUESTAS Y AGRUPACIONES	CANTIDAD DE ALUMNOS	LUGAR	PROGRAMA	DIRECTOR	ESPACIOS ESTUCHES
ENSAMBLE DE CORNOS	12	LOBBY	- HIMNO DE LA ALEGRIA -CORNOCOPIA	LUIS VALLADARES	C6
NIÑOS CANTORES DE MONTALBÁN	60	A2	- CAMPANAS SOBRE CAMPANAS. - ADORACIÓN	RAQUEL CAMPOMAS Y PAOLA OTERO	
INICIACIÓN ORQUESTAL	60	A4	-MI PRIMERA CANCIÓN - HOLA AMIGUITO	EDWIN MIJARES	A3
ORQUETA INFANTIL "MOZART"	140	C1	-OVERTURA 1812 ARREGLO	ANABELL ASTUDILLO	C5
ORQUESTA INFANTIL MONTALBÁN	120	SE	-TOREADORES - MAMBO	MANUEL CAMPOS	B9
BANDA DE VIENTOS VENEZUELA	50	SALITA	-GUILLERMO TELL - CARTOON SYMPHONY -DANZON JUAREZ	LUIS MELO	B2

The printed schedule for my tour of Montalbán núcleo.

try."[1] The program began in 1975; according to official figures, by 2012 it comprised approximately 200 music centers (called *núcleos*), nearly 400 orchestras, and some 350,000 participants, around two-thirds from the country's two poorest social strata.[2] Two distinctive elements are its emphasis on collective learning through orchestral practice and its intensive schedule. Many students may spend around four hours a day in the núcleo, five or six days a week. Tuition is offered at low cost or for free, and instruments are loaned to students according to availability.[3]

According to the Inter-American Development Bank (IDB), its major nonstate funder, "the primary individual benefits attributed to the System include improvements in academic achievement and in the psychological development of children and young people. Its social benefits include reducing the school dropout rate and the rate of youth violence.... [I]t has transcended the artistic world to become a social development project that aspires to imbue citizens from a very early age with civic values and teamwork" ("Program to Support" 2007, 1 and 8). The idea that this nationwide network of youth orchestras is in essence a social project aimed at the poor, designed not so much to train musicians as to forge citizens, has put El Sistema firmly on the global map. The centering of music education on classical music has been increasingly questioned since the 1970s, yet El Sistema has sent the pendulum swinging back the other way, representing symphonic music as a route to socioeconomic and moral salvation.

Gramophone magazine declared El Sistema the second most important development in classical music of the new millennium (after the invention of the iPod). Sir Simon Rattle went one better, describing it as "the most important thing happening in music anywhere in the world," and proclaiming: "If anybody asked me where is there something really important going on for the future of classical music I would simply have to say here, in Venezuela...I say I have seen the future of music in Venezuela and that is a resurrection."[4] Other major figures (Claudio Abbado, Placido Domingo) and prestigious institutions (UNESCO, the Organization of American States) have enthusiastically endorsed The System and its founding director, José Antonio Abreu. The SBYO has captured the world's imagination: its concert at the 2011 Proms was the first to sell out, in just three hours.[5]

Combining children, a repertoire of classical favorites, and a heartwarming backstory, El Sistema has an extraordinary capacity to appeal to the emotions, and I am just one of many who has shed a tear during a documentary or felt my hair stand on end in a concert. Rattle fought a losing battle to contain his emotions during a visit to Montalbán in 2004 (Borzacchini 2010, 32). Yet judging from my own visit, this emotional effect is carefully calculated. With the tour designed for maximum impact, El Sistema aims at the heart, not the head. Bolivia Bottome, head of Institutional Development and International Relations at FESNOJIV, stated: "In Venezuela, we don't show numbers—we do a lot of large showcase demonstrations to fundraise. We sit people down and make them listen to a huge orchestra of children playing Mahler 2 and then they fund us."[6] A senior IDB figure admitted privately that its loans to El Sistema—some $160 million over seventeen years—had been made primarily on the basis of hearing the children in action, rather than robust evidence of the program's social effectiveness. José Antonio Abreu is famous for utilizing the impact of a huge youth orchestra to persuade politicians and funding bodies: one of his favored techniques in the early days was to ambush politicians with surprise concerts in unlikely places, and he has led lavish performances to celebrate the inauguration of new presidents throughout El Sistema's history. Abreu understands the power of music—and the music of power.

Emotion also dominates virtually all attempts to analyze El Sistema. Chefi Borzacchini (2010, 7) admits that her book, the most substantial on the program, is not objective but rather "permeated, from start to finish, with emotions and sentiments." Chapter 1 opens: "We may close our eyes and let our ears and hearts guide us." Jonathan Govias, a leading commentator on El Sistema, wrote on his blog on April 6, 2012, that for those who have studied the program and experienced it in action, "it's extremely difficult not to believe completely and utterly in the power of the idea on primarily an emotional rather than rational level." He noted a tendency toward "intellectual intoxication" in discussions of El Sistema overseas—"to lose sight of all perspective, to buy into propaganda, to be unreasonably passionate."

El Sistema seems to repel rational analysis—Rattle stated, "if people cry two minutes into the concert, there's nothing more to say" (Aloy 2013)—yet this is my aim. I arrived in Venezuela with my heart full of the program's amazing sights and sounds; but during a year of research, I tried to use my head. It became clear that El Sistema had rarely been analyzed properly. There was a lot of relevant material circulating—documentaries, TV programs, books, a PhD, master's and undergraduate theses, blogs, and a vast number of newspaper and magazine articles—but none combined an independent, objective approach with in-depth research on the everyday realities of El Sistema beyond the guided tours and showcase núcleos. Almost all started from the premise that El Sistema was a great success, a miracle even, and then tried to explain its secret. They began, overawed, with the conclusion—and worked backward from there.

Cook (2003, 254) identifies this procedure as commonplace: "writing about music is generally designed to look as if it is working from causes to effects, but is better understood as working backward from a valued belief to reasons for believing it." This is particularly true in the Venezuelan case: most foreigners arrive (like me) inspired by a rousing concert, a hagiographical documentary, or a delirious article, and thus with our valued belief firmly in place. But a research project ought properly to start from a blank slate and ask: Is El Sistema successful? At what? What are its strengths and weaknesses? What do Venezuelan musicians think about it?

Such basic questions had rarely been asked outside Venezuela, yet any large organization, and especially a publicly funded one with lofty, expansive aims, deserves rigorous analysis and public debate. El Sistema is a huge, powerful institution that has hundreds of thousands of students and employees, moves hundreds of millions of dollars, and lobbies intensively at national and international levels, and it is no more deserving of automatic adulation than any other such organization. Plenty of corporations, such as pharmaceutical, oil, or technology companies, claim to be making the world a better place. Their claims are considered fair game for scrutiny, since institutional discourses are constructed instrumentally and often conceal as much as they reveal, but El Sistema has been a conspicuous exception. Its powerful public narrative seems to have overawed observers.

El Sistema plans to expand its capacity to one million children in Venezuela before the end of the decade, and it is becoming a global franchise for music education—one of the fastest-expanding and most-discussed initiatives in the world, now operating in more than sixty countries. In April 2013 the Brazilian government committed to creating three hundred orchestral núcleos and serving half a million children under the guidance of El Sistema ("Brasilia" 2013). Shortly afterward, at the Salzburg Festival, Abreu declared that El Sistema would eventually have a presence in every country in the world. As the idea of the orchestra as a powerful tool for social inclusion takes root internationally and Abreu accumulates international prizes, there is a growing sense that El Sistema provides a model for the world to follow. However, this model lacks support from rigorous, objective research, and its extraordinary boom makes in-depth, critical scrutiny more important than ever. Issues like inclusion and social justice are complex and need to be considered carefully. It is not enough simply for an organization to state them as priorities; researchers must examine what actually takes place and whether it promotes or undermines those goals. What lies behind the impressive surface? Does the program deliver on its promises? Is an orchestra really a model for a better society? As Kartomi (2012, 864) asks of youth orchestras in general: "Is the 'evidence' of educational outcomes anecdotal and a perception generated by mission statements, websites, and other publicity material?"

Given El Sistema's rapid international expansion, the aims of this book go beyond an examination of the Venezuelan program to encompass a broader critical analysis of the youth symphony orchestra as a vehicle for a rounded, inclusive education in music and citizenship. Ethnographic observations will be placed in comparative and theoretical context, exploring how local findings are bolstered by scholarly literature on music, education, and their institutions, and may thus be considered both representative and of wider significance. In ordinary núcleos, the detail of El Sistema's day-to-day practices was largely unremarkable in relation to the conventional practices of European music education; the most notable feature was quantity—of musicians, hours, and sound. My focus is therefore less on extensive ethnographic detail than on analysis of the program's broader implications.

It is remarkable that such a significant music education project, nearly four decades old and with a global reach, has been the object of so little critical examination and informed debate. Why is this the case? One reason is that, for all the recent writings and films, there is relatively little hard information about it available. El Sistema is an opaque organization, verging on the secretive, sometimes described as a state within a state; external monitoring and evaluation have been minimal, and most reports have not been made public. Even the most basic facts and figures are thus hard to pin down. Researching El Sistema presents a challenge: when I inquired, FESNOJIV told me that it did not have an archive, though Borzacchini's (2010, 250) official history reveals that it does. A high-level informant explained, "José Antonio [Abreu] doesn't like things to be written down because then it is hard to adjust to the political interests of the moment." What the world knows is essentially what FESNOJIV tells it.

Additionally, the public circulation of information is extremely constrained. While many Venezuelan musicians, administrators, and journalists know a lot about El Sistema, hardly any speak out publicly because they are bound by loyalty or afraid of the consequences. El Sistema functions through the strict exercise of power and control. Abreu has a near monopoly on the classical music sphere in Venezuela, and many stories circulate about his ruthless approach to those who cross or simply disagree with him. Critics of El Sistema have allegedly been fired and blacklisted, and some have ended up leaving Venezuela. El Sistema not only takes a zero-tolerance approach to criticism but also has a formidable PR machine to keep information under tight control. Public debate is thus severely hampered: few are willing to go on record with critical opinions, and the outlets for their views are minimal.

Behind the scenes, I became aware of a climate of fear. Some internationally known musicians and cultural figures expressed private concerns but would not say anything publicly against El Sistema, and did not want their name to reach Abreu's ears. Some interviewees simply ducked questions about the program's deficiencies; one lowered her voice and omitted Abreu's name in public. I asked another for further contacts: "It's difficult," he replied, "because people are always afraid that El Sistema may somehow persecute them."

Musicians see Abreu as omniscient and omnipresent, but for some he is a vengeful god. One, who had devoted more than twenty-five years to El Sistema, claimed that criticizing the project meant "musical death...they crucify you without a word of warning...that's what they did to me." After El Sistema vetoed a major initiative that he had organized, without giving him a reason, he felt it was "killing him musically," and he left Venezuela.

The wide circulation of similar stories in Venezuelan musical circles made research complex and frustrating. Informants described a culture of fear, self-preservation, and *amiguismo* (looking after friends) that constrained open discussion. "He won't tell you what he really thinks," said the daughter of one interviewee. "I'm only going to tell you half the story," began the director of a music school; having suffered the consequences of a disagreement with Abreu earlier in his career, he confessed, "it's not in my interest to be completely open with you." Four of my key informants were urged by their spouses not to speak to me in case their collaboration got back to Abreu. One's wife said, "We have already suffered enough at the hands of El Sistema."

To criticize the program publicly is to risk career suicide, said a former Sistema director. I met leading musicians who criticized the program in private but occupied prestigious posts within it and formed part of its public face. The program's financial resources and monopolization of institutionalized music make it hard to resist. Eric Booth (2008, 3) was amazed that "at every nucleo, all the educators and staff can tell you exactly what the goals of El Sistema are—a stunningly unified vision and purpose," yet he seems unaware of the forces that produce this unity. Its unified vision tells us more about its power than what its members really think.

This climate of fear also began to affect me. Musicians advised me of the risks of taking a critical line, believing that I might be fired from my job, though some warnings were considerably more dramatic. One musician predicted dire consequences if I published my findings before Abreu's death. They remembered the case of the Argentinean theater director Gustavo Tambascio, against whom Abreu waged a vicious public campaign after Tambascio wrote a critical review of a concert by the SBYO, and claimed that other newspaper music critics had lost their jobs for similar "crimes." Abreu's power over other organizations, even overseas, was taken as a given. A former senior Sistema figure claimed that Abreu had ex–police detectives on his payroll doing surveillance work, while a current senior figure revealed that he avoided contacting Sistema dissidents or criticizing the program by phone or email, just in case his communications were being monitored.

I had no way of judging the veracity of the rumors or the seriousness of the warnings, but I was more interested in the fact that Sistema employees found them believable. Whether founded or not, they circulated widely and worried Venezuelan musicians, who thought that getting on the wrong side of Abreu could bring serious consequences. These stories are worthy of consideration because they form part of El Sistema's belief system, and also because they have real effects on musicians, inducing behavior like the self-censorship that makes understanding the program so complicated. A musician with whom I had had many long discussions wrote to me after I left Venezuela, saying that he had become "frightened by the possibility of physical damage to my family or property," and he stopped writing to me for a long time, also shelving his long-standing plan to author a critical article about El Sistema. The metaphor of the mafia recurred like a leitmotif in private conversations about the program, and there were moments when researching El Sistema felt more like investigating organized crime than an arts education project. I came to understand why few critics showed their hand in public.

FOREIGN PERCEPTIONS

The predominant vision of El Sistema overseas rests heavily on good PR. El Sistema is determined to present its best face to foreign visitors, providing them with red carpet treatment and carefully choreographed events at model institutions like the Center for Social Action through Music (Centro de Acción Social por la Música, CASM), La Rinconada, and Montalbán, where I witnessed its willingness to organize an entire afternoon at a school to impress a single guest. The focus on spectacle makes it hard for foreign visitors—even serious, thoughtful, and experienced ones—to comprehend El Sistema. Most make short trips to Venezuela and, lacking long-term exposure to everyday realities, fail to grasp fully the inculcation of positive impressions through careful control of access and information and a combination of discipline, choreography, and PR—what I call its "politics of impact."

If the polished displays are intended to suspend disbelief, Tunstall's (2012, 38) invocation of "an international pilgrimage" also underlines how most visitors are driven by faith in the "Venezuelan musical miracle" rather than a spirit of critical inquiry. This belief colors all subsequent discussion and over-

El Sistema's Caracas headquarters, the Centro de Acción Social por la Música (CASM). Photo by Geoffrey Baker.

rides conflicting evidence. Booth (2008, 5) was well aware that he was witnessing a show for foreign consumption, while Wakin (2012a) writes of "an elaborately choreographed showcase" for visiting Americans, noting that El Sistema "is a well-oiled machine when it comes to welcoming outsiders," yet neither writer pursues this thought. Wakin notes a number of potentially disturbing features, including El Sistema's resemblance to a cult; displays for which children are "rehearsed to within an inch of their lives"; Abreu's metaphorical wielding of the whip and intolerance of dissent; and his Machiavellian-sounding tendency to "dictate career moves among the top echelon of musicians." Despite this unusually perceptive analysis, however, the author concludes by comparing Abreu not to a dictator or cult leader, but to a saint and pope. He even quotes without comment the extraordinary line of an anonymous informant: "When there are saints, there is no room for dissidents." Swed (2012), too, manages to draw highly positive conclusions from unpromising materials, such as "lock-step learning" in "endless daily rehearsals" that "hammer in" Abreu's message. Wakin's extended simile of El Sistema as a religion and its leaders as evangelists neglects an important element—the role of foreign observers as the converted.

Glowing reports of El Sistema may reflect the fact that some of the best-known foreign commentators have little Spanish and limited knowledge of Venezuela, and so, for all their other expertise, may not be best placed to tease out the complexities of everyday life in the núcleo. Foreign analyses have also often foundered on excessively close relationships between observers and the program, leading advocacy to elide critical examination. Several leading voices are employees of El Sistema or its affiliated programs, or have hitched their careers to its success.

As a consequence, much commentary in the English-speaking world is profoundly shaped by advocacy, and consists of El Sistema's PR materials given an extra spin by foreign intermediaries. There is another reason, however, behind the overwhelmingly positive narrative overseas, and it is a familiar one: there are well-placed figures who are critical of El Sistema's national and international operations but who remain largely silent in public for fear of vilification by its supporters. A lack of public debate should not therefore be taken to signify unanimity.

CRITICAL RESEARCH ON CLASSICAL MUSIC AND EDUCATION

As a classical musician, former youth orchestra member, music teacher, and researcher of Latin American music, institutions, and cultural policy (e.g., Baker 2008a; 2010; 2011), I was captivated the moment I first read about El Sistema in the early 2000s, though the idea lay dormant until the 2007 Proms. I arrived in Venezuela with a glowingly positive view of El Sistema. I was fascinated by the idea of mass-scale, socially transformative music education and wanted to find out more about this apparent miracle. However, a year of ethnographic research in Venezuela between 2010 and 2011 changed my view. As I watched, listened, and read, I saw a gulf open up between theory and practice, between official narratives and everyday realities. Conceptions of El Sistema were, I realized, highly idealized, overlooking significant drawbacks and contradictions. Furthermore, there was far more debate around El Sistema than had been visible from overseas. Its national and international activities provoked questions, concerns, and criticisms. Abroad, the project's image was going from strength to strength, but at home doubts were commonplace in cultural circles.

I went to Venezuela looking for an uplifting story, for Rattle's "future of music," and I was disappointed to find something quite different, more akin to its past dressed in appealing rhetorical garb. I also became concerned as I learned how El Sistema operated, yet this concern was instructive: it taught me about the program's power. The cautionary tales left me rethinking my project and at times considering abandoning it; like my informants, I weighed the advisability of self-censorship and silence. When I shared these thoughts with two founder members of the SBYO, they chuckled approvingly: I was now "up to my eyeballs in the same craziness" that they had lived with since the 1970s.

My change of direction was also underpinned by my prior experience of critical ethnography (Baker 2011). If skepticism and interrogating common assumptions are cornerstones of intellectual inquiry in the humanities and social sciences, ethnography is a particularly suitable tool. Its slow, indirect techniques allow the researcher to probe strong, deeply internalized official discourses and unearth internal conflicts and divergent opinions that may be obscured in surveys and official interviews. As Born (1995, 7) writes, since institutions and systems "have the capacity to absorb and conceal contradiction, it takes a method such as ethnography to uncover the gaps between external claims and internal realities, public rhetoric and private thought, ideology and practice."

Hollinger's (2006, 119) attempt to discuss social values with Sistema children saw ten-year-olds stating that "playing in the orchestra teaches us responsibility, confidence and discipline"; "we learn to work together in the orchestra"; "it is like a family here"; and "playing music changes our souls." Though these answers may be sincere, and perhaps even true, the author recognized that they were not exactly "personal responses." Here we see Booth's "stunningly unified vision" in its early formative stages. Ethnography opens up the possibility of going beyond such formulaic statements and reaching for deeper understanding. As Robert K. Merton put it succinctly, social science asks "is it really so?" (Roach 2011). This is a question that ought to have been asked a lot more of El Sistema.

A significant obstacle to the social analysis of musical practices is the tendency toward idealization. There is a lot of myth making and romanticization around El Sistema, as with much youthful musical activity (Etherington 2007), and the affective impact of children making music can make clear-eyed analysis particularly difficult. Furthermore, El Sistema is, among other things, a discursive edifice, constructed by a master rhetorician. Abreu has all the best aphorisms—"culture for the poor should never be poor culture," "the huge spiritual world that music produces in itself ends up overcoming material poverty"—and his followers know them by heart. The highly polished and seductive nature of this discourse seems to ward off proper examination, provoking instead the urge to quote it frequently, as if invoking the sayings of a guru. Ethnography may serve as a means to penetrate this idealized rhetorical carapace, grasp its political and marketing functions, and uncover realities that it masks.

Particularly notable is the prevalence of musical metaphors, above all harmony, which can often obscure actual goings-on. Borzacchini's (2010, 7) comment that "everyone needs to be fully in tune in order to achieve unison" is emblematic of the blurring of El Sistema's realities through musical discourse and the dressing-up in softening symbolism of what is, actually, a distinctly authoritarian view. As Born (1995, 20) notes, metaphors can be drawn into "strategies of authority, legitimation, and power"—a warning to be skeptical of musical metaphors when dealing with musical institutions. Abreu subscribes to the view that "music is not just artistic expression, it is the global concept of cosmic harmony" ("Música, Armonía" 2012). Yet does musical harmony really engender social harmony, or is it a metaphor for it? In reality, while music making may be sociable and participatory, it is also frequently riven by issues of power, conflict, and competition. Abreu's idealized view is appealing and has deep historical roots, but does it reveal or obscure the actual workings of a real music program in the twenty-first century?

In a review article on studies of music and conflict transformation, Bergh and Sloboda (2010) demonstrate a healthy skepticism from which observers of El Sistema could learn. Among the problems they identify are that projects' power dynamics are downplayed or ignored; ordinary participants' opinions tend to be overshadowed by the views of those in charge; and music's role is often exaggerated via sweeping statements about its power. It is in everyone's interest to claim success, which is usually vital for funding, so evaluations are often done by project organizers themselves and rely on anecdotes as proof. Bergh and Sloboda are personally invested in the processes they study, yet they maintain the critical attitude necessary for meaningful research.

There is an existing tradition of critical analysis of classical music culture, much of it written by scholars who respect this music but are not afraid to shine a harsh light on its institutions and practices (e.g., Born 1995). Kingsbury (1988) and Nettl (1995) have critiqued North American conservatoires, while

Small (1977; 1998) has done the same with classical music institutions more generally. Symphony orchestras, too, have been a topic for critical study by sociologists (e.g., Faulkner 1973; Kamerman and Martorella 1983) and ethnomusicologists (e.g., Cottrell 2004; Ramnarine 2012), though youth orchestras have been largely overlooked.

A one-day conference in London in mid-2014, "Classical Music as Contemporary Socio-cultural Practice: Critical Perspectives," pointed to a new wave of activity in this area, building on earlier studies, and the coalescence of a critical field. Scholars have recently shone a spotlight on Daniel Barenboim and Edward Said's West-Eastern Divan Orchestra (WEDO), a project often mentioned in the same breath as El Sistema. There is now a body of critical literature examining this orchestra's rhetoric and power relations, and uncovering the micro-interactions and internal contradictions beneath its public discourses (Etherington 2007; Beckles Willson 2009; Cheah 2009; Riiser 2010). Wakeling (2010), reviewing such critiques of WEDO, concludes that while its "blend of musical excellence and apparently humanitarian vision has proved a heady mix for liberal European audiences, provoking intense, proselytising excitement among commentators...the orchestra functions more as Euro-American fantasy of cooperation and a vehicle for individual musical ambition, than a positive contribution to Middle Eastern social dynamics." Such a critical appraisal of El Sistema, a far larger and more influential project, is distinctly overdue.

Similarly, many scholars have asked penetrating questions about classical music education (e.g., Jorgensen 1997 and 2003; Green 1988, 2002, 2003a, and 2003b; Regelski and Gates 2009; Wright 2010a). Jorgensen (2003), Allsup (2007), and Gates (2009) have underlined the need for unflinching critical inquiry in the field of music education research, even though, as Jorgensen (2003, xiii) warns, "the search for truth is often uncomfortable and disconcerting, especially when those things one has held dear are challenged." Commitment to music education thus encompasses a willingness to question dominant institutions and unsettle their advocates. Campbell (2004, xvi) provides a prime example: "School music programs in North America, Europe, Australia and New Zealand, and in parts of Asia and Latin America have been successful in developing Western-oriented musical skills and understandings, and are celebrated for the effectiveness of pedagogical approaches that produce musically literate singers and players. Yet this is but one model, and a colonial one at that, which fixes European music (and its staff notation) and its pedagogical processes highest in a hierarchy atop the musical expressions and instructional approaches of so many other rich traditions. Should such a model be continued in the twenty-first century, in a time of post-colonial and democratic reconsiderations of cultures and their perspectives?"

The object of my critique, like Campbell's, is not classical music per se but rather the institutions, pedagogies, and practices that mediate it. The ethical values fostered by music education institutions may be quite different from those informing the music itself. Classical music has emancipatory potential (Harper-Scott 2013) and an important part to play in music education if taught in ethically and educatively sound ways. But there are problematic issues to address, such as the gulf that can emerge between the experiences of orchestral audiences and performers: "although the results of an orchestral performance can be exceptionally uplifting, the means of attaining these results are often anything but uplifting to those whose job it is to achieve them" (Seifter 2001). Similarly, the thorny questions and lively debates about postcolonial Venezuela's devotion of huge resources to a musical culture implanted by colonialism cannot continue to be brushed under the carpet. Such questions may be answerable; perhaps a case can be made for placing classical music at the center of cultural and educational policy; but it needs to be made. In El Sistema, that classical music should take the leading role is an implicit and unexamined assumption. Bizarrely, its predominance is even denied by some ardent supporters, impeding deeper understanding of the issue. Classical music is too important for its potential, both positive and negative, to be obscured in this way.

I am indebted to the work of many critical scholars of music education, on whose work I draw extensively. There has been a disconnect between existing music education research and El Sistema, and my aim is in part to make this connection. A particular influence on me has been the work of Jorgensen, who makes an argument that is crucial to this book:

> Oppressive structures are endemic to music education as to society, and these oppose civility and humanity. By privileging some and marginalizing others, the establishment ensures that some voices are heard while others are silenced in the public spaces, some cultural expressions and visions of civility are advocated while others are repudiated. This exclusivity, under whatever guise, no matter how well meaning, is to the detriment of all. However, where these oppressive structures are undermined, society is enriched in terms of the discourse, conduct, and cultural expressions of its members. By tackling the dehumanizing forces in music education, music educators and those interested in their work can create a miniature society that presages a more civil society; in this way, music education can model not only general education but also society yet to come. (2003, 120)

Jorgensen's language has close parallels with El Sistema's, yet there are crucial differences: she envisions music education as a model for a society yet to come, not one that is already disappearing; and the pursuit of social justice requires the critique of oppressive structures and exclusive forces in conventional music education, not their perpetuation and expansion in new guises. Her miniature civil society is founded on tackling long-standing problems, not strengthening tradition. This means grappling with El Sistema's weaknesses, not engaging in bourgeois fantasies about the power of Beethoven to save the poor.

ACCOUNTS OF EL SISTEMA: ADULATION AND SKEPTICISM

Most reports on El Sistema display the problems that Bergh and Sloboda identify and veer more toward celebration than critique, revealing little to no hint of debates in Venezuela or the critical literature on orchestras and music education.[7] Carvajal and Melgarejo (2008) focus exclusively on current senior figures in El Sistema, ensuring zero deviation from the official line. Indeed, this "study" reads like an extended press release, aping not just FESNOJIV's claims but also its mystical, metaphorical language. Mora-Brito's (2011) account is considerably more insightful, but also weakened by its reliance on interviews with on-message managers. Booth (2008) and Tunstall (2012) marvel at El Sistema's consistent vision, yet they, too, rely mainly on a narrow constituency of official spokespeople and núcleo directors. Texts on El Sistema that have become canonical in the English-speaking world are rapturous visions designed largely to promote rather than probe.

Yet critical analyses are available, though most are in Spanish and therefore little known in the international Sistema sphere. The renowned Uruguayan composer and musicologist Coriún Aharonián (2004) published a short but sharp account, attacking the program's authoritarian, Eurocentric conservatism. The Venezuelan composers Diego Silva (winner of the prestigious Casa de las Américas prize) and Emilio Mendoza (professor at the Universidad Simón Bolívar) have put their critiques in print, at considerable risk and cost to their professional activities.[8] The musician and political activist Freddy Argimiro, frustrated at the lack of public debate, started the blog *La Otra Cara del Sistema* (The Other Face of El Sistema), on which he has published both his own critical reflections and articles by a range of left-wing cultural commentators.

Outside Venezuela, only the occasional voice has been raised. Tom Service at *The Guardian* has questioned some of the claims and suggested that similar work has been going on for decades, unheralded, throughout the United Kingdom (e.g., Service 2010). Marco Frei (2011) was even more forthright, noting the lack of critical distance in existing accounts, with one recent book "reading like an official announcement"; the difficulty of posing critical questions in Venezuela; the program's "self-confidence bordering on hubris"; the fact that most members of the Teresa Carreño Youth Orchestra (TCYO)—El Sistema's number two ensemble—were middle class, not from the slums; and the disconcertingly commercial orientation of the project, with its lucrative festival appearances and CD contracts. In the academic field, Borchert (2012) provided a penetrating analysis of the relationship between the Sistema philosophy and the production of subjects for capitalism, while Logan's (n.d.) bracing critique of El Sistema's politics constitutes a significant step forward in understanding the program.

The most public break in the English-language consensus came in the form of two critical articles by the U.K. journalist Igor Toronyi-Lalic (2012a and 2012b). His principal charge concerned the flimsy evidence for El Sistema's alleged positive impact. He went on to suggest that even if intensive investment in this program were proven to produce better results than no investment in anything, it would do nothing to show that El Sistema was a particularly efficient way of achieving its social goals. Questioning the idea that classical music is better for people, and especially for the poor, than other kinds of music, he accused Sistema supporters of ignoring the sometimes unpalatable realities of the professional music world. He also turned his fire on the press, whom he accused of delivering an "unthinking whitewashing": "few have thought it appropriate to ask even the most basic questions of the enterprise.... Only blind devotion is permitted. Scepticism and inquiry, even of a musical sort, is forbidden" (2012a). Toronyi-Lalic's tone was confrontational and he provoked the wrath of leading Sistema advocates; yet despite his superficial acquaintance with the program, he put his finger on some key issues.[9] Indeed, his criticism of the press could be extended to academia, where references to El Sistema are now commonly found in mainstream works such as *The Oxford Handbook of Music Education*, yet all too often rely on problematic sources like Wikipedia, promotional websites, and under-researched newspaper articles.

In Venezuela, criticisms have at times been stronger still, and they may come as a shock to readers overseas. An Internet article about Abreu winning the Alternative Nobel Prize turned into a public forum on El Sistema, with nearly two hundred comments, most from current and former members of the program and many of them lengthy and detailed.[10] "All that glitters is not gold," begins one poster. "Over time I have realized that FESNOJIV is a big lie, it's all a world of dreams, but when you wake up you understand everything and it's a horrible blow," writes another. The feted documentary *Tocar y Luchar* comes in for repeated criticism: "All of us in El Sistema know that it's a despicable lie and a farce designed to brainwash people!" Many of the program's best-known features are denounced as emotional manipulation. One poster writes of "the supposed social work that the foundation does, which is all a front to make it look like a phenomenon to other countries so it can fill its boots with resources sent from overseas...they don't do genuine work on values and principles with the children, but rather work them to the bone for a week before some stupid conductor from overseas comes in and is blown away by the racket."

Behind the appealing appearances, according to numerous posters, lie harsh realities: corruption, maladministration, discrimination, nepotism, favoritism, bullying, poor pay and working conditions, strife between management and teachers, and exploitation of staff and children. Hourly paid teachers complain of having no labor rights or social security. FESNOJIV's personnel department and higher bureaucracy are repeatedly slated for their contemptuous treatment of lower-ranking staff. Posters describe an excessive concentration of power in the hands of senior figures, one of whom in particular receives severe criticism for his overbearing behavior. There are allusions to alleged sexual relationships between staff and students and the persecution of teachers who speak out against internal problems.

Contributors from the regions report a lack of facilities, equipment, and teachers, and gross inequalities in resources and pay. Disgruntled provincial teachers complain that the Caracas HQ ignores them or treats them with disdain, and carries away their best students to the capital. However, there are also reports of deplorable conditions in some núcleos in the capital itself. Conditions in the "front line" núcleos are contrasted with the lavish expenditure on the SBYO. Bitter rivalries between Sistema orchestras rear their head. Question marks over the destinations of large sums of money and the true quantity of children in the program lead several commenters to call for an immediate government audit.

This forum throws doubt on El Sistema's claims to be modeling an ideal, harmonious society. To be sure, the Internet needs to be treated with considerable caution; however, the detail of some comments (including names and places) and the repetition of key themes are suggestive, and my fieldwork provided frequent corroboration. I met many people who enjoyed being part of El Sistema; but I also witnessed enough disappointment and disillusionment for the criticisms to ring true.

This is not to deny that El Sistema has numerous positive aspects. It has brought cultural activity to many children; its scale and intensity are impressive; and youths from humble circumstances have been given extraordinary opportunities. Dedicated music teachers are at work in all four corners of Venezuela. Thousands of children are enjoying making music under their direction, in many cases benefiting from the personal attention of an adult, from sociability with their peers, and from the cognitive benefits of childhood musical learning. But it is essential to examine broad forces that impact on this educational program, reducing its effectiveness or steering it in undesirable directions. All teachers know their work can be compromised by systemic problems—an overly rigid curriculum, poor working conditions, excessive numbers of pupils, low pay and status—and the Venezuelan program, too, has ideological and structural weaknesses that go beyond the best efforts of individuals within it.

Institutions and cultural practices potentially have both positive and negative effects simultaneously, and claimed benefits may come with hidden costs or countereffects. As Bowman (2009, 11) argues: "Music and music education are not unconditional goods. They can harm as well as heal.... [I]ntended results on one level may be undesirable on another." A fuller range of outcomes thus needs investigating. Furthermore, an intensive program like El Sistema involves so much normalization and naturalization that many individuals within it may not be aware of the complex forces operating on them. This is why detailed, critical research is necessary.

Of course it can be fun for young people to do group activities with their friends, meet boyfriends and girlfriends, play loud music in big ensembles, and be part of a prestigious project. Research has a part to play, however, in digging beneath this surface to uncover less obvious (and potentially more problematic) realities. Certainly, many children enjoy participating in El Sistema, though it is also true—if less widely grasped or discussed—that many do not and leave. (Núcleo observations and interviews only reveal part of the picture, since they focus on a self-selecting group and render dissenters largely invisible and inaudible.) But the fact that children are enjoying themselves does not necessarily mean that they are receiving a good education, any more than enjoying fast food means that it is nutritious. The Third Wave, an educational experiment in a California school, demonstrated that children enjoyed studying in a fascist environment, yet few adults would regard this as a validation of such methods (see Chapter 8). My critique does not therefore deny that El Sistema is a source of pleasure. Many of the ideological forces I identify are ethically problematic yet perfectly compatible with enjoyment.

El Sistema as a musical and social miracle is a story that has been told endlessly and hyperbolically in recent years and many readers will know it already; those who do not can turn to the books and articles that I cite or the hundreds more that are available at the click of a mouse. Rehashing these well-worn and often ill-informed tales would serve little purpose here, especially since there are many lesser-known stories that urgently need to be told. Unbeknown to most observers, El Sistema consists of a plurality of narratives. The dominant one, propagated by the institution itself and perpetuated by the media and supporters overseas, has captured public attention around the world, but, like most public narratives, it is selective and simplistic; up close in Venezuela the picture is more complex, ambiguous, contradictory. This book focuses on the narratives that are currently inaudible and the ways that they complicate the official one; it brings out into the open debates that normally take place in private.

El Sistema has accrued obscuring layers of rhetoric and myth. Analysis requires peeling back those layers and puncturing some myths. A key role for academic studies is to interrogate grandiose claims, to complicate simplistic accounts, and to reveal other sides to a story, particularly where private narratives have been elided by institutional ones. Taking such an approach to El Sistema will hopefully contribute to more informed discussion among those who are interested in understanding the program.

A prime example of such analysis (and a clear illustration of the value of ethnography) can be found in Wald's (2011) study of two Sistema-inspired programs in Buenos Aires. Journalists and producers were captivated by the sight and sound of young people from poorer neighborhoods engaging in orchestral music, so the programs were the object of innumerable press articles and television reports, as well as two documentaries. Wald explores the gap between such official narratives (formal aims and media characterizations) and unofficial ones (the experiences and perceptions of participants). Young musicians learned about the orchestras' formal, social objectives through the media, and often disagreed with them: "We're not more integrated into society through the orchestra; if I want to integrate myself into society, I'll go and get a job and that's it," said one; "I was doing worse in school because I spent my time studying music," added another. The young musicians were critical of what they saw as the romanticization of their music education and exaggeration of its benefits by both the media and project leaders. They also attacked the stereotyping and stigmatization of their social realities in order to play up the transformative effects of music: "they talk about us as though we were savages who have a violin instead of a bow and arrow"; "we're not at risk, in my house we've never lacked anything"; "we don't feel vulnerable because we're strong, we live here and we can work, study, get ahead." Participants may not have had a complete understanding of the effects of their music education, and the benefits that they discounted may nevertheless have been present; but their skepticism suggests that a critical approach to official and media narratives would be wise.

Participants in Buenos Aires perceived benefits from their music education, just not the same ones described by the media. They focused on enjoyment and sociability. No one would dispute that these are positive outcomes, but they are hardly unique to orchestral music. More pertinently, governments and development banks would not fund expensive orchestral programs just because they were fun and sociable, and El Sistema would not have achieved national hegemony and global fame on such a basis. The key question for researchers is therefore not whether playing in an orchestra is enjoyable—something that is unquestionably true for some people, some of the time—but rather whether it is a particularly effective vehicle for positive personal and social transformation. Do the more grandiose claims derive from benefits of which participants may be unaware or from the necessity of positing outcomes that are in tune with wider social and political trends in order to secure funding? The fact that many such claims predate research, remain unproven, and are queried by participants suggests that the latter possibility needs to be taken seriously, particularly in the light of Belfiore's (2002, 6) analysis of the broad shift toward justifying cultural expenditure through assertions of economic and social benefits as "originally a defensive strategy of survival, aimed at preserving existing levels of cultural expenditure."

My "activist ethnomusicology" (Bohlman 2008; Ramnarine 2008) is thus on behalf of the voices and narratives that have been marginalized in the public realm rather than those that have dominated it. The problems identified by teachers and students, rather than success stories or Abreu's finely crafted aphorisms, will form the core of this book, which is underpinned by C. Wright Mills's (2000, 187) contention that the task of a politically engaged social scientist is "to translate personal troubles into public issues." Rather than dictating how these successes, failures, benefits, and costs should be weighed against each other—creating an arbitrarily balanced account—I provide a counterweight to the official story that has dramatically skewed the scales and leave the reader to decide which has more substance.

RESEARCHING EL SISTEMA

My account draws on published critical analyses from Venezuela, but rests primarily on approximately a hundred interviews and many times that number of informal conversations with Venezuelan musicians, conductors, administrators, and cultural authorities, ranging from students to teachers to international concert artists. I spoke to former as well as current Sistema employees, musicians of all ages both inside and outside the institution, and knowledgeable figures in other organizations. My aim was to elicit candid views from a cross-section of Venezuelan cultural life, rather than just the "usual suspects" (El Sistema's directors, spokespeople, and top students). Frequently talking off the record, I discovered a mass of divergent opinions and visions behind the surface uniformity that has so impressed foreign observers. (I did not attempt to speak to Abreu. His views have been extensively documented in speeches and interviews, and, like Born [1995], I preferred to analyze a charismatic leader through the eyes of those who worked and played under him.)

Some of the most penetrating analyses came from members of the first generation of the National Youth Orchestra—"the founders," as they are called. They had known Abreu and El Sistema for decades, and some had reached the upper levels of the Sistema pyramid. The many hours they spent talking to me have shaped this book's critique in crucial ways. Contemporaries of the founders also proved to be valuable sources of information, having maintained long-term friendships with their Sistema counterparts but being less bound to silence by loyalty or fear.

Alongside many semistructured interviews and informal conversations, I observed the day-to-day business of El Sistema, sitting in on rehearsals, lessons, and administrative activities in different núcleos. Social media were very useful for observing debates that were excluded from official narratives. As such, my focus will be more qualitative than quantitative, with a couple of important exceptions. Ethnographic studies are concerned less with counting or proving than with analyzing perceptions, meanings, and the construction of social worlds. I am primarily interested in culture, ideology, and understandings of El Sistema; quantitative analysis of the impact of music learning on individual achievement or the national economy will have to be left to others.

Both kinds of research are necessary, because they cover different ground. Current evaluation by the IDB may shed light on El Sistema's short- and medium-term impact on easily measurable factors (see Chapter 11), but other, more complex questions—cultural, political, or ethical ones—will not be so easily answered and require different kinds of analysis. There are also other potentially fruitful approaches to studying El Sistema. Abreu's life and work once provided rich material for investigative journalists, and they would be fertile territory for renewed examination by those with the requisite skills.

For all the difficulties in finding people willing to talk openly to a foreign researcher, writing as an outsider has advantages. Primarily, I have no prior history with the project, no ax to grind. Without exception, I was treated well by staff and students, and I had no personal problems with anyone in the program. In contrast, most classical musicians in Venezuela have had some dealings with El Sistema, and so their critical views may be dismissed (however unfairly) as sour grapes—and critics who have *not* been part of El Sistema are accused of being envious of its success. My relationship with El Sistema, however, is entirely neutral.

While I endeavored to embrace a variety of interlocutors and locations, the scope of my research is inevitably limited. El Sistema has been running for nearly forty years and has trained hundreds of thousands of children; Abreu's career has lasted half a century. This book is not, therefore, a comprehensive or conclusive narrative but rather a critical, informed analysis of some of El Sistema's key actors and core claims, pointing to existing questions and debates around Abreu and his program. I can only open a window onto these complex realities; there is much more to explore, many other research methods to be applied, and a vast number of stories still to be told.

In my final in-depth conversation in Venezuela, two founders stated that El Sistema had been filling musicians' heads with illusions, in Venezuela and around the world. The program needed purifying from top to bottom, they said, and for that to happen—they looked at me meaningfully—the truth had to come out. What follows may not be *the* truth, but it contains some (inconvenient) truths, and their publication will hopefully animate Sistema debates to a greater extent than the mirroring of official institutional discourses, which has led to intellectual and practical stasis. I am motivated by the words of a former senior figure in El Sistema: "unfortunately there is resistance to thinking. It is more comfortable for people to accept things as they are and not to disturb. But I am sure that one day the truth about El Sistema will come out—not to destroy it or finish it, but to strengthen it and make it more honest." Another long-term Sistema figure wrote: "I love everything that El Sistema stands for—it has been my life—but I am not going to keep quiet in the face of its huge faults." Skepticism, critique, and the raising of uncomfortable issues should not then be confused with a desire to weaken El Sistema—quite the opposite. It is a lack of scrutiny, criticism, and public debate that puts the program at risk.

*   *   *

A NOTE ON PLACES AND NAMES

I undertook my research in different parts of Venezuela, ranging from Caracas to small towns in the interior. The main focus of my research was a provincial city that I will call "Veracruz." I have chosen to use this pseudonym partly to bolster the anonymization of research informants—most of the names in this book are not real, and in some cases other identifying information has been altered as well—and partly to underline that this book's critique is not aimed at a particular city or any specific individuals who live there. My intention is ultimately to go beyond the details of what took place to address systemic issues and raise broader questions about social action through music, the institutions and practices of music education, Venezuelan cultural policy, European culture in a postcolonial context, and classical music in the twenty-first century.

Articles and further discussion about El Sistema can be found at http://geoffbakermusic.wordpress.com.

PART ONE

The Institution and Its Leaders

CHAPTER 1

El Maestro: José Antonio Abreu

He is many things: musician, administrator, executive, minister, psychologist, technician, philosopher and dispenser of wrath.... Above all, he is a leader of men. His subjects look to him for guidance.... He has but to stretch out his hand and he is obeyed. He tolerates no opposition. His will, his word, his very glance, are law.
—H. C. Schonberg, *The Great Conductors* (1967)

To understand the triumph of El Sistema, we first need to understand the triumph of José Antonio Abreu. Founder, director, day-to-day manager of El Sistema for thirty-nine years; conductor, keyboard player, music educator; economist, politician, man of letters: Abreu is an extraordinary individual. His list of international awards is seemingly endless, and grows by the month. It includes the Swedish Parliament's Alternative Nobel Prize for an "exemplary life." He is deified by his admirers. In Venezuela, Hollinger (2006, 125) heard him described as "father and mother to The System and to us," as the "creator, life and soul" of El Sistema, and as possessed of a "great love of mankind." He has been likened to Gandhi, Mother Teresa, Nelson Mandela, and the Pope (Wakin 2012; Eatock 2010; Aloy 2013). Since Claudio Abbado calls him "a saint," it seems fitting that it was the International Academy of Hagiography—devoted to "the study and dissemination of the life and work of saints and virtuous people"—that proposed Abreu for the 2012 Nobel Peace Prize. Beatification and the ultimate earthly reward appear to be drawing ever closer.

This is the Abreu of documentaries, articles, and prize committees, the image that circulates globally. It is also the public persona constructed by El Sistema's PR department and the many overseas enterprises to which he is linked. The FESNOJIV website portrays him as a "visionary" and "creator of dreams and realities," and as single-handedly responsible for El Sistema's successes, while Deutsche Grammophon describes him as "tireless, devout and universally respected." The classical music world, with its tendency to deify great composers, conductors, and performers, is fertile ground for such a cult of personality.

Beyond the PR pitches, however, lies another Abreu: the one nicknamed Machiavelli, the Godfather, the Führer, the Pharaoh. The journalist Rafael Rivero (1994) famously labeled him "The Philanthropic Ogre." A dominant—and, some would say, domineering—figure of Venezuelan cultural life, Abreu is a far more complex character than the modern-day saint of public discourse. In his home country, he arouses strong feelings—great admiration, but also, from those who have had close dealings with him, fierce criticism and even palpable fear. Some describe his huge charisma; others his huge ego. He shares with the legendary conductor and musical dictator Toscanini more than just the title of "The Maestro" (as though no other existed). His critics accuse him of tyranny, pointing to the enormous and unelected power he wields in Venezuela, where, they claim, his word is all but law.

Prominent musicians privately described him as vengeful, malevolent, even an "evil genius." They talked about working with Abreu as "selling their soul." He was likened to a wolf in sheep's clothing, or an octopus extending tentacles throughout Venezuelan political and business circles, squeezing his contacts for support and throttling potential threats. The writer Eduardo Casanova (2009) described Abreu as "totalitarian and opportunist" and driven by "money, power and fame." A well-known conductor called him "a sinister genius, powered by narcissism," and likened his saintly public persona to "the devil dressed as an angel." A highly decorated musician compared him to Ronald Wilford, the shadowy maestro of maestros who pulls the strings of the classical music world in Norman Lebrecht's *The Maestro Myth*. For Abreu, he said, music is primarily a means of influencing people and events. Numerous well-placed observers believed that politics was Abreu's true calling and power, where his greatest interest lay.

Abreu's friends and foes agree that he is an exceptionally brilliant, powerful, well-connected individual who has shone in political and cultural life. He wields influence across the highest levels of Venezuelan politics and the media, aided by his tremendous skill as an orator. There is a mystique around him, exemplified by his famous color-coded notebook—an indecipherable mess of multicolored scrawls that suggests the encoded plotting of a higher life form—and the stories that he and his closest allies wear black opal rings. Two musicians who had known and worked with Abreu for decades claimed he rarely signed anything; he pulled many strings yet left few traces.

El Sistema is, to all intents and purposes, Abreu writ large, made in his own image and shaped by his strengths and weaknesses, his preoccupations and prejudices. If to his supporters he is the architect of all the program's successes, to his critics he is equally the source of all its failings. To begin with Abreu is to begin with the seed from which El Sistema grew.

To understand Abreu we cannot confine ourselves to his much-recounted official biography, but must rather explore how he is perceived in Venezuelan cultural circles—and how these perceptions are founded on episodes that have been largely obliterated from the official record but live on in the memories of his contemporaries. These alternative perspectives have rarely if ever been voiced internationally, but with El Sistema's influence and fame growing, they deserve attention. In order to understand El Sistema's success, we need to understand Abreu's rise to and wielding of power. The social order is the outcome of perpetual processes of competition and conflict; as Peter Martin (1995, 178) notes, it reflects "the power of some groups to impose authoritative definitions on others, to accumulate the resources with which to protect their positions and render them legitimate, and to resist challenges to their supremacy." Beneath the rhetoric of spirituality and art, the story of El Sistema unfolds as "a massively unequal contest" in a cultural field of "vigorous and dynamic struggle" (1995, 180–81), one that Abreu has fought with uncommon tenacity and skill.

THE HISTORICAL RECORD

Abreu is a hard man to investigate. Musicians speak of a "conspiracy of silence"—a combination of his extensive alliances and his habit of quieting his critics. I sought out the recollections and opinions of those who had worked with or encountered Abreu at different periods, as he rose from a student of music and economics to a leading figure in Venezuelan politics and culture. Their views made more sense after I read two articles published by investigative journalists in the early 1990s, focusing on the apogee of Abreu's political career—his tenure as minister of culture and president of the National Council for Culture (Consejo Nacional de la Cultura, CONAC) during the second government (1989–1993) of President Carlos Andrés Pérez (known as CAP). The history of these articles is intriguing. They were particularly significant when published, yet hard to find today. According to myth, the magazines they appeared in were mysteriously rounded up and very few copies made it into public circulation. Nevertheless, a few photocopies had been preserved in the cultural sphere in a samizdat-like manner, and two were presented to me by a musician.

The first article was written by Roger Santodomingo (1990), who would go on to serve as president of the National College of Journalists. Santodomingo underlines the lavish spending overseen by Abreu as minister. Despite the economic crisis at the time, "culture remains in spendthrift Saudi Venezuela," as the country was nicknamed in the 1970s when oil prices were high. Santodomingo identifies irrationality and compulsivity as hallmarks of cultural expenditure under Abreu. Two-thirds of CONAC's budget went on bureaucracy: lavish spending thus produced scant visible results, and frequently disappeared off the books as it passed through other ministries. Since, according to Santodomingo, Abreu had emasculated CONAC's internal audit office, it was impossible to guarantee that money was being used properly.

Santodomingo identifies a pair of funds, entitled "Transfers to persons" and "Various transfers to persons," which he claims constituted a *partida secreta* (slush fund) for Abreu's personal use. More than fifty million bolívares went into this account from cuts to personnel and programs including "Cultural Planning and Research" and "Promotion and Diffusion of Cultural Events." The money was spent in one week, says Santodomingo, in a "strange, improvised movement" of funds.

Santodomingo also claimed to have seen checks and contracts that revealed Abreu hired consultants and journalists as part of a media campaign to polish CONAC's image. The reams of uniformly positive press suggested that this policy was working well. Santodomingo's principal source, Joaquín López Mujica, a member of CONAC's consultative council, claimed that Abreu had approximately forty journalists among his consultants and asserted: "Abreu's management has been characterized by covert control of information. It's what could be termed a totalitarianism of cultural information." Santodomingo concludes "Abreu loves the press."

CONAC's principal objectives at the time supposedly included decentralization, but its director of regional development revealed that only half the relevant targets were ever achieved, with less than 4 percent of its total budget spent on decentralization. Most of the budget continued to be eaten up by a few Caracas groups, and regionalization consisted mainly of symbolic acts.

One of Abreu's defining features emerges as a fixation with display. López Mujica states baldly that "culture for Abreu is spectacle," and "the priority is the show." Abreu is criticized for neglecting research and, interestingly, education, with Santodomingo asking why, given the booming culture budget, Venezuela's conservatoires are in a state of abandonment. (As minister, Abreu not only secured considerable funding for his personal orchestral project, but he did so at the expense of other music education institutions—his competitors, in Martin's terms.) Large sums were assigned to new programs and institutions "that fulfill the requirement of having an instructional aim and national character," but, according to López Mujica, many resulted in "phantom institutes or programs that have never been launched."

López Mujica does not spare El Sistema from criticism, describing it as "an illusion." The SBYO started with the aim of democratizing high culture but has ended up competing "disloyally" with other orchestras. Huge amounts are spent on foreign tours yet most provincial núcleos are far from impressive. El Sistema appears as overfunded and underachieving.

For López Mujica, Abreu "is definitely divorced from the reality of the country. He is floating on a planet made of candy. The problem is that underneath there are great inequalities in the assignation of resources and priorities are neglected. Money is being spent and spent but results are scarce." Popular culture, education, and research have all been sidelined, while "a billion has been invested in a great spectacle. That is Abreu's style."

López Mujica also published many articles himself, such as a critical overview of the arts scene (1992a). As minister of culture, Abreu had broad responsibilities, yet "the favorite son is classical music," and "clientelism, preferential treatment, and favoritism" were widespread. Half of the large investment in symphony orchestras went to Abreu's youth orchestra foundation, while support for composition was minimal.

López Mujica (1991) homes in on Abreu's overwhelming favoritism for his own project in an article on CONAC's budget, questioning why expenditure on youth orchestras was over four hundred times higher than on provincial concert bands and over five hundred times that spent on a program called "Extension into popular zones." He criticizes "the strangulation of the national system of bands, the elitist conception of musical culture, [and] the rigidity of projects imposed on the provinces." In López Mujica's view, El Sistema's founder used his responsibility for the country's culture budget to pursue his own plans and ultimately redefine the nation's cultural order according to his own interests.

Elsewhere, López Mujica (1993) criticizes Abreu's CONAC for its lack of planning, bureaucratic stodginess, and institutional narcissism, and for providing insufficient support for the research, composition, and recording of Venezuelan music, accusing the institution of "musical Eurocentrism." He lays the blame for an alleged failure of cultural policy at Abreu's door, citing centralization, elitism, the sidelining of research, and a focus on the ephemeral and the spectacular (1992b).

It would be easy to dismiss López Mujica as someone with a grudge against Abreu, were it not for the foundation of his arguments in facts—to which he presumably had access as a member of CONAC's consultative council—and their echoes in articles by other journalists. Manuel Quintana Castillo (1994) wrote of a huge culture budget being handed out according to the whims and to the benefit of very few. Many projects had been announced, but "apart from the youth orchestras there are no concrete results." María Teresa Boulton (1992) argued that the Ministry of Culture had little time for minority activities, "since it is clear that in a context of vertical leadership—like that which exists at present in CONAC—other more ostentatious, eye-catching, spectacular activities will be the only ones to benefit."

In an article entitled "The Humiliated of CONAC," Earle Herrera (1994) describes the offices of Abreu's institution as full of humble artists queuing to be paid, only to be told "your cheque hasn't been issued—come back in a month," a process that might go on for six months. Artists traveled overnight from all over the country to receive inefficient and often rude treatment in the "dictatorial centre of culture." The pay was so poor and so hard to extract that some artists simply gave up. "Venezuelan artists and intellectuals are treated poorly and paid worse everywhere, but CONAC sets the standard and leads the pack. To be sure, there is a little group that has nothing to complain about: the same old 'big names' that look down on popular culture." Herrera mocks the neoliberal language of CONAC's managers and the paid hacks who sing their praises, claiming that "the current leadership of CONAC owes much of its 'shine' to these shameful and pricey pens." He describes a starkly divided cultural world: those at the top enjoy "overseas trips, self-publication of books, the traffic of influence, legions of flatterers, fine food and fine wine, self-promotion and carte blanche in the press," while "the artists from the provinces and the barrios, people who are all about hard work rather than show," are forgotten. The president of this elitist organization was soon to reinvent himself as the champion of Venezuela's poor.

Oscar Ramos's critique begins with Abreu's uncannily and uniformly positive press.[1] "Do you recall any criticism of the cultural policy of Pérez-Abreu appearing at any point in the press?" He mocks Chefi Borzacchini, Abreu's leading supporter at *El Nacional* newspaper, for painting the minister as a hero "in language that recalls the odes of Gómez" (Venezuela's early-twentieth-century dictator). Ramos's criticisms are by now familiar: disordered cultural management, excessive and poorly controlled spending (particularly on bureaucracy), and a focus on culture as spectacle. Decentralization appears again as a weakness: regionalization was interpreted as sending out the occasional group from Caracas, "and the provinces? They don't exist."

The second major article about Abreu was published by Rafael Rivero (1994), who makes some disturbing claims about "The Philanthropic Ogre." Rivero's opening gambit is that "the minister is sad," and the cause, he concludes, is the death of Abreu's chauffeur, his "right-hand man who accompanied him everywhere, even on tours on which a driver was unessential, taking care of matters like his boss's outfit." The driver's wife "began to resent her husband's inability to resist being absorbed by the famous baton. In the small hours of the 25th of December, after a dramatic argument, the drama reaches a climax worthy of a Greek tragedy: the Othello-like lady takes out a revolver, shoots her husband in the head, and immediately afterwards commits suicide." Two of the three members of the triangle died, leaving only Abreu—the sad minister.

Though this alleged scandal is the article's most infamous detail, its other contents are more revealing of Abreu's role in Venezuelan culture, politics, and economics. In his public life, too, controversy has not been in short supply. First of all, he was sent on a mission by political allies to open up a dialogue with the former dictator Marcos Pérez Jiménez, who had "led a government notorious for brutality and corruption" and was "feared and hated inside his country and mocked elsewhere as the prototype of the Latin American military despot" (Rohter 2001), and was now living out his autumn years in exile in Madrid. Abreu's longtime associate Pedro Tinoco was the 1973 presidential candidate of the Movimiento Desarrollista (Developmentalist Movement), which had emerged from and remained closely aligned to that of Pérez Jiménez. Tinoco sent Abreu to Spain as his envoy in order to rally the convicted and disgraced leader's remaining followers to their cause.[2] According to a U.S. State Department document: "Following Pedro Tinoco's talks with PJ [Pérez Jiménez] in January, *desarrollista* José Antonio Abreu carried on talks with PJ and [his advisor Pedro] Estrada to draw up program agreeable to PJ and *desarrollistas*."[3] Abreu's political affinities and abilities are hard to mistake in his negotiations with one of Venezuela's most infamous caudillos. Pedro Tinoco, meanwhile, went on to notoriety as a key figure behind the 1994 Venezuelan banking scandal.

The article also refers to a financial pyramid scheme whose collapse, according to Rivero and other sources, was blamed on a relative of Abreu. No charges were made against Abreu himself, and there is no evidence that he was involved, but Rivero notes that a "malicious journalist hinted that behind it all there had to be hiding a brilliant mind." Suspicions were aroused, and rumors have continued to circulate to this day. In interviews, several older musicians remembered well this drama that had engulfed the Abreu family; it had clearly colored their views of El Maestro. With his genius beyond doubt, Abreu's critics struggle to view him as ignorant when scandal erupts close by.

A third cause célèbre erupted in late 1979, when the exiled Argentinean theater director and music critic Gustavo Tambascio dared to criticize Abreu's youth orchestra in his column in *El Nacional*, describing a recent concert as "orchestral chaos," and comparing the event to the raucous finale of a children's party. Abreu responded in print the next day, unleashing a merciless attack on the critic, but he did not stop there: "He [Tambascio] should know that in Venezuela there are many legal means to hit back hard in every sphere against those who try to insult or denigrate the country." The threats continued: "we will make any gatecrasher respect us . . . his article will not go unpunished." Abreu's heavy-handed, almost xenophobic response took the exchange beyond the usual skirmishes of the cultural sphere. Like the pyramid scheme, this incident, seen as emblematic of Abreu's vengeful character and intolerance of criticism, is still clearly remembered over three decades later.

Abreu's media fixation soon comes to the fore. The former head of publicity at CONAC describes Abreu as "obsessed as far as the media are concerned . . . more than capable of calling me at 3 am about a small detail of an information leaflet." Rivero describes Abreu's abhorrence of a publicity vacuum—somewhat typical in politicians—and also points to its darker side: he claims that *El Nacional* critic Enrique Moya's negative report of an Abreu-sponsored event saw the author given his marching orders, and alludes to a practice of cultural institutions defanging journalistic reports. An attempt at revolution by a group of journalists, fed up with constant interference, fizzled out after a number of signatories to a mordant open letter mysteriously withdrew their support; coincidentally, almost all of them were subsequently given jobs as cultural advisors to CONAC.

According to Rivero, Abreu's micro-control of the media extended into the provinces, where journalists who published critical opinions in local newspapers were instantly reprimanded or their employers urged to take punitive action. Those who dared question his management of CONAC put their careers at risk. The governor of a distant state received a phone call urging him to fire an advisor who had criticized Abreu. The governor not only refused, but gave Abreu a public lesson in democracy, stating: "Dr. Abreu, you must learn that criticism is necessary." Rivero portrays a bitterly divided cultural sphere, riven by confrontations between Abreu's unconditional supporters, who occupied multiple posts and absorbed large sums of money destined for the cultural sphere, and his critics, who considered El Maestro "an individual with Machiavellian intentions" and "a lover of applause at any cost."

Abreu was a genius at securing funds: not only did CONAC's budget rise exponentially under his stewardship, but he was famed for his capacity to extract further money from other ministries, leading Rivero to liken him to a snake charmer. Abreu is also portrayed as a neoliberal stooge: "his true function in the Pérez package was to silence the voices of intellectuals before the predictable neoliberal storm, and that explains why all these huge resources were devoted to an elite with a powerful influence over public opinion." As a result, the cultural sector was the least vocal during the upheavals of the time, which saw two abortive coups d'état while Abreu was minister.

Abreu may have been the master fund-raiser, but, according to Rivero, he also presided over great wastage and unfulfilled commitments: "it is no secret that in this most recent period everyone travelled [overseas], or received money for X project which, in many cases, was never carried out." Rivero alludes to slush funds for the use of cultural bureaucrats. Hordes of artists were sent off on lavish, state-funded tours to Europe on which they sometimes did little; the SBYO famously ended up in Paris and London without its instruments. Rivero signs off with the opinions of two cultural observers who claim that "for Abreu, culture is a fashion show, a swindle, without true quality, after which nothing will remain," and that "under Abreu there has been no culture, just a lavish and self-congratulatory spectacle."

These articles provide a detailed picture of the controversies that surrounded Abreu at the height of his political career.[4] When I received them, I discovered that many of the criticisms I had encountered during fieldwork had been foreshadowed in print two decades earlier, pointing to long-standing and unresolved issues. The articles tell us much about Abreu's record in cultural management, and especially about his reputation—which was far from saintly or Gandhi-esque. They portray a politician known—at least to some—for his wasteful, opaque financial administration; his predilection for vertical, authoritarian management; his highly unequal distribution of resources and marked preference for high culture; his favoring of show over substance; and his illusory projects and unimpressive results, dressed up by a compliant press. They also provide a valuable backdrop to understanding the new phase of his career that began in the mid-1990s as he left formal politics and devoted his energies to El Sistema. Yet perhaps the most striking historical record of all comes from the end of that decade, and from the very heart of his orchestral project.

THE OTHER GUSTAVO

Gustavo Medina joined El Sistema as a violinist in 1976, and rose to become one of Abreu's right-hand men. For eight years, he occupied the post of conductor of the National Children's Orchestra, a position in which he was succeeded by another Gustavo—Dudamel. On November 28, 1999, he resigned, and on December 3 his resignation letter appeared in the newspaper *El Mundo* under the headline "Abreu Denounced" ("Crisis en Orquestas" 1999). According to the article's subtitle, Medina "reveals management blunders and the persecution that he suffered."

Medina writes of his early enthusiasm for the program, which turned into all-absorbing dedication. However, "today, 24 years later, I find myself before the greatest disillusion of my life, with the unpleasant sensation of having devoted it to a project in which I, like many others, was used to serve not music but the interests of José Antonio Abreu."

Medina believed fully in the project and its leader. Yet as the turbulent decade of the 1990s wore on, fundamental political changes loomed, Abreu approached his sixtieth year (and twenty-fifth in charge of El Sistema), and Medina started to believe that "the intellectual grandeur of José Antonio Abreu would be confirmed by his propelling a process of change in order to adapt the institution to the necessities of the new moment." Medina was increasingly concerned that El Sistema's administrative structure and politics were like a suit made to measure for Abreu; he believed that changes and plans for succession needed to be made, so that the program would not fall apart on El Maestro's retirement or death.

It soon became apparent to Medina that transformations were not high on Abreu's agenda. "Events showed categorically that all this was nothing more than an illusion. They revealed a conduct that was diametrically opposed, and the desire for improvement and change that any evolutionary process logically requires was taken as a betrayal or an attempted coup, as though our institution were a state within the country." According to Medina, he was the victim of a whispering campaign by other members of Abreu's inner circle, which culminated in his removal from his conducting position without warning or explanation to the orchestra.

Medina describes manipulations and pressures from El Sistema's leading figures: "they ordered the editing of the videos of the concerts that I did with the children's orchestra so that 'only children appeared.'" Sistema orchestras are often very varied in age, and attempts are sometimes made to project a more youthful image. "The final straw was Dr. Abreu's order not to allow me to have copies of the music that I needed to study unless I solicited them directly from him in writing, as though a symphony by Saint Saëns or Beethoven were 'secrets of state.'" In the light of the pressures that he and his family were subjected to, Medina resigned, accusing the organization to which he had devoted his life of being "a gigantic flattery machine designed to satisfy the interests of its founder José Antonio Abreu, without regard for the fact that the cost may be generations of young people who believe that their future depends on their efforts and dedication, without realizing that without the 'unction of the maestro' that future does not exist."

This is of course the view of a single disgruntled ex-employee; but as Dudamel's predecessor, he was no ordinary employee. Furthermore, his account coincides with those of others, both published and private. He paints a sobering portrait of an institution shot through with manipulation and intrigue, resistant to debate and change, and hinging on Abreu's word.

POLITICIAN

Internationally, Abreu is usually portrayed as either an apolitical figure or a reluctant politician, but the facts (and Venezuelan observers) tell a different story. His first stint in parliament began in 1964, when he was just twenty-five, and he went on to become minister of culture. Under the government of Hugo Chávez, he acted as a kind of cultural ambassador and moved steadily closer to the center of power, eventually operating out of the Office of the President. His half-century near the top of the political tree, barely ruffled by dramatic shifts in the winds, shows him to be a consummate politician.

His most striking achievement has been to obtain massive state funding for a single project, working effectively over decades with successive governments and riding out a political about-turn. In Venezuela, large-scale projects started by one government are often abandoned by the next. Abreu, however, did not just survive but thrived off the seismic shift from forty years of social democratic governments to Chávez's socialist revolution (labeled "Bolivarian" in honor of the president's hero, Simón Bolívar)—a remarkable outcome given that Abreu was minister when Chávez launched an unsuccessful coup in 1992.

As a profoundly conservative figure who moved in the highest right-wing circles, Abreu was a very odd bedfellow for Chávez. In his youth, Abreu formed part of a conservative political group at the Universidad Católica Andrés Bello (UCAB) with Pedro Tinoco and Marcel Granier, two key architects of Venezuelan neoliberalism, and he was a right-hand man of CAP during the sharp turn toward neoliberalism from 1989. Another associate is conservative icon Lorenzo Mendoza of Grupo Polar, who declared in 2009 that his company had been supporting El Sistema for thirty-two years and "since then we have been allies and have been growing and working together" (Ocando 2009). He is also closely connected to ultraconservative elements of the Catholic Church.

Not only were Chávez and Abreu historically political enemies, but they represented antagonistic ideological positions. Chávez embraced socialism, participatory democracy, and political consciousness-raising, whereas El Sistema, as discussed in subsequent chapters, models the values of corporate capitalism, is an autocracy, and resolutely avoids political discussion. The contradiction between Chávez's brashly anti-imperialist stance and El Sistema's Eurocentrism has been a target for left-wing critics like Diego Silva and Freddy Argimiro, who regard Abreu as a lackey of U.S. cultural and economic imperialism and hence deeply implicated in Venezuela's social problems rather than the savior of its youth. For them, but also for some scholars (e.g., Hellinger 1991, 191; Fernandes 2010, 70–71), the need for state-sponsored social programs of the 1990s (including El Sistema) was provoked by the neoliberal structural adjustment enacted by CAP's second government, in which Abreu served as minister.

How, then, did Abreu and El Sistema thrive in Chávez's Venezuela? One view is that these two charismatic leaders have more in common than meets the eye. "They're very similar," opined a university professor. "From the point of view of how they function, how they invade territory, it's very similar. They're caudillos [strongmen]." Nevertheless, the path was very rocky to start with. Following his own tradition, Abreu organized a huge orchestral concert preceded by a grand trumpet fanfare to receive Chávez after his electoral victory, but the president barely acknowledged him at the event. Two knowledgeable informants suggested that Abreu then shifted his focus to persuading Chávez's wife. According to others, however, Chávez's distaste for Abreu was eventually overcome by the appeal of the project itself, above all the social benefits that it claimed to offer the president's key political constituency, the urban poor.

As I argue in Chapter 7, there are good reasons to believe that the program underwent a politically expedient and predominantly discursive transformation around this time, one that was necessary for its survival but also allowed it to thrive. Any discussion of El Sistema as a social project needs to bear in mind the crisis Abreu faced in 1998 when his political foe came to power, with zero interest in classical music but considerable concern for social inclusion. El Sistema's subsequent expansion testifies to Abreu's unparalleled lobbying skills and his ability to blur the disjunctures between El Sistema and the

Bolivarian Revolution by framing the project in the language of social justice. However, El Sistema's social rhetoric emerged clearly during the decade that also saw the consolidation at an international level of an ideology that Yúdice (2003) calls "the expediency of culture"—making the case for culture in terms of its social and economic impacts. El Sistema's "turn to the social" in the 1990s may thus be seen as responding to broad ideological shifts at both national and international level.

While the language of social inclusion undoubtedly appealed to Chávez, supporting El Sistema offered him advantages. Associating himself with a highly regarded project made sense. Also, orchestras are effective political tools, and supporting the SBYO added another weapon to Chávez's political-ceremonial armory. The concert for the bicentenary celebrations in July 2011 was a Chavista jamboree with a triple-sized orchestra and "greatest hits" program. Later that year, the Community of Latin American and Caribbean States summit in Caracas was opened by the SBYO. Throughout 2011, important bi- or multinational occasions involving Venezuela were marked by either a Sistema concert or the promise to create a youth orchestra, and Dudamel and El Sistema appeared on TV infomercials on behalf of the state National Electoral Council encouraging people to vote in the 2012 elections. Under Chávez and Abreu, El Sistema took its place at the heart of Venezuelan political ceremony.

El Sistema's Chávez-era boom thus depended on an incongruous meeting of political minds, which seems to have rested on pragmatism and mutual opportunism, in addition to a shared love of demagogic display. As an illustration, a journalist reported that in the mid-1990s Abreu's office was decorated with photos of El Maestro with a succession of presidents and first wives, dating back to the mid-1970s. When the journalist returned some five years later, all the old photos had gone—there were just new ones picturing Abreu with Chávez. Eduardo Casanova, a writer, retired diplomat, and contemporary of Abreu, described the latter's entry into politics under the wing of presidential candidate Arturo Uslar Pietri: "Abreu, who had previously been a member of the Christian Democrat party, joined [Uslar Pietri] at the end of the campaign and managed with great opportunism to enter parliament at the expense of many young people who had actually worked and were more qualified than him." In this account, Abreu entered parliament by switching political parties—useful preparation for Chávez's ascent to the presidency.

Abreu's unmatched capacity to move with the political winds is viewed by supporters as evidence that his project is above politics, and by critics as the sign of a truly political animal whose success rests on an ability to lobby both sides, and a man with few convictions beyond the pursuit of power. With Abreu's influence extending into every corner of Venezuelan musical life, a founder described him as a modern Jean-Baptiste Lully, the superintendent of music who took absolute control over French music under Louis XIV. The composer

René Rojas, too, compared Abreu to the supreme musician-courtier and flatterer of monarchs, and added: "when there are changes of government or cabinet, the first thing he does is offer up a concert to the new leading figures" (quoted in Rivero 1994, 52). Casanova (2007) claimed that successive governments had given Abreu "the power so that music in Venezuela became what you said, only you had the power to decide. You were and you are the little dictator (*el dictadorzuelo*) of music in Venezuela."

By allying himself with both neoliberals and socialists, Abreu has kept governments onside and himself in power, but alienated people across the political spectrum. Many on the Left distrust Abreu for his conservatism and close ties to CAP, and are offended by his high profile in a socialist revolution. Others on the Right, meanwhile, have been critical of Abreu's alliance with Chávez. Abreu's symbolic support for the closure of the opposition-slanted Radio Caracas TV in 2007 was the final straw for many: on the stroke of midnight, the channel went off the air, to be replaced immediately by a Sistema choir and orchestra conducted by Dudamel performing the national anthem, inaugurating the government-run TVES channel on the same frequency—a politically charged move that created a host of enemies for Abreu at a stroke.

In October 2011 Abreu lent his weight to the Venezuelan government's defense of its human rights record, sending the SBYO to perform a concert in conjunction with the government's presentation to the United Nations in Geneva. Abreu's actions again infuriated the government's critics, who accused him of being an apologist for Chávez's abuses. However, the sense that Abreu was shifting El Sistema's weight squarely behind the government reached a new peak in January 2013.

Venezuela had been going through a tense political moment since the New Year, with Chávez gravely ill in hospital in Cuba and therefore missing his inauguration on January 10. Nevertheless, as part of the official events to mark the noninauguration, Abreu, Dudamel, and the Simón Bolívar Symphony Orchestra (SBSO) offered a concert for Chávez's health, performing Beethoven's 9th Symphony. Abreu expressed his solidarity with Chávez, thanking the president for promoting "the revolutionary rescue of 400,000 and up to a goal of one million children and young people" ("Abreu: Vaya Nuestra Gratitud" 2013). Abreu seized the chance to underline his conviction "that the President will continue to offer his enthusiastic support to this musical project," and Vice President Nicolás Maduro rewarded him with a promise to continue expanding El Sistema. This enthusiastic and very public display of Chavism was too much for many opposition supporters, and as with the closure of RCTV, it unleashed a barrage of criticism. Abreu's appearance, smiling and applauding, in the front row at Maduro's controversial investiture in April 2013 left yet more observers disenchanted (Silva 2013).

Yet, ironically, Chavistas were also railing against Abreu. Just two days earlier, and equally controversially, he had been photographed warmly embracing two VIP guests, the Colombian singer Juanes and the Spaniard Miguel Bosé—both well-known, outspoken critics of Chávez. Leftists were immediately up in arms. Facebook and the political website Aporrea were bombarded by journalists, musicians, and cultural activists, lambasting Juanes and Bosé for their views and Abreu for supporting them, accusing the three of being the friendly face of the international Right.[5] Soon afterward, 146 of them signed a petition repudiating Abreu for "attack[ing] the image of our country in the world" and demanding "that Dr. Abreu give an explanation that justifies his invitation to two enemies of Comandante Chávez and the Venezuelan people at a particularly sensitive moment for the Bolivarian Revolution" ("Artistas Venezolanos" 2013).

Abreu's two public and contradictory political gestures in the space of three days provoked a flurry of debate. In Venezuela, far from being seen as apolitical, Abreu's every move is considered politically significant and is scrutinized for its meaning. Which (if either) of these gestures revealed Abreu's true colors, and which his political calculations?

Whatever his underlying intentions, through his overt association of his project with Chávez, Abreu politicized El Sistema. In return for massive government investment, he offered unquestioning public support for Chávez, including the use of El Sistema's young musicians in political ceremonies. (A member of the Veracruz regional youth orchestra claimed that many of its concerts were organized for political events and key dates in the revolutionary calendar.) On January 10, 2013, as Abreu's display of loyalty earned him a public promise from acting leader Maduro, the political nature of the deal could hardly have been clearer. This was an effective strategy, but it alienated part of his natural conservative constituency, and it did not win Abreu many friends; as Casanova put it, "Abreu's political opportunism is a terrible example for young people."

After such political contortions in a country as polarized as Venezuela, the idea that Abreu is "universally respected," as Deutsche Grammophon puts it, is clearly a fiction. Opposition supporters accused Abreu and Dudamel of collaborating with a dictator, comparing them to Herbert von Karajan under the Nazis; Chavistas, meanwhile, labeled Abreu a Trojan horse, smuggling conservative ideology into the heart of the Bolivarian Revolution—all a far cry from the serene, depoliticized depiction overseas.[6] El Sistema's recent history displays Martin's "vigorous and dynamic struggle," and if Abreu's political skill enabled him to consolidate his position, he made enemies along the way. Nevertheless, while musicians' networks and social media buzzed with polemical debates, criticisms found no space in the mainstream media and were unknown to most Sistema enthusiasts overseas until the major outbreak of civil unrest in Venezuela in February 2014.

As trouble flared on February 12, Abreu and Dudamel contributed to official celebrations for the Day of Youth with a gala concert. Days later, pianist

Gabriela Montero wrote a critical open letter ("Carta Abierta" 2014) to Abreu and Dudamel about their failure to react to the political upheaval going on around them, sparking a mass of newspaper articles, blog posts, and social media commentary. It appeared that many Venezuelans agreed with her and harbored critical opinions of El Sistema's twin figureheads. For the first time, critics broke cover in numbers and attacked *publicly* what they saw as collaborationism with a repressive government, while a political dividing line appeared in the classical music sphere, with opposition-supporting musicians organizing protest concerts in Europe and the United States, setting themselves apart implicitly or explicitly from Abreu, Dudamel, and their de facto alignment with the government. The two conductors' allegiances, maneuvers, partial statements, and silences came under repeated scrutiny. In *El Nacional*, long one of Abreu's strongholds in the media, Arroyo Gil (2014) articulated a common source of disquiet: Abreu's personal identification with and closeness to power. He described El Sistema's founder as a serial flatterer of political leaders who appeared "smiling, like Caesar's special guest." For Álvarez Pifano (2014), meanwhile, Abreu was "one of the most astute and mysterious politicians of the last fifty years.... A wolf in sheep's clothing. A politician camouflaged by the modest attire of a musician." The criticism was reported and repeated around the world in major newspapers like *The Guardian* and the *Los Angeles Times*. In *The Huffington Post*, a former Venezuelan minister described Dudamel as "a musical giant but a moral midget" (Goodman 2014). In *The Telegraph*, Sistema sympathizer Ivan Hewett (2014) accused him of "intransigent evasiveness" and suggested that unless the conductor took a stand, "we'll have to conclude that all his high-sounding stuff about music being a 'universal language of peace' is so much hot air." At the time of writing, the fallout from this transnational debate is hard to predict, but for the first time Abreu and Dudamel have been subjected to widespread critical scrutiny in the international media, and the claim that the former is above politics has become much harder to sustain.

LEADER

Abreu is unquestionably an exceptional leader. His capacity to influence others takes various forms. One is his legendary oratorical skill. His public speeches are often interrupted by applause and cries of approval. He is also described as a "snake charmer," possessing a hypnotic power. People say that if you get into an elevator with Abreu, he will have persuaded you to do something for him by the time you reach your floor.

Abreu has other tools at his disposal as well. A distinguished musician claimed that Abreu's "Plan A" was usually to try to bring the opposition into the fold, flattering them, making extravagant offers, creating jobs or projects for them. If he has to fight, said my interviewee, Abreu will do it—but he prefers to pay. "Everyone has their price," Abreu allegedly told a journalist. Some of the most trenchant critics of El Sistema in Veracruz ended up with plum jobs inside the system. Most work opportunities for classical musicians are within El Sistema, and Abreu can create jobs at will; few musicians can resist his offer. Several informants also echoed Santodomingo and Rivero's claims that Abreu channeled money to culture reporters and editors at leading newspapers. In the 1990s Abreu's control of the media was legendary.

Abreu allegedly handles potential adversaries with the stick as well as the carrot. Several people I interviewed appeared afraid to speak their minds. One prominent figure was visibly nervous, adding the suffix "but I'm not criticizing!" to a series of negative stories. He was worried about the survival of the non-Sistema institution that he directed. I heard several reports of individuals being fired from their jobs for criticizing or displeasing Abreu. Informants recalled threatening phone calls, sometimes in the middle of the night, to musicians who announced a desire to leave El Sistema. Abreu reportedly snapped at one such musician, a founder, "one day I'm going to cut you down to size." A Ministry of Culture official who crossed Abreu left his job after anonymous threats and an Internet campaign against him.

While it was impossible for me to verify these stories, a former senior figure in El Sistema alleged that "espionage and persecution" had been part of Abreu's decades of "trampling on and taking advantage of so many people." He went on: "there is a long list of people who have been persecuted for a range of reasons, from the most trivial (like disagreeing publicly with Abreu more than once) to those who really took some action against him," and the latter "will have to suffer the consequences for the rest of Abreu's life." He claimed that after a dispute broke out between Abreu and a provincial music school director in the late 1970s, "Abreu waged a merciless campaign to destroy, in the literal sense of the word, any work or musical group that was linked to [the director]. In this war, no holds were barred: from coaxing the musicians away from [the director's] school with offers of scholarships and instruments, to the constant publication of accusations of corruption in the press to finish him off morally." I asked him about the darker stories that circulated: "I saw the business of persecution many times," he replied, "and after I left I experienced it firsthand. There were various spies who appeared, looking for the opportunity to screw me over. Why? Perhaps because I knew too much and one day I might talk!"

These accounts, even if they cannot be verified, reflect widespread beliefs about the extent of Abreu's power and his vengeful streak. But beliefs aside, Venezuelan musical life is littered with musicians who have fallen out with Abreu, though most keep silent. Furthermore, several well-known musicians, while they praised Abreu in public, reported difficult experiences with him in private, ranging from simple lack of support to more problematic interventions in their professional lives. In her hagiography, Borzacchini (2010, 48) writes that Abreu "offers the world a key to peace: tolerate, include, and recognize one's neighbor," but numerous musicians portrayed a man who is intolerant of criticism and willing to persecute those who do not submit to his will.

Reports surfaced frequently of tensions over musicians wanting to leave to study or work overseas. Abreu sometimes tried to persuade them to stay by offering them a better job or a pay rise; but numerous musicians reported cases or fears of blacklisting or instruments being taken away. Interviewees, including current and former members of the SBYO, in Venezuela and overseas, recounted fallings-out and punitive action. Leaving El Sistema is unquestionably a touchy subject. Those who have left have sometimes been labeled as "exiles" and treated as deserters. There are signs, however, that Abreu's position has softened recently and overseas study has become more acceptable, as El Sistema's production of talented musicians has outstripped the opportunities available to them in Venezuela.

Abreu's vision is Manichean. He demands total commitment and absolute allegiance, and drives his followers hard. One of his favorite lines is "rest comes with eternal rest, my dear." Abreu sleeps very little and is unconcerned about making others do the same; he is notorious for phoning his acolytes in the middle of the night, keeping them in a constant state of nervous tension. A former SBYO member recalled a rehearsal back in the days when Abreu conducted the orchestra. It was one o'clock in the morning, and a violinist said to Abreu, "we're tired, let's give it a break." Abreu replied: "Fine, have a break," and that—goes the story—was the end of the violinist's career in El Sistema.

MACHIAVELLIAN

Santodomingo wrote of Abreu that "the word which best identifies him seems to be 'power,' and with it he is capable, just like Mephistopheles, of drawing in Faust." The term "Machiavellian" appeared in Rivero's investigation, and arose repeatedly in my own, as musicians described Abreu's strategies to reward supporters, silence critics, absorb or curb competitors, and consolidate his political influence. Several prominent musicians claimed that Abreu disliked alternatives and independent initiatives, preferring to incorporate or eliminate, and they portrayed him as a Machiavellian puppet-master, pulling the strings of Venezuelan music from behind the scenes. A founder described Abreu as a master chess player, moving his pieces around the board. Abreu's vision is purely strategic, he claimed; the maestro trains young musicians to be his foot soldiers and, with a few exceptions, is uninterested in what happens to them as individuals. Machiavellianism is ultimately a pragmatic philosophy, and Abreu is a pragmatist at heart.

"There was always an element of manipulation and espionage," said another founder. "That role was played loyally in that period by X [today one of

El Sistema's top figures]. He played with us in the orchestra and transmitted information back and forth for Abreu, something that we as kids didn't suspect. There were always individuals like X who infiltrated the orchestra itself to keep Abreu informed about the most intimate details of everyone, to be used to control and manipulate at the appropriate moment. Sexual transgressions, infidelities, financial problems, family problems, everything went through Abreu to keep control over the musicians. When there was some 'scandal' with an orchestra member, Abreu would intervene immediately and 'adopt' them to 'help' them and from then on they would become one of Abreu's favorites. The most awkward thing is that he would demand the most intimate details possible of the situations that came to light, supposedly to protect the 'institutional prestige.'" He compared Abreu to J. Edgar Hoover, gathering compromising information on those close to him in order to ensure their silence.

Some of Venezuela's best-known concert artists have reportedly been on the receiving end of Abreu's Machiavellian side. Stories of manipulative interventions abound, with Abreu allegedly ensuring that one artist's career moves rapidly ahead while another's stalls. Two musicians with international solo careers claimed that they had had foreign engagements (unconnected with El Sistema) cancelled immediately after disputes with Abreu. Such stories apparently reached the ears of Wakin (2012c), who alludes to Abreu's tendency to "dictate career moves among the top echelon of musicians." As one musician put it, Abreu wants to be there with his baton, pointing to those who get to make it and those who do not. Naming three famous Venezuelan musicians whom he knew personally, a music critic reported: "Abreu maintains his image through people whose excellence has been proven overseas. He hired [the three artists], people who, in return for a lot of money, played a part in El Sistema for years, but did not emerge from it. They are not keen on working for him, and they only do it for the money."

Several interviewees reported that Abreu had used his large network of influence in order to preempt projects that other musicians had in the pipeline. A conservatoire director had been offered an enticing space for a music school. He met with Abreu to ask him to lend his weight to the proposal. Three days later he went to present the proposal, only to find that Abreu had intervened and claimed the space for El Sistema. Another senior musician alleged that he had been about to present a proposal for music education in prisons to the Ministry of Justice, but Abreu got a proposal in first; he marveled at the way that Abreu's network of contacts enabled him to catch wind of plans, intercept them in motion, and replace them with his own. Another eminent musician described the genesis of the Camerata Criolla project: he claimed that Abreu had intercepted the project proposal at the Ministry of Culture, copied it, and presented it himself. This alleged scheme was scotched, however, by the current minister's dislike of Abreu. This musician summed up Abreu as an "intellectual vampire."

Abreu's reputed Machiavellian tendencies are also in evidence on a more personalized scale. A senior musician who fell out with Abreu described his astonishment that the first person on the phone to congratulate him on a new job or commiserate on the illness of a family member was El Maestro, who was at the very same time undermining his professional projects. A journalist described Abreu as a consummate actor, turning up at events to lavish public praise and affection on people who are his adversaries in private. Don't believe everything you see, said this journalist; it is all judged for effect. According to these accounts, Abreu's capacity to offer public support while placing obstacles in private makes him simultaneously the most solicitous and the most implacable of enemies.

VISIONARY

One of the most common descriptions of Abreu (not least by FESNOJIV) is "visionary." There is certainly some truth in this, but what distinguishes Abreu from many other cultural managers is not just his vision but also his capacity to back it with political power and economic resources. As we will see in Chapter 3, Abreu's National Youth Orchestra grew out of various existing initiatives; what he contributed, according to several informants, was not so much vision as managerial skill, a talent for persuasion, and money to pay the musicians.

As minister of culture, Abreu had the opportunity to strengthen his authority, assign resources to his project, and give full rein to his vision. A journalist connected to CONAC in the 1990s described the institution as Abreu's personal fiefdom, and claimed that the disproportionate spending on El Sistema continued long after Abreu had left. CONAC's next president was stunned when Abreu gave him instructions about apportioning funds, and a dispute broke out between the new CONAC leadership and Abreu's followers, but Abreu had allegedly put in place a network of contacts and support that ensured the continuation of his plans. A journalist with close connections to CONAC caught another journalist (an Abreu ally) going through the institution's bins during this period; the latter replied defiantly: "Don't you know who I work for?" The leakage of important information led to a sweep of the CONAC offices; according to my informant, they turned out to be bugged. As late as 2003, a decade after Abreu left CONAC, a group of education and culture workers wrote in an open letter to the institution's president that Abreu "has managed to maintain significant parcels of power within CONAC, through which he exercises enough influence to be able to prevent any progressive action outside his immediate control" (López Mujica 2003).

Something similar took place at the Ministry of Culture. The Fundación Vicente Emilio Sojo mooted a law that all ensembles that received money from the state should devote 1 percent of their budget to supporting composition. A representative spoke to an official at the ministry (from which Abreu had already departed), who responded: "they'll never approve this, because El Sistema will never agree to it." The official refused even to consider the proposal, because Abreu—not the minister—would be against it.

Emilio Mendoza (n.d.a), formerly director of the Orchestra of Latin American Instruments (Orquesta de Instrumentos Latinoamericanos, ODILA), recounted a dispute with Abreu that centered on the issue of expansion and, indirectly, vision.[7] Abreu wanted to spread ODILA all across Venezuela, whereas Mendoza argued that they should ensure that the existing núcleo, in poor shape at the time, was working properly first. Abreu accused him of lacking vision, and the relationship (and ODILA's prospects) ended there. An internationally renowned Venezuelan music group described being summoned to Abreu's office, where he announced a grand vision of hundreds of copycat ensembles across Venezuela, offering the musicians large salaries, cars, and perks. Another musician received a similar proposal; Abreu called him in and pointed to the sixth floor of the CASM: "from there you are going to create your kingdom." In both cases the musicians refused Abreu's offer, unwilling to become pawns in his master plan. In all these examples, the relationship between vision and political or economic power is clear.

CONTROVERSIAL PUBLIC FIGURE

José Antonio Abreu is unquestionably a highly charismatic figure. His reputation in Venezuela, however, is somewhat mixed. A hallmark of his personal history, lost in the international eulogizing but not forgotten at home, is the series of controversies that has punctuated his career. These episodes came up repeatedly in my private conversations with current and former figures of authority in El Sistema and other institutions, who recalled Abreu's close association with controversial political figures and raised concerns about the integrity of his cultural management.

Abreu's political support for Pedro Tinoco and his dealings with the deposed dictator Marcos Pérez Jiménez aroused doubts, and the pyramid scheme scandal apparently damaged his reputation, even though there was no evidence of his involvement. Even the pinnacle of his political career in the early 1990s turned into a difficult time, because of his close ties to public figures who fell spectacularly from grace. His political mentor, CAP, was ousted from the presidency after a corruption scandal in 1993. His long-term ally Tinoco—a conservative politician, supporter of ex-dictator Pérez Jiménez, and figure with "dubious democratic credentials" (Karl 1997, 143)—was at the heart of the 1994 Venezuelan banking crisis and came to be seen as the epitome of the corruption of CAP's inner circle. The banking crisis saw Abreu's family brushed by financial scandal for a second time: his brother, Rafael Enrique, was a director at Banco Latino, the eye of the financial storm, and was investigated, his assets frozen, and his office and home raided, though he was not charged with any offense.[8]

Abreu was a minister and a brilliant economist in the midst of a government and banking system riddled with corruption (Hellinger 1991; Coronil 1997). As the U.S. Department of State reported in 1992: "CAP has shown a remarkable tolerance for corruption...members of his inner circle have been responsible for some of the most egregious recent excesses."[9] Abreu was never implicated personally, but key members of his circle were, and notoriously so.

For historian Fernando Coronil, Venezuela during this period was also characterized by ostentatiousness. He labels Venezuela "the magical state," one "endowed with the power to replace reality with fabulous fictions propped up by oil wealth" (1997, 2). Spectacle, characteristic of the Venezuelan state since the oil boom of the early twentieth century, reached its apogee under CAP's first government (1974–1979). Venezuela was presided over by a master magician and exhibitionist, who kept "frenetically advancing from one spectacular undertaking to another and keeping the expectant collectivity open to the marvels of his power" (375).

A preference for spectacle over substance; control and manipulation of the media; lavish and unregulated expenditure; a social sphere driven by clientelism and riven with divisions and intrigue—these salient features of journalistic and private accounts of Abreu were commonplace at the top end of Caracas society from CAP's first to second terms, reveals Coronil. He concludes: "If changes were ultimately ineffective, what remained—short of a radical transformation—was the spectacle of change, the show" (317). This sentence could have been plucked straight from the articles about Abreu, who appears, then, to have been very much a man of his time. But history has not judged that time, nor many of Abreu's former associates, kindly. The question is whether he rose above the failings of his milieu and his own family, or whether two decades of forgetfulness, media whitewash, and superficial research have combined subsequently to provide him with a saintly sheen.

CONCLUSION

It is often said that El Sistema was created in Abreu's image—and, going back in time, that image appears somewhat tarnished. In the early 1990s, Abreu was perceived less as a paragon of virtue than as a typical politician. El Sistema seems like an undeniable success story, yet historical records and interviews provide different angles on this narrative, constructed in part by the "shameful and pricey pens" of compliant journalists. The triumph of symphonic music in Venezuela came with notable costs—both literal and figurative. Furthermore,

Abreu launched the National Youth Orchestra under CAP's first government and rose to minister under the second. His program is a child of Venezuela's "magical" era: How much is reality and how much "fabulous fiction propped up by oil wealth"?

Why are the kinds of episodes and opinions aired in this chapter not more widely known? One reason may be that El Sistema's supporters simply do not want to hear them. One informant's explanation was darker: "we are talking about very clever people, who try to ensure that irregularities remain hidden. And in general they succeed." Musicians told me of complaints ignored, problems hushed up, and critics fired. Consequently, few are prepared to speak up.

Nevertheless, it was not hard for me to learn about Abreu's less-than-saintly past, which makes the International Academy of Hagiography's comment regarding its proposal of Abreu for the Nobel Peace Prize—"a series of serious, very formal steps has been followed, including the examination of the person"—somewhat surprising ("Postulan Al Maestro" 2012). Then again, two of the three proposers who traveled to Oslo were professors at his alma mater, UCAB.

More of a barrier is establishing the veracity of oral accounts. My sources were seemingly reliable—founders, former senior Sistema figures, directors of cultural institutions, university professors, journalists—and their reports often coincided with published articles, but like Hellinger (1991, 176) and Coronil (1997, 359), I bumped up against the lack of definitive proof for many explanations that circulated widely. Private conversations, backroom deals, and string pulling rarely leave traces. Thus, like these historians, I came to be more interested in the fact that certain explanations were considered believable, and what these beliefs revealed. Abreu's actions were unknowable to me, but his reputation was not.

As I was starting to write this book, Steve Jobs died, and Daisey's (2011) subsequent article could not fail to remind me of Abreu. He portrayed a genius who had created a kind of magic, but also a ruthless operator whose project had become the epitome of a "Big Brother" organization that triumphed at the expense of exploited workers. "We can admire the design perfection and business acumen while acknowledging the truth," argued Daisey; "with Apple's immense resources at his command he could have revolutionized the industry to make devices more humanely and more openly, and chose not to. If we view him unsparingly, without nostalgia, we would see a great man whose genius in design, showmanship and stewardship of the tech world will not be seen again in our lifetime. We would also see a man who in the end failed to 'think different,' in the deepest way, about the human needs of both his users and his workers."

Jobs was a capitalist entrepreneur; thinking differently about human needs was not, therefore, at the top of his agenda. Making Apple into a dominant corporation was a desired end in itself, providing a logic to his priorities and practices.

El Sistema, however, is not supposed to revolve around directors and share-holders, but precisely around its users and workers. An authoritarian CEO may be an effective manager of a corporation, even of an arts organization, but whether this model is equally suitable to a project for social change is a moot point.

Officially, El Sistema's success is all down to Abreu's dedication, vision, and saint-like persona. Many musicians and cultural observers, however, see his mastery of the dark arts of politics and economics, his autocratic management style, his intolerance of competing visions, and his relentless pursuit of power to be just as important. Abreu started out conducting eleven students in a garage and became one of the most famous and powerful cultural managers in the world; the conclusion is indisputable, but there is more than one way of telling the story.

CHAPTER 2

Gustavo Dudamel and the Simón Bolívar Youth Orchestra

He is the perfect music director for the orchestra of a city that celebrates youth, glamour
and beauty and whose chief business is the creation and marketing of illusions.
—*Baltimore Sun* on Esa-Pekka Salonen, Dudamel's predecessor
at the Los Angeles Philharmonic

"The dapper gentleman in the tuxedo and wearing a very expensive Rolex
watch is not a model. He's the L.A. Phil's very own Gustavo Dudamel,"
reported the *Los Angeles Times* (Ng 2009). "The ad on the back of the programs
at today's 'iBienvenido Gustavo!' concert at the Hollywood Bowl features
Dudamel in ultra-suave mode, endorsing the luxury watch brand." The adver-
tisement reads: "Musical force. Electrifying conductor. And music director of
the Los Angeles Philharmonic. Catalyst for change for Venezuela's youth
through El Sistema. A passion for his art that will be felt forever." The article
concluded: "Not everyone can afford a Rolex but every member of today's concert gets a free Dudamel hand-held fan with a built-in sun visor."

Gustavo Dudamel is El Sistema's poster-boy. The son of musicians from the
city of Barquisimeto, he rose rapidly through the ranks of his local youth orchestra and was then whisked off to Caracas to be Abreu's conducting protégé.
He was put at the helm of the SBYO after Gustavo Medina's dismissal, and his
meteoric rise continued; after winning the Gustav Mahler conducting prize in
2004, he went on to be appointed conductor of the Los Angeles Philharmonic
and become, according to *Time* magazine, one of the "100 World's Most
Influential People." With his dark curls and aura of freshness, Dudamel has
seduced audiences and critics around the world, often portrayed as a conductor who has revolutionized the stuffy world of classical music.

As a Hollywood resident, Dudamel was largely absent from Venezuela
during my research. Like most people, I know him only through music industry

PR and the media. Nevertheless, even from afar it was evident how he had emerged simultaneously as the crown jewel of El Sistema and an icon of multinational corporations, two roles that—as the *L. A. Times* article hinted ever so lightly—sit together somewhat uneasily.

ROLEX MAN

Tensions started to emerge publicly in 2009, when Dudamel was appointed conductor of the L.A. Philharmonic and chosen to front the advertising campaign for Rolex "timeless luxury watches." The public face of Abreu's "revolutionary social project" had now embraced the role of the superstar, jet-set maestro. Sporting his luxury watch and installed in his Hollywood mansion, he had become a prominent symbol of capitalist success—the very ideology that Hugo Chávez's socialist government, El Sistema's major financial backer, had roundly rejected. In Caracas, Dudamel played a prominent role in the revolutionary government's 2011 bicentenary celebrations, while overseas he was promoting one of the ultimate symbols of conspicuous consumption.

The "Rolex man" issue caused a minor fuss in Venezuelan musical circles in 2009–10.[1] Leftist critics were furious that Dudamel projected the conservative values of Rolex and the conductor star system, and kept quiet about the Bolivarian Revolution that sustained El Sistema and thus his own rise to fame. They argued that Rolex was profiting from the socialist government's investment in El Sistema, and using it (and Dudamel) to advance a set of values to which that government was ideologically opposed.

El Sistema's most famous product slid seamlessly into the world of multinational labels, marketing budgets, artist agencies, and globetrotting celebrities. Far from suggesting that he has "sold out" the project that produced him, however, this scenario points to the opposite conclusion: that there is a close fit between the two systems and their values. Dudamel's trajectory tells us less about him than it does about El Sistema's ideological basis. Lubow (2007) suggests light-heartedly but perceptively that Dudamel's rise to stardom originated in Abreu's monitoring of "in-house talent as closely as a studio mogul of the Hollywood golden age." For all the social rhetoric, El Sistema is a project with a markedly commercial slant, indeed one that fits hand-in-glove with global music capitalism.

Dudamel epitomizes classical music's grotesquely unequal star system, according to which one individual—the conductor—may earn ten or twenty times as much as an orchestral musician (in 2013 his salary from the L.A. Philharmonic alone was over $1.4 million).[2] In *Capital*, Marx (1887) uses the figure of the conductor to explain the idea of a capitalist extracting surplus value and exploiting labor power to the maximum. A celebrity conductor is thus a strange hero for a socialist state. Dudamel is a perfect example of a winner-takes-all ethos. His fame and economic success, and that of the orchestra he leads, the SBYO, point to a System in which a tiny percentage of aspirants reap most of the rewards. In other words, this is a System that, for all its lavish funding by the Venezuelan state, produces inequality and models the capitalist American, not the socialist Venezuelan, dream.

DUDAMEL AND THE MUSIC BUSINESS

Much has been made of Dudamel's rise to become the conductor of the SBYO and the backing he has received from classical music luminaries like Sir Simon Rattle, conductor of the Berlin Philharmonic, and Claudio Abbado. Interestingly, as noted on the blog *On an Overgrown Path* on August 4, 2005, these three conductors and two orchestras were all signed to the leading concert management agency Askonas Holt during Dudamel's rise to fame (he moved on in 2010). Diego Matheuz and Christian Vásquez, the two prime candidates for the role of "the new Dudamel," also signed to Askonas Holt. After Dudamel won the Gustav Mahler conducting prize in 2004, but well before he became a household name, he and the SBYO were signed up by Deutsche Grammophon. One of the "documentaries" about El Sistema that eulogizes both Dudamel and the SBYO is *The Promise of Music*—released by Deutsche Grammophon, to which the Berlin Phil and Abbado have very close links. There is nothing untoward in any of this, but it does cast a new light on all their mutual praise and promotion.

As the blog noted, "fairytales just don't exist anymore in today's music-like-water world of classical music—except in the minds of PR men and management agencies." On August 5, 2011, the same blog pointed out that "both the Simón Bolívar Orchestra and Gustavo Dudamel record for Deutsche Grammophon, which is part of Universal Music, the world's largest record company. Universal Music is owned by French media conglomerate Vivendi, a global corporation with annual revenues of 29 billion Euros. El Sistema's work with the socially disadvantaged is highly laudable, but success does bring its rewards." El Sistema is, among other things, big business, and the close alignment of a supposed social project for the poor with the interests of major international corporations deserves further attention.

In a blog post on September 26, 2012, Marshall Marcus described the scene at the Sistema headquarters:

> the front yard of La Sede filled with the Caracas Youth Orchestra gathering together to leave for Maiquetia airport and a tour to Italy, Russia, the Czech Republic, Belgium, Austria and Germany, a tour which they are by now well into. At the same time, the Simón Bolívar choir are on tour in New York, and as soon as both groups get back, the Teresa Carreño Youth Orchestra prepares to leave

for Europe. By that time the Sistema's Percussion Ensemble will have been to the UK, and the Simón Bolívar String Quartet during 2012 will have been performing in Canada, Europe, and the Far East. The Brass Ensemble will be in the US, and later in the autumn Gustavo Dudamel and the Simón Bolívar Symphony Orchestra also head to Washington, New York and other points North American. From now until Christmas there is hardly a day without one of seven El Sistema groups on tour abroad in one continent or another, something that must surely be on the minds of Askonas Holt, the unflinching music agency charged with regularly moving these approximately one thousand people around the globe.

Impressive though this portrait may be, it raises a number of questions, not least—given that El Sistema is funded from social development sources—how much it costs, who pays for it, and who benefits. Should resources be concentrated on this extraordinary international mobilization of a fraction of 1 percent of El Sistema's students—and the most talented, not the most needy? For whom do the sellout concerts around the world generate income? Why does El Sistema focus on displaying its products overseas, preferring to send its elite ensembles to London or New York rather than to the Venezuelan provinces? There are distinct echoes of the WEDO, which primarily "projects a utopia in Europe and for European audiences" (Beckles Willson 2009, 2). It is hard to square Marcus's description with claims that El Sistema is primarily a social rather than musical project, run for the benefit of Venezuelan youth. Here it resembles a new branch of the old global music business, focused on creating elite ensembles to fulfill the desires of middle-class audiences in the Global North.

Eatock (2010) suggests that this business is in the interest of everyone in the classical music world, which might explain (up to a point) why so many have been queuing up to praise El Sistema: "The motives of El Sistema's supporters may not be entirely altruistic. These days, classical music is struggling with its own problems: declining popularity and a growing sense that the art form has lost its relevance. Some musicians (such as Simon Rattle) aren't adverse [sic] to hoping that El Sistema could provide the shot in the arm that classical music needs." Rattle has praised El Sistema as the future of classical music, but is it more accurately the future of the classical music industry?

Jorgensen (2003, 2) provides a different slant, noting that aggressive commercial practices (of the kind that have made Dudamel a household name) can have a broader negative effect on musical culture: "International marketing of music and artists makes some music widely available. At the same time, it silences others who cannot obtain venture capital and afford to distribute their music extensively. And it undermines and devalues amateur participation in music making by subjecting it to comparison with exacting professional and commercial standards." Indeed, the rise of Dudamel and the SBYO has had problematic repercussions on the broader sphere of Venezuelan music (see Chapter 12). Their impact may even be felt further afield: focusing on the Ulster Orchestra, on October 12, 2011, *On an Overgrown Path* questioned the reduction in BBC broadcasts—an important source of funding for the orchestra—at the same time that the corporation was paying out handsome sums for the visit of Dudamel and the SBYO to the Proms. In this competitive sphere, one orchestra's gain may be another's loss. Eatock's suggestion thus needs to be modified: Dudamel's success benefits a few key players at the top end of the classical music industry, but whether these benefits trickle down is a different matter.

The image of Dudamel as a breath of fresh air and "revolutionary" talent should therefore be balanced against its construction and employment in the service of capital and consumerism, and contrasted to the conservative musical, social, and economic order that his success rests on and affirms. As *On an Overgrown Path* pointed out on August 5, 2011, behind Dudamel's media sound bite—"I think the most important thing is to make the music accessible"—lay a superstar-sized fee and two concerts at the Salzburg summer festival, "probably the most expensive and least accessible music event in the world." By idolizing Dudamel, El Sistema is not so much revolutionizing classical music as reaffirming many of its traditional structures and practices. What we see is an image of revolution—what we get, in most respects, is business as usual.

THE SIMÓN BOLÍVAR YOUTH ORCHESTRA

The SBYO has rapidly become one of the world's most high-profile orchestras, selling out major concert halls around the world, receiving lavish praise from the press, and delighting audiences everywhere. Nevertheless, little is known about how it really works, and it has attracted minimal analysis. A founder member warned me that it was difficult to get a true image of the orchestra: membership brings earnings and perks like no other job in Venezuelan classical music, so its musicians keep their opinions under wraps.

The SBYO is a very unusual orchestra. It was called a "youth orchestra" until 2011, when it changed its name to "symphony orchestra," and yet it included musicians in their thirties (the average age of a musician in the Berlin Philharmonic is thirty-eight) and paid top salaries. It was thus much closer to a professional orchestra than a normal youth orchestra, yet its musicians are both more pampered and more constrained than the norm; they receive lavish benefits but have few rights. Musicians who do not please their superiors may be fired, without any formal procedure or right of appeal.

The process of joining the orchestra is equally distant from professional norms. Recruitment usually results from an invitation from Abreu or one of his inner circle, or a musician seizing an opportunity to play for one of these top figures in private. Cara, a member of the orchestra, explained that there were no fixed, publicly advertised audition dates. The orchestra is essentially full, she said; there are rarely auditions anymore, and certainly not open ones. There were different ways to join. One way in was to send a letter to FESNOJIV asking for an audition, and then wait to be called, which might be never. Another was to try to be included on a closed audition roster by knocking on Abreu's door or catching him and playing for him in private. Cara herself had entered by this route: the SBYO has internal auditions to determine who gets promoted, and by playing for Abreu she managed to persuade him to include her in one of these internal auditions even though she was not part of the orchestra.

The complexity and arbitrariness of the process are striking. Even the orchestra's members were unable to give me a clear, succinct explanation of how to join it. Compare this to the United Kingdom's National Youth Orchestra, which has a webpage that explains the audition process in detail.[3] In Venezuela the process is highly personalized, and most musicians believe that it is almost impossible to get into the orchestra without direct contact with Abreu or his inner circle; they do not perceive recruitment as the result of transparent, meritocratic auditions. Both joining and remaining in the orchestra are understood as relying on patronage, and the lack of formal processes leaves individuals at the whim of their superiors. A former SBYO member claimed that her section principal took a personal dislike to her and had her fired, nominally for missing a rehearsal. We may recall that Gustavo Medina claimed (after being fired himself) that El Sistema is creating "generations of young people who believe that their future depends on their efforts and dedication, without realizing that without the 'unction of the maestro' that future does not exist."

PLAYING FOR THEIR LIVES?

The SBYO has attracted great interest for its dynamic performances but also because of its social mythology: the belief that it is rescuing disadvantaged youth from a life of crime in the slums and instilling them with noble values, leading to frequent media descriptions of the musicians as "playing for their lives." "Gustavo Dudamel brings music from Venezuela's slums to the Proms," trumpeted *The Independent* (Duchen 2011). Spain's *El País* lauded "Abreu, Dudamel and their young legion of musicians rescued from marginality" (Mantilla 2011). Yet the current and former SBYO members to whom I spoke all concurred that it is in fact a largely middle-class orchestra. There are a few cases of musicians who come from more disadvantaged backgrounds, but they are the exception rather than the rule. However, El Sistema's marketing and foreign media representations have given them great prominence, leading to distorted perceptions of the social balance. *The Promise of Music*, a film about the SBYO, includes images and talk of the Caracas barrios, but rather than being set inside these neighborhoods, it shows them from the window of a violist's apartment; they are not her reality, but her view. She is later filmed driving off to work in a smart-looking hatchback. Revealingly, the photo accompanying the *Independent* article showed the SBYO's concert in the Caracas barrio of La Vega—a famous PR stunt that took the orchestra's music *to* the barrio for a single day, but produced enough photos and footage to propagate a connection between the orchestra and slums for years to come (see Chapter 7).

Former and current members expressed to me their irritation at the distortion that leads international audiences to see these predominantly middle-class musicians as former delinquents and drug addicts. Hardly a mention of the SBYO goes by without a long disquisition on poverty and crime in the Caracas barrios, but this is not the reality that most of its musicians inhabit. Both Dudamel and the orchestra's concertmaster, Alejandro Carreño, come from middle-class musical families, and they are broadly representative of the orchestra in social terms. As Spich and Sylvester (1999, 27) note, when there are many similar orchestral products, "the act of making and marketing a specific value-laden image to the minds of the consumers" becomes very important. The SBYO has been highly successful in marketing itself through its "value-laden image" of rescuing children from the slums, but the reality is quite distinct.

In order to grasp how the SBYO is perceived within musical circles in Venezuela, it is worth noting some well-known puns that are associated with it. One changes the Sistema slogan "tocar y luchar" (to play and to struggle) to "tocar y cobrar" (to play and to get paid), reflecting the perception (and the reality) that the orchestra represents an economic as well as musical elite. Eatock (2010) writes of a concert by the orchestra in Toronto: "The performance was impressive by professional standards—but, astoundingly, this was an amateur youth orchestra." There is nothing remotely amateur about the SBYO, whose members' salaries are the envy of professional musicians across Venezuela. "It's amazing that they earn so much," said one musician. "What other profession allows you to earn so much money with nothing more than a high-school certificate?" A senior university professor reported that rank-and-file members of the orchestra earned two-and-a-half times his salary. One Sistema student stated ironically that if I wanted to see social action through music, I should spend some time in Caracas with the SBYO: guys carrying a top-end Blackberry and driving the latest SUV. Indeed, one member of the orchestra posted a photo of his new sports car on Facebook. Despite its funding by a socialist government and portrayals as a symbol of social change, the orchestra reproduces the inequalities of capitalism, with its members cast as the ostentatious nouveaux riches.

DISCIPLINE

Some Venezuelan musicians talk about those who join the orchestra as selling their soul to El Sistema (or even to the devil). This idea is captured by another insiders' pun: the Orquesta de la Juventud Venezolana (Venezuelan Youth Orchestra) is tweaked to the Orquesta de la *Esclavitud* Venezolana, or Venezuelan Slave Orchestra. One of the SBYO's lesser-known aspects is its extraordinary rehearsal schedule, far more intensive than the professional norm, which sees its members sometimes rehearsing ten or twelve hours a day. Rehearsals have no fixed end time and go on until the conductor is satisfied. A violinist described twelve-hour days when preparing for a tour or a recording, with rehearsals starting at 9 a.m. and, after breaks, continuing until late at night. One musician reported having fallen asleep while rehearsing at 2 a.m. Complaints of tiredness are not tolerated, however, and are likely to be met with Abreu's famed line: "rest comes with eternal rest, my dear."

Founder members revealed that Abreu imposed this grueling routine from the start. In the earliest days, rehearsals would go on until midnight most nights, with a seemingly endless rehearsal on Saturdays. Even through the rose-tinted spectacles of Borzacchini's hagiography, Abreu's strictness with the young musicians shines through: "the rehearsals with José Antonio were fierce, he did what we call 'stand by stand,' one by one, playing through the parts," said one founder. "Every rehearsal could bring a surprise and a terrible challenge, and if you weren't ready, well, you'd better be: he made us play the most difficult passages one by one, at any moment, when you were least expecting it" (Borzacchini 2010, 73). This "stand by stand" technique—scaring students into practicing harder by shining a spotlight on one at random in a full rehearsal—is a signature feature of Sistema practice to this day, and the speaker's choice of words points to the role of psychological pressure in producing results. Abreu's rehearsals had no fixed end time—another practice that has become generalized. Abreu, a conservative Catholic, would tell tired musicians that "the body should be mortified."

In an anonymous post on the Internet forum discussed in the Introduction, an SBYO member wrote: "we are at the beck and call of the telephone, waiting to hear when our sectional rehearsal or workshop is, since at many points in the year the orchestra works up to nine hours a day for a whole week, sometimes without lunch and with no right of reply ... you don't even have a social life, because your house is like a hotel, you leave in the morning and get back at night and it's practically impossible to get a university degree with decent marks since there is no time to study."

A questionnaire elicited similar concerns about a lack of scheduling and its effects on musicians: "The orchestra members often lack information about rehearsal times and locations until the last minute. The orchestra managers, equipped with each of the members' FESNOJIV-supplied cell phone numbers, call them at odd hours of the day. Only Abreu chooses the repertoire, and sometimes he does not decide until the week of the concert. Musicians must scramble to prepare his selections, dedicating only a few days of frantic preparation to each concert. Some suggest that he intentionally keeps them in the dark to maintain his control over the organization" (Chang 2007, 102).

One informant described the musicians of the SBYO as "imprisoned" by their benefits and commitments. Former members, and friends and siblings of current members, often used the word "exploitation," claiming that musicians' personal development was sacrificed at the altar of the orchestra. In the eyes of some musicians, the SBYO is just the tip of the iceberg of a System whose musicians are permanently "on call," and in which children are routinely overworked and obliged to play difficult music for long hours on instruments they are still coming to grips with, leading in some cases to playing-related injuries. "Those are the things no one talks about," said one musician, "but there is always money to cover it up—everything is paid for, medical treatment and so on."

The tone of such private responses somewhat contradicts Dudamel's official line: "The lovely thing about Venezuelan musicians is their energy and willingness to work.... There is no schedule, but there is a great desire to have fun doing what we know best: making music" (quoted in Carvajal and Melgarejo 2008). Claudio Abbado, one of the SBYO's famous collaborators and cheerleaders, enthuses that the musicians, "when playing in the orchestra, give their soul, without restrictions, hours, union rules. They are crazy about music" (Mattioli 2009). Dudamel displays a relaxed, "typically Latin" attitude, while Abbado's vision is more romantic. Off-the-record responses by orchestra members, however, reveal beliefs that the running of the orchestra is about more than just charming, carefree Venezuelan disorganization; they show considerably less enthusiasm for the arbitrary, disempowering, all-consuming working practices that give rise to the widespread metaphors of slavery and selling one's soul.

Levine and Levine's (1996, 23) study of stress and discontent in orchestras reveals that professional musicians respond to a situation in which they have a chronic lack of control by insisting on strict limits on rehearsal time and on the conductor's authority over them: "to musicians, the necessity of such limits is painfully obvious. The root issue is one of pure and simple control. Conductors resent having control taken away from them after 150 minutes of complete autonomy. Musicians, having experienced 150 minutes of total lack of control, want their lives back." In other words, the restrictions, hours, and union rules whose absence Abbado celebrates are designed specifically to make orchestral life bearable for musicians. Dudamel and Abbado's cheery words are thus understandable: these conductors marvel at a System that gives free rein to the maestro's autocratic desires and renders his subject-musicians entirely powerless to resist.

The orchestra's publicity and media reports emphasize its "natural" Latin swing. There is something undeniably powerful about the orchestra's famous swaying during Márquez's "Danzón" or dancing during Bernstein's "Mambo"; now a key component of El Sistema's identity, it never fails to move the audience. The orchestra is held up as an emblem of physical freedom, a New World loosening of classical music's straitjacket.

The reality is, as ever, a little more ambiguous. Paradoxically, this New World swing is the product of extreme, and extremely Old World, discipline. The idea that it springs spontaneously from some kind of Latin essence is simplistic and misleading. As one musician told me, most children in El Sistema do not grow up playing Latin music: for all their exposure to Latin music in their everyday lives, their studies instead focus on European classical music. She and her colleagues actually struggled more with the occasional Latin repertoire than the Beethoven and Tchaikovsky that was their normal fare.

When I visited the Caracas Children's Orchestra at Montalbán, I was struck by the difference between the children's movements in the Latin repertoire and the classical. They bopped around during a Pérez Prado mambo, but their moves were entirely choreographed, and I had seen a very similar routine a few months earlier in a distant city; the Beethoven, meanwhile, did not look much different from a U.K. youth orchestra. I came away with the sense that the movement is highly planned, evidence of drilling and a desire to impress rather than the simple, spontaneous physicality that many foreigners fondly imagine.

Luis, a former National Children's Orchestra member, told me that some musicians hated the dancing and found it humiliating, but they had no choice. For Márquez's "Danzón No. 2," the Veracruz conductor would tell them to plan their choreography and rehearse it in sections. Luis recalled two instances in Veracruz when front-desk violinists had been relegated to the back of the seconds or thrown out of a rehearsal for refusing to "monkey around" at the conductor's insistence. I watched a video of the Veracruz youth orchestra on YouTube with Luis, who pointed out certain synchronized physical movements by the leaders of the string sections in Tchaikovsky 4: this is what they had learnt in the National Children's Orchestra with Dudamel. He claimed that Dudamel explicitly told the players what to do physically as well as musically at key points.

In a blog post on October 3, 2010, Jonathan Govias recalls the moment he grasped that "Danzón" had a standardized, rehearsed choreography: "Until that moment, I'd never considered the possibility that the onstage mambos were anything more than spontaneous manifestations of group exuberance." Nevertheless, he continues to associate movement with freedom, which entails arguing that complete freedom is the result of continual disciplining. It is unclear why an orchestra in which everyone performs a routine in lockstep should be considered freer than one in which every musician moves as they wish, but audiences have been conditioned to understand Venezuelan youth orchestras in this way.

It is possible that, as Govias suggests on January 23, 2012, synchronized movement stimulates emotional responses and social bonding in students. Yet the research he cites tests the hypothesis that "synchronous activity may serve as a partial *solution to the free-rider problem* facing groups that need to motivate their members to contribute toward the collective good," and its first example is of an army training by marching in step (Wiltermuth and Heath 2009, 1, emphasis added). Whatever positive effects choreographed movement may have, promoting freedom is not one of them. Far from a sign of Latin spontaneity, it is in fact a form of training and disciplining the body, a practice closely linked to Foucault's *dressage* (see Chapter 8).

Tunstall (2012, 126) notes that the soloists in the TCYO's rendition of "Danzón" made the same expressive gestures as those of the older SBYO, and that the Caracas Children's Orchestra, too, had adopted the SBYO's choreographic tricks. She reads this positively, yet an alternative interpretation would be that El Sistema has raised dressage in classical music to a new level and that its intensive rehearsal schedule serves to discipline bodily expression, iron out physical freedom and individuality, and replace them with a simulacrum. Contemplating how young musicians are trained not just to sound but also to move the same, one may understand why some describe themselves as replaceable cogs in the Sistema machine (see Chapter 9).

In the puns associated with the SBYO, we may glimpse some roots of the orchestra's striking performances. Dudamel and other leading figures claim variously that the orchestra's distinctiveness comes from its members growing up and making music together for years, their sense of fun and friendship, the social changes they have undergone, or a natural Latin musicality. Yet the slavery pun points to other, less romantic factors—uncommonly hard work and strict discipline—while *tocar y cobrar* nods at the financial inducements that make such hard work feasible.

Potentially more provocative is research by orchestra expert Richard Hackman on the correlation between performance quality, funding level, and authoritarian leadership (Judy 1996). Hackman's conclusions seem highly applicable to the SBYO, an orchestra created by a disciplinarian economist and fundraiser extraordinaire. They suggest that the thrilling sound of the SBYO may reflect not as much fun, friendship, and Latin swing as its autocratic leadership model and the huge sums that are spent on the orchestra. "Swing" looks a touch less attractive in this light. The combination of authoritarian management, strict discipline, and high expenditure produces results, but its compatibility with El Sistema's proclaimed social mission deserves greater scrutiny. It seems an odd basis for a revolutionary social project and a problematic model for progressive music education.

Abreu's eye has been firmly fixed on foreign stages since he took the helm of the Juan José Landaeta youth orchestra in 1975. Within little more than a year, it had performed in Scotland, Mexico, Colombia, and the United States (interestingly, this information leads the "Social Impact" section of the Sistema website).[4] Today, celebratory accounts often focus on the SBYO's tours around the world's great concert halls and El Sistema's success in placing conductors with foreign orchestras (e.g., Guarache Ocque 2012), but this over-seas orientation has its critics. As one blogger wrote (Guanipa 2013): "Look at the enormous amounts of resources and money (belonging to the people) that the government expends on transporting and performing classical music with the aim of entertaining, captivating or delighting the ears of the European elite! ... Why on earth doesn't Dudamel's symphony orchestra make a tour around all the state capitals of Venezuela, open and free to the public, to entertain the ears of the Venezuelan people, who own the money that pays those musicians with their uniforms, instruments and everything?"

Today, the SBYO has two principal roles: first, to accompany important po-litical ceremonies (such as Chávez's funeral); second, to project world-class performances of great orchestral music onto the world stage. (It is a nice irony that the orchestra can fit hand-in-glove with socialist political ceremony and global music capitalism at the same time.) What is beaten into a distant third place here is the idea of a social project at the service of the Venezuelan people, since it is easier to see the SBYO in Europe or North America than a provincial city in Venezuela.

El Sistema is often held up as something radically new, yet beyond populist gestures like the colorful jackets and the dancing, the SBYO rarely breaks the conventions of symphonic music on its overseas travels—indeed, its program-ming and performances are often quite conservative. Now that the novelty of Bernstein's "Mambo" has worn off, it is easier to see that the nature of the symphonic concert experience remains largely unchanged. Through its over-seas circulation, El Sistema reveals its ideology and priorities—music as spec-tacle and commodity—and the conservative thinking that lies behind the revolutionary surface.

The SBYO's programming tends to fall into two camps: heavyweight European symphonies and lighter Latin American works. This formula is rarely inverted. Venezuelan music plays only a small part in its repertoire, with anything more than an orchestrated folk tune an uncommon sighting (unlike most national youth orchestras around the world, which usually make promoting new national music a signature feature). Programming thus tends to hold up the European canon as the gold standard, with Latin American music generally presented as the lightweight Other of this repertoire of "great works" (for example, as encores). The transaction between El Sistema and overseas audiences thus involves the buying and selling of sameness and difference of a predictable, comforting kind; there is little challenge to conventional assumptions about "serious" Europeans and "exuberant" Latin Americans. In this transaction, the Europeans are the true guardians of great culture, while the Venezuelans are "typically Latin" entertainers.[5]

The orchestra's focus on recirculating the European canon back to Europe has clear political implications. It fits with the modernization or developmentalist paradigm that dominated Venezuela for much of the twentieth century: icons of modernity were seen as lying outside Latin America, and oil wealth was used to purchase them and copy them in Venezuela, then show them off to the outside world for validation (Coronil 1997; see Chapter 4). The SBYO's focus on the European canon and marginalization of Venezuelan music on its travels encapsulates and perpetuates this ideology, according to which the West is seen as the locus of modernity and matching the metropolis is considered the highest goal—a political ideology, ironically, to which the Chávez government was firmly opposed.

The SBYO has done a huge amount to publicize Venezuelan musical culture internationally, yet the circulating images and music hide as much as they reveal. They largely elide Venezuela's tradition of "serious" art music composition, and place Venezuelan music in a subsidiary position to European. The SBYO shows Venezuelan musicians to the world as expert performers rather than creators, reproducing a colonialist dynamic that dates back to the Spanish Conquest.

CONCLUSION

The SBYO is often projected as an antidote to classical music's image problems: young, fluid, colorful musicians from an "exotic" country, performing accessible repertoire in dynamic ways. The contrast with (the caricature of) Old World classical musicians—old, stiff, dull, penguin-suited, playing "difficult" music—is clear. In reality, the differences have much to do with marketing and image management: the SBYO's performances are the result of discipline that would put the Germans to shame, and the Venezuelan musicians place the Berlin Philharmonic on the highest pedestal.

Under the astute management of Abreu, Askonas Holt, and Deutsche Grammophon, the SBYO and Dudamel have become household names in classical music and even beyond. The next steps may well prove interesting. Recent critical reactions suggest that the delirious honeymoon stage may be drawing to a close. For example, responses to the orchestra's return to the Proms in 2011 were much more mixed than to its 2007 debut. Dudamel's conducting has come under scrutiny at home and abroad; after all the hype, a certain amount of critical backlash was perhaps inevitable. Venezuelan conductors to whom I spoke acknowledged his natural talent and charisma but doubted—perhaps with a hint of professional jealousy—that he had the musical education or the intellectual tools to take his interpretations to the highest level. One felt that much of the hype came from a neocolonialist amazement that the "natives" were capable of making European music; another questioned the overseas fascination with the SBYO in similar terms: "The world is hugely hypocritical: what moves people about our orchestra is that they are Latinos and blacks who play Shostakovich from memory. If they were blond with blue eyes, they would be of less interest."

Perhaps of more significance than subjective debates over Dudamel's skill are the perceptive comments by Anne Midgette (2010) at the *Washington Post*. Alongside her even-handed remarks about Dudamel's strengths ("hugely charismatic...scarily talented") and weaknesses ("his conducting can be uneven, superficial, moment-to-moment"), she makes a key point: "Dudamel is not the future of classical music. He's not even trying to be. The people who are trying to move classical music into the future are thinking about alternate kinds of programming, new venues, different repertory....But Dudamel's whole training appears to have been about perpetuating the status quo—about the idea that leading an orchestra in standard repertoire is the highest thing to which a musician can aspire. I think this is one reason he's been so exciting to many people in the field: He represents a future without radical change." Midgette identifies a crucial point: the conservatism of El Sistema's leading figures beneath the surface detail.

Not everyone agrees that Dudamel represents the future or the savior of classical music, then, or even that saviors are necessarily a good thing. On his blog *The Rest Is Noise*, Alex Ross asked on February 16, 2012: "What is it that classical music needs to be saved from? Among other things, from media outlets that have all but eliminated classical music from their coverage, paying attention to it only on the rare occasion when an artist acquires the weird chemistry of 'star value.' Stardom in the American mode is a devouring force." Stardom in the American mode is precisely what Dudamel represents, and again, it is suggested that a huge success story at the apex of the classical music pyramid is not necessarily good news for the whole edifice.

Dudamel's hallmark is his conducting style. As Javier Vidal commented, "Dudamel is the show [*espectáculo*] of symphonic music" (Borzacchini 2010, 177). The young conductor is not just Abreu's musical protégé and heir but also the flowering of his philosophy of culture as spectacle. Among the ample praise, Dudamel has been criticized for showmanship over depth and an excess of PR spin—precisely the same criticisms that were made of Abreu in his prime.

The SBYO displays a similar duality as its conductor. Like Dudamel, it presents an image of youthful revolution and Latin flair, but behind the surface lies a conservative organization that thrives on old-fashioned discipline and reproduces the disparities of power and resources that mar both wider Venezuelan society and the classical music industry. It represents less the future of classical music than its past with an appealing makeover. Both orchestra and conductor have been forged in the image of El Maestro, archconservative and showman extraordinaire.

CODA: THE LATIN GRAMMY AWARDS

In November 2011 Gustavo Dudamel and the SBYO played a starring role in the opening show of the Latin Grammy Awards in Las Vegas, where they accompanied the Puerto Rican artists Calle 13 in a rendition of their song "Latinoamérica." This moment, rich in symbolism and contradictions, sealed the SBYO's status as the world's great show orchestra. This moment, more than the idea of social action through music, could be seen as the logical conclusion of the program Abreu started in 1975.

The contradictions were multiple: an orchestra dedicated to social change and funded by a revolutionary government performing at a Las Vegas showbiz ceremony and celebration of music capitalism. Calle 13's anti-imperialist song accompanied by an orchestra was regarded by its critics as the very epitome of Eurocentrism. The song's vaguely anticapitalist chorus, "you can't buy the wind, you can't buy the sun, you can't buy the rain," was sung to an audience of industry movers and shakers, harmonized by a music education program with unprecedented economic power, and led by a face of Rolex and an economist trained in business management.

However, perhaps we should see not contradictions but revelations. For critical observers in Venezuela, the SBYO has always been a show orchestra, Abreu has always been interested in power and money for his project, and El Sistema has always promoted conservative capitalist values—in which case nothing could be more fitting than the orchestra's opening of a glitzy industry extravaganza in Las Vegas. Participants and leaders reaped propaganda rewards that day, but the ease with which the SBYO slotted into the occasion was revealing. Dudamel and the SBYO's script is about radicalism and revolution, but its setting (Hollywood and Las Vegas) and major characters (Rolex, Vivendi, Askonas Holt, the Grammys) tell a different story.

CHAPTER 3
Organizational Features and Dynamics

Between both of us, El Sistema and our bank, we saw from day one an exceptionally clear convergence of values.
> —Miguel Ignacio Purroy, president of Bancaribe

When everyone thinks the same, nobody is thinking.
> —Attributed to Walter Lippmann

When subjected to careful scrutiny, classical music institutions have not always appeared in a glowing light (e.g., Born 1995). In their studies of conservatoires, Kingsbury (1988) found competitiveness, cliques, authoritarianism, and the reproduction of social hierarchies, while Nettl (1995) identified conflict, inequality, and jockeying for position, concluding that Western musical culture is based on principles "characteristic of an unkind society" (1995, 42). Jorgensen (2003, 5–6) argues that the institutions of music making and education have a dark side, "disciplining and excluding those who do not meet or accede to the group's expectations.... Notions of freedom, equality, inclusiveness, and humanity invariably collide with systemic pressures toward conformity, injustice, exclusivity, and inhumanity; as a result, they are only ever achieved partially, if at all." Oppressive forces are embedded in institutional beliefs and practices, their ubiquity and apparent normality making them hard to identify and uproot. Consequently, "Action for Change in Music Education"—the manifesto of the MayDay Group, an international consortium of music education scholars—argues that such institutions *must* be critiqued: "Despite their good intentions and the high claims often made for institutions . . . institutionally mediated expressions of musical culture are unpredictable and often self-destructing or self-limiting" (2009, xxxiv).

Discussion of El Sistema's organizational culture needs to take place against this background of scholarly skepticism over the institutions of music learning. Does El Sistema, as many believe, exemplify a much-needed transformation, or has it inherited problems from Europe and North America? This chapter will suggest that neither conclusion is sufficient. After reassessing El Sistema's origins, it will trace how salient features of Abreu's personality, background, and career have left their mark on his grand project. It will also explore the contradictory dynamics of centralization and expansion (both hallmarks of his management as minister of culture) that continue to shape it today. Prominent themes from Chapter 1 will thus resurface as the contours and mechanics of Abreu's project emerge. The result is a distinctive problematics—neither straightforward continuity nor transformation—and tensions between (self-)characterizations of El Sistema and the effects generated by its corporate model.

THE ORIGINS OF EL SISTEMA

"The condensation of history, our desire for clean narratives, and the need for elites and organizations to project an image of control and purpose all conspire to convey a false image of historical causation," warns Scott (2012, 140). It is therefore worth reconsidering El Sistema's oft-recounted creation myth, which portrays Abreu as a lone visionary, gathering a handful of children in a garage, dreaming of transforming Venezuela's youth. This story elides significant details and is shaped by present needs and desires.

The orchestra Abreu formed in 1975 did not appear out of nowhere. There were other youth orchestra projects at the time, in particular the Orquesta Experimental de la Orquesta Sinfónica de Venezuela, founded in 1970 at the José Angel Lamas (JAL) Conservatoire, where Abreu had studied. There were also existing youth orchestras in Carora and Trujillo. Pedroza (n.d.) explores the creation of the Sistema myth, as events were transmuted into an epic history—"the rise of a *hero*, the *democratization* of music, the *transformation* of society"—not just through the mythification of its leading character but also through the devaluation or elision of the surrounding reality.[1] She debunks the idea of Venezuela as a land without classical music before El Sistema, revealing a wealth of choral and instrumental ensembles in the twentieth century— just not many symphony orchestras. It is only through the conflation of "music" and "symphonic music" that claims about musical deficiency could be sustained. Similarly, depictions of the art music sphere as elitist until Abreu appeared—a key element of his rhetoric today—are misleading; Venezuela had at least five major conservatoires in the early 1970s, which offered a comprehensive music education free of charge.

Pedroza's alternative reading of events in the 1960s and 1970s stresses continuities rather than changes. Here, it is Orquesta Sinfónica de Venezuela (OSV) president Pedro Antonio Ríos Reyna who is the true visionary of the youth orchestra movement, and Abreu figures as executor rather than originator. The birth of this movement is identified as the creation of the Orquesta

Experimental in 1970, not the National Youth Orchestra five years later; hence it emerges from the heart of the existing symphonic context (the OSV) rather than in opposition to it, as the story is told today.

Abreu's orchestra also grew up alongside one in the town of Carora, illustrating that he was less of a voice in the wilderness than is sometimes supposed (Carlson 2012). The Carora orchestra was strongly influenced by the arrival of three musicians from Jorge Peña Hen's pioneering youth orchestra project, created in the Chilean town of La Serena in 1964. Key elements of Abreu's discourse, such as critiques of traditional conservatoires and the promotion of classical music education to all social classes, were articulated in Chile ten years before El Sistema's appearance, and a conduit for their transfer to Venezuela is clear. Again, Abreu emerges as a highly effective manager and promoter of an existing vision. This is of course a rather less epic story.

Furthermore, ideas identified today with El Sistema—musical training as a tool of social mobility and cultural assimilation (or social inclusion, in today's language), and blurring the distinction between art and popular music—can be traced back to the eighteenth century in Venezuela, argues Pedroza. In the nineteenth and early twentieth centuries, large ensembles were commonplace across the country and occupied a space between the academic and the popular. Philharmonic societies, chamber orchestras, and student orchestras existed alongside ensembles known as *estudiantinas* and *orquestas típicas* that mixed art, popular, and folkloric music. This rich ensemble life provides an important backdrop to El Sistema, but also sheds light on Abreu's claims about "overcoming the false distinction between popular and classical music": not only was this distinction blurred long before El Sistema—for example, by iconic figures such as Juan Bautista Plaza and Vicente Emilio Sojo in the 1920s and 1930s (Labonville 2007, 8–9)—but it was arguably deepened by Abreu's system, which focused more closely on the European canon than earlier variants.

Abreu thus built on various musical and ideological antecedents, assimilating much from his predecessors and contemporaries. His hyperidealization of the symphony orchestra merely intensified an existing current in Venezuela's classical music world, and even the linking of youth orchestras with social action was already in the air. In 1971 a journalist commented on the potential social repercussions of the Orquesta Experimental: "it represents the labor of the true rescue of the youth" (quoted in Pedroza n.d.). Abreu's subsequent depiction as a revolutionizing figure thus has much to do with mythification and political expediency.

Given all these antecedents, why did Abreu's orchestra prevail, allowing him to move center stage? Several older musicians remembered the mid-1970s as a period of rupture. According to one, the Orquesta Experimental was well established, but it was an unpaid student ensemble; Abreu, however, secured scholarships from the Fundación Gran Mariscal de Ayacucho, and young musicians began to move over to his orchestra. Two musicians who had been students at the time claimed that Abreu took musicians from existing music schools; fellow students left, seduced by the promise of money, tours, publicity, and, above all, rapid success—without having to finish their studies. As a result, some of their contemporaries never graduated. Ulyses Ascanio, a senior Sistema figure, recalls how Abreu drew him in with such promises (Borzacchini 2010, 81), and we may glimpse the carrots that El Maestro dangled in front of young musicians in the words of Domingo Sánchez Bor (quoted in Logan n.d.): on the night of the orchestra's inaugural performance, "we knew it was for real, all that about the scholarships, the chances for work, our careers as musicians, it was all possible, it had come true."

My informants contrasted Abreu with Vicente Emilio Sojo, the legendary director of the JAL. Sojo led the school with firm moral, ethical, and political values, said one; he strictly believed that students should complete their formal training before turning professional. It would have been inconceivable for one of Sojo's students to provide music for advertising and political events, putting their studies at risk.

Some claimed that Sojo had banished Abreu from the JAL after an argument. While explanations varied, one saw this souring of relations as the catalyst for Abreu to turn his attention to a new youth orchestra that had been founded at the Juan José Landaeta Conservatoire by its director, Ángel Sauce. Abreu and Sauce jointly conducted the inaugural concert of the Juan José Landaeta National Youth Orchestra, but Abreu soon took over musical direction. The JAL orchestra could not compete and eventually died out. The Landaeta Conservatoire is in Chacao, one of the wealthiest sectors of Caracas, and the first members of Abreu's orchestra were mainly middle-class music students, not the impoverished children so often imagined today.

These oral histories emphasize Abreu's economic clout, Machiavellian side, and disruptive influence in pursuit of his goals. They identify the production of the social and cultural order through conflict and one-sided accumulation of resources, as explored in Chapter 1. In these accounts, two features of Abreu's orchestra marked it out from other projects: his legendary powers of persuasion and the scholarships that he secured.

A RELIGIOUS MISSION

Abreu's "concern and rebellion in the face of social imbalances impelled him, at the age of 35, to conceive a project that would allow him to synthesize and channel, in an ingenious and nationalist way, the experience and knowledge that he had gained in the fields of economics, management, pedagogy, and, of course, music since his adolescence," according to the FESNOJIV website. While the first part of this claim displays the mythification discussed above,

Abreu's education and training did indeed shape his program. He was educated by the Jesuits, earned a PhD in petroleum economics, and worked as director of planning for the state economic agency Cordiplan. It is no coincidence, then, that his great project is characterized variously as a religious mission, a music corporation, and a state within the state.

"The sistema is a kind of religion, and among its initiates, I grew accustomed to hearing Abreu described in Godlike terms (all-seeing, all-knowing, never-resting) and Dudamel celebrated as his charismatic, filial prophet," writes Lubow (2007). Wakin (2012a) spins an elaborate simile of Abreu as "venerated high priest," El Sistema as the Catholic Church, and its founding musicians as apostles: "Mr. Abreu and his inner circle are persistent evangelizers for El Sistema, proclaiming its advocacy of social justice with the zeal of missionaries." Abreu is widely known to be a highly religious man, and less widely known for his close links to Opus Dei, the ultraconservative Catholic sect. His rhetoric is infused with spiritual fervor, and he compares himself to a priest devoted to his flock and a servant of Christ (Borzacchini 2010, 66); his sanctification by admirers and journalists thus ties in with his self-depiction.

More than a saint, however, Abreu—devoted to taking European music to the farthest corners of Venezuela in the name of salvation—is heir to the missionaries who spearheaded the cultural conquest of the continent in the sixteenth century. El Sistema is not just underpinned by Catholic ideology, then, but also shows intriguing parallels with the Church's establishment of European music schools across Latin America in the colonial period. The most famed foot soldiers of the Spanish "musical conquest" were the Jesuits. El Sistema's mixture of mystical rhetoric, military discipline, theatrical displays, and music as civilizing project carries distinct echoes of Jesuit ideology and specifically the order's colonial-era colleges (van Orden 2005).

The Church's aim was a dual one: to train up an indigenous musical workforce and to "civilize" the participants in the process (Baker 2008a). The colonial musical culture that was transmitted to the indigenous population focused on ensemble performance of European(-style) repertoire. The Spaniards were more interested in hearing indigenous musicians perform European(-style) music than in teaching them to compose their own. When non-European music did rear its head, it was in stylized, Europeanized reworkings (Baker 2007; 2008b). The parallels with El Sistema are unmistakable.

Early colonial accounts by missionaries demonstrate a belief that the skillful performance of European music signified civilization. Five centuries on—and as amply demonstrated by the film *Dudamel* (2010), with its leitmotif of "Hymn to Joy"—one still finds the same belief that a group of Latin American children performing European music is a sign that they are being "saved." El Sistema's language of rescue and salvation underlines its role as the successor to colonial missionary music.

Borzacchini (2010, 103–4) appropriately titles her section on El Sistema's efforts to spread the word overseas "the musical missionaries": one proselytizer talks about creating orchestras in Paraguay despite local resistance; another discusses the challenges of implanting El Sistema in the Caribbean islands in the face of local attachment to steel bands. The colonialist overtones are inescapable. A leading figure at Bancaribe, one of El Sistema's key sponsors, spoke approvingly about the program's mission to inculcate values such as discipline and order, and ultimately to forge good citizens and a "well-tuned Venezuela" (2010, 213); this language harks straight back to the colonization project five centuries earlier, when musical metaphors and practices were coupled to a program to "civilize" the New World (Baker 2010). The "missionary zeal" of El Sistema's leaders and advocates has often been noted, but it is more than a metaphor—it is indicative of an organization deeply infused with Catholic ideology.

Abreu was involved in an infamous experiment in 1979 with the minister for the development of intelligence, Luis Alberto Machado, who was researching the role of nurture in human intelligence. Members of the Pemón indigenous group were taken from Venezuela's eastern interior to Caracas and taught to play symphonies by Haydn and Beethoven in two and a half months using a sped-up variant of the Suzuki method. This experiment became something of a cause célèbre in Caracas: with its clear echoes of colonial missionary practices and its manifest ethnocentrism, it unleashed "an anthropological and cultural storm" and was accused of "cultural violation" and "ethnocide."[2] This "anthropological barbarity," to quote an experienced music educator, shows a darker side to Abreu's creed of social engineering through classical music.

Forming orchestras of poor children in the barrios is thus the contemporary version of Jesuit missionaries who set off into the Paraguayan jungle in the seventeenth century to form choirs of Indians. Both projects are underpinned by an urge to save and civilize the Other at the point of a violin bow, and they met in the infamous Pemón musical experiment. If the seventeenth-century Jesuits had used today's language, they would have spoken about social inclusion and "schools of social life." Analyses of colonial Spanish musical policy in the New World illuminate modern-day developments, revealing ethical complexities and a coercive streak beneath the sweet-sounding tales of order and harmony. Missionaries have a mixed history in Latin America, combining fervor, vision, and creation with ruthlessness, monoculturalism, and destruction.

A MUSIC CORPORATION

El Sistema looks and functions, in certain respects, like a large business. Its scholarships to its more advanced young musicians have a distinct resemblance to salaries. In 2010 the Veracruz regional youth orchestra paid more than the adult, professional symphony. Young musicians are treated as employees of El Sistema, though they do not have certain basic rights such as maximum working hours or guaranteed free days. In Veracruz, the director decided when he wanted to rehearse and the musicians were expected to be there. If they missed a rehearsal, they had to present a medical note or their pay would be docked. A senior Sistema teacher described its young participants as workers rather than students, since they were required to be constantly available. A renowned conductor argued that because it started by removing young musicians from music schools halfway through their studies and putting them to work, El Sistema was more of an industrial than educative project. Even a pro-Sistema alumnus described the program as a perfect, pyramidal capitalist enterprise, resting on a huge base of low-paid workers. Such views are substantiated by the link between the development of the symphony orchestra and the corporations of business and industry as part of European industrialization (e.g., Small 1998). Nettl (1995, 34–35, 80) regards the organization of classical music schools as transferring the industrial model of corporations to the educational environment.

Abreu is an economist who studied business management at the same time as music, and his corporate capitalist background has left an unmistakable imprint on his project. As Borchert (2012, 47) notes, the language in which El Sistema is described is frequently indistinguishable from that of contemporary corporate culture. Particularly revealing is the preface to Borzacchini's book by Miguel Ignacio Purroy, president of Bancaribe, the bank that published the book and also sponsors El Sistema. Purroy praises the organization of the project "according to clear relations of discipline, order, division of labor, and clear targets to achieve" (2010, 3)—curious language for an arts education project. Continuing with the industrial theme, he describes El Sistema's students as "indefatigable and creative workers" (2010, 5). Most tellingly, he concludes (4): "between both of us, El Sistema and our bank, we saw from day one an exceptionally clear convergence of values."

The vision of Bancaribe's president is hard to dispute: El Sistema does indeed show clear parallels to industrial corporations and financial institutions. It also merges seamlessly with the international music industry, as discussed in Chapter 2; the links are not just ideological but also practical. El Sistema schools young people in the values of industrial and corporate capitalism, and serves as a feeder and moneymaker for the classical music business. One of its most distinctive features is the extent to which it has converted music education into an economic resource. Abreu gives his most concerted attention to conductors, forming future stars of the global music industry. Purroy's summary of recent Sistema highlights underlines the emergence of Dudamel, recordings for international labels, and high-profile international tours—all industry-related achievements.

The figure of the conductor has often appealed to management gurus as a model for business leaders. Roger Johnson (2009, 21) notes that "the orchestra with its conductor have long been interpreted as a representation or even idealization of the smooth-running capitalist organizational structure." An article in *Business Management* magazine titled "Orchestrating the Organization" describes how a group of business managers sought to explore the parallels between the conductor and company leadership (Miller 2006). The author's enthusiasm is undented by a conductor describing his job as "the last refuge for dictators" and the realization that conductors and musicians are in "a relationship which is not based on being 'nice' to one another, in fact conductors are often despised." Miller concluded that "conductors are definitely underpaid for what they do. Who cares that they earn 10 times as much as the first violin?" (Tindall [2005, 298], a professional orchestral musician, answers this rhetorical question: conductors' high salaries "destroy morale within the ranks of musicians who earn a fraction of their bosses' pay.") Business managers' admiring glances at conductors derive from a shared cult of leadership: an ideology of drastic inequality between the workforce and hyperrich, hyperpowerful figureheads. The pay of conductors, like that of CEOs, skyrocketed in the late twentieth century. El Sistema, with its focus on producing star conductors, normalizes this model, and—as Purroy reveals—fits snugly with broader capitalist ideology. Admirers may see a "revolutionary social project," but Venezuelan critics talk revealingly of a "big business."

Given that, as a young man, Abreu's studies focused on classical music and oil, it may also be worth noting intriguing parallels between El Sistema and the operations of multinational oil companies in Venezuela (Tinker Salas 2009). The latter "promoted the image of the model worker and the ideal public citizen" (2009, 10); to that end, they attempted to "remake the Venezuelan character" (195) via a moralistic program focused on order, hard work, and the importation of foreign practices and values; and they sought to create a new, exemplary, corporate social order, often imagined as a broad family. Tinker Salas notes: "The experiences acquired in the oil industry influenced several generations of Venezuelans who after 1960 took the reins of power in the country" (203). To what extent were Abreu's orchestral training program and its social engineering along corporate lines influenced by his expertise in the oil world?

A STATE WITHIN THE STATE

Over time, Abreu has attached his project to an array of government ministries, with significant consequences: he has managed to secure considerable funds by drawing on the budgets of larger ministries; and he has developed a cultural program beyond the control of the Ministry of Culture and an educational program outside the reach of the Ministry of Education. The largest cultural organization in Venezuela thus operates independently of (and sometimes in opposition to) national cultural policy and the Venezuelan constitution, which in Article 100 grants the highest priority to Venezuelan popular culture. It has also been free to ignore the Ministry of Education's 1964 music education curriculum, which included instrumental and vocal lessons, solfège and music theory, complementary harmony, music history, aesthetics, and composition. When critics describe El Sistema as "a state within the state," they allude not just to its size and economic resources but also to its capacity to ignore the state's cultural and educational priorities.

According to a Ministry of Culture official, his institution and El Sistema were two separate worlds that barely communicated. The ministry was developing two responses to El Sistema: one was the National System of Arts Education, intended to provide the rounded music education that El Sistema did not; the other was the National System for Popular Cultures (NSPC), which aimed to train and provide work for popular culture practitioners sidelined by Abreu's project. Most notably, this official described national cultural policy as responding to Abreu, rather than vice versa. No sooner had the NSPC been created, however, than Abreu founded Alma Llanera, a very similar project (see Chapter 12), though under his control and with a 50 percent larger budget.

El Sistema operates according to its own logic and obeys its own rules. Its fuel is the language of vision, inspiration, and the power of art; it has little time for prosaic notions like monitoring, accountability, and evidence-based decision making, which might be expected of a state foundation. Its supporters argue that its independence has been a source of strength, but others believe it has become too powerful, perceiving it as a black hole for funds and, in Gustavo Medina's words, "a state within the country."

ORGANIZATIONAL CULTURE

El Sistema has "a flexible, open, and democratic management style that is adapted to the local needs of each region," according to its website. My informants, however, painted a very different picture. A well-known conductor compared it to Oceania in Orwell's *Nineteen Eighty-Four*. At the top is Maestro Abreu, the "Big Brother." El Sistema's structure exists primarily to carry out his orders. In theory his decisions are subject to scrutiny by a Consultative Council, but in 2011 there was no information publicly available about this committee. A former senior figure described it as "one of the foundation's most closely guarded secrets": "Obviously they are all 'unconditionals' of José Antonio [Abreu] because that's the basic requirement for being there."

According to FESNOJIV's founding document, its board of directors is made up of an executive director and four directors. In recent years Abreu has been referred to as the founding director, a post not mentioned in the original constitution. So while he runs El Sistema, the precise dynamics are somewhat obscure. For example, when El Sistema reformed its constitution in 1996 and became FESNOJIV, a number of Sistema leaders were present and signed the notarial document, but Abreu's signature was not among them.[3] When I located this document, I recalled the claim by two senior figures that Abreu's signature rarely appeared in official documents. Why was he legally absent at this key juncture in the program's history?

Beneath Abreu are the directors, several of whom were originally members of the National Youth Orchestra. The hierarchical relationship between them thus has a long history. As one former high-level figure put it, Abreu demanded that his inner circle show "not just loyalty but devotion to their leader, both publicly and privately"—something aided by appointing former students who owed their success to El Maestro. At the regional level, each state has its own director. In Veracruz, this leader oversaw all the Sistema music schools and also served as conductor and director of the regional youth orchestra, combining musical and bureaucratic power. Every decision—logistical, economic, musical, disciplinary—passed through him. At the state level, too, the director's word is law. Far from "a flexible, open, and democratic management style," the cult of leadership is evident everywhere.

Some leaders, like Abreu himself, appear soft-spoken and genial, though there is reputedly an iron fist inside the velvet glove. Others are famed, however, for their abrasive ways and domineering treatment of subordinates. One was nicknamed "The Dog" because of his savage temperament. A former senior figure described this inner circle as despots, while another claimed that Abreu was very careful to keep his image clean, making sure that members of his inner circle did his dirty work. According to some of their contemporaries, these right-hand men—known unofficially as *verdugos* (executioners)—were "yes men" chosen for their willingness to carry out Abreu's orders. Abreu received a broad education and gained wide working experience before starting El Sistema, but the next generation grew up inside the program and reflects the "following orders" culture of orchestral music.

El Sistema itself is organized like an orchestra: Abreu is the conductor; the directors are the section principals, with power over others but less room for decision making. Conducting has often been described in terms of dictatorial leadership (e.g., Nettl 1995, 77), and those who have studied or worked within El Sistema regularly use such terms. Abreu's stereotypically conductor-like management style has transmitted itself throughout his institution and beyond into the professional orchestral world where many of his protégés occupy positions of authority. For all the images of freedom and fiesta, the tyrannical maestro is alive and well in Venezuela. A musician in the Veracruz Symphony Orchestra recounted:

> We were doing a warm-up concert before a trip to Caracas. We were playing Mahler 1, in which the score indicates that the big final horns solo should be played standing up. During the rehearsals the horns kept trying to stand up, but the conductor said no they couldn't, because in order to stand up the horns had to know the part perfectly, and it wasn't good enough. So the concert began and it had never gone so well; everything came out perfectly, all the solos, everything. Anyway, this bit comes about 30 bars before the end of the symphony. The horns had made a plan to stand up at that point anyway. We were getting towards the end, everything was going marvelously, we got to that bit, and boom...the horns stood up. And the conductor went mad. He started shouting in mid-concert, "Sit down! Sit down!" The horns carried on standing up. "Sit down! For fuck's sake, sit down!"—swearing and everything, red in the face, literally spitting mad. He threw down the baton and shouted, "Stop! Stop! Silence! Shut up!" Because of the layout of the venue, half the orchestra couldn't see what was going on. "Sit down! Sit down!" The horns sit down. And the guy says, "OK, from letter N." And he starts beating time. The symphony finished as badly as you can imagine. It was totally humiliating.

The musicians had committed the unpardonable sin of challenging the conductor's authority. The trip to Caracas was cancelled.

Authoritarianism runs right through El Sistema. One young musician reported that he could not think of anyone who had become a better person through playing in the orchestra—but he knew plenty who had become worse: "It's a question of ego, of power." The orchestra gives authority to section leaders, who exercise this power over the rank and file. He claimed that principals and assistant principals tended to mix socially, separating themselves from the rest of the orchestra, and admitted that it felt great to be at the top of the pile—and that trampling on others was part of that feeling: "I've lived it, it's kind of crazy, but sometimes you find yourself doing things where you say 'hang on, this isn't me, why did I do that?' And maybe you realize this, but others don't and they spend years doing it, treating others badly, trampling on them, humiliating them.... It's fun when you're at the top of it, but if you're one of the ones further down...I've been there and it's horrible." From this perspective, if El Sistema serves as a school of social life, one of the main subjects it teaches is despotism.

Authoritarianism goes hand in hand with hierarchization. There is a clear prestige structure in classical music and especially orchestras, with conductors at the top and different status accorded to different instrument groups (Bensman 1967, 57–58). The musician's position within the section (desk or chair) is another important marker of status. One young musician reported:

"Just like there are classes in society, it's the same in the orchestra—there are strata." Yet El Sistema's institutional culture emphasizes such stratification and status differences. Young musicians are ranked according to a descending scale: principal, assistant principal, A, B, C, and practice-level. This hierarchy is accentuated by pay differences between the ranks and, at least in Veracruz, the tendency to mix socially with people of similar rank. The inequalities of the outside world are supposedly left behind as children walk through the doors of the núcleo, but they are simply replaced by other forms of stratification. One interviewee claimed that principals only respected others of similar status: "It's not total integration or anything like that....I don't know half the orchestra—and it's the half that's level B downwards."

Another of Abreu's traits that has become generalized is his intolerance of criticism. One high-placed informant, noting Abreu's insistence on devotion, claimed: "when you start to question him, that's the end of your relationship." Despite El Sistema's obvious failings, "it is forbidden to talk. Worse still, it is forbidden to think. As soon as you are old enough to make a critical comment about what you see every day, from that moment you start to be watched and if you do not 'rectify' your behavior, look out, because you will be out in no time." The consequences of standing up to Abreu are dire: "no one can criticize him openly because that means condemning their musical career in the country." At every level of the program, dissent may lead to ejection. The result is a generalized lack of critical reflection and debate.

CAUDILLO

El Sistema reproduces a long-standing Latin American tradition: dependence on and worship of the authoritarian *caudillo* (strong leader) who operates through charisma, patronage, and clientelism and maintains his own private army—in this case, of musicians. Venezuela's particular authoritarian tradition was labeled "democratic caesarism" by the early-twentieth-century intellectual Laureano Vallenilla Lanz, who believed that the national character made caudillo-style rule essential. El Sistema also perpetuates the paternalist power dynamics of the political sphere in which Abreu moved as a young man (Fernandes 2010, 46). The main parties operated in a highly disciplined, "verticalist" or hierarchical style, exercising a "politics of patronage" (Hellinger 1991, 155). The government of CAP I, when El Sistema was formed, saw "the concentration of power at the highest levels of government" and "a vertical style of policy making which often led to arbitrary and contradictory actions and undermined democratic practices" (Coronil 1997, 11). El Sistema's organizational culture thus draws on Abreu's political background, and here, too, patronage is crucial. Power can be measured by proximity or access to El Maestro.

Carvajal and Melgarejo (2008) claim that the program "is open to people who come with divergent but complementary projects" and "tends to favor change instead of blocking it," but interviewees painted a picture of independent initiatives taken over or arbitrarily curtailed. A senior figure revealed that behind his high public profile, his activity was restricted; everything he did had to be approved by Abreu, and anything that smacked of independence—such as solo or chamber music projects—was turned down. Several middle-aged musicians described themselves or their Sistema contemporaries—including founders—as trapped in limbo, their destiny in Abreu's recalcitrant hands.

A former member of the National Children's Orchestra recalled Abreu's urge to interfere in everything—rehearsal plans, repertoire, interpretation. He would contradict the conductor during rehearsals and demand that the orchestra play music that was beyond it. Another member reported: "Abreu was always there in the rehearsals—all the time, sitting there with his score. When we finished playing a passage, the conductor would turn round and look at Abreu, who would say whether it was OK or not, what needed changing, whether to play it again or go on." Such accounts are echoed by Lubow's (2007) description of Gustavo Dudamel's "audition" to become Gustavo Medina's replacement: "For the teenage novice, the challenge was heightened by the conspicuous and audible presence of his mentor, José Antonio Abreu, who was seated front-row center and calling out suggestions. 'Woodwinds up!' Abreu urged his protégé. 'Tell the strings more bow!' The conductor sailed ahead confidently. 'I think that was the test,' Dudamel told me." The test was apparently less one of conducting ability than dealing with an overshadowing mentor, something that the new Gustavo was more willing to accept than the old one.

The paradox of El Sistema, it is often said, is that there is no system. This also means no fixed, transparent, accountable processes. El Sistema's institutional culture is a contradictory mix of hyperorganization and disorganization, stemming directly from Abreu's total control. El Sistema has the capacity to mobilize huge resources at short notice, especially for distinguished foreign visitors; yet plans change constantly according to Abreu's whim. Informants described a vast state foundation run according to the caprice of a single individual. Booth (2010, 4) reads this disorganization in positive terms: "There is an improvisational feel to the work, a pride in continual rediscovery of how to do things as they go." He quotes Abreu: "We believe a certain level of chaos is important for us." Carvajal and Melgarejo (2008) concur, suggesting that "disorder is conceived as a renewing factor, giving rise to new and higher forms of self-organization." Another possible reading is that The System feels no compulsion to provide order for its rank and file. Such disorder may seem positive to those giving the commands, but less so for those on the receiving end, for whom the lack of transparent processes morphs easily into arbitrariness, forced passivity, and powerlessness. As Chang (2007, 102) reported, some

SBYO musicians believe that Abreu "intentionally keeps them in the dark to maintain his control over the organization."

A longtime Sistema director spoke of the precariousness that El Sistema brings to professional musical life. Musicians are hired, fired, and moved on with a wave of El Maestro's baton. Decades of work and dedication are worth nothing without Abreu's blessing, he said, recalling the damning conclusion to Medina's resignation letter. The only stable element in El Sistema is Abreu's will, on which everything depends.

The society that El Sistema models is thus an intensely hierarchical one of powerful, authoritarian leaders, clearly defined strata, and the performance of fixed, assigned roles. With its opaque procedures, it has echoes of the Catholic Church, which "demands authority, without offering accountability" (Deveney 2013). It constitutes a detailed classificatory system and, as discussed in Chapter 8, a microcosm of Foucault's "disciplinary society."

CENTRALIZATION

If power is highly concentrated at the top of El Sistema, it is almost as clearly consolidated at the center. One of the issues that I encountered with greatest regularity was centralization—both the accumulation of resources in the capital, and the pull that Caracas exerted on provincial musicians. In Veracruz, there was a widespread belief that things were better in the capital, and that local problems were due to distance from the center. One musician asked me why I was bothering to do research in Veracruz—a fairly large city—given that "El Sistema is Caracas."

If Abreu is highly adept at securing funds *for* El Sistema, their distribution *within* it is more of a problem. The program mirrors the nation, for which the concentration of resources in the capital has been a perennial issue; during the post-1958 democratic period, when Abreu's political apprenticeship occurred, "oil wealth produced a highly centralized state apparatus" (Fernandes 2010, 20). CAP attempted to promote decentralization from 1989, but was largely unsuccessful. As minister under CAP, Abreu came under fire for perpetuating centralization and highly unequal distribution of resources in the cultural sphere. Similarly, in El Sistema, as a senior informant reported, "everyone criticizes, though under their breath, and asks why there's so much money for [foreign] tours when there are núcleos that don't have teachers or instruments, that don't pay, or the núcleo is in a bad state."

El Sistema's showcase orchestras lack for nothing in their breathtaking home, the state-of-the-art CASM in Caracas, yet in one provincial núcleo I watched the administrator hauling instrument after battered instrument out of a storage space—all broken or missing strings that could not be bought locally and were not being provided centrally. The núcleo also had no internal doors—hardly ideal for a music school. Another spent its first two years without instruments and had not gotten beyond a dozen string instruments in nearly four years of functioning; yet another was given ten violins to start with, but only one bow. Similar tales emerged from small núcleos across Venezuela: students complaining of having no teacher, no instrument, no classroom, or no electricity. Even in some state capitals, the teaching conditions were mediocre at best. Such conditions would be understandable in a project on a tight budget, but El Sistema is handsomely funded.

One Veracruz musician questioned how the concentration of resources in Caracas fitted with the idea of a national program. Many state capitals were lacking experienced staff in some key instruments, partly because of the poor pay, and the situation in their satellite núcleos was worse still. Many students thus had to travel overnight to Caracas every two weeks for lessons (often at their own cost). If El Sistema were serious about decentralization, he said, it would address the unevenness of teaching quality across the country.

In March 2013 a group of provincial music teachers posted a series of petitions on the Facebook page "Yo soy 100% FESNOJIV" (I am 100% FESNOJIV), complaining that their pay was not only painfully low but also much delayed. Following this, reports filtered in suggesting that the capital's teachers had already been paid. "That's what's wrong, they always look after those from the capital and they don't care about the rest, as if they didn't play from the same score," responded one poster. Another wrote: "El Sistema isn't just Caracas, it's the whole of Venezuela . . . it's a joke for us workers—we're devoted to this passion called music but we still need to be paid enough and on time . . . how sad the reality of El Sistema is becoming." By late May, the tone was becoming increasingly militant: "most of the [government] support stays in Caracas (Simón Bolívar Orchestra A and B, directors with mega-salaries, etc.). . . . They are the ones who enjoy all the benefits, comforts and quality of life, bonuses, hyper-expensive travels, among others . . . these rewards should be more balanced and such stark differences should not be created; the sharing-out of this money should be fairer and include us all."

One does not need to leave Caracas, however, to see notable imbalances: just a few miles from the CASM there are núcleos suffering from shortages of basic necessities. A teacher with sixteen years' experience claimed that the difference between Montalbán and the Caracas núcleos where he taught was like night and day. Foreign visitors always get taken to the same few núcleos, he said. He was highly critical of the lack of spending on ordinary núcleos, yet lavish expenditure on showpiece events and foreign tours. Reports of poor conditions, broken instruments, long waits for equipment, and deserting teachers filtered out from the less favored núcleos. Looking also at the CASM and the SBYO, El Sistema's production of inequality is abundantly clear.

The centralization of resources in El Sistema is institutionalized: individual Sistema núcleos that I visited did not manage their own budgets, so all significant decisions were taken at the center, and even insignificant matters often required endless waits for funds from higher up. Forged in the political culture of the Punto Fijo period (1958–98), the program had not followed the lead of the Chávez government, which sought to devolve budgets and decision making to local communal councils. In one provincial núcleo, an older student was left as the head of his family when his father died, and he stopped attending the orchestra regularly because he needed to feed his family. The núcleo's director went to Caracas and petitioned Abreu in person, taking reams of documents with her, and chased up the case every few months. It took a year, but he was finally given a job as a handyman in the núcleo. This is a characteristic Sistema story, involving direct and benevolent intervention from Abreu, yet also revealing the problematic verticalist structure and inefficient functioning of the program.

El Sistema's showcase ensembles are also highly centralized. It is easier to see them in London than in the Venezuelan regions. Provincial musicians who received their scholarships or salaries months behind schedule sometimes claimed that the delay was due to the diverting of funds to cover the flagship orchestras' foreign tours. El Sistema's finances are not publicly available, but the belief itself is revealing.

Another form of centralization is the "national curriculum" of orchestral repertoire. This standardization allows students from different núcleos to collaborate easily, but it also contributes to the concentration of power. A former provincial núcleo director claimed that the stipulation of repertoire by Caracas had left him with little artistic autonomy. He recalled a directive to put on Mahler 1 with the children from the state's núcleos, a demand that he considered completely unrealistic, given the playing level at the time. Despite the claims of adaptability, then, local autonomy is often limited.

CENTRIPETAL FLOWS

El Sistema's distribution of resources constitutes a form of trickle-down economics, with núcleos in small towns and many Caracas barrios—where core work is supposed to happen—at the bottom. This model combines with a much more efficient upward flow of talent toward the capital, where the best orchestras and teachers are concentrated. If we focus on the most gifted students, the centralizing forces are unmistakable.

Many members of the Veracruz regional youth orchestra traveled in several times a week from surrounding small towns, growing apart from their local núcleos as their city commitments increased. Their scholarship was provided by the city orchestra, so they were obliged to prioritize their commitments in Veracruz. This systemic form of centralization prevents many talented students from participating fully in their local musical life. Each day they travel to the city is a day they cannot attend their home núcleo. This siphoning off of talent does not appear an efficient means of transforming local communities.

Some students simply move to the city, leaving their family and community for the surrogate family of the orchestra—and not necessarily voluntarily. Three young students from Santa Ana, a small town two hours from Veracruz, became section principals in the regional youth orchestra. The director then announced that they had to move to Veracruz, as he wanted them to be available every day; if they did not, they would be demoted. For the most talented provincial students, further progress may mean leaving for the capital. With the best orchestras and most powerful patrons there, the pull of Caracas is hard to resist. When Abreu saw Dudamel conduct in 1998, "after the concert, he went to speak to Dudamel's grandparents and said, 'I have to take him to Caracas.' They were shocked, but they could not refuse. 'We cried a lot,' Engracia recalls. 'And my husband told Dr. Abreu, 'You are taking the light out of this house'' " (Lubow 2007).

Abreu had little respect for rural núcleos, which were simply regarded as feeders for Caracas, claimed a senior musician. A musician who spent twenty-five years in El Sistema left because he was fed up with Caracas "talent-hunting" in the provinces. A leading Veracruz teacher reported that he faced constant entreaties to move to Caracas. Executive Director Igor Lanz claimed that Abreu undertook a "process of decentralization and deconcentration of musical teaching and practice" (Borzacchini 2010, 197), but provincial musicians told a different story.

The director of a major regional núcleo claimed the talent flight to Caracas would continue as long as each state did not have control over resources proportional to its size. The day that I visited, a guest conductor due to start a two-week stint with the orchestra pulled out at four days' notice after being called to Caracas to receive some visitors from overseas; the brass section was leaving for a weeklong seminar in the capital; and the Caracas HQ decided to send a soloist to do a dry run of a concerto before performing in the capital, to which the director responded, "if that's an order from Caracas, then we just have to do it."

THE VIEW FROM A SMALL PROVINCIAL TOWN

The núcleo in Santa Ana was a joint effort, supported by local parents (who joined together into a Society of Friends), FESNOJIV, and the mayor, though the parents felt that the input had been very uneven. They said that they had worked extremely hard to make the orchestra function, and that FESNOJIV gave them some support but also created obstacles, while the mayor, they claimed, was mainly interested in the shine that the orchestra gave to his image. They appreciated that without El Sistema, there would be no orchestra in Santa Ana, but they felt it could function much better.

FESNOJIV's centralization made for constant phoning and letter writing to Caracas to ask for the release of funds and instruments. The núcleo was underresourced, for example lacking spare strings for its instruments. Too much money and attention went toward flagship projects in Caracas and foreign tours, they felt, leaving the regions with the scraps. The pay was low, making it hard to attract a good director. Recent changes in leadership had led to a decline in morale and standards at the núcleo, so they saw it as important to create stability in the town.

The Society of Friends was putting together a list of proposals. They planned to push for greater independence and self-sufficiency and a stronger, more active, more connected local music scene; they were no longer happy to serve as a feeder for Veracruz and ultimately for Caracas, bringing in teachers from outside and then losing the best local talents to the cities. They felt that El Sistema discriminated against keen young musicians from small towns, who were required to travel to the city three or four times a week, using up most of their scholarship and their free time and leading to disengagement from their home community.

Ultimately they wanted to manage their own budget. Pointing to the decentralization of the Venezuelan political process under Chávez, they argued that FESNOJIV should replicate the communal council system: every núcleo should have a Society of Friends, empowered and funded to take decisions. They also aimed to create a network of local sponsors, since FESNOJIV provided insufficient funds for the núcleo's basic needs.

Concerned by the minimal music-theory teaching in El Sistema, they decided that the solution was for children to learn theory in school before they came to the núcleo. They planned to link up with local schools in order to provide basic music education from five years old. Also, there was some resistance to El Sistema from nonclassical musicians in the town, so they intended to open up the núcleo to other musical genres and instruments, bringing musical worlds together.

Soothing words about local customization and experimentation appear in official statements and are echoed by foreign supporters (e.g., Booth 2008, 10–11), yet in Santa Ana FESNOJIV showed little sign of flexibility, local adaptation was something of a battleground between institution and parents, and experimentation was constrained by the lack of local financial control. Had local customization been a reality, by 2010 Venezuela would have been littered with núcleos specializing in popular or traditional music. In Santa Ana, the Society of Friends planned to tell FESNOJIV about most of their changes after the event, as they believed that an advance request would simply be turned down.

The IDB has regarded the decentralization of El Sistema as a priority since its Phase I loan in 1998, when it proposed the construction of seven regional CASMs to remedy the problem, but the pace of change has been glacial. In its 2007 summary of the Phase I loan, the IDB reported that "the original design for the construction of the CASPM [the Caracas CASM] underwent successive changes that led the resources earmarked for FESNOJIV's institutional development to be channeled to construction of the CASPM, which in turn left the institutional progress only partially achieved." For all the talk of decentralization, then, El Sistema devoted most of the loan to building a showpiece conservatoire in the middle of Caracas. Hence the loan "did not effectively deconcentrate FESNOJIV's administrative-financial and music education areas" ("Program to Support" 2007, 1, 7).

The 2007 Phase II proposal prioritized the as yet unrealized seven regional centers as the core of its efforts to decentralize El Sistema. Four were supposed to have been completed by the end of 2010, but in 2011 I saw no signs that work had even begun. Fourteen years after the initial proposal, it appeared that decentralization was not a high priority, since it was constantly being deferred. Recalling Abreu's stewardship of CONAC, it appears that decentralization is his Achilles heel.

In late 2012 the Latin American Development Bank, CAF, approved the second part of a $350 million loan for the construction of a new Sistema center, the Simón Bolívar Complex for Social Action through Music ("El Sistema" 2012). Building had already begun—next door to the Caracas CASM, which had only been fully operational for a couple of years. The IDB's Phase II loan was realized in 2008, yet signs of progress were still scarce in the provinces. In contrast, construction of a massive extension to the sumptuous Caracas headquarters, including three more concert halls, was already well under way, even though the CAF loan was not approved until 2010. The bricks and mortar tell an eloquent story.

This vast (and vastly expensive) new complex will stand as a testament to Abreu's influence over national and international institutions, but it will also exacerbate the disparity between center and periphery. A musician from Veracruz who had visited the CASM on several occasions claimed that the building was usually quiet, with a number of rooms standing empty, whereas in his núcleo there were often four people practicing simultaneously in every cubicle. Why was another huge center being constructed beside the CASM, he asked? Without a doubt, the new complex will have some impact on the lives of musicians outside Caracas, who will continue to travel to the capital; but the expenditure of $350 million on a single complex in central Caracas, next door to the best facilities in the country, seems a highly centralizing move.

Sala Simón Bolívar, Centro de Acción Social por la Música. Photo by Geoffrey Baker.

Most of the $500 million in development bank loans since 2008 is thus destined for a small number of large, imposing music centers. Creating impressive temples to classical music is hardly a new idea, and part of their social action is undoubtedly to inspire awe and reverence for a cultural tradition and its patrons. In El Sistema's monumental Caracas HQ, Abreu is literally cementing his musical preferences at the heart of Venezuela's cultural life. It may also be seen as a facet of Abreu's "politics of impact," manifested in attempts to convince observers of his program's effectiveness through performance and spectacle (see Chapter 11). Abreu seems to have learnt from President Pérez Jiménez's luxurious building projects, with their "fetishistic vision of modernity as a collection of grand material achievements" that "had in common the quality of spectacular display," designed to impress foreign visitors (Coronil 1997, 178).

Whether such grandiose schemes bring the maximum possible benefits to local users is another matter; as the urban planner Stanley Tankel stated (quoted in Scott 1998, 144), it is easy "to confuse great building projects with great social achievements." It might be argued that a focus on decentralization and social change should entail starting from the margins, following the lead of Medellín, Colombia, a city with dramatic social problems that attempted to reverse its fortunes via a program of "library parks." Instead of creating a single, dominant focal point in the city center, it spread resources out to nine poor neighborhoods on the periphery, which were provided with innovative cultural and community centers (Nichols 2012). In contrast to monumental construction projects of the past, the library parks were designed in consultation with local communities rather than imposed from a central office, embodying the devolution of power to the local level. The meanings of these new spaces remain fluid, as do the activities within them. The buildings are designed to be shaped by their users; they are not places to learn a particular skill or absorb a paternalistic vision.

El Sistema operates in some barrios, but facilities are often decrepit, and in many towns the Sistema núcleo is in fact far from the poorest areas. With $350 million, El Sistema could have transformed its infrastructure across Venezuela. Such a move would have had symbolic as well as practical consequences, letting the country know that every community's cultural life was valued equally. A $350 million complex in Caracas, on the other hand, is likely to exacerbate existing inequalities and centripetal flows. Medellín's library parks enact a progressive, contemporary philosophy for urban and social development, whereas El Sistema, by planting another high temple of European culture at the center of the map, is creating the musical equivalent of the New York Public Library—the thinking of a century ago.

EXPANSION

Paradoxically, El Sistema combines a centralizing impulse with a continuous drive for expansion. A key aim of the Phase II loan was to double the size of El Sistema to five hundred thousand children, and by 2013 the figure of one million was being cited. How realistic is it for the program to expand so far and so fast, and is it likely to benefit the children, the project, or Venezuela?

El Sistema does not fully fund núcleos: it provides some salaries and instruments, but not normally the physical infrastructure. As a result, many existing núcleos are already struggling. Thousands of Sistema students are lacking either a decent instrument, or a reliable supply of strings or reeds, or regular lessons, or a respectable learning space, and the constant expansion just puts greater pressure on resources. Teachers argued that El Sistema should devote more attention to looking after existing núcleos and their staff and students, rather than constantly creating new ones. Even if the seven provincial CASMs are eventually built, what impact will this have on the two-hundred-odd existing núcleos, many of which are borrowing premises or occupying decrepit buildings?

In his article on ODILA, an abortive traditional music program of the early 1980s, director Emilio Mendoza (n.d.a) recalls its sudden suspension after a disagreement with Abreu. Mendoza argued that it was essential to ensure that the pilot núcleo in Caracas was functioning properly before expanding, but Abreu wanted to push ahead and create traditional music núcleos all across Venezuela. Mendoza was concerned that Abreu was more interested in quantity than quality. "Since Abreu insisted on starting the multiplication of ODILA immediately, without any heed for the lamentable state of the only existing orchestra in Caracas, there was no possibility of agreement or dialogue."

Conversely, there are some impressive initiatives, such as the early childhood education program, that have become well established in show núcleos in Caracas like La Rinconada and Montalbán. Why is El Sistema focused on doubling in size rather than rolling out such attractive pilot schemes to the existing núcleo network? Critics suggested that a few high-quality show núcleos, bolstered by some extraordinarily large figures, was the most efficient route to impressing observers and funders.

Expansion has produced a notable problem of personnel. There is an oversupply of competent orchestral players, yet everywhere I went, I heard complaints of a shortage of teachers. Who will actually implement the vast project of doubling or quadrupling the number of students? As Uy (2012, 15) argues, without a dramatic increase in the number of teachers, the planned expansion will simply be impossible.

Another obstacle for El Sistema's expansion plans is a lack of qualified and charismatic núcleo directors. Some satellite núcleos around Veracruz had been quite successful, but others were considered partial failures. One had no director and hence few students; this was apparently a long-standing problem. An excellent director in a remote rural núcleo admitted that she would rather be closer to the city so that she could go to concerts, and indeed, she was trying to leave. Symphony orchestras are urban organizations, in that they depend on a concentration of musicians, audiences, facilities, and resources; hence few active, dynamic orchestral musicians want to be based very far from a city. Provincial expansion may therefore be inherently problematic. As long as they continue to focus on preprofessional orchestral training, provincial núcleos may be destined to remain feeders for the cities rather than thriving cultural centers in their own right.

There is an obvious solution to this problem, but it would require a complete reversal of El Sistema's corporate capitalist model: to make núcleo teaching the best-paid job in El Sistema rather than the worst. Another solution would be to refound the project around traditional, community-based musical genres, which would be more suited to a locally oriented social project than orchestral music.

Along with attracting more teachers, the biggest challenge of rapid expansion is quality. The combination of centralization of talent and expansion tends to produce weakness on the periphery. A long-term Sistema participant complained that massification had brought a loss of human and musical quality, while an orchestral administrator concurred that overexpansion and a fixation on quantity had impacted negatively on musical training. Borzacchini and Tunstall write that in the earliest days, Abreu would lead group discussions of art, music, literature, and philosophy. This rounded education has been lost with the SBYO's conversion into a show orchestra and its reproduction hundreds of times over. Doubling in size may double the project's budget and Abreu's prestige, but will it really make Venezuelan music education twice as good?

AN INSIDER'S VIEW ON EXPANSION

A former senior figure in El Sistema discussed a second phase of its history, beginning around the time that Abreu became minister of culture, as "the phase of growth and recruitment":

> We understood that as El Sistema grew in numbers, the state's interest in it would grow too, and it would have more political weight to influence the decisions of the state. So there was a policy of constant growth and of recruiting ever more people. A group of us would get together to make an orchestra out of nothing. We would arrive [in a new town] in the holidays (which was ideal because the kids weren't in school) and we'd go to the main square and recruit kids. We had a whole spiel prepared.
>
> There were also political decisions behind this, because, for example, if we knew that there was a deputy in the national congress who was on the finance committee and who could have an important bearing on the foundation's budget, then we would have the political aim of creating an orchestra in that deputy's home town so as to win him over and commit him [to the project], so that he would look favorably on the proposed budgets when he came to take part in the congressional commission.

He claimed there was usually a political interest, rather than an altruistic urge for social transformation, behind the creation of an orchestra in a particular location.

> One of the things that has enabled José Antonio to survive all these years through all these governments is his clear understanding of the political structure of the country, above all what its defects are and what its faults are and how it works, in order to be able to manipulate the political process, by means of those weaknesses, to the benefit of the orchestra and, at the end of the day, to the benefit of himself.

My informant suggested there were similar political motivations behind El Sistema's expansion overseas. He claimed Abreu had shown interest in Uruguay because the president of the IDB at the time was Uruguayan. "There was a lot of international political strategy behind this," he said; "it was the same national mechanism applied on an international level." The IDB subsequently played an important role in financing the expansion of El Sistema in Venezuela. Abreu told my informant that El Sistema and the overseas orchestras were part of the Venezuelan government's regional political strategy. "This came as a response to questions that I raised about the way we were creating the orchestras (with no musical future or real sustainability), and it was when I realized that didn't matter...it was all about politics."

In 2010 Abreu accompanied the SBYO to Oslo for a concert and a major speech. In 2011 he sent the Caracas Youth Orchestra (CYO) to Norway to cement this binational relationship, which resulted in the creation of the Norway-Venezuela (NOVE) Orchestra. My informant commented that Abreu "is trying finally to land the Nobel Peace Prize, talking about poor children around the world and so on...he's softening up the Nobel people." Indeed, FESNOJIV's press releases spoke less of Oslo than of "the cradle of the Nobel" and "the capital of the land of the Nobel Prize."

In early 2012 Abreu was formally proposed for the prize. At this point, the campaign appeared to move up a notch. In May El Sistema sent enough CYO members to Norway to allow their division into two blocks: one formed the Venezuelan half of NOVE, while the other constituted its own orchestra and gave half a dozen concerts around Oslo, ensuring a double dose of Sistema publicity in Norway just a few months before the Nobel decision. Back in Venezuela, El Sistema's references to "peace" increased. The year began with the huge joint Mahler project with the L.A. Philharmonic, labeled "With Dudamel for Peace." In April, FESNOJIV's website described the CASM as "promoting a culture of peace." Dudamel and the SBSO's collaboration with Rubén Blades in July was another "concert for peace." Older musicians described a discursive shift in the 1990s that had seen El Sistema insert the word "social" into its self-presentation; in 2012 "peace" was the *mot du jour*.

Harford (2012, 40–41) presents a commonplace view of how effective organizations work. A strong leader sees the big picture; he is surrounded by a supportive team with a shared vision; and clear reporting lines ensure that information flows up the system and instructions flow back down in response. But this is a "dangerously misleading view" in Harford's eyes: "Every one of these assets can become a liability if the task of the organization is to learn from mistakes. The big picture becomes a self-deluding propaganda poster, the unified team retreats into groupthink, and the chain of command becomes a hierarchy of wastebaskets, perfectly evolved to prevent feedback reaching the top. What works in reality is a far more unsightly, chaotic and rebellious organization altogether" (42). By chaos, he means not the capriciousness of leaders, but rather internal diversity of opinion.

Harford's critique of President Johnson's handling of the Vietnam War finds multiple echoes in El Sistema. "His three aides, who viewed themselves as 'a kind of family,' were careful always to harmonize their advice before meeting Johnson, which was just the way he liked it. McNamara himself looked for 'team players,' declaring that it was impossible for a government to operate effectively if departmental heads 'express disagreement with decisions' of the President. This was the idealized organization at its worst. Loyalty wasn't enough. Merely to 'express disagreement' was a threat" (42). The "family" discourse, the "harmonized" message, and the confusion between following and teamwork are all familiar from El Sistema, and there are striking parallels with my informant's aforementioned comment about Abreu demanding not just loyalty but also devotion. A culture of unanimity and the suppression of dissent foster efficiency of action but are damaging to an organization, cultivating inflexibility and leaving little space for productive alternatives. "The right decisions are more likely when they emerge from a clash of very different perspectives" (60), meaning that embracing criticism and even "internal dissidents" is very important. Contrary to received wisdom, "a strong team—a 'kind of family'—can quickly fall into the habit of reinforcing each other's prejudices" (62). The "stunningly unified vision" that so impressed Eric Booth when he visited El Sistema looks rather different in this light.

El Sistema's culture of devotion to its leader and its discouragement of dissent sometimes lead to an extreme level of identification with the institution. Senior figures used terms such as "indoctrination," "cult," and "brainwashing"; one claimed that musicians gave up their life to the program. A Sistema parent compared it to a drug: children are obsessed with it, he said, giving up all their free time to it and prepared to do anything to get ahead. He was happy that his children were involved in cultural activities but concerned by the cult-like absorption. Abreu's TED prize speech was intercut with the words of a student: "After all this time here, music is life. Nothing else. Music is life." Booth's

(2010, 9) urging to "become our own distributed version of Dr. Abreu" and "infuse Dr. Abreu into our own thinking" carries similarly eerie overtones (and its reversal of the idea of distributed cognition is highly revealing).

Several senior musicians, including founders, alluded to a bizarre atmosphere in the program. One claimed: "There's a lot of psychological play that goes on...you realize it as soon as you arrive in El Sistema, you realize that there's something strange going on, that you don't find with people who just go to work or play in their orchestra, but rather a very strange relationship... like this guy [Abreu] is the genius, we all owe him sacred obedience...crazy, strange things like that." An atmosphere of secrecy and mystery surrounds Abreu and his inner circle; as one former CONAC employee put it, the group has "something Masonic" about it. Several founders mentioned a black opal ring that Abreu supposedly wore. One reported that Abreu's closest allies in the National Youth Orchestra wore identical rings; another said that the stories around the ring bordered on magical realism, suggesting that those who touched it were believed to accrue special powers. A third was more dismissive: "His closest flatterers got to the point of asking him for a ring because they thought it was 'pretty.' Sometimes José Antonio himself gave them one, or they bought one themselves and then said Abreu had given it to them—all this was a way of demonstrating that they were close to the center of power and making the most of their supposed invulnerability."

Given that several informants compared El Sistema to a cult, it is noteworthy the extent to which the program exemplifies what Tourish and Vatcha (2005) term "corporate cultism." They argue that some corporations develop features that are characteristic of cults, including emphasis on charismatic leadership; excessive devotion to a person and/or idea; power concentrated in the hands of a leader who is the sole source of doctrine; a transcendent or totalistic ideology (often [quasi-]religious); promotion of a single "common culture" (in reality defined by leaders) and uniform values and behaviors; top-down, unidirectional communication; marked status differentials; demand for a high level of personal commitment from participants (often evidenced by intensive work schedules and the monopolization of individuals' time); promoting the organization as a surrogate family; manipulative or coercive techniques of persuasion and control; rewarding conformity, discouraging alternatives, and penalizing dissent; and strict control of information, ensuring opacity to participants and external observers alike.

El Sistema is a corporation in which such cultic dynamics are quite pronounced. Cults, notes Tourish (2011, 218), tend to be organized around "a 'totalistic' (i.e., all-embracing) vision of a new world order, way of being or form of organization. The group's leaders suggest that their vision constitutes an inspirational new paradigm, capable of transforming an otherwise impure reality." Again, we see Booth's "stunningly unified vision" from a different angle: "such organizations promote all-embracing cultures, decreed by the leader, and with which everyone is supposed to agree. Difference from the vision of the leader is banished to the margins of the group's tightly policed norms" (2011, 221).

"Total conformity along these lines leads to the disabling and well-documented phenomenon of groupthink," continues Tourish (2011, 221), illustrating how corporate cultism is accompanied by downsides and risks for participants and the organizations themselves, for all that it may also produce benefits. Excessive and unthinking deference to leaders can curb critical thinking and lead to dependence. Tourish and Vatcha (2005, 476) argue that overalignment with an organization and its leader can make individuals "liable to lose their original sense of identity, tolerate ethical lapses they would have previously deplored, find a new and possibly corrosive value system taking root, and leave themselves vulnerable to manipulation by the leaders of the organization." Tourish believes that charismatic, autocratic leaders are prone to regard criticism as a threat and react accordingly; the resulting discouragement of dissent limits the debate and corrective feedback that are essential to healthy institutional functioning. Like Harford, he suggests that embracing dissent and distributing power more widely are important steps to fostering sustainable organizations and creative participants. Citing Keith Grint, Tourish and Vatcha (2005, 459) argue that "the most successful leaders are liable to be those with the least compliant followers, 'for when leaders err—and they always do—the leader with compliant followers will fail.'"

Tourish and Vatcha hold up Enron, an archetypal cultic corporation, as a cautionary tale. It was a company with a powerful vision, grand plans, high ideals, and a committed workforce of "believers." It appeared rosy, even miraculous, to observers, and was lauded by many (including experts from the Harvard Business School), yet it ended in disaster. Enron reveals how presumed strengths (such as charismatic leadership and strong vision) may actually be weaknesses. Numerous parallels with El Sistema may be noted in Enron's compelling and totalistic vision; equation of vision with expansion; hyperbolic rhetoric and extraordinary goals; requirement of high levels of commitment; predominantly young employees who were prepared to work long hours and rarely questioned authority; great benefits for a chosen few; high levels of social control and correspondingly low levels of critical reflection; focus on drama and spectacle in order to convince participants and observers; and the abundance of hagiographic (but flawed) accounts of the organization. Enron employees understood that dissent would not be tolerated, and there were no spaces to discuss problems or concerns. Similarly, as Frei (2011) noted, "anyone who asks critical questions of El Sistema in Venezuela will make no friends. If you ask the creative director and founder Abreu to talk about problems in El Sistema, he looks irritated. 'Problems?' he asked with a questioning glance through thick glasses. 'We grow, grow, grow.'" At Enron, "a punitive culture was established, in which all that had been so painstakingly gained could be withdrawn at the whim of senior managers" (Tourish and Vatcha 2005, 470), recalling similar claims by former senior Sistema figures. El Sistema's parallels with cults and cultic corporations reveal much about its ideological foundations and organizational dynamics.

Tourish and Vatcha's work provides significant pointers for students of El Sistema. One concerns the potential gap between benign (even emancipatory) official rhetoric and more controlling or coercive realities. For example, Enron had a heavily promoted code of ethics, yet one that was disregarded in daily practice: "The code of ethics was thus a dramaturgical device, whose theatrical display cultivated the illusion of noble ideals and generated a convincing spectacle of ethical practice for both the organization's internal and external audiences" (Tourish and Vatcha 2005, 474). The importance of probing beneath official narratives is clear. Indeed, a lack of scrutiny and understanding, combined with an exaggerated belief in charismatic leadership, may allow corporate cultism to flourish. Another notable conclusion is that participants in a cultic organization may paradoxically experience their decrease in personal autonomy as the opposite—as personal freedom and self-fulfillment. This should be borne in mind when considering Sistema participants' self-reports. Finally, Tourish and Vatcha (2005, 476) conclude that "Enron 'traded' on the desire of many people to believe that ever increasing profits could be manufactured by means of accountancy conjuring tricks, by an organization that was also serving a greater good—a secular miracle." The word "miracle" is also used frequently with reference to El Sistema, underpinned by a desire to believe that old-fashioned excellence in orchestral performance (in other words, classical music's status quo) can go hand in hand with social change. The case of Enron suggests that apparent miracles should be treated with a modicum of caution and that widespread belief does not necessarily make them true.

Another organization that is often described as cult-like is Opus Dei. According to its critics, its cult-like aspects include a hierarchical structure in which few people have a clear picture of institutional functioning, expectations of obedience, control of dissent, a system of rewards and punishments, monopolization of members' time, cultivation of groupthink, rejection of critical reflection (especially about leaders or policies), and use of platitudinous catchphrases that curtail deeper analysis (Clasen 2003). Opus Dei has been portrayed as secretive and manipulative: James Martin (1995) writes of the difficulty of ascertaining its basic corporate practices, and quotes a former member who claims "Opus Dei plays by its own rules. If they don't want to have something out in the open, they won't make it accessible." It was once described as a "holy mafia" (Boston 2006). It is ultraconservative, in areas ranging from political alliances to attitudes to women (who rarely take leadership roles). Similar characterizations of El Sistema emerged through my research, and these parallels may be more than coincidental, given that Abreu has close links to Opus Dei and his project is thoroughly imbued with his religiosity.

CONCLUSION

El Sistema is increasingly being taken as a blueprint or inspiration for music education around the world, yet there are reasons to question the viability or desirability of its generalization. One is that El Sistema is Abreu writ large: it is shaped by his education and training, his personality and preferences. It is also very much a project of its time and place—the upper echelons of Caracas society in the 1970s. As such, it is a very particular project. Its functioning is highly dependent on Abreu; a Sistema without him might therefore have considerably less ideological or practical coherence. A model that revolves around a single, highly unusual individual, and is molded by his religious beliefs and corporate capitalist ideology, is not an obvious candidate for reproduction in a diverse array of countries and contexts. A second reason is that El Sistema functions in problematic ways, ones that would perhaps be best avoided rather than reproduced by arts education programs in other countries. El Sistema embodies the predilection for vertical, authoritarian management that Abreu's critics noted in his ministerial years, and its centralizing tendencies and infrastructure decisions maintain widely critiqued approaches of the past.

El Sistema has produced some impressive achievements, but the question remains: Could it have achieved much more had it adopted a more inclusive, forward-looking organizational philosophy, and had it not been defined so closely by Abreu's personality and preferences? What might El Sistema look like if it had embraced "internal dissidents" rather than only "team players" prepared to assume the role of "a kind of family"? If it had opened up its top levels to more than just Abreu's "unconditionals" and protégés, including instead a more diverse array of figures better prepared to propel it into the twenty-first century? Perhaps it would have softened or shed some of the features that it inherited from its founder and from elite Caracas society of the 1970s—corporatism, centralization, clientelism, a disciplined and hierarchical management style, and a focus on cultural importation and spectacle—and become more like the revolutionary social project of contemporary myth.

CHAPTER 4
Demographics and Development

Two of the most striking claims about El Sistema concern its number of participants and their socioeconomic background. This chapter raises questions about calculations of the program's size and, particularly, its alleged targeting of the most deprived sectors of Venezuelan society. The analysis then opens out to address the broader issue of music and development. I argue that El Sistema is an ambitious project of social engineering, underpinned by the ideology of modernist developmentalism, and should therefore be examined through the lens of critical studies of development, which have highlighted the drawbacks of large-scale, top-down, centralized schemes for social transformation.

NUMBERS

Behind the official figures lie inconsistencies and question marks. The FESNOJIV website stated in 2011 that there were 180 núcleos and 350,000 participants; Borzacchini's official history, however, published in the same year, claimed that there were 230 núcleos and 300,000 participants, while a press release gave the figure of 400,000. Variations of 50 music schools and 100,000 students are striking. Does anyone actually know how large the project is?

The answer appears to be no. One former senior Sistema figure asked: "Why is there no reliable census of how many participants El Sistema really has?" He argued that the program was able to make such grandiose claims because it took visitors to the same handful of large núcleos, but that most schools were smaller. Another former senior figure claimed that the true figure was probably nearer 100,000.

The website figures imply an average of almost 2,000 participants per núcleo. Some of the largest urban núcleos may have this many students—though according to Borzacchini (2010, 143), Montalbán, one of the most important, has only 1,200—but the small-town núcleos I visited contained closer to 200 students than 2,000. Even some state capitals, like Veracruz, appeared to have considerably fewer than 2,000 students. Most núcleos simply did not have the facilities for anything like this number.

Borzacchini (2010, 198) also quotes another set of figures: Caracas has 32,000 students and the five most "populous" states have an average of around 6,500. The median state would therefore have around 6,000 students at most. Taking 6,000 as the average figure for 23 states, and adding 32,000 for Caracas, produces a figure of 170,000—approximately half the official number. The contradictions within Borzacchini's own figures are noteworthy. While rough calculations and participants' skepticism do not substitute for a proper survey, they do raise doubts about claims for El Sistema's size. Uy (2012, 18) points to a motivation for exaggeration: the greater the numbers presented, the larger the budget allocation. El Sistema's impressive figures have concrete effects, and have played a key role in building its reputation internationally.

A crucial question is what these numbers actually mean. A teacher at Veracruz confided that the dropout rate was high, above all among beginners: the staff "shout at them and tell them 'you're no good, don't come back' and little by little they drift away." He claimed that at least 50 percent of students dropped out within a year of inscription, with only 10 to 20 percent remaining after three years. Many children tried out a range of activities—orchestra, football, swimming, ballet—and stuck with the one they enjoyed, dropping the rest. Children often preferred sports, he said, because they had to commit less time and were treated better. If a núcleo has a thousand students, does this mean that a thousand started the school year or a thousand finished it?

CLASS

One of Abreu's famous rhetorical conceits is that "the huge spiritual world that music produces in itself...ends up overcoming material poverty. From the minute a child is taught how to play an instrument, he is no longer poor." This much-quoted line does not stand up to scrutiny; history is littered with impoverished musicians. To suggest that learning to play the violin instantly banishes poverty is to deny that deprivation has any material reality or any structural causes. One might argue that music has spiritual effects or that scholarships reduce material poverty, but Abreu's esoteric claim about music's power to transcend socioeconomic realities begs numerous questions.

One concerns the very linkage of El Sistema with poverty. A key to the program's fame is its claim to focus on deprived children. FESNOJIV's mission statement refers to the "rescue of the most vulnerable groups in the country," while in his TED prize speech, Abreu claimed that "the large majority of our children belong...to the most vulnerable strata of the Venezuelan population."

Borzacchini (2011, 7) describes El Sistema as "saving our children from the horror of violence, drugs and material and spiritual poverty." Lennar Acosta, a former juvenile delinquent rescued by El Sistema, is often held up as representative of the program.

Overseas, Booth (2008, 1–2) claims that the project "teaches 300,000 of Venezuela's poorest children" and "turns around the lives of hundreds of thousands of at-risk kids." According to Deutsche Grammophon's publicity, 90 percent of El Sistema's students come from poor socioeconomic backgrounds, and this figure appears in a range of widely dispersed sources. Such accounts suggest that extreme poverty is the norm, but how accurate are they?

My research with musicians of all ages in different parts of Venezuela suggested that all kinds of children can be found in El Sistema, from reformed delinquents to the children of the rich; but the majority, at least in the provinces (where most live), are from the middle strata of society, and while some dwell in low-income households, only a few could be described as deeply deprived, at-risk, or Venezuela's poorest. The núcleo in Veracruz was located on a leafy central square, and those in the surrounding towns were not oases in the middle of desperation. One administrator told me cheerfully that his small town had few social problems, and that the main issue children faced was how to choose from the many after-school activities offered. In another, the children were running around with BlackBerries, "friending" visitors on Facebook. Certainly, there are some núcleos in poorer zones, especially in large cities, and some deeply deprived children in the program, but the key issue is whether the vast majority of El Sistema's participants could accurately be described as "the most vulnerable and excluded children and young people in Venezuela" who were "escap[ing] from a background of drug abuse and crime."[1]

In interviews, I consistently heard skepticism about such claims from El Sistema's own musicians and, in some cases, its senior figures. One former Sistema musician responded: "it's sad to think that's how they see us from overseas. Where are all of us—the great majority—who are or were there out of desire, passion, and love?" One musician who had spent fourteen years in El Sistema, traveling around the country, claimed he had never met anyone who fit the "deeply deprived" profile. A second questioned the idea that Sistema orchestras were made up of poor children from barrios, and expressed a strong distaste for the social project "propaganda." A third had toured Spain with a Sistema ensemble; the local press had reported that they were reformed delinquents, even though not one of the group was from a disadvantaged background. He criticized documentaries like *Tocar y Luchar* for focusing on a small minority of extreme cases and distorting public perceptions. The top Sistema musician I interviewed held up Dudamel—an ordinary middle-class boy—as representative of its social makeup.

None of my interviewees regarded themselves or their friends as having been saved from drugs or the street. Students in Veracruz described themselves and their entire musical-social circle as middle class; they talked about their scholarships as a bonus rather than a necessity. One reported that all his Sistema friends had stable lives and money to pay their monthly subscription, even to buy their own instrument. A Sistema parent in Santa Ana saw the program as fairly bourgeois; he remarked that poor children were the exception rather than the rule in the local núcleo, and alluded to financial and cultural barriers to their participation. Abreu's statement that "for the children that we work with, music is practically the only way to a dignified social destiny" was patently untrue in Veracruz and its satellite núcleos.[2]

There is a crucial question here over the definition of poverty. Fernandes (2010, 73–74) identifies a "downwardly mobile middle class" that she traces to the 1980s and 1990s, when its members increasingly turned to activities traditionally associated with the urban poor. Opposition supporters, however, blamed Chávez for a decline in the economic status of the middle class, resulting in an increasing number of people who might be considered culturally middle class but were struggling economically. Wherever responsibility lies, the category of "poor" is a very broad one in Venezuela and overlaps with the middle class. Indeed, according to the National Statistics Institute, nearly three-quarters of children lived in poor households in 2006 (Cuesta 2008, 1). Many "poor" children may therefore come from "downwardly mobile middle class" households that have reduced income and employment options, yet remain far from "the most vulnerable strata of the Venezuelan population."

Clearly, there is a world of difference between the 70th percentile and the 1st, so it is vital to know where (if anywhere) on this broad spectrum of poverty the average Sistema child lies. A child in the 70th percentile may be officially "poor," yet is unlikely to be "deeply deprived" and is certainly not one of "Venezuela's poorest." Much of the rhetoric around El Sistema results from a slippage that labels nearly three-quarters of Venezuela's children, many from stable working- and lower-middle-class homes, as highly vulnerable or at-risk.

TARGETING

Another closely related question is whether El Sistema is a program aimed at poor and at-risk children, or whether it is a program aimed at all children, including the poor and at-risk. This is not a quibble over semantics but a crucial issue. El Sistema works in some poor barrios, but it cannot be concluded from this fact alone that it targets the most deprived children in those neighborhoods or helps young people escape from drugs, prostitution, and crime. The poor and at-risk are clearly the heart of the project's rhetoric and the justification for its lavish funding, but is the program targeted at them, or is their inclusion more contingent?

The IDB, in its Phase I loan decision, declared ("Program to Support" 1997): "Although the proposed operation is intended to consolidate a program targeted to low-income children and youths, *it does not qualify as poverty-targeted* in the terms of paragraph 2.15 of the Eighth Replenishment document" (emphasis added). The relevant paragraph gives two possible criteria for identifying investment as poverty-targeted ("Report" 1994, 19): "first, the project or program is geographically targeted to poor beneficiaries or, second, it is determined that a significant majority of the beneficiaries of a project or program, according to conditions prevailing in each country, are poor." El Sistema met neither criterion. Its international funder thus concurred with the anecdotal evidence from my informants. It appears that Lennar Acosta, however inspiring his story, is not representative of the program after all.

This IDB statement also contradicts the description of the program as having a "pro-poor profile" in Cuesta's (2008) report—produced, ironically, for the IDB. However, Cuesta's conclusions are perplexing: he states that "approximately 67% [of Sistema participants] reportedly come from the country's two poorest social strata," yet footnote 1 says: "An estimated 74% of children ages 0 to 9 and 71% of children ages 10 to 15 live in poor households" (2008, 1). If the definition of "poor" is consistent, how could 67-percent participation by poor children be considered a "pro-poor profile" if more than 70 percent of Venezuelan children are poor?

There are further problems with this report. Cuesta notes that the supposed pro-poor profile "is achieved despite the System is [*sic*] a universal program that does not include explicit mechanisms for targeting of its beneficiaries." Except in a handful of núcleos, El Sistema does not actively recruit children from more deprived backgrounds. As Rafael Elster, the director of Sarría núcleo, put it bluntly in the film *La Tierra de las Mil Orquestas*: "We haven't gone looking for anyone anywhere." How, then, would El Sistema achieve a pro-poor profile?

The question of geography is thus crucial, since the location of núcleos affects their intake, yet the IDB stated in 1998 that El Sistema was not "geographically targeted to poor beneficiaries." In Caracas, many of the núcleos are located in poorer parts of the city, and they undoubtedly cater to *some* very disadvantaged children, but Caracas only accounts for 10 to 20 percent of El Sistema's children (depending on which official figures are used). Outside the capital, children from deprived backgrounds have been the exception rather than the rule for most of El Sistema's history, claimed a former núcleo director, because núcleos are not generally located in deprived neighborhoods.

There are many reasons, therefore, to regard a high proportion of Sistema children as coming from the middle rather than lowest strata of society, and from relatively stable rather than deeply vulnerable family contexts. As one former Sistema musician stated: "Most of the kids in El Sistema, even the poor ones, are there because their parents take them there. El Sistema isn't rescuing them. Do you think they'd be there every day if their parents neglected them?" Indeed, almost all my interviewees said their parents gave them their full support, and several argued that parental investment was important. In the provinces, where núcleos are often far away from the poorest barrios, just getting children to classes usually requires a certain degree of parental involvement. One might wonder how many children would progress far if their parents did not want to drop them off or collect them, would not sign for their instrument, or did not want them practicing at home. There was no mechanism to ensure that the most disadvantaged children arrived at the núcleo in the first place, or to combat the heightened risk that they would drop out again, raising the questions about El Sistema's effectiveness in reaching and sustaining the involvement of the most vulnerable children.

Strikingly, the Veracruz núcleo operated entrance auditions, and rejected not just the least musically talented children, but also, according to one teacher, those who showed signs of poor attention or behavior—quite possibly symptoms of social disadvantage. The núcleo was thus weeding out some of those whom it was explicitly designed to serve. This teacher also claimed that children from the most deprived families would struggle to complete the process of joining the program, which involved pre-inscription and then inscription, requiring a parent or guardian to bring in papers and wait in long queues. El Sistema does not go out into the barrios looking for the poorest children, she said, but just deals with whoever turns up at the núcleo—and the chances of a deprived child managing inscription and regular attendance without parental or adult support were slim. For her, children's regular attendance pointed away from extremes of deprivation and vulnerability.

There are a few núcleos that focus specifically on at-risk children, but these are the exception rather than the norm. Even there, matters may not be as clear-cut as they seem. Borzacchini (2010, 134) interviewed a seventeen-year-old tuba player at Los Chorros, one of these núcleos: "I arrived here via a special program for street children called 'Forging the Future.' Since I was already fifteen, they didn't accept me here, so a teacher who gave classes here told me that I could get in via this special program for street children; although I wasn't one, it was the only way."

Patricia, who had studied and taught in Sistema núcleos in Caracas, exclaimed: "the business about street children—these aren't street children! If only street children could have access to all that luxury that the Bolívar [SBYO] has! If only they gave 3,000 of the 11,000 [Bolívares] that they earn to an institution that takes care of street children! But it's not that way." She described El Sistema as mainly middle- and lower-middle-class. She knew musicians who lived without luxuries, but they had the essentials, came from stable homes, and did not live in particularly bad neighborhoods.

My findings are closely echoed by Wald's (2011) study of Sistema-inspired orchestras in Buenos Aires, where several parents explained that not any child from their neighborhood could sustain involvement in the orchestra, since it required parental involvement in dropping off and collecting children from rehearsals. Furthermore, participants insisted that their values and behavior were conditioned largely by their families, not their music education, and that if they were not in the orchestra, they would be playing football or studying at home rather than up to mischief in the street. Their "social inclusion" was thus prior to joining the orchestra rather than a consequence. In Venezuela, too, key informants ascribed their achievements to a disciplined and supportive family background rather than any transformative effect of El Sistema.

A final question concerns the relationship between socioeconomic status and achievement. A founder claimed that few children from the poorer núcleos of Caracas made it to the national orchestras. Similarly, a current member of the SBYO stated that there were few players in the orchestra from poor backgrounds; poverty was something she saw more in the lower-level núcleos— implying that poorer children faced more barriers to progress. A detailed statistical study would be invaluable in determining whether middle-class youths are more likely to reach the higher levels of the program, and thus whether El Sistema ensures equality of opportunity all the way through or simply at the start.

A qualitative study has obvious limitations, so my research raises questions rather than providing answers; but it is significant that many Sistema interviewees were skeptical about the claims surrounding their program's social composition and its supposed rescuing of the deprived. Figures circulating internationally suggest that nine in ten participants come from deep deprivation, yet my informants claimed not to have met more than isolated examples. A teacher in a Caracas núcleo estimated that one in ten was closer to the truth. Even if these musicians are wrong, their skepticism is worthy of further examination; *something* makes them disbelieve El Sistema's official line and view the program as predominantly middle class. Above all, the multiple, contradictory narratives point to the urgent need for a rigorous demographic study.

MUSIC, DEVELOPMENT, AND DEVELOPMENTALISM

One of the most striking features of El Sistema has been its conversion from an orchestral training program into a social development project, one that received over $500 million in loans from international development banks in the five years since 2008. Yet it is not set up to target consistently the poorest sectors of society and there are question marks over the extent that it does so. What kind of development project is it, then? It is, I would argue, a broad, ambitious project of social engineering, one that is expanding rapidly and aimed ultimately at the whole of Venezuelan society and beyond. If it is to be considered and funded as a social program first and foremost, then it should be taken seriously *qua* development project and judged by the relevant standards, which means engaging with scholarship in development studies and its critiques of such large-scale, top-down, centralized schemes for social transformation.

To understand Abreu and his project, we should note that, along with Pedro Tinoco, he formed part of a political group called The Developmentalists at the UCAB in the early 1960s.[3] A decade later, he was still closely involved with Tinoco and the Developmentalist Movement, now formally constituted as a political party. Although the party itself never flourished, developmentalism was a major feature of Venezuelan politics and society in the mid-twentieth century. Coronil (1997, 4) describes the "magical" Venezuelan state as casting its spell via "dazzling development projects that engender collective fantasies of progress." Under Pérez Jiménez, in particular, "Venezuela was literally bulldozing its past" (Hellinger 1991, 79), as a drive for modernization underpinned by oil wealth saw radical transformation of urban environments. Pérez Jiménez's goal was the "moral, intellectual, and material improvement of the inhabitants of the country and the rational transformation of the physical environment" (quoted in Mayhall 2005, 126). Tinoco and Abreu's political movement not only courted the dictator's supporters after his fall from power but also inherited his developmentalist ideology.

Modernist developmentalism, exemplified by new cities of the 1950s like Brasília and Chandigarh, as well as Pérez Jiménez's simultaneous attempt to transform Caracas into an international tourist center and conference site, was characterized by centralized planning and the urge for social transformation from above. It was underpinned by a belief that creating the right macrostructure was the route to social improvement, and that the central planner knew best; the role of the ordinary citizen was to slot into the structure and be improved, rather than to participate in (much less critique) the planning process. What already existed on the ground was paid little attention (or even razed). What replaced it were projects that "had in common the quality of spectacular display" (Coronil 1997, 178).

Abreu was a card-carrying developmentalist and his great project displays many of the hallmarks of modernist developmentalism: the imposition by a member of the social elite of a huge Eurocentric project, marginalizing local traditions; the desire to transform individuals by placing them in a centralized, disciplinary macrostructure; strict, top-down control of the project; the exclusion of alternative visions and critical participation in shaping the program; and a predilection for dazzling spectacle.

El Sistema's focus on European culture—the National Youth Orchestra's first concert consisted of Bach, Handel, Mozart, and Vivaldi—was characteristic of the mid-twentieth century, when "[t]he pursuit of modernity in Venezuela [was] cast by official discourse as the nation's quest to resemble metropolitan centers" and cultural importation became increasingly the norm

(1997, 367; Hellinger 1991, 77–79). The leaders of the Venezuelan transformation of this period embraced both North Atlantic developmentalism and its accompaniments, deciding "to import an entire way of life—politics, consumer habits, architectural conventions, economic and social organizations" (Lombardi 1982, 248). El Sistema was born during a developmentalist peak, fueled by oil wealth, when "the symbols of civilized life—metropolitan history, commodities, institutions, steel mills, freeways, constitutions—were transformed into potent tokens that could be purchased or copied" (Coronil 1997, 229–30). Classical music was one such symbol, and its choice as the cornerstone of Abreu's project reproduces a dominant ideology of the time and, particularly, of Abreu's social and political milieu—one that saw icons of progress and modernity as located outside Latin America.

A powerful critique of modernist developmentalism can be found in James C. Scott's *Seeing Like a State* (1998), a book worth examining in detail given the centrality of this ideology to El Sistema. Scott prefers the term "high modernism," which he defines as "the aspiration to the administrative ordering of nature and society" (1998, 88). He explores how and why so many grand twentieth-century schemes to improve the human condition, particularly in the developing world, went wrong. High modernists were often "the avant-garde among engineers, planners, technocrats, high-level administrators, architects, scientists, and visionaries" (88), who sought a more rational design of social order, and they were usually utopians: they believed that their social engineering would transform society for the better. The problem was not intentions, then, but unintended outcomes, since many grand schemes proceeded in the name of progress, emancipation, and reform, yet ended in failure.

Abreu fits precisely Scott's high-modernist profile. He came of age in the mid-twentieth century, the high point of high modernism. As a member of The Developmentalists, his ideological leanings were already clear in his early twenties, and his PhD in petroleum economics sealed his technocratic training. He spent five years in parliament in the 1960s, working as an economist for the central budgeting office. As Borzacchini (2010, 58) notes, he emerged with "all the necessary tools to construct a great institution." By the time he launched El Sistema, Abreu literally "saw like a state."

There are also echoes of Abreu's famous political malleability in Scott's (1998, 5) assertion that high-modernist faith "was no respecter of traditional political boundaries; it could be found across the political spectrum from left to right." Scott argues that high modernism "is the ideology par excellence of the bureaucratic intelligentsia, technicians, planners, and engineers. The position accorded to them is not just one of rule and privilege but also one of responsibility for the great works of nation building and social transformation" (96). High modernists tend to revel in their self-assigned role as educator of the people (or shepherd to their flock). They also incline toward authoritarianism and a "tendency to disallow other competing sources of judgment" (93). Those who do not agree need to be educated or swept aside. High modernism exalts the planner, since "the order in question is most evident, not at street level, but rather from above and from outside" (57)—from "a God's-eye view, or the view of an absolute ruler" (or that of a conductor on the podium).

Scott's critique of high modernism focuses on its problematic, at times disastrous, outcomes and seeks explanations in its schematic approach, which ignores local complexity, distinctiveness, and forms of knowledge. He underlines the double-edged nature of utopianism: "Utopian aspirations per se are not dangerous.... Where the utopian vision goes wrong is when it is held by ruling elites with no commitment to democracy" (89). Not only may noble aims for social improvement be present, they may even be partially fulfilled in high-modernist projects—all have had *some* beneficial effects, in some cases quite dramatic ones—but Scott emphasizes the need to analyze longer-term or partially hidden costs. The effect of rationalized, simplified designs and the pursuit of massification, uniformity, and standardization is to undermine diversity and thereby weaken social and ecological systems over time. Thinking big can be impressive, particularly in the short term, but not necessarily beneficial to those on the receiving end.

Taking the case of scientific forestry in the eighteenth century, Scott shows how rationalization was at first a great success. It took about a century for the negative consequences to appear, but eventually the dangers of dismembering a complex ecology and isolating a single element of instrumental value became clear. Radical, utilitarian simplification was an effective way of maximizing production in the short term, but its drawbacks came back to haunt it, as monoculture unbalanced the forest ecology. The importance of diversity and complexity only became clear long after they had been removed.

As with scientific forestry, so with high-modernist agriculture. The narrowing of attention to a single outcome dramatically increased yields but led to pernicious long-term outcomes, problematic third-party effects, and greater vulnerability to crises. Short-term goals were prioritized over the health and quality of the ecological system, and despite lavish funding, many projects eventually failed, as excessive confidence led to shortsightedness and blind spots. If we think about El Sistema as a program of musical simplification and intensification, in its concentration on orchestral practice, and if we consider culture as an ecological system (see Chapter 12), then we may find important lessons in these apparently distant case studies.

A point of particular interest is the regular invocation of musical metaphors. Scott attributes the birth of high modernism to Walther Rathenau, the architect of German mobilization during World War I. Rathenau characterized the modern era as "a consolidation of the world into an unconscious association of constraint, into an uninterrupted community of production and harmony" (100), and Lenin became an enthusiastic advocate of German systematic management, extolling "the principle of discipline, organization, and harmonious cooperation based upon the most modern, mechanized industry, the most rigid system of accountability and control" (100). The linkage of harmony to high-modernist social engineering, constraint, and control is an important point to bear in mind when considering El Sistema's flights of rhetoric about "a well-tuned Venezuela" or "a harmonious society."

A discourse of order and harmony was employed by the urban planner Le Corbusier as he dreamt of new cities, yet Scott underlines how this discourse was allied to authoritarianism, one-size-fits-all plans, ignoring local difference, a production-line mentality, and an ideology of centralization, hierarchization, and control. Le Corbusier may have been a utopian, but he conceived of pleasure in terms of fitting others into a rational plan, not their freedom and autonomy. The opinions of urban residents were of little concern to him. In Le Corbusier's vision, just as a single brain (that of the city planner) directs activity, the city is the "brain" of society, dominating and colonizing the provinces: "the lines of influence and command are exclusively from the center to the periphery" (112). Le Corbusier's thinking finds many echoes in the orchestra, where the single brain of the conductor directs musical activity, and in El Sistema, where commands fan out from the center but talent flows toward it. In Le Corbusier's world, "[o]ne's status can be directly read from one's distance from the center" (115)—as in the microcosm of the orchestra or the macrocosm of El Sistema. High modernism prefers starting from a tabula rasa rather than working on an existing model; in Venezuela, Abreu largely rejected existing music education establishments and ignored most musical traditions once his project was underway. It also tends toward universalism; Le Corbusier's motto was "city planning everywhere" (117), and Abreu's could easily be "orchestras everywhere."

Jane Jacobs's book *The Death and Life of Great American Cities* provides a riposte both to high-modernist urban planning and to the blurring of aesthetic and social harmony. For Jacobs, harmony is the vision of the urban planner; places where people would want actually to live would be much more discordant. Planners were distracted by an aesthetic view of order, failing to appreciate that "[m]ost complex systems...do not display a surface regularity; their order must be sought at a deeper level" (133). Jacobs argued that "modern city planning has been burdened from its beginnings with the unsuitable aim of converting cities into disciplined works of art." However, she states firmly: "*A city cannot be a work of art*" (quoted in Scott 1998, 134, 139). Jacobs's work is an important rejoinder to El Sistema's propensity to read across from aesthetic to social realms and imagine the orchestration of Venezuela into a "harmonious society," confusing visual and aural harmony with an enriching social environment. It highlights the risks of trying to convert social complexity into ordered, aesthetically pleasing structures.

Scott develops further this critique of the visuality of rationalization, or the "optics of power." He considers the high-modernist idea of a national plan, which would be devised at the capital and would then reorder the periphery after its own image into quasi-military units obeying a single command.... The image of coordination and authority aspired to here recalls that of mass exercises—thousands of bodies moving in perfect unison according to a meticulously rehearsed script. When such coordination is achieved, the spectacle may have several effects. The demonstration of mass coordination, its designers hope, will awe spectators and participants with its display of powerful cohesion. The awe is enhanced by the fact that, as in the Taylorist factory, only someone outside and above the display can fully appreciate it as a totality; the individual participants at ground level are small molecules within an organism whose brain is elsewhere. The image of a nation that might operate along these lines is enormously flattering to elites at the apex—and, of course, demeaning to a population whose role they thus reduce to that of ciphers. Beyond impressing observers, such displays may, in the short run at least, constitute a reassuring self-hypnosis which serves to reinforce the moral purpose and self-confidence of the elites. (254)

This analysis is hugely important for a consideration of El Sistema. It reveals the shared ideological underpinnings of a centralized national plan and carefully choreographed displays. The spectacle of massed bodies "moving in perfect unison according to a meticulously rehearsed script" cannot fail to evoke El Sistema's huge orchestral showcase performances. Scott's invocation of "an organism whose brain is elsewhere" and his suggestion that the prime locus of impact and benefit lies *outside* this organism—in impressing observers and strengthening elites—is highly significant and finds numerous parallels in Venezuela, for example in the reports of young musicians who see themselves as cogs in a machine as Abreu's list of prizes grows ever longer. Impressive displays of order and harmony have problematic subtexts, and the fact that these subtexts tend to be obscured by the overawing impact of the spectacle—in Venezuela, by the emotional contagion of watching children play moving music—makes clear-eyed analysis all the more important.

Scott makes the provocative claim that such grandiose projects may in fact produce the opposite of their intended effects, and actually create the kinds of problems they claim to be solving: "high-modernist designs for life and production tend to diminish the skills, agility, initiative, and morale of their intended beneficiaries.... Complex, diverse, animated environments contribute, as Jacobs saw, to producing a resilient, flexible, adept population that has more experience in confronting novel challenges and taking initiative. Narrow, planned environments, by contrast, foster a less skilled, less innovative, less resourceful population" (349). For Scott, then, "the logic of social engineering on this scale was to produce the sort of subjects that its plans had assumed at the outset" (349). These conclusions, which imply that high-modernist projects may create more social problems than they solve, need to be tested by future assessments of El Sistema.

Given that such projects "may impoverish the local wellsprings of economic, social, and cultural self-expression" (349), Scott makes the case for small institutions that are "multifunctional, plastic, diverse, and adaptable" (353). In the natural world, diversity and complexity may not be as productive in the short run as monoculture, but they are more stable, more self-sufficient, and less vulnerable. The same is true with human institutions, argues Scott: large, rigid, single-purpose institutions founded on repetition and routine may be efficient, but they are weak in other ways. Small, adaptable organizations are better suited to postindustrial societies and provide a superior training ground for democratic citizenship. Meanwhile, El Sistema plans to expand its one-size-fits-all model to one million participants.

At the heart of Scott's study lies a critique of rationalization, so it is well worth noting that Max Weber saw the orchestra as exemplifying the rationalization of society (Sica 2004, 112). Accordingly, El Sistema's project to orchestrate musical life and wider society may be understood as eminently susceptible to Scott's critique. There are many aspects of El Sistema that tie it clearly to high-modernist ideology: Abreu's personal history, his desire to orchestrate society, utopian dreams of order and harmony, authoritarianism, standardization, minimization of local difference, narrow focus, and emphasis on quick results. El Sistema might be seen as attempting to do in the cultural realm what had previously been done in the spheres of urban, industrial, and agricultural planning, pursuing the rationalization that was central to the developmentalism that Abreu espoused. The shortcomings and risks of this approach are laid bare in Scott's study, which has parallels with Harford's critique of centralized, top-down organizations in Chapter 3. Scott's analysis has two main thrusts: first, high modernism is politically questionable (authoritarian, antidemocratic); second, impressive short-term results often give way to long-term damage. The first has been applicable to El Sistema since it began; time will tell more about the relevance of the second, to be discussed further in later chapters.

POST-DEVELOPMENT

Scott's study is part of a broader field of critical approaches to development that has emerged since the 1990s, sometimes referred to as "post-development." Scott builds on the work of Ferguson (1994), a seminal figure who warned about the dangers of applying blueprints for development in widely varying contexts without consideration of local specificity. Ferguson claimed that development projects routinely fail to meet their stated objectives, but succeed in achieving something else—the expansion of bureaucratic power. Drawing on this analysis, it might be argued that by presenting Western classical music as a solution to poverty in Venezuela, El Sistema both depoliticizes poverty, by suggesting that it has cultural causes rather than stemming from the policies pursued by previous governments (including that in which Abreu served), and constructs an arbitrary cultural hierarchy, since it implies (on the basis of no evidence) that other musical traditions do not possess the same uplifting power.

Ferguson claims that development institutions generate their own forms of knowledge as part of their justification for intervention. In its mission statement, FESNOJIV declares its vision as "rescuing children and young people from an empty, disorientated, and deviant youth." El Sistema rests on its salvation narrative, which depends in turn on the definition of young people as "empty, disorientated and deviant" and hence in need of saving. There are clear echoes of Foucault's (1991, 251) argument that the category of delinquent was produced by the penitentiary system to rationalize its project to reform individuals. As discussed in later chapters, justifying intervention by El Sistema also requires generating ideas about Venezuelan barrios and popular music as culturally deficient and thus urgently in need of a transfusion of "art." Categorizing every child as a potential delinquent and every poor neighborhood as a cultural desert strengthens El Sistema's hand.

The salvation narrative has the effect of disempowering those being saved and empowering those doing the saving. Freire (1974, 15–16), for example, critiques "assistencialism" as a passifying model of development, stating: "Pedagogy which begins with the egoistic interests of the oppressors (an egoism cloaked in the false generosity of paternalism) and makes of the oppressed the objects of its humanitarianism, itself maintains and embodies oppression" (2005, 54). As Karpman's (1968) "drama triangle" psychological model suggests, the language of rescue implies a persecutor, a victim, and a rescuer (in our case, Venezuelan society, the child, and El Sistema/Abreu, respectively). This dynamic, argues Karpman, sets up a relationship of dependency between victim and rescuer, and the rescuer in fact benefits more (in the form of enhanced status and self-esteem). There are clear echoes in Scott's analysis of developmentalist programs as flattering to elites, demeaning to the ordinary population, and creating the kinds of problems they claim to be solving.

Escobar's (1995) work, too, may be read as a critique of top-down development projects—he strongly disapproved of the way that development projects tended to impose norms and dictate behavior—but it also promotes alternatives. Escobar supported local agency based on local traditions and valorized grassroots initiatives such as Latin American new social movements. Relevant examples might include the Venezuelan hip hop projects EPATU and Tiuna el Fuerte, contrasted with El Sistema at various points in these pages, which demonstrate a respect for local traditions that is neither conservative nor curatorial but rather fully engaged with globalization. One of Escobar's central concerns is that development intervention becomes a mechanism through which the West reasserts its supposed moral and cultural superiority over the developing world and thus constitutes a form of cultural imperialism—an issue that is clearly relevant to El Sistema, even if it is led by a Venezuelan, given its manifest Eurocentrism.

The contrast between El Sistema and the Latin American new social movements that Escobar promotes is striking, but unsurprising if we think that these new movements grew up precisely as a rejection of older ideologies epitomized by the Venezuelan program. El Sistema, like Venezuelan politics of the twentieth century, is strongly verticalist, whereas a central pillar of the new social movements is horizontalism, a repudiation of the hierarchical structures and top-down organizational models characteristic of earlier social and political movements (Hammond 2012). El Sistema is a blueprint that is applied across Venezuela and, with minor adjustments, internationally; the new social movements are more localist and tend to focus on concrete problems in particular places. Abreu's program relies on close ties with the government and lavish state subsidy; the new movements prefer self-management and autonomy, and often minimize their involvement with the state. El Sistema emerges clearly from this comparison as an "old social movement" based on an ideology that has been widely rejected by progressive activists and thinkers across Latin America.

CONCLUSION

This chapter has raised questions about El Sistema's effectiveness as a social development program and about the development ideology that underpins it. El Sistema constitutes a cultural and educational continuation of mid-twentieth-century modernization theories that posited the Global North as the standard to which the South should aspire (Carballo 2014). It pays almost no attention to the Latin American development alternatives that emerged from social movements associated with Liberation Theology and Radical Pedagogy in the late 1960s and 1970s, despite its creation at this very time. It also shows little trace of the later alternatives to development proposed by Latin American post-development theorists like Escobar, and it is highly susceptible to their critiques. In sum, it adheres to an old development paradigm that has been widely questioned in Latin America over the last half-century.

Elsewhere, too, criticism of large, centralized, top-down development institutions and projects has been building for some time. Modernist developmentalism has been characterized as paternalistic, authoritarian, exclusive, and, in its elision of local perspectives and local distinctiveness, founded on a presumption of Western cultural superiority and of the West as the only locus of modernity (e.g., Sundaram 2005). Universalist approaches to development have been accused of failing to respect cultural rights and diversity (e.g., Gould and Marsh 2004). Arts-based development projects are sometimes seen as offering a counternarrative to increasingly discredited mainstream development practices; El Sistema, however, fits squarely with conventional developmentalist ideology and is swimming against the tide of progressive thinking.

Critiques of El Sistema are sometimes articulated in similar terms in Venezuela. A senior music educator pinpointed El Sistema precisely as an example of developmentalist thinking, criticizing its tendency to measure success through the quantity of orchestras and its attempt to change the musical taste of the country from above. Another interviewee wrote: "cultural plurality is being swallowed by the culture of the symphony orchestra...does our paradigm have to continue to be that of development, of achieving the standards of a developed country, of competing with the cultural, economic, and consumerist standards that the capitalist system upholds? If we blindly follow that paradigm we're screwed."

PART TWO

Music Education

CHAPTER 5

The Orchestra in Theory and Practice

At the heart of El Sistema lies the orchestra. Among its most enduring images are the energetic, colorful displays of the SBYO and the vast National Children's Orchestra under the baton of Sir Simon Rattle. The orchestra is also the core of the project's social dimension. The FESNOJIV website is subtitled "the orchestra as a means of social organization," and El Sistema is based on the idea of the orchestra as "a model and school of social life" and a miniature "harmonious society." "My education was sitting in an orchestra," claims Dudamel. "And what a beautiful model for a society. Everyone together, listening to each other, with one goal. This is the best way I can think of to build a better world" (Higgins 2011). The orchestra is "a model for an ideal global society," he states in a *Newsweek* article (Lee 2012). The SBYO's concertmaster, Alejandro Carreño, concurred, telling Tunstall (2012, 127): "the way you behave in an orchestra is the perfect way to behave in society."

Those who make such utopian pronouncements are usually either conductors or principals, and it is no wonder they are so enthusiastic about a social microcosm that invests them with great authority and material rewards. But what is the view from the ranks? I put Dudamel's words to an experienced Veracruz musician; she replied: "Yes, it's a model ... of absolute tyranny: a society where someone will always be telling you what to do, depending on what *they* need and what *they* think, where you'll never be able to rise up. Yes, it'll be organized, of course, because you have someone with *lots* of power who tells you exactly what to do, and you keep your mouth shut, end of story."

Films and articles on El Sistema present the orchestra in a glowing light. Govias (2011, 22) enthuses about "the collaborative, interdependent environment of the ensemble. As members of an orchestra or chorus, students must learn and contribute simultaneously; they receive immediate, practical support from their peers while confronting challenges as a team, and must build and model the cooperative attributes of a healthy symbiotic community in order to achieve success." The FESNOJIV website waxes idealistically about "harmonious

The Teresa Carreño Youth Orchestra performing at the Sala Simón Bolívar, Centro de Acción Social por la Música. Photo by Geoffrey Baker.

interdependence," "the formation of a spirit of solidarity and fraternalism," and "the cultivation of ethical and aesthetic values." Yet the basis for these oft-repeated sound bites is unclear and rarely examined. There are innumerable studies of the benefits of music education in general, but very few consider the specific example of the youth orchestra. Professional orchestras, however, have been more widely researched, and this literature may be very relevant to El Sistema, since its higher-level ensembles are salaried and require almost daily attendance. Significantly, there is a marked—if largely unexplored—tension between El Sistema's hugely positive rhetoric and the negativity of these studies.

This chapter outlines some general lessons that can be learned from the orchestral literature, before moving on to a comparative examination of Venezuelan professional orchestras. The gaps between rhetoric and reality that emerge are analyzed by considering the orchestra as a metaphor as well as a musical ensemble. The symphony orchestra is then examined critically as a pedagogical tool and motor of social action, and is held up against alternative ensemble-based musical practices.

STUDIES OF ORCHESTRAS

"As a vocation, orchestral playing cannot satisfy the craving for freedom and self-expression latent in the musicians' heart," wrote Bernard Shore in 1938 (quoted in Love 2006, 60). Couch (1983, 118) paints a bleak picture of the profession in the United States more recently: "The powerlessness of American orchestra musicians within their work environment combines with physical and mental stress factors inherent in playing long seasons in professional orchestras and helps provide an explanation for the very high rate of physical and psychological problems found among professional orchestra players." The United Kingdom seems little different. Cottrell's (2004) study of orchestral musicians in London reveals an ambivalent, dissatisfied group suffering from economic insecurity, overwork, frustration, and a sense of having lost their individuality. He concludes by quoting an orchestral musician (2004, 199): "I'm often asked if I would like my children to become musicians, and the answer is a categorical no."

Faulkner's (1973) study of orchestral musicians portrays a stratified, competitive world marred by frustration and entrapment. Channing (2003, 181) acknowledges that during the twentieth century the authoritarian structure of orchestras was "a recipe for wonderful music-making, but surely it took its toll on the psyche of the musician whose subservience was only compounded by the narrow work pattern." Martin (1995, 214) seems justified in concluding that orchestras "are far from the cohesive, responsive social groups which figure in the mythology of the 'classical' music literature."

A similar picture emerges from Tindall's insider's account of North American orchestras: "a full-time symphonic job evolves into monotony for many players. Orchestra musicians saw away like factory workers, repeating the same pieces year after year. Once a player is employed by a desirable orchestra, career advancement is severely limited. Perfectionism and injuries wear musicians down. Nighttime and holiday work disconnect them from mainstream life. Players complain they forfeit autonomy to an omnipotent conductor who works a third of their schedule, is paid as much as twenty musicians, and gets credit for the music they make" (2005, 215). Tindall's colorful story veers from the pervasive stress and boredom to the prevalence of sexual promiscuity, heavy drinking, and drug use among orchestral musicians, particularly in New York in the 1980s. While she occasionally implies a causal link between orchestral life and these behaviors, another explanation is that they were commonplace among middle-class New Yorkers at the time—in other words, that orchestras simply reproduced the characteristics of their surrounding society. What is entirely absent in both academics' and musicians' accounts is the notion of the orchestra as an embodiment of social harmony and a defense against social ills, which seems to rest on a high degree of idealization.

Many problems stem from placing total authority in the hands of a single, unelected individual—the conductor. The musician and management guru Harvey Seifter (2001) points out: "In most orchestras, the conductor directly supervises each musician; the conductor not only decides what music will be played but how it will be played as well. There is little room for the opinions or suggestions of the musicians themselves; such input is rarely solicited and even less often welcomed. Like workers reporting to an autocratic manager, orchestral musicians are expected to unquestioningly follow the direction of the conductor—anything less invites humiliation before one's colleagues and may be grounds for immediate dismissal." The conductor Benjamin Zander (2000, 68) describes his profession as "one of the last bastions of totalitarianism in the civilized world." He takes the conductor as an emblem of old-fashioned, patriarchal, autocratic social organization, and admits that "vanity and tyranny are prevalent in the music world even in these enlightened times" (2008.).

Zander likes to quote a study that showed that orchestral musicians came below prison guards in terms of job satisfaction (see Allmendinger, Hackman, and Lehman 1996, 201–2). Interestingly, chamber musicians came top in the survey. As Cottrell (2004, 85) notes: "Orchestral musicians often enjoy playing chamber music because it gives them more opportunity for self-expression, something which they may feel is denied to them in their orchestral job." Even among those with sympathetic views of classical music, then, the orchestra is often viewed askance; many musicians prefer to play in smaller, unconducted ensembles, where they have more freedom and responsibility.

Seifter (2001) makes a crucial distinction between production and reception: "Clearly, although the results of an orchestral performance can be exceptionally uplifting, the means of attaining these results are often anything but uplifting to those whose job it is to achieve them." This raises a glaring problem for a project that promotes playing in an orchestra as a positive educational experience. Conventional symphony orchestras put the show above the needs of those who produce it, who traditionally dress in the style of nineteenth-century servants. An orchestra is an obvious tool for a politics of spectacle that serves its patron and impresses its audience, but the benefit to its players is more questionable.

A particularly damning assessment can be found in Levine and Levine's (1996) study of stress and discontent in the orchestral workplace. They affirm: "Orchestras are fundamentally patriarchal. Underlying the behavior of conductors and musicians in the orchestra is the myth of the conductor as omniscient father ('maestro,' 'maître') and the musicians as children ('players') who know nothing and require uninterrupted teaching and supervision" (18). This myth allows orchestras to operate efficiently, but it blocks communication from musician to conductor, and "musicians pay a very high price in the form of chronic stress, job dissatisfaction, and infantilization" (19). Musicians have little control over the work environment, and research shows that lack of control is a major cause of stress; and stress, in turn, can lead to learned helplessness, depression, and reduction in cognitive skills. This is a particularly important conclusion, considering that music education is often associated with (and justified by) increases in cognitive skills in children. Also of considerable interest to a study of youth orchestras is "another, more subtle effect of this chronic lack of control on orchestra musicians: infantilization. Forced to play the roles of children, musicians can behave childishly. Musicians who, when not at work, are perfectly responsible adults, can regress to the level of five-year-olds at work" (22). El Sistema claims to prepare children to become responsible adult citizens; yet here its primary tool, the orchestra, is seen as reducing responsible adults to the level of infants. The article concludes by likening orchestral musicians to "rats in someone else's maze" (24). Dudamel's "ideal global society" is starting to look less like the egalitarian utopias imagined since the time of Plato, and more like the dystopia of Oceania in Orwell's *Nineteen Eighty-Four*.

With criticisms of the orchestra coming from multiple angles—sociology, psychology, musicology, and naturally from musicians themselves—El Sistema's central claim that the orchestra is "a model and school of social life" and a "harmonious society" does not stand up to much scrutiny. If one turns away from conductors and concertmasters, and toward rank-and-file musicians and those who have studied them, one finds a troubled profession. Symphony orchestras are in fact widely perceived as autocratic, hierarchical structures, reproducing the values of the European societies from which they emerged (e.g., Osborne 1999). Aharonián (2004) argues that the orchestra transmits "the reaffirmation of an extremely authoritarian order, with a single will imposed on all the members of the group, and the removal of any possibility of interaction between its members." Is this organizational structure a sound basis for a progressive social project, or is El Sistema actually imposing an outdated and dysfunctional social model on contemporary Venezuelan youth?

CHALLENGES TO THE SYMPHONY ORCHESTRA

Given the manifest problems around the symphony orchestra, it is hardly surprising that it has been challenged at various times, though curiously not in the midst of Venezuela's Bolivarian revolution. In Holland around 1970, radical musicians and composers sought to transform the hidebound practices and ideologies of the classical music sphere (Adlington 2007). The head of the Dutch Musicians' Union, Maurice Ferares, argued that "the musicians are just as alienated from their product as the workers in industry, and both take the role of wage laborers in businesses. Just as a laborer loses his freedom when he enters a business, so the musician loses his individual freedom when he goes and works in an orchestra" (2007, 551). Dutch musicians critiqued the authoritarianism of orchestral organizations, recognizing that the problems lay not just in the ensembles' power dynamics, but also in the whole bureaucratic structure supporting them.

Similar developments were afoot in Germany (Kutschke 2010). Musicians associated with the New Left rebelled against authoritarianism and "called attention to aspects of the old-fashioned, uptight German educational methods and mores oriented toward practice and discipline which still prevailed in conservatories and orchestras" (2010, 574). The composer Konrad Boehmer described German conservatoire education as "drill and coercion—both socially sanctioned—that seek to produce musicians who perpetually reproduce musical values with a reactionary ideological basis" (575).

Radical figures were inspired by Theodor Adorno, who had stated: "The orchestral apparatus is alienated from both itself—because no member ever precisely hears everything that happens around him—and the unity of the music to be presented. This conjures the alienated institution of the conductor in whose musical and social relationship to the orchestra this alienation is prolonged" (quoted in Kutschke 2010, 574). Adorno had also argued that a broader and even more problematic political process was at play: "the conductor acts as though he were taming the orchestra, but his real target is the audience—a trick not unknown to political demagogues" (quoted in DeNora 2003, 51). The spectacle of conductor and orchestra "provides a means for rendering listening subjects amenable to authoritarian rule" (2003, 52). Sennett (1976), too, conceives of the rise of the conductor as a musical authority in the nineteenth century in terms of the imposition of discipline on musicians and audience alike, and he highlights the parallels between this new musical figure and a new political one: "the politician who had become a believable, moving public performer, a personality who could impose [discipline] on his working-class audience" (1976, 224). In these analyses, which underline the connection between orchestras and political authoritarianism, we may hear echoes of Abreu—conductor, politician, demagogue, and disciplinarian.

Such critiques point toward the ideological charge of musical "spectacle" (a word so frequently attached to Abreu), epitomized by the symphony orchestra. Spectacle has been the object of much critical attention, accused of generating or exacerbating a power discrepancy between viewer and viewed. In Marxian formulations, it is the viewer who is alienated, pacified, stupefied, distracted, or stripped of agency; from postcolonial and feminist perspectives, however, it is the viewed who is objectified or controlled (Butterworth 2014, 77). Either way, interesting questions arise about the place for musical spectacle in a program of education for social justice.

Radical European musicians of an earlier revolutionary moment thus understood clearly the problems that ran through conventional classical music culture, particularly the orchestra, and grasped that social change had to go hand in hand with challenges to authoritarian structures and musical practices. In Germany, "[t]he New Leftist spirit manifested itself particularly clearly in the new enthusiasm for improvisation and musical creativity. Both were seen as pedagogical instruments that served to performatively change social behavioral modes in the musical field, and were believed to be transferable to the practices of everyday West German society" (Kutschke 2010, 561). Again, social change would stem from musical transformation, above all from the prioritization of creativity over reproduction. In 1968 students sought to "'break up the authoritarian structures of the orchestra and the whole musical enterprise and to convey to the musician a new critical consciousness' that would go beyond the mindless reproduction of music on cue. Paying tribute to these insights into the intertwining of authority and orchestral performance structures, avant-garde musicians as well as those of the early-music movement developed ensemble structures and performance practices that avoided not only a conductor and hierarchal relationships between the musicians, but also the use of a score" (576).

Symphony orchestras and classical music education thus came under intense scrutiny and fierce criticism in Europe at precisely the moment that the idea of El Sistema was starting to gestate. Dutch and German musical radicals recognized the orchestra as an inherently flawed structure and a microcosm of a hidebound society; yet they could not have had less influence on the Venezuelan project, whose management and educational practices embody the reactionary forces that the European musicians rejected.

INNOVATIONS AND FUTURES

More recently, Richard J. Hackman posed some challenging questions about the continuing viability of the orchestra as institution: "Are we ... trapped and limited not only by the classical repertoire but also by the classical orchestral form? Are fundamental changes in the very *idea* of the 100-person symphony orchestra required if serious music is to survive, let alone prosper, in contemporary American society? Must the institution of the professional symphony orchestra be dismantled and reconstructed in order to make it manageable?" (quoted in Judy 1996, 12).

These are not questions that are widely heard, much less addressed, in Venezuela. For all its radical political context and progressive rhetoric, El Sistema is a traditionalist organization. To see adaptations of the orchestra, one must turn to other countries. The Bolshevik Revolution saw the creation of Persimfans, a conductorless orchestra that attempted to mirror political ideas about equality in the artistic sphere—an experiment not repeated under the Bolivarian Revolution. More recently, we can find more exercises in radical musical democracy, such as the Lahti Symphony Orchestra (Wagner and Ward 2002) and the Orpheus Chamber Orchestra (Seifter 2001). The Orpheus removed the conductor—the figure at the heart of many musicians' gripes. It was founded by a group of musicians "with the goal of bringing the chamber music ideals of democracy, personal involvement, and mutual respect into an orchestral setting" (Seifter 2001). Ramnarine (2012) presents three case studies of United Kingdom symphony orchestras that are striving to be "socially aware participants in orchestrations of civil society" (2012, 348), all of which depart from conventional practices by introducing non-Western musicians and instruments or interactive digital technology. Echoing the aforementioned Dutch and German examples, but in contrast to Venezuela, social inclusion is enacted through the transformation of musical practices and repertoire, rather than simply including a wider spectrum of people in business as usual. In Ramnarine's examples, orchestras have recognized that the institution has been much questioned, and that in order to resolve deep-seated problems, improve musicians' experiences, and impact more positively on wider society, it needs to make bold structural and artistic changes. El Sistema's silence on such questions is telling.

Orchestral innovation may be seen as driven by two principal forces: ideological discomfort with the past (how to address problematic aspects of the orchestral tradition), and practical concerns about the future (how to maintain audiences and secure economic foundations). El Sistema, however, has persisted with traditional structures and has resolved the financial issue, for the time being at least, by persuading the state and the IDB to bankroll it. Innovation has been primarily discursive—reframing the project in social terms. This has proven an extremely successful move, but questions remain: Can Venezuela buck the international trend over the longer term? Is "a country sown with orchestras" (one of El Sistema's catchphrases) a viable proposition for the twenty-first century or a hangover from the nineteenth, dependent on unprecedented access to petro dollars and social funds? Above all, does the symphony orchestra not require reform if social objectives are to be prioritized?

Osborne (1999, 73), a stern critic of the conventional orchestra, looks forward to a more positive future: "*new artistic genres* will evolve in the global village that differ from those created by artist-prophets representing the feudalistic, nationalistic and monolithic political ideologies of European history. *Connective technological developments*—such as collaborative musical composition via the Web and the ability to quickly disseminate and retrieve information worldwide—will generate *new concepts of community*. Notions of stylistic orthodoxy will be diminished, and disenfranchised groups such as women and minorities will have greater access to the avenues of power provided by new forms of large-scale networking. Advancements such as these will weaken the patriarchal cultural concept of the artist-prophet and replace the authoritarian, hierarchical social structures of the symphony orchestra that was his instrument" (emphases added). Some traditionally underrepresented social groups are being included in Venezuelan orchestras (though women face a clear glass ceiling—see Chapter 8), but Osborne envisions something much more radical: new genres, new technologies, and new ways of creating community.

He sees the orchestra as a remnant of a dark period in European history and an organization in need of fundamental change.

Similarly, Spich and Sylvester (1999, 30) envisage profound revolutions. "Can the symphony orchestra transform itself from a dinosaur to some other beast more of this day?" they ask. "The answer is simply that it probably cannot under the present structure, culture, and functioning of the symphony orchestra. Transformational strategies require a willingness to change in such ways that the past might become unrecognizable." They dream about possible developments: an orchestra "that creates leading-edge, high-art music using high-technology sound mixing to combine newly instrumented, traditional high-art music forms, computer-generated sound, and high-art visuals (borrowed from local museums) to invent unique new listening and feeling experiences" (1999, 31). However, their examples of attempts to revolutionize symphony concerts through new technology, programming, marketing, presentation, and use of space find few echoes in Venezuela. Once again, El Sistema looks more like the past than the future of classical music.

PROFESSIONAL ORCHESTRAS IN VENEZUELA

Turning to the professional orchestral sphere, one might hope for a more positive story from the home of El Sistema, but in Venezuela the picture is, if anything, more troubled than in the Global North. FESNOJIV claims that it "contributes to the promotion of a successful image of professional Venezuelan musicians, giving participants the possibility of developing a professional career that brings status and social recognition." In fact, there is often a gulf between image and career realities. El Sistema's publicity makes much of the quantity of orchestras in the country, but quality—of music making, of professional life—is often a casualty of this constant drive to expand.

When I arrived in Veracruz, morale in the symphony orchestra was low: many of the best older musicians had left for Caracas or simply stopped playing, while the talented younger ones generally preferred to play in the regional youth orchestra, which paid better. There were frictions between the conductors of the two orchestras and regular disputes over which musicians should play in which orchestra. An ex-member of the symphony described a dispiriting work environment: "in the rehearsals there was *always* someone arguing—almost always about money, or because they weren't being paid their *cesta tickets* [food stamps], or because of internal problems—in the symphony, everyone gossips, everyone argues. Everything was always a struggle, it wasn't really enjoyable to play in the symphony." She described it as a "military regime" and a "tyranny," led by "a lunatic who shouts at you, who says everything is rubbish and the world is about to end, who shouts until he loses his voice or starts crying." She was on the lowest rung, which meant that it was impossible for her to play interesting parts unless the principal died or retired. When the regional youth orchestra was created, she switched ensembles, and her salary increased dramatically. Even so, many of her companions dropped out because they simply saw no economic future in music.

The main problem was the endemic one of classical music in Venezuela: low and late pay. Some provincial orchestras would go for months at a time without paying their musicians. A top-level soloist told me an anecdote: he went on tour to the island of Margarita, took a taxi from the airport to his hotel, and was surprised when the driver hailed him by name. It turned out that the driver was a principal in the state's professional orchestra. He had not been paid for a year, so he was working as a taxi driver to make ends meet.

There were great imbalances between the provinces and the capital. The concertmaster of the Veracruz Symphony had recently left to become a section player in a Caracas orchestra, where he was earning several times his former salary; in Veracruz, he had been earning the same as an unskilled laborer. A member of the symphony reported in late 2012 that he was earning 2,000 bolívares a month, equivalent to the minimum wage, while a friend in the Caracas Youth Orchestra, El Sistema's third-ranking ensemble, was earning 9,000. He also claimed that the SBSO salary was in the region of 20,000 (a former member of the orchestra confirmed that it was 22,000). Additionally, he had not been paid for several months. "I'm out of here," he said, fed up with scraping a living.

Compared with professional ensembles in Europe, standards were low. A former member of the symphony suggested that high turnover of personnel worked against quality. While the number of graduates from El Sistema was expanding exponentially and Venezuela boasted many orchestras, he said, the general standards were not very impressive.

Conditions in Veracruz were mirrored in other cities that I visited, where I heard stories of declining standards, talent draining toward the capital, poor morale, low and irregular pay, lack of benefits, and poor relations with the local politicians who held the purse strings. Many of the provincial symphonies seemed to be struggling, with some reportedly close to folding and others having recently survived similar scares. In one case, a historically strong provincial orchestra was suspended due to its poor financial situation; a few musicians carried on as a chamber orchestra, playing for free, to try to prevent the institution from dying altogether. These orchestras grew out of El Sistema (as youth orchestras turned professional), but they are no longer funded by it; they are thus tied to Abreu in a historically subservient relationship, yet financially orphaned and thus dependent on limited regional funding and local politicians who do not necessarily regard classical music as a priority. Youth orchestras are well funded by the state and transnational institutions, but adult orchestras' subsidies are harder to justify, since they do not push the "social" buttons that open coffers. There does not seem to be the potential to generate much income through ticket sales; although concerts are often free, audiences are usually modest. With many provincial professional orchestras run on a budget that is not only tight but under threat, their prospects are doubtful.

Venezuela therefore lacks a nationwide professional infrastructure commensurate with its preprofessional training program. It might seem to make perfect sense for El Sistema to focus on training the young rather than worrying about adult professional musicians; but as a result, the world of work that awaits its trainees is a precarious one. Venezuela is not historically prepared to support an abundance of orchestras and orchestral musicians. As the SBYO transformed smoothly into the SBSO, it was easy to imagine that the future of Venezuela's young musicians was assured; but the solution of creating a new professional orchestra when a youth orchestra grows up, and putting its wages on the public tab, is a very expensive one, and there are only so many times this process can be repeated in a country already oversupplied with orchestras. Outside Caracas, with the existing professional orchestras already struggling, this step seems unrealistic. For many aspiring professional musicians, especially in the provinces, the future is cloudy.

A well-known musician summed up the problems, accusing Abreu of failing to promote the creation of well-structured professional orchestras that would provide Sistema graduates with an appealing career path: "You cannot imagine the frustration that exists within El Sistema, since when the applause is over at the Proms, in New York, in Vienna, around the world, what is left is the silence of the everyday life of Venezuelan classical musicians. Working for a low salary and realizing that all that sacrifice served only to end up in an orchestra without a clear artistic direction. Then the twin serpents of drugs and alcohol start to knock on the door."

THE ORCHESTRA AS METAPHOR AND REALITY

In order to comprehend the gaps between rhetoric and realities, it is instructive to turn to Spitzer and Zaslaw's (2005) argument that the orchestra has been enmeshed for centuries in a "web of metaphors," which plays a crucial role in understanding it today. The ideology underpinning the birth of the modern orchestra in the mid-seventeenth-century French court was, unsurprisingly, one of autocratic absolutism. Under Jean-Baptiste Lully, orchestras became "disciplined, hierarchical, polished ensembles, simulacra of a well-functioning autocratic society" (2005, 99). In the metaphorical realm, too, the orchestra was seen as intimately linked to royal absolutism, with harmony achieved by the imposition of authority. Orchestral metaphors changed over time, however, and by the late eighteenth century the influence of the vocabulary and values of the Enlightenment and the French Revolution started to be felt, as metaphors of cooperation began to predominate.

During the eighteenth century, then, the meaning of the orchestra changed from a model of top-down, divine-right authority to the promise of a new social order of voluntary association. "Under the ancien régime where social hierarchy and deference were highly valued, the orchestra was understood in terms of order and discipline. As individual initiative and responsibility became preferred social values, the orchestra became an example of participation and social solidarity" (530). The crucial point here is that *metaphors* changed under the influence of social and political transformations—but the orchestra itself did not change accordingly. In fact, most changes in the orchestra in the late eighteenth century "were in the direction of tighter coordination and discipline" (527), as exemplified by the subsequent rise of the conductor. Thus a gulf opened up during the eighteenth century between the orchestra's realities, which remained rooted in the absolutism of the previous century, and its role as a metaphor for newly emerging sociopolitical formations.

What we see with El Sistema today is an extension of the process that Spitzer and Zaslaw identify, as the orchestra has been drawn into contemporary progressive discourse about social inclusion, solidarity, and teamwork. Yet those who employ this rhetoric overlook or even blur the fact that the orchestra's role here is *metaphorical*: the association of the orchestra with this discourse reflects current social values and sensibilities rather than the nitty-gritty of what takes place within these ensembles, which remain quite close in spirit to Lully's simulacra of an autocratic society while also displaying a range of social and professional problems. The propagation of appealing orchestral metaphors of order and harmony depends on an ignorance or denial of their distance from the challenging and sometimes sordid realities of orchestral life and thus on a suspension of disbelief (Cottrell 2014).

Cook (2007, 338) posits the argument that "the experience of music-making in a face-to-face situation is prototypical and that its values are thus generalized to orchestral performance, so that we *hear* the music of large groups as embodying social interaction even when that is not literally the case; music, in short, symbolizes social interaction even when it doesn't actually present it." So Cook, too, points to a gap between metaphor and reality (as well as a gap between the experiences of listeners and orchestral musicians, since social interaction is experienced by the audience, not the players). An orchestra may symbolize social interaction but not enact it, or it may enact social interaction of a very different kind to that of chamber music, with its more egalitarian, collaborative dynamics.

This point, which reveals a fundamental flaw in the Sistema concept, may be illustrated by a comparison between El Sistema and the WEDO. These projects have traits in common: both are famed for their social discourse and display a reverential attitude to European Romantic orchestral music. But there is a crucial difference. One might argue that the internal micropolitics of the

WEDO are of secondary importance, since the orchestra's function is more symbolic than practical. The number of young people that it directly affects is very small, but it is held up as an emblem of hope and possibility for the entire Middle East. Its social action is envisaged as deriving primarily from its symbolic force—from witnessing the orchestra more than playing in it. Beckles Willson's (2009) exploration of the gaps between the project's high-flown rhetoric and the realities for participants is illuminating, yet since an orchestra "symbolizes social interaction even when it doesn't actually present it," in Cook's words, the WEDO could still potentially fulfill its mission.

The same is not true of El Sistema, which is claiming nothing less than a reeducation of society through the direct experience of playing in an orchestra. While the SBYO, too, may have become a symbolic orchestra (symbolizing more than enacting the "rescue" of young people), El Sistema's raison d'être today is that playing in an orchestra changes its young members, so the realities of orchestral life become very important. If the WEDO successfully propagated the *idea* of harmony to a wide public, then its job would be largely done, but El Sistema is supposed to produce the real thing for the musicians themselves. If the orchestra is inherently dysfunctional, El Sistema's work is fundamentally undermined in a way that the WEDO's is not.

In one sense, then, the cornerstone of El Sistema is a simple misconception: a confusion of orchestra as metaphor with orchestra as reality. Discussions of El Sistema are usually muddied by a failure to distinguish between these two ideas, and this blurring of lines is something that the program itself is ready to promote. El Sistema's expansion has depended on persuading politicians and institutions that there is a direct correspondence between metaphors and realities, thereby securing funding not just for a symbolic orchestra but also for a nationwide program.

The masking of problematic reality by seductive metaphor is Abreu's specialty. For example, he claims that an orchestra is "a model society...whose essence is *concertación*; because *orquestar* is precisely *concertar*" (quoted in Maidana 2012). *Concertar/concertación* has a dual meaning—to agree/agreement, but also to harmonize/harmonization. *Orquestar*, to orchestrate, also has a double meaning, as in English. The result is a richly layered, appealing aphorism, yet one that is largely untrue; with the exception of unusual cases like the Orpheus and the Lahti, the essence of an orchestra is to obey, not to agree. Abreu uses the dual meaning of *concertar* in order to transmute authoritarian reality into democratic illusion and thereby present the orchestra as a model society—something that few orchestral musicians actually believe to be true. Abreu crafts such authoritative, natural-sounding aphorisms with uncommon skill, yet they serve to obfuscate rather than elucidate musical realities.

Concertación is a word that also has particular political connotations in Venezuela. It was employed by CAP as part of his neoliberal restructuring of the economy immediately after his reelection in 1989 (when Abreu joined the government as minister of culture). Yet behind the language of national consensus lay a familiar concentration of power and decision making in the hands of the elite. Hellinger (1991, 194) argues that the policy failed to shift the burden of sacrifice to the rich and produced little benefit for workers. CAP's government spoke of *concertación* as strengthening popular participation in decision making, but in practice understood the term to mean "unconditional support for a national commitment considered to be beyond dispute" (Lander 2006, 88).

Concertación was the "magic word of the current political order" in 1989, yet there were concerns that "its current ambiguity and apparent breadth are only a novel packaging that holds inside a package of firmly established economic measures and political alliances that will serve to strengthen existing tendencies in our society to concentrate the mechanisms of decision-making in the hands of the few and to channel the economic process according to neoliberal orthodoxy" ("Concertación" 1989, 2). The word thus has a history of camouflaging unpalatable realities. Abreu's aphorism harks back to a particular historical moment—one in which his political authority was greatest and a discourse of "agreement" served as a euphemism for the concentration of power. The disconnect between *concertación* and a "model society" may be gauged from the explosion, just weeks into CAP's new term, of the Caracazo, a wave of riots and protests against free-market reforms that constituted Venezuela's most serious social upheaval of the late twentieth century.

That the discourse of *concertación* serves as a cloak for top-down decision making illustrates the importance of critically examining El Sistema's seductive claims. For example, El Sistema's website alleges that "the orchestral and choral routine involving children and young people implies, *necessarily*, the formation of a spirit of solidarity and fraternity, a vigorous development of self-esteem, and the cultivation of ethical and aesthetic values" (emphasis added). But studies of orchestras reveal that there is nothing remotely inevitable about the link between orchestral practice and solidarity; Faulkner (1973, 336) writes of "one of the most complex, competitive, and stratified organizational sets in existence." Since it would also be hard to argue seriously that orchestral musicians are more ethical than other kinds of people, such statements should be viewed with skepticism.

A considerable part of El Sistema's success has been due to Abreu's expertise in rhetoric, and his seduction of politicians and funders through discourses of concertizing, orchestrating, and harmonizing. Understanding El Sistema requires unpicking its linguistic constructions and exploring the potential gulf between metaphor and reality—evident in the tensions between El Sistema's utopian rhetoric and scholarly studies of orchestras. The orchestra may have come to *symbolize* social harmony, inclusion, teamwork, and solidarity, but it does not necessarily foster those values and may even engender the opposite (see Chapters 8 and 9). The orchestra as metaphor has served El Sistema very well indeed, but the orchestra as reality is more important if we are interested in the ensemble as a "school for social life." Without substantial changes, the orchestra may never be more than a metaphor for an ideal society—which is not much use for a real-life music education system or social development project.

The orchestra is often described in Venezuela as "a big family," a phrase that is possibly more revealing than intended. The family is used here as a metaphor for a harmoniously functioning community, yet the reality, as the poet Philip Larkin famously noted ("They fuck you up, your mum and dad"), may be quite different. For the anthropologist Edmund Leach, the family was not the basis of a good society but rather "the source of all our discontents" (Purvis 2013, 47). A Veracruz musician mocked the oft-repeated line about the orchestra: "Yes, it's like a big family—everyone has fallen out with someone, and everyone has their favorites... at the end of the day, families are all about fighting."

ORCHESTRAS AND PEDAGOGY

El Sistema's signature pedagogical practice is to put children into an orchestra as soon as they start playing, providing a communal learning environment with obvious social attractions. I observed a beginner's orchestra, and it was an impressive sight: it was only four days old, so the children were playing just single notes in unison, but they *looked* the part. They sat up straight, holding their instruments high, like "real" orchestral musicians. They did not have written music, and the conductor's sole point, made repeatedly, was "follow the baton." The results may be impressive, yet it is essential to examine critically the orchestra as a pedagogical tool.

Playing together was not so much about listening to each other as following the conductor, a strong leader who issued commands that had to be obeyed. Orchestral discipline is inculcated as soon as the children can play a single note on their instrument. As Tunstall (2012, 158) remarked of her visit to La Rinconada: "Most of the children in this group were in a two-year-old Baby Vivaldi orchestra last year, and it seems likely that they have already absorbed a great deal not only about music, but about group discipline; these three-year-olds sit startlingly still when they are not singing or shaking maracas." El Sistema's learning process thus foregrounds certain aesthetic and social values, such as uniformity, hierarchy, and obedience, and downplays others often associated with the arts, such as creativity, freedom, exploration, and play.

A typical full orchestral rehearsal depends on maintaining discipline among a group of underoccupied youths. It involves different members to different degrees, with certain instrumental sections sometimes experiencing long periods of inactivity. Many youth orchestra rehearsals are thus punctuated by the conductor telling (or yelling at) the brass and percussion to stop talking. A North American music educator who observed members of the SBYO leading workshops in the United States commented: "The kids weren't really engaged during sectionals/rehearsals (I watched as the woodwinds were ignored for at least 30 minutes while the brass were focused on a wind sectional, and lots of kids getting antsy and impatient)."

Price (2010) focuses on this issue in his discussion of a TV series about a Sistema-inspired initiative by Manchester's Hallé Orchestra. "Several young lads were asked why they were being 'naughty' in rehearsals: 'because when we're playing in brass bands, we're busy all the time, but with this music, we have ages where we're not doing anything' was their perfectly sensible response." Price critiques the orchestral learning model, which involved a lot of shouting by the conductor: "The kids, of course, had no say in what music they would play, nor given any opportunity to express themselves, nor, apparently, given any reason *why* the pieces had been chosen for them." He contests the "myth" that "a symphony orchestra is a fantastic vehicle for learning. No, it's not—it's one of the most didactic, even dictatorial, modes of learning, where you have lots and lots of nothing to do, but become bored."

Increasing numbers of scholars, too, have been critiquing the role of large performance ensembles in music education. Kratus (2007, 45–46) claims that large classical ensembles enact an autocratic model of teaching that is being abandoned in other school subjects, which "have come to terms with the cognitive revolution." Hebert (2009, 44–45)—a conductor as well as an academic—describes a moment when he was directing a wind band:

> While...I am earnestly seizing the intensity of each moment in the rehearsal described, it is entirely possible that the fourth-chair Third Clarinet player is not in the slightest experiencing that musical intensity, as she incessantly blows through the repetitive and uninteresting passages, failing to grasp how each fits into the fabric of the ensemble and the larger or holistic experience of the piece, and how (or whether) we are collectively progressing "ever nearer to ideal." Despite my careful choice of repertoire and eager efforts to provide inspiring conducting and effective instruction, such inherent limitations associated with the fundamental structure of this instructional vehicle demonstrate that large ensembles are simply not conducive to the learning of much of what really matters in music. Learning the notes for the next concert is not a proper "curriculum."

Hebert identifies a form of fundamentalism or neoconservatism in U.S. music education, manifested in a tendency to persist with a focus on large ensembles playing canonical repertoire and arrangements of traditional music despite the obvious problems with this approach. He argues that future historians will look back in bewilderment on the fact that "many leaders of our field supported an extraordinarily misguided agenda in diametric opposition to the scholarly discourse of music education" (2009, 43).

O'Toole's (1994) Foucauldian study of choral singing highlights an issue that is equally applicable to Sistema orchestras—the musicians' lack of "voice." She argues that "the conventions of choral pedagogy are designed to create docile, complacent singers who are subject to a discourse that is more interested in the production of music than in the laborers" (1994, 65). Part of the ideology of classical music, according to O'Toole, is that the needs of the music—to be performed "well"—come first; musicians' training is molded by those needs rather than their own. Efficiency dictates that it is "common sense" that a single person direct the choir, and musicians internalize the "necessity" for a structure that leaves no room for their views. She concludes: "The purpose of choir is to create a quality product, not a quality experience" (73)—a prioritizing of results over processes that is pedagogically suspect, particularly if social goals are supposedly paramount.

The first step in designing a better pedagogical model for large ensembles is to acknowledge that there are problems with the traditional one—something that would be heresy in Venezuela. Davis (2011) identifies the same problem as O'Toole, and explores ways to give children a "musical say." This say includes "opportunities to contribute in ensemble settings and the development of musical voice through ownership, agency, relevance, and personal expression" (2011, 267). Through such efforts, "band became more than a performance setting with the conductor at the helm. It became an opportunity for composing, arranging, and improvising through both formal and informal learning processes" (267). The band made musical decisions collectively and thus fostered true collaboration rather than the simulacrum that large ensemble performance under a conductor often provides. Morrison and Demorest (2012, 827), too, recognize that "[t]he traditional autocratic model of the school conductor appears to be in direct opposition to contemporary educational thought." Most musical thinking is carried out in private by the conductor; since students rarely see the process, it is hard for them to learn from it. They are primarily expected to put the conductor's ideas into practice. "However, if our goal is to give students the tools to become self-sufficient learners, then something must change" (2012, 836). To allow students to develop independent musicianship, they should be involved in choosing repertoire, determining the rehearsal process, and identifying and solving problems.

El Sistema operates on the basis that the more children play in an orchestra the better, but there is considerable evidence for the opposite conclusion. Numerous progressive educationalists argue that performance-focused, results-driven music education via large ensembles is deficient, and the dynamics of such ensembles need to be transformed if sound educational goals are to be met. Playing in a symphony orchestra should perhaps be regarded as best indulged in moderation.

ORCHESTRAS AND SOCIAL ACTION

For all El Sistema's fame, a wealth of studies suggests that an orchestral program is not an obvious place to look for progressive social action. An authoritative vision of the tensions between symphony orchestras and social work can be gleaned from the work of Richard J. Hackman, interviewed by Judy (1996). Hackman undertook an exhaustive survey of seventy-eight orchestras in four countries, and concluded that, in comparison with other professions, orchestral musicians were below average in terms of satisfaction with growth opportunities. "The professional symphony orchestra, it seems, does not provide as rich and rewarding an occupational setting for musicians as one would hope," he notes; "what audiences appreciate may not always be that which stretches and pleases musicians" (1996, 4, 6).

Hackman's key findings, however, were that orchestral performance was determined to a large extent by financial resources, and financial strength depended on management, with top-down structures more effective than democratic ones. Yet a large body of research demonstrates that in music education and orchestral contexts, musicians' happiness and sense of worth is directly related to their participation in decision making (e.g., Green 2008). Logically, then, Hackman reports a *negative* association between orchestral performance and player satisfaction, since "the most powerful influence on orchestra players' professional satisfaction is the degree to which their organizations provide them opportunities for meaningful involvement in orchestral affairs" (Judy 1996, 9), yet such democratic involvement tends to lower standards.

Hackman's study demonstrates a clear contradiction between the pursuit of musical goals and social ones, and thus poses a major and empirically grounded challenge to one of El Sistema's key philosophies: that the pursuit of excellence and social inclusion go hand in hand. A Sistema spokesman stated: "we have to insist on musical excellence. The idea of good social care and mediocre music-making makes no sense" (Hewett 2010). In an article personally approved by Abreu, Govias (2011, 21) wrote: "The primary objective is social transformation *through* the pursuit of musical excellence." Yet this first and most important of Govias's five fundamental principles of El Sistema is challenged by Hackman's exhaustive research, which shows that to maximize their artistic performance, orchestras tend to relegate their musicians' satisfaction to a lesser priority, while to maximize inclusion and player satisfaction would mean accepting a probable lowering in quality.

Furthermore, there is a question here about definitions of "excellent" and "mediocre." In large classical ensembles, excellent music-making is defined to a significant degree as playing the notes accurately, together, and in tune. El Sistema places a particular emphasis on *quantity of music and musicians* as a sign of excellence. Turino (2008), however, draws on other musical traditions to define excellence in terms of the *quality of the social bonds* created through music making. Following Turino, another way of understanding excellent music-making would be musical practices that stimulate democratic, nonhierarchical, noncompetitive values and interactions—something that mainstream orchestral practice rarely does. Many of Turino's informants would probably agree with El Sistema's view that "the idea of good social care and mediocre music-making makes no sense," precisely because they would regard good social care *as* excellent music-making. El Sistema, however, regards excellent music-making as good social care—a very different proposition. As Hackman's work suggests, and as I will explore in the following chapters, there is a strong case for considering the insistence on musical excellence in orchestral settings as frequently working *against* good social care, because it usually emphasizes the undemocratic, hierarchical, competitive values of classical music (though research by Green [2008] and Abrahams [n.d.] indicates that introducing informal learning methods can alter this dynamic).

Hackman's study implies that El Sistema may need to decide whether it wants to prioritize great orchestras or good citizens. A project that prioritized the social over the musical would take risks with aesthetic quality in order to maximize social benefit. But El Sistema was launched as a preprofessional orchestral training program and quickly came to aim at overseas concert stages, and all the subsequent rebranding cannot hide the fact that its priority is still to dazzle foreign audiences, meaning that it puts musical quality first.

This point was illustrated by a U.S. student band's visit to Veracruz to stage joint concerts with the Sistema núcleo. At the first rehearsal, the Veracruz musicians did as they always did: the section leader (a student) told his subordinates where to sit and which part to play, according to their preestablished order. But the U.S. musicians sat according to alphabetical order, and it soon emerged that they expected to rotate for each piece so that each player had an equal opportunity. According to one Venezuelan participant, the Veracruz musicians were not just shocked but unimpressed by seeing musical democracy in action, since having weaker players on the most important parts at times resulted in a loss of musical quality. The U.S. band was organized along more inclusive lines than El Sistema—and the Venezuelans did not approve.

Hackman's study highlights the clash between social and professional values in orchestral music. Likewise, Jorgensen (1997) and Bohlman and Bohlman (2007) draw distinctions between music education for (aspiring) professional musicians and for amateurs. They suggest that a preprofessional program has to make sacrifices as a social project. Consequently, it might seem a good idea, if social goals were paramount, to keep youth orchestras quite separate from the professional world. El Sistema, however, still bears the imprint of its original mission to stock Venezuelan professional orchestras, so there is considerable blurring between the two spheres. Youth orchestras now routinely pay their members, while there are adolescents in their early to mid-teens in provincial professional symphony orchestras. Young musicians in Veracruz moved back and forth between the two, and while this unusual model may speed up the acquisition of skills and experience, one might question whether young musicians should be propelled into the stressful, messy realities of professional musical life (Martin 1995, 205–16) while still in their mid-teens.

ALTERNATIVES

Orchestras show some signs of innovating, as Ramnarine suggests. Price compares the Sistema-derived initiative in Manchester with the Guildhall School of Music and Drama's Connect ensembles, which work with whatever instruments appear, focus on composition, and actively promote equality (see also Renshaw 2005). The informal learning movement (e.g., Green 2008; Abrahams n.d.) argues that conventional school ensembles and curricula can also be transformed by a pedagogical revolution. However, other musical traditions may provide more promising examples of progressive social models.

Many scholars interested in social issues regard jazz improvisation more positively than orchestral music. Skyllstad (2008, 178), for example, argues that "a special case of team-building through music in many Western countries may be observed in the way jazz ensembles cooperate in working out a musical concept." Improvisation relies on dialogue: "In order for jazz to work, players must develop a remarkable degree of empathic competence" (2008, 179).

Barrett (1998, 605) proposes that jazz musicians provide a good example for modern, flexible organizations to emulate. He contests the idea that the orchestral conductor is a good model for a twenty-first-century manager, arguing that "[t]he mechanistic, bureaucratic model for organizing…is no longer adequate," and explores the jazz band as "an example of an organization designed for maximizing learning and innovation" (1998, 620). "To be innovative, managers—like jazz musicians—must interpret vague cues, face unstructured tasks, process incomplete knowledge, and yet they must take action anyway. Managers, like jazz players, need to engage in dialogue and negotiation, the creation of shared spaces for decision making based on expertise rather than hierarchical position" (620).

Eagleton (2007, 172) sees the jazz band not just as a positive social model but as encapsulating the very meaning of life—and he, too, expressly contrasts it with the orchestra. "A jazz group which is improvising obviously differs from a symphony orchestra, since to a large extent each member is free to express herself as she likes. But she does so with a receptive sensitivity to the self-expressive performances of the other musicians. The complex harmony they fashion comes not from playing from a collective score, but from the free musical expression of each member acting as the basis for the free expression of the others." Eagleton's vision may be idealistic, but unlike idealizations of the orchestra, it seems to concord to a reasonable degree with scholarly analyses (e.g., Fischlin and Heble 2004).

Cope (1998; 1999; and Smith 1997) presents another alternative: community-based traditional fiddle-playing in Scotland. He finds classical music problematic, since many children struggle with reading it or do not have the motivation for scales and exercises. Consequently, he argues that developing musical competence through learning traditional music in traditional ways makes more sense to more people than classical training, which has the concert performer as its explicit or implicit goal. He also suggests that classical music skills are of limited use for many people in adult life; many musicians stop playing once they outgrow youth music programs, since they have no obvious context within which to carry on. El Sistema is no different. Its best, most determined, or best-connected students may continue, but many give up El Sistema in their teens, at which point their classical skills may lose most of their meaning, since there is little adult, amateur classical music-making in Venezuela. Cope's model does not offer participants a professional future; it does, however, attempt to cultivate modest skills that may have lifelong relevance.

Broadening the curriculum to include a range of musical genres, ensembles, and learning styles may, if done well, allow the temporary flourishing of alternative forms of social and political relations. Jorgensen (1997, 36) cites John Blacking, who "contrasted Western classical music, which reflects Western hierarchical social structures and mores and values individualism and competition, with the indigenous music of the Venda people of South Africa, which reveals egalitarian social values and beliefs and values communalism and cooperation." Turino (2008, 35) argues that presentational music reproduces the values of capitalism whereas participatory music offers an alternative vision: more democratic, less competitive, less hierarchical. For him, the virtue of pursuing diverse musical activities lies primarily in the chance to explore different value systems. An ideal music project would expose children to different kinds of music, ensembles, and the values associated with them, allowing them to experience and reflect on a variety of notions of citizenship.

Bramley (2012), for example, describes an educational project based on free improvisation. By allowing conflicts to be played out rather than suppressed through authoritarian action, it challenges a unitary view of community. He invokes Deleuze and Guattari's concept of "minoritarian" group formations:

While majoritarian formations attempt to reduce chaos, difference and conflict by imposing a "standard" and fixed identity that all participants must subscribe to, minoritarian formations on the other hand expand difference by allowing contradictions, chaos and conflict to remain in view.... To take a musical example, if someone joined a group with absolutely no prior musical experience, but wanted to participate, a majoritarian group would usually require that person to be able to meet the group's requirements without conflict, or face exclusion, whereas a minoritarian group would find ways of adapting to allow that person to add to the group and participate meaningfully. (2012, 6–7)

It is clear that a conventional symphony orchestra is a majoritarian formation and that the kinds of social values that might be learned through collective free improvisation would be quite different, providing students with experience of an anarchist rather than an authoritarian political model (see also Ford 1995). The point is not that one should be deemed a priori more valuable than the other, but that children should be exposed to both and encouraged to reflect critically on them.

CONCLUSION

The orchestra is El Sistema's "unique selling point"—from playing in an ensemble at the very start, all the way up to the showcase SBYO. Its social mission also focuses on the orchestra, which it claims serves as a model and school of social life. If orchestras were widely considered to be positive social and professional environments, then there would be some basis for El Sistema's position; but its claims founder on the numerous accounts by orchestral musicians and experts that reveal large classical ensembles to be permeated by social dysfunction, questionable ideologies, and pedagogical flaws. The symphony orchestra appears to be a problematic institution, in Venezuela as much as elsewhere, leaving El Sistema's core idea looking rather threadbare. There is clearly more debate needed about the suitability of a nineteenth-century adult organization as a school for children in the twenty-first century, but it seems that El Sistema's USP might actually be a source of weakness rather than strength, and that progressive social goals might be achieved more effectively via other kinds of ensembles.

CHAPTER 6

Learning and Teaching in El Sistema

It's an absolutely primitive system. It's just repeat, repeat, repeat, until it sounds OK. El Sistema isn't interested in educating the child. It's just about the show.
— Venezuelan musicologist

This chapter examines El Sistema's music teaching program and philosophy. Clearly, the musical and social are entwined and often need to be considered together. Nevertheless, for the sake of clarity, El Sistema is approached here through the lens of musical practices, whereas the next section of the book focuses more on social values and ideals. Issues of curriculum and pedagogy form a central thread: I consider both El Sistema's distinctive approaches—its orchestral focus, its emphasis on peer teaching—and its more conventional elements, such as a hierarchization of musical genres that favors classical music and a marginalization of critical reflection. Musicians' distinction between training and education informs the analysis. These discussions shed light on the core issue of promoting social justice through music education, which is also illuminated by accounts of students' work schedules, teachers' working conditions, and núcleo life that bookend the chapter.

WORK SCHEDULES

El Sistema is a labor-intensive organization. Attached to an old-fashioned kind of rote learning, it relies on long, regular rehearsals. The beginners' orchestra in Veracruz rehearsed for ninety minutes, three times a week. Borzacchini (2010, 132) interviewed an eight-year-old violinist who did four hours of music every afternoon, got home at 8 p.m., and then had to do homework. This level of time commitment makes for an impressive pace of learning, in one sense, because children may be playing "real" orchestral music within a year or less of starting. Moving up the age and ability range, the provincial youth orchestras rehearse five or six times a week. The national orchestras thus draw from a huge pool of musicians who have been rehearsing almost daily (and playing the same repertoire). At the showcase end, the TCYO standardly rehearses between twenty-five and thirty-five hours a week, but often more, and the SBYO up to double this—schedules that are unheard of in European or North American youth orchestras.

The *seminarios* (intensive courses) of the National Children's Orchestra involve children, some of them preteen, getting up as early as 5 a.m. and rehearsing from breakfast time until as late as midnight. A musician who had played in a national orchestra had seen people faint from tiredness in late-night rehearsals. Musicians who complained of aches and pains were told to take some painkillers and keep going: "There was someone there giving out paracetemol like it was sweets." Even Booth (2008, 7–8) notes the workload: "They may spend as much as three days on 12 bars of music, culminating in the whole orchestra coming together to work on those 12 bars. Almost all students join in annual retreats around holidays and vacations, for one to three weeks. While on retreat everyone works on pieces in a variety of ways for ten hours a day; no wonder they jokingly call it boot camp." This kind of drilling produces results, but whether spending three days on twelve bars of music is a good educational program is a moot point, as is the physical and psychological impact of playing ten hours a day on children as young as eight.

One musician recounted his experience of a grueling seminario routine to prepare for a visit by members of the Berlin Philharmonic: "[A well-known Sistema teacher] started saying to me, 'again, again, again, again,' the same two bars, until I got a cramp in my arm. At the end of the class he asked me if it hurt, and I said of course, I was really tired, and he said, 'now that it's all swollen, when you try it tomorrow the passage will come out fine—first you have to damage the muscle, and then it will come out.' Afterwards I couldn't move my arm, I had to see the FESNOJIV doctor, and the guy obviously gave me Ibuprofen, and he told me to put my arm in hot water and then cold water and that the swelling would go down and the next day I would be able to play. But after that my arm carried on hurting me for a week, but still you can't stop—still, you play 10 hours a day or more, sometimes more. It's one thing if you're playing on your own, you can just stop if your arm starts to hurt. But if you're playing in the orchestra, then you have to keep going as long as you've got notes to play." Years later, he was still suffering from injuries that stemmed, he believed, from overplaying in the orchestra.

El Sistema's orchestras provoked concern among experienced Venezuelan musicians, who compared them to the Chinese circus or Soviet gymnasts. Teenagers can perform jaw-dropping physical feats, said one, but once you know the intensive and unbending training regime behind them, it is hard to look on them with unalloyed enthusiasm. A former top figure in El Sistema argued that people are impressed by the SBYO because they think that it has a normal rehearsal schedule and approach to repertoire, whereas "if you grab any old bunch of kids and you get them playing the same music for ten years, even the least talented kid is going to learn and is going to be able to play it." He argued that Sistema orchestras required an "absurd" number of rehearsals to learn music; the challenge is to produce good results *efficiently*, he said, in other words with a *normal* investment of time and effort.

Cara, a member of the SBYO, reported that long rehearsals and the consequent lack of time for personal study was the biggest problem for the orchestra's members and the principal reason why they left. Marco, a former member of the CYO, described a work schedule that routinely ran from 9 a.m. to 10 p.m., with the musicians at the beck and call of the conductor. Marco left because he felt like a slave to the orchestra and believed his playing could not improve under such a regime. The University Institute of Musical Studies (IUDEM) was created to provide older students with the opportunity to study at the same time as playing, but members of the showcase orchestras report not having time to go to classes, and some never graduate because the orchestra keeps them so busy. Even Sistema director Valdemar Rodríguez told Tunstall (2012, 180) that SBYO members "may take five years or seven years or nine years to get degrees—and that's fine."

Several advanced students in Veracruz explained their decision not to move to Caracas in terms of their desire to avoid "exploitation" by the showcase orchestras. One stated that she did not want to spend twelve hours a day in orchestra rehearsals and acquire only a limited range of skills. She preferred to study at university rather than end up with nothing more than a high school diploma, a common occurrence in El Sistema.

PEDAGOGY AND CURRICULUM

Channing (2003, 193) states that "orchestras are gradually repositioning themselves as a vital resource for the whole community. The challenge for those who train orchestral musicians is to reflect these developments in the range of skills taught without compromising the learning of basic instrumental techniques, and to balance specialisation with a broader understanding of the musical and cultural issues which face everybody working in the arts." The increasing social mission of orchestras is thus seen as linked to a shift in pedagogy and curriculum.

El Sistema, however, has undergone no such shift. The lessons and rehearsals that I witnessed and heard described in interviews reproduced conventional practices of institutional music education: sequential and repetitious; teacher-centered and hierarchical; emphasizing the transmission and "banking" of existing knowledge rather than creativity; dedicated to performance rather than composing, improvising, arranging, or listening; and marginalizing discussion of broader social and cultural issues. Interestingly, only one of Govias's five fundamental principles of El Sistema refers to teaching, stating simply: "the focus of El Sistema is the orchestra or choral experience" (2011, 21). Four are discursive or organizational, and none refer to pedagogy. It is perhaps unsurprising, then, that classroom activities often look unremarkable.

Tunstall's (2012, 161–63) report of a class at La Rinconada núcleo is illuminating: "We watch her [the teacher] lead the group in playing a D scale as she claps out a beat so strong it cannot be resisted. Over and over, they play that D scale...over, and over, and over." Eventually the children move on to a piece by Corelli; but "it is rehearsed in the same way the D scale was—phrase by phrase, over and over and over. The teacher is as ruthless as any symphony conductor about their entrances and cutoffs being exactly, precisely together."

Deutsche Grammophon presents Abreu as architect of a "unique pedagogical approach. 'Our pedagogy is based on individual creativity on the part of the teachers,' says Abreu. 'They are very inventive.'"[1] As Tunstall reveals, however, with her description of rigid instruction focused on repetition, discipline, and precision, El Sistema's approach is neither unique (it has clear historical precedents) nor, in its narrowness and intensity, inventive. It is a traditionalist program, retaining practices and methods that were normal in the 1970s (and long before), and paying little heed to subsequent critical thinking about music education.

Emilio Mendoza raised the question of pedagogy in his appraisal of a concert of contemporary music at the CASM.[2] His delight at seeing a large group of children at a concert of somewhat recherché music soon turned to unease, as he recalled El Sistema's well-known disinterest in discussing music with its students. It might seem ironic that a contemporary composer should question the presence of a large, young audience, but his point was that difficult contemporary music was challenging even for adults and needed to be presented to young children in particular ways. He was concerned that children were being taken to concerts to keep them busy (and to fill seats at the CASM) rather than to educate them.

His concerns were echoed by a Sistema teacher who reported that children in her núcleo were obliged to sit through long, conventional concerts every weekend: "they were so fidgety, and falling asleep, and starving." She went on: "one time the pastoral staff took them out because they were throwing stuff and just not paying attention, but [a senior Sistema figure] said 'no, they've got to go back in.' The concerts were really good, but that was probably a bit excessive, to make the kids sit through that every Saturday."

Jonathan Govias wrote on his blog on May 9, 2012: "Many orchestras still import busloads of children once a year for shows explaining the profound and poignant difference between 'high' and 'low,' or for those of more advanced age and intellect, 'soft' and 'loud,' and then consider their civil obligations duly discharged and return confidently to their funders proudly boasting of their commitment to outreach. 'Playing for poor kids,' or in more fashionable parlance, 'access to excellence' is cheap and easy, requiring relatively little money and even less thought." El Sistema falls into this category. For an organization that specializes in working with children, it is remarkably disinclined to tailor its activities to young performers and audiences. Jorge Peña Hen composed a children's opera for the youth orchestra in La Serena in 1966, but Abreu took a less ambitious route. El Sistema has little time for experiments like Tod Machover's *Toy Symphony*—"a collaboration between professional orchestral players, an international soloist and schoolchildren...intended to explore new relations between trained and untrained performers, adults and children, music-makers and audience" (Chang n.d.). The showcase orchestras devote far more time to touring the world's great concert halls with mainstream symphonic repertoire than to providing stimulating, pedagogically innovative experiences for ordinary Venezuelan children.

With regard to curriculum, the program focuses primarily on the Romantic orchestral canon, which is held to be "universal." It echoes pre-1970s music education in the United Kingdom, when "music in schools was overwhelmingly concerned with Western classical music and settings of folk songs by prestigious composers" (Green 2003a, 265). For most of its history, traditional and popular Venezuelan music have been largely absent, except in the form of orchestrations, much to the chagrin of many defenders of national musical traditions. Moves to create small spaces for these musics began in 2008, and during my fieldwork, recently formed groups like the Simón Bolívar Conservatoire's Latin music ensembles, Montalbán's cuatro orchestra, or Guárico's traditional music orchestra were brought out on important occasions to demonstrate inclusivity, but this handful of groups needs to be considered in the context of a program with some four hundred symphony orchestras (Borzacchini 2010, 214).

While the Alma Llanera initiative, launched in 2011, may alter this picture (see Chapter 12), many ordinary núcleos did not offer traditional Venezuelan music up to that point, and those that did usually offered only basic cuatro lessons as a preparatory step before moving on to a "real" (i.e., orchestral) instrument, demonstrating the relative importance attributed to European and Venezuelan traditions. A Sistema leader, trying to impress the program's adaptability on Mora-Brito (2011, 39), inadvertently revealed this hierarchy of values: "If the program will be implemented in a small community that is oriented toward the development of folkloric expressions, the Foundation ties itself to those genres at first to then bring the orchestral format to the fore." Veracruz—the largest núcleo in its region—only offered traditional music to special needs students, and provision in its satellite núcleos was minimal. In one, there was a cuatro teacher, but he was paid by the municipality rather than El Sistema; a second also had a cuatro teacher, but only because the núcleo's administrator had insisted in the face of resistance from his superiors. At a third, some of the pupils wanted to learn cuatro but El Sistema would not oblige, so the núcleo was arranging for a non-Sistema teacher to come in. In all three cases, FESNOJIV only paid for classical tuition; cuatro was offered despite, and not because of, institutional policy. An advanced cuatro student at a major regional núcleo revealed that he received no scholarship since he was not in the orchestra; in other words, El Sistema provided a financial incentive to focus on orchestral instruments.

This kind of educational philosophy has been critiqued since the 1970s, the very time that El Sistema was being launched (Philpott 2010). Woodford (2005) and Bowman (2009) are just two of the many scholars who have questioned a universalist approach more recently. Bowman (2009, 5) rejects the assumption that "the music simply 'has' value of a kind that is good for everyone, equally," and criticizes attempts "to universalize instructional systems and strategies that are effective only under certain conditions" as a "naïve faith in one true way of being musical" (7). Their positions challenge Abreu's philosophy that what works for one poor child should work for any poor child, and that El Sistema is a template that can be applied in any community anywhere in the world.

In response, music educationalists have increasingly embraced a shift toward multicultural or popular music education. Hebert (2010, 105) argues that "there are many exclusively musical rationales for including genres other than European art music in the curriculum, including the fact that other genres are more readily conducive to the development of compositional, improvisational, and multi-instrumental skills, and more often permit creative experimentation." Claiming that cultural diversity questions the hegemonies created by societal institutions, Jorgensen (2002, 39) locates diversity in music making itself (rather than those exposed to it) and imagines "a polyglot of instructional programs...fostering early musics, contemporary musics, popular musics, classical musics, and traditional musics of all sorts, each focusing on the array of musical experiences such as composing, improvising, performing, listening, producing, and distributing" (2003, 137).

El Sistema's disciplined orchestral training looks very narrow in comparison, and one of its prominent weak spots is creativity; even a Sistema fan admits that "the fostering of individual creativity is simply not, for Abreu, a goal" (Swed 2012). However, scholars such as Burnard (2012) and Cee (2013) have made impassioned pleas for the re-centering of creativity and problem solving in music education. Creativity would be stimulated much more by education in an improvisatory tradition (Bramley 2012) or composition and arrangement (Burnard and Younker 2010); when these activities are tackled collaboratively, they may promote empathy as well as creativity (Cross, Laurence, and Rabinowitch 2012). Koutsoupidou and Hargreaves (2009) demonstrated experimentally that learning musical improvisation promotes the development of creative thinking to a greater extent than didactic teaching. They also noted that "musical creativity has been associated with children's cognitive and emotional development and its value is increasingly acknowledged in psychological and therapeutic studies" (2009, 251).

Outside Venezuela, emphasis is thus shifting from performance skills to creativity, which is increasingly recognized as essential to a rounded musical and social education; forward-looking programs are placing less emphasis on reproducing the canon and more on improvising, composing, and arranging (Levin 2013). Yet as Odena (2012, 516) notes, for creativity to flourish, "students would need to feel safe to take risks and to experiment without frequent fear of failure." Divergent thinking is a key aspect of creativity, so "teachers need to eliminate negative attitudes toward divergence ... and reduce anxiety about correctness or incorrectness." Orchestral conductors rarely have much time for divergent thinking, however, and one of El Sistema's signature techniques, originated by Abreu and maintained by the conductors he has trained, is the "public audition" or "stand-by-stand technique"—picking out a musician during a full rehearsal and making them play a difficult section on their own, in front of a hundred of their peers. This technique, described by young musicians as one of ritual humiliation, clearly promotes conformity, not divergence or creativity.[3]

Many of the numerous critiques of conventional music education (e.g., Green 1988; Jorgensen 1997, 2003; Woodford 2005; Regelski and Gates 2009; Wright 2010a) thus apply to El Sistema. Jorgensen (2003, 46) could be describing Venezuelan núcleos when she writes: "Their prevailing ideas and practices have been designed by and for men. Their worldviews represent the old scientific and technocratic paradigm. Their musical and educational values are primarily those of the Western establishment. Their educational values and methods are primarily those of banking education that emphasizes the logical primacy of the subject matter and the active role of the teacher in transmitting knowledge to the receptive student. They are preoccupied with the traditional beliefs, values, and practices of the past." Nevertheless, there are two features of El Sistema that are distinctive and thus worth further discussion: the central place of the orchestra, and peer teaching.

PUTTING THE ORCHESTRA FIRST

The previous chapter raised multiple doubts about a program focused on orchestral practice, but there is another to consider. The program focuses on the public performance of a set repertoire of orchestral works, and, to echo O'Toole (1994), the music comes first. El Sistema's educational philosophy is work-centered (rather than child-centered) learning. A former núcleo director reported that putting on set works was prioritized over musical or technical training; learning was dictated by commands from Caracas about repertoire rather than by abilities or desires at the local level. Another former director recalled that when he started, he found children playing big Romantic symphonies without having taken the basic steps first. He wanted to start with Haydn, Mozart, Vivaldi, or Corelli, but his superiors demurred, insisting on Tchaikovsky and Mahler. The role of the young musicians was to stage these great works.

Musicians play the same pieces repeatedly rather than constantly exploring new repertoire. Youth orchestras have a set of well-worn pieces known informally as "Serie 33," which they know almost by heart and can bring out at a moment's notice; it is used primarily to impress visitors. A typical Sistema sight is rousing music (the last movement of Tchaikovsky's Fourth Symphony is a favorite) played extremely fast and largely from memory. The repetition required builds confidence and makes for a good spectacle. When an orchestra of 640 played from memory to impress visiting Americans, the L.A. Philharmonic's president, Deborah Borda, told them: "You have worked a miracle" (Wakin 2012a). Yet what is miraculous here? What does playing a symphony from memory show, other than (in Wakin's words) children being "rehearsed to within an inch of their lives"? As Jonathan Govias blogged on August 4, 2011: "Memorization of the repertoire sounds impressive, but without the flexibility or the capacity to change or correct, it's largely meaningless."

One of Venezuela's best-known orchestral musicians marveled that children learnt to play Tchaikovsky 4 faster than a professional orchestra when they could barely play their instruments or read music; don't ask them to play Tchaikovsky 3, though, he added. The risk of El Sistema's approach is that children's skills serve only for the specific task for which they have been trained. A number of musicians claimed that if you ask ordinary Sistema violinists to play on their own, many cannot play a simple scale in tune. Clearly, a violinist who can play scales beautifully but cannot play Mahler is not the answer, but should El Sistema not aspire to produce children who can play both scales *and* Mahler?

Christine Witkowski (2010) attended a National Children's Orchestra course: "I sat through their second round auditions that took place toward the end of the seminar and was shocked. The majority of the [French horn] students were 10 or under and could hardly play a single requested passage. But, only a few hours before, I had watched them play a full orchestra rehearsal at a high level. I turned to the horn professor after the auditions, baffled. 'It is incredible. There is something like magic that happens to them when they are playing in a section.'" There is indeed something undeniably magical about this tale of individuals surpassing themselves through collective endeavor, but the other side of the coin is a story of inflexibility: young musicians with a narrow range of skills that only function in a specific context. El Sistema's philosophy of putting the orchestra first conflicts with developing independent musicians—a key aim of contemporary music education (Morrison and Demorest 2012, 834). Is a child who can only play orchestral parts with the full orchestra really on their way to becoming a rounded, self-sufficient musician? If their skills are not transferable even within the narrow field of classical music, how much benefit will this training bring to their wider musical and social lives?

PEER TEACHING

Another distinctive feature of El Sistema is peer teaching—older students teaching the younger ones, even if they are only a step or two ahead. Much teaching in and around Veracruz was carried out by teachers in their late teens or early twenties. Peer teaching can bring notable benefits, such as counteracting hierarchical structures, providing accessible role models, and injecting freshness into learning (e.g., Green 2008). An experienced Sistema teacher argued, however, that positive spin on peer teaching covered up a lack of systematic teacher training (to which Abreu's remark about teachers' creativity and inventiveness elliptically points). Unprepared students, some still in their teens, are sent into difficult núcleos to teach difficult children, said a Caracas teacher; how could this be considered a good model for an educational project? A Veracruz student reported that a lot of teaching was carried out by young musicians who could barely play themselves; teachers came and went, in some cases lasting just a week or two, and she—like many others—had ended up with very patchy skills. El Sistema did not believe in teacher training, meaning that peer teachers often lacked pedagogical skills. A Sistema graduate who went on to study pedagogy at university was critical of the fact that the program bred advanced players rather than advanced teachers.[4]

"Teach as you were taught" is El Sistema's philosophy, one that emphasizes less inventiveness than the reproduction of established ways and encapsulates a conception of peer teaching that replicates the hierarchical dynamics of conventional teacher/pupil instruction or adult/child interaction. The rightness of this philosophy is treated as self-evident in El Sistema, yet it is flatly contradicted by progressive educational thinking as set out in "Action for Change in Music Education" (2009, xxxiii), which argues: "A musical culture is a living process, not a set of works or of given practices. It . . . cannot simply be passed on as a timeless, unchanging set of traditions. Music educators, thus, must not be satisfied simply to perpetuate any musical culture as a matter of received 'fact.'" This manifesto asks: "To what extent and how can we free music teachers from uncritically mimicking their own teachers' techniques and instead develop rational, reflective, and effective personal teaching approaches based on new evidence, rather than on tradition alone?" (2009, xxxv).

Teachout (2012, 686) critiques the perpetuation of teaching practices down generations as producing stasis rather than revolution, claiming that current practice in music education, including "the myopic attention to achieving large ensemble performance excellence," is "encased in a 'closed-loop' system." Jorgensen (2003, 111), too, argues: "where one's perspective is uncritical—for example, when instead of challenging or subverting a music practice, a teacher accepts it as it is and seeks to pass it on largely unchanged or unadulterated to one's students—one fails to take sufficient cognizance of practices that are flawed, oppressive, and in need of change, even transformation" (2003, 88). El Sistema's teachers have considerable freedom to create their own approach, but the program has little time for the critical engagement with teaching practice that Jorgensen demands.

It is clear that Jorgensen envisages the ideal teacher as a professional who has studied and then transcended conventional approaches, rather than a teenager who has not even embarked on this journey. She argues that music teachers need a broad, liberal education in the humanities and sciences to enable them to think critically, and that experienced, educated, reflective teachers are required for musical and social transformation to occur. Most Sistema peer teachers do not have such a broad preparation, however, and are still too young to have developed the critical skills to surpass conventional methods.

Jorgensen also underlines the importance of professional meetings, seminars, and symposia in promoting improvements in music education. Opportunities for group discussion of teaching practices are extremely rare in El Sistema, however; such symposia take place almost exclusively overseas. Diverse educational philosophies or practices are simply not a topic for discussion at most levels, so pedagogical innovation is the exception rather than the rule. As a music educator who observed members of the SBYO leading workshops in the United States remarked: "I was really unimpressed by the teaching by the Simon Bolivars. After all the talk on good teaching practices for over a week [at two North American Sistema symposia], I didn't really see anything new or promising modeled by the Bolivars."

TOCAR Y LUCHAR (PERO NO PENSAR)

The issues of peer teaching and teacher training encroach on a fundamental question: the place of critical reflection in music education. El Sistema's motto is *tocar y luchar*—to play and to struggle. The problem with El Sistema, in the eyes of its critics, is that *pensar*—to think—has no place. Abreu's pragmatic philosophy prefers action to reflection, and his program gives students little encouragement and few opportunities to stop and think. I found many students surprisingly unreflective about the social aspects of music making, considering their program is labeled "social action through music." Those social aspects are not necessarily absent, but there is little consciousness-raising taking place.

As Shieh (2012, 7) reports, El Sistema's avoidance of debate is so thorough that "[c]ertain understandings, like the possibility that classical music is not an inherent good (my question 'Why classical music?' surprised most teachers), may even be unintelligible to its actors." He continues: "More than a few teachers quote for me José Antonio Abreu, El Sistema's founder, as saying 'material poverty can be defeated by spiritual wealth'" (2012, 7). El Sistema's thinking goes on at the top; those further down often regurgitate it rather than grapple with issues themselves.

Orchestras do not generally prize independent thinking. As one Veracruz musician remarked, "the people who can really voice an opinion are the high post holders [i.e., section leaders]. I can speak up because I have a high post...now; but when I didn't have a high post, I had to keep my mouth shut, full stop." El Sistema appears to be an extreme case, however. "If you're a thinking person, you can't be in El Sistema," a senior orchestral administrator confided. Abreu makes a show of soliciting advice from foreign visitors, but he is famously intolerant of internal criticism, and this attitude percolates downward through the organization. El Sistema's ideal society rests on values of discipline, respect, following orders, and knowing your place.

Extraordinarily for a man who is universally recognized for his intellect and learning, Abreu has failed to support research or intellectual reflection in El Sistema, echoing reports of his stewardship of CONAC in the 1990s. Tunstall's (2012, 43) PR handler claimed: "Maestro Abreu is eager to encourage music students to pursue musicology and related academic disciplines as well as performance"; in the núcleos, however, evidence of this eagerness was desperately thin. In El Sistema's earliest days, things were different: David Ascanio talks of studying privately with Abreu and "learning everything about music: history, aesthetics, mythology. He would surround the music I was playing with books and art" (Tunstall 2012, 64). But massification has reduced this eclectic education to *tocar y luchar*.

If anything, El Sistema has exacerbated a trend in Latin American music education to grant minimal value to scholarly inquiry and reflection, including about music education itself, leading to a prevalence of untheorized music teaching (Estrada Rodríguez 2012). El Sistema's orchestras appeared largely divorced from the academic world. Although older students had the opportunity of studying at IUDEM, the number of places was tiny considering the size of the program. An SBYO member spoke of timetable clashes, inflexible attitudes, and substantial obstacles to missing rehearsals. She estimated that only around ten string players from the orchestra had graduated from IUDEM in the previous six or seven years. A TCYO violinist stopped taking classes at the Sistema conservatoire because they clashed with her orchestral rehearsals.

El Sistema's organizational arrangements confirm that a rounded and complete education is low priority, something that has been clear ever since Abreu attracted conservatoire students in the 1970s with the promise of wonderful opportunities without having to finish their studies.

There was no discussion of repertoire, composers, or contextual history in any rehearsals that I attended. The children did not need to know who wrote the music, or even how to read the music. All that mattered was that the notes should sound.

In Europe and the United States, however, educationalists have shown increasing interest in exploring the relationship between music and its social context. One of the seven pillars of "Action for Change in Music Education" (2009, xxxiii) is: "The social and cultural contexts of musical actions are integral to musical meaning and cannot be ignored or minimized in music education." It is thus dismissive of context-free instruction (2009, xxxiii): "Aesthetic theories, with their claims that musical meaning and value transcend time, place, context, and human purpose and usefulness, fail to account for the fullest range of meanings inherent in individual and collective musical actions." Similarly, Detels (2002, 13–14) criticizes "the systematic separation of the teaching of artistic practice and performance from the intellectual teaching of the history, theory, and philosophy of those practices," arguing that it leads to "a singular emphasis on practical issues of getting students 'ready' for contests, concerts, and exhibits, and a neglect of philosophical questions and historical information that would add intellectual meaning to the performances." El Sistema is thus swimming against the tide of progressive music education: classical music is held to be universal, notes are just to be played, and struggle is physical rather than intellectual.

Simon Rattle, a leading Sistema fan, told Borzacchini (2010, 243) a story about Brahms. A group of students asked the composer how they could play his music better. He replied: "Practice one hour less a day and instead read a good book." It is ironic to read this anecdote—the polar opposite of El Sistema's philosophy—in the program's official history.

The banishment of critical thinking gets short shrift from critical scholars of music education, many of whom are influenced by Freire's *Pedagogy of the Oppressed* (2005), first published in 1970. Freire emphasizes the importance of awakening critical consciousness: "learning to perceive social, political and economic contradictions, and to take action against the oppressive elements of reality" (2005, 35). Critical reflection is thus essential to meaningful action and liberation: "[t]o surmount the situation of oppression, people must first critically recognize its causes" (46).

A liberatory pedagogy requires critical dialogue with the oppressed; reflection cannot be pursued by social elites on behalf of the disadvantaged. "To substitute monologue, slogans, and communiqués for dialogue," argues Freire, "is to attempt to liberate the oppressed with the instruments of domestication.

Attempting to liberate the oppressed without their reflective participation in the act of liberation is to . . . transform them into masses which can be manipulated" (65). In talking to Sistema students, however, I became very aware that the program's rhetoric was indeed a monologue, expressed in communiqués for external consumption and Abreu's frequently repeated aphorisms; since it was not the outcome of dialogue, many students were uninterested or even skeptical about it. "That's what they say," or more cynically, "that's how they sell it," were common responses. In sum, Freire exhorted educators not to broadcast messages but to engage in horizontal, dialogic, critical conversations. Comparing Freire's radical vision with El Sistema—another child of the 1970s—is highly revealing.

There are numerous contemporary calls for "critically reflective musicianship" (Johnson 2009), "mindful music-making" (Langer, Russell, and Eisenkraft 2009), and continual rethinking in music education (e.g., "Action for Change in Music Education" 2009, xxxii). "Musical and instructional activity that is unreflective or critically uninformed lacks both substance and integrity. It is more about mimicry than true musical or educational engagement," states Bowman (2009, 3). "To execute one's duties unreflectively, unthinkingly, or mechanically—even if with considerable fluency, efficiency, and passion, and even in ways that are widely sanctioned by the profession at large—may well be antithetical to the basic aims and purposes of music education" (2009, 4). Woodford (2005, 87) and Jorgensen (2003, xii and 115) regard critical reflection in music education as necessary to promoting a healthy political culture and positive social change, and the latter suggests that cultivating social and political awareness ought to be a central part of music teacher training. Such perspectives present a clear challenge to El Sistema's philosophy of *tocar y luchar (pero no pensar)*.

EDUCATION VERSUS TRAINING

El Sistema emerged in the 1970s as an alternative to traditional Venezuelan conservatoire education, offering a shortcut to becoming a professional musician. In this it was very successful, but only by providing a much more limited training. The program provides little space for music theory, and even less for historical or musicological perspectives. Many students emerge as skilled orchestral players, but their practical skills often have little foundation in knowledge.

Some musicians thus insisted that El Sistema provided training rather than education. One suggested that El Sistema was creating not *músicos* (musicians) but *tocadores* (players); another described Sistema students as technicians rather than artists, and a founder spoke of the difference between *ensayar* (rehearsing) and *estudiar* (learning). These kinds of binary oppositions are revealing of widespread attitudes to El Sistema's pedagogical approach.

A scholarly echo of such emic discourses can be found in Weeks's (1996, 278) study of a youth orchestra rehearsal: "whereas lessons are a form of instruction that aims at the cultivation of generalized skills, *rehearsals* are directed toward achieving a concerted, specific *rendering* of specified texts for the anticipated critical occasion of the public concert.... In lessons, it appears that the students are deliberately given ample opportunity to practice their skills, with occasional guidance and the even rarer providing of the correct renditions of bits of the text.... However, in rehearsals, the tasks are to shape a specific realization of the conductor's interpretation of the music-at-hand." Weeks's analysis supports the education/training distinction and challenges one of El Sistema's core principles: that orchestral rehearsals and performances provide a rounded education.

FESNOJIV claims on its website to "contribute to the integral development of human beings," yet a member of the SBYO argued that núcleos were not so much schools for educating musicians as training centers where children learnt orchestral parts in preparation for possible promotion to the showpiece orchestras. One prominent musician stated: "Abreu created a huge façade, without worrying about providing young people with a rounded musical education." The director of a music institution likened El Sistema to a school that taught only thirteen letters of the alphabet. Many musicians and educators question whether such narrow training can lead to holistic personal development.

Even Sistema teachers sometimes harbored doubts about the notion that orchestral playing provided a solid education. Revealingly, some were reluctant to hand over their own children entirely to the project. A former SBYO member put his talented son in a non-Sistema conservatoire. Similarly, the son of two Sistema graduates was taking violin lessons in a non-Sistema school: they did not want him to start playing in the orchestra until he had several years of lessons behind him, as they had seen too many children pick up bad technical habits. The quality of El Sistema's program is thus questioned in Venezuela, including by some of its former senior figures. One founder claimed that if you pulled the average child out of a Sistema orchestra and put a sheet of music on a stand for them to sight-read, they would be stumped. He saw the SBYO as the glittering tip of an iceberg of mediocrity. Sistema supporters praise its ability to excel both musically and socially, but some critics suggest that neither aspect functions properly, since it fails to foster either rounded musicians or rounded human beings.

El Sistema has come to dwarf Venezuela's older conservatoire system, but some musicians believe that the latter, though much maligned and mistreated, still provides a more thorough music education. The conservatoires offer a traditional education and, as such, are susceptible to the critiques of classical music schooling found in innumerable scholarly studies. One could certainly argue that music education in Venezuela was ripe for transformation in the 1970s—but also that El Sistema was a step in the wrong direction. The conservatoires were supposed to follow the Ministry of Education's 1964 music education curriculum, which included instrumental and vocal lessons, solfège and music theory, complementary harmony, music history, aesthetics, and composition (Pedroza n.d.). El Sistema narrowed down the curriculum markedly, when what was needed was arguably *more* breadth, flexibility, and critical thinking, not less.

I interviewed three former state-level Sistema directors, all of whom had distinctly equivocal views about the program. One was shocked at the paucity of music theory and history being taught when he took over. He attempted to make orchestral rehearsals more informative, encouraging reflection on repertoire as well as practice, but his initiatives were viewed askance by his superiors. Also, he was unimpressed by the conservativeness of El Sistema's repertoire and took a more experimental approach, using his own and others' arrangements. He felt that the program would have been stronger if more directors had been composers or musicologists, rather than performers handpicked from the orchestral ranks by Abreu. His Sistema career was short-lived.

The second made similar observations: when he took up the post, the students knew only about playing instruments, and had little knowledge of history or theory. He had tried to persuade Caracas to provide professional teachers, but they had refused. He left El Sistema feeling that the music education it offered was inferior to that of a traditional conservatoire.

The third was critical of the abilities of satellite núcleo directors, and like the others, he described El Sistema's training as intellectually impoverished. He taught at the local university and claimed that students making the transition from El Sistema often arrived with big gaps in their musical knowledge, meaning that the first part of their degree was spent covering the basics. Many Sistema students struggled with anything beyond playing a limited repertoire of tutti orchestral parts.

The education/training dichotomy points to a lack of aspiration beneath El Sistema's utopian rhetoric. Abreu's project marginalizes many activities that were crucial to his own musical education, such as creating music and thinking, reading, and talking about it. It has the children onsite for twenty or more hours a week; it could aspire to educating them, rather than simply training them how to play great orchestral works.

MUSIC EDUCATION, CRITICAL REFLECTION, AND SOCIAL JUSTICE

Critical reflection is a central pillar of social inclusion and social justice (Wright 2010b; Spruce 2013). Pursuing social justice through music education requires considerable thought, effort, and debate. As Allsup and Shieh (2012, 49) argue, social justice music educators are made, not born: "Critical self-reflection takes time and emotional investment." This raises the question of what, precisely, is taking place in El Sistema, and whether its philosophy of *tocar y luchar* (*pero no pensar*) should be considered a positive model for social action through music.

In 2007 *Music Education Research* produced a special edition on "Music education, equity, and social justice," and these essays reveal a gulf between El Sistema and prevailing notions of equity and social justice. Younker and Hickey (2007, 218) describe a visit to a school in Budapest that sounds much like a Venezuelan núcleo: "the children sang beautifully, with energy, conviction, and pure tone quality. Their bodies were engaged as they moved, reflecting pulse, rhythm, and phrasing. Their faces were alive as they sang for their music teacher and us." Yet Younker had nagging doubts. "I was curious, however, about what they were thinking musically. Did they know when their intonation faltered and how to fix it without direction? Did they understand why the songs they sang were chosen? Did they examine the text of the songs and discuss the meaning and inferences? Did the experiences contribute to their growth as musical thinkers?" She goes on: "Musicianship is defined [here] by how well students can imitate, acquire skills, and apply them in future settings for future performances.... Might musicianship also be defined by application that involves critical reflection on musical decisions made, or by the utilization of imagination and divergent thinking as possibilities are investigated and evaluated?" These authors are concerned by classrooms in which standards are high, but so are levels of control and discipline. They see a gap between such a traditional, performance-centered music education and social justice, which arises from "a participatory, democratic community, in which opportunities for opinions, informed decisions and justification are understood and accepted at the tacit level" (2007, 225).

Writing about U.S. school music education, Richardson (2007, 205) argues: "The master/apprentice and conductor/ensemble models institutionalized in our profession are *not* democratic; the typical teacher/student exchanges at the core of our studio lessons, rehearsals and music classrooms are *not* models of shared musical decision-making power." Consequently, as Woodford (2005, 84) writes, civility cannot be learned just through conventional music instruction: "Rather, it must be inculcated and developed in children. They require instruction and practice in learning how to behave appropriately." He draws a distinction between "music as a drug to which mere exposure or immersion is supposed to make children happier and more civilized (albeit rendered passive)" and "music classes as occasions for the development of musical, intellectual, and moral character" (2005, 85). Yet, as Richardson (2007, 210) laments, "the big issues of democracy, social justice, and social consciousness typically have no place in our foundations or music methods syllabi." Critical music education scholarship thus challenges the ancient idea (revived by El Sistema) that musical participation alone deals with these questions, through mysterious, implicit processes.

Reimer (2007) argues that projects based on performing in large ensembles and sidelining popular music have little to offer from the perspective of morality or social justice. He suggests that popular music is richly saturated with moral issues, and that if it is marginalized, "our attention to music's social justice dimension can only be meager at best, and artificial at worst" (2007, 201). This collection of essays thus raises awkward questions for El Sistema.

Elsewhere, Laurence (2008) focuses on the issue of music and empathy. Noting that music has more often been used in the exercise of power, she holds up the orchestra as *the opposite pole of empathy*: "Creating empathic relationships is hardly the purpose in such contexts; music is doing other work" (2008, 23). She asks: "what if we take another kind of musicking? A musicking based, for example, upon cooperation, democratic participation, mutual, respectful listening, and care for each other's differing musical values" (23–24). Such music making—which sounds more like chamber music, jazz, or traditional music—would be a step toward a "non-hierarchical, other-enhancing empathic relationship" (24).

Laurence (2010, 246–47) also critiques top-down institutional music education as implicated in the "selection, stratification and arguably the objectification of children." Drawing on Christopher Small, she argues that music making is not an inherently virtuous activity: "We can *music* according to, and making, ideal relationships which promote inclusion and peace, but equally in a way which celebrates relationships of hierarchy, power and alienation" (248)—a point that would not be lost on many classical music students and orchestral musicians. For Laurence, encouraging children to participate in decisions about their learning promotes empathy. Echoing O'Toole (1994), she suggests that giving children a voice is very different from giving them a part to play.

Laurence is careful to contrast empathy with Edith Stein's "emotional contagion," which is linked with music's dark political history. She describes a concert of children performing their *own* works as educating, not emotionally overwhelming, the audience. If we recall Sistema spokesperson Bolivia Bottome's words—"we do a lot of large showcase demonstrations to fundraise. We sit people down and make them listen to a huge orchestra of children playing Mahler 2 and then they fund us"—we may understand that key performances in El Sistema are intended to elicit something from listeners (emotions, tears, money) more than edify them. Performances are designed (through repertoire, choreography, dress, and size) to be emotionally contagious rather than promote empathy, and are thus *instrumental*—children are being used for a larger purpose, rather than using performance for their own ends.

A key issue for both El Sistema and scholars interested in social justice is social inclusion, yet Wright (2010b, 267) argues that "issues of inclusion in music education are more complex than they might first appear." Exclusion takes cultural as well as social form—the marginalization of cultural images to which children are already attached. Wright defines genuine inclusion as: "The chance to see one's own cultural image reflected as valued in the school mirror, and to perceive one's voice as heard in the school acoustic.... The right to remain musically and culturally autonomous—not to be absorbed or have to conform to the dominant culture" (277). These are challenging words for a project that has traditionally demanded obedience to the conductor and the orchestral canon. Over the course of El Sistema's history, most long-term participants have had to adapt themselves to the norms of European classical performance; few whose skills lie primarily in other musical areas have advanced far in the program. Wright raises significant doubts over the applicability of the word "inclusive" to this scenario.

Wider literature on general education and social justice is equally revealing. Bell (1997, 10) critiques the imposition of a supposedly universal culture—that of the dominant group, and invariably of European origin. Hardiman and Jackson (1997, 20) identify social oppression in hierarchical educational contexts, and their discussion of agents and targets of oppression resonates with orchestras: target groups have "their choices and movement restricted and limited; are seen and treated as expendable and replaceable, without an individual identity apart from the group; and are compartmentalized into narrowly defined roles." For Adams (1997, 39), "[t]he democratic classroom becomes, in effect, a laboratory of democratic social practice," pointing up the illogicality of assuming that social justice could emerge from a non-democratic organization like a conventional symphony orchestra.

In sum, El Sistema's ideology and practices lie far from much recent research on music education, equity, and social justice. Critical thinkers are pushing music educators to engage ever more directly with urgent social and political issues, and thus with broader questions of artistic citizenship and social justice (e.g., Elliott 2012; Woodford 2014). El Sistema appears more interested in its world tours and new flagship buildings. Musical learning within El Sistema usually involves autocratic social models, hierarchical relationships, and the transmission of fixed knowledge—all elements that scholars of social justice have criticized. El Sistema's watchword is discipline, which implies the imposition of authority; music education experts increasingly call for the development of critical consciousness, a first step toward the challenging of authority (Spruce 2013). El Sistema argues that learning to play orchestral music will make you a better person; critical educational theory suggests that focusing on orchestral music may curtail genuine education and lead to social oppression rather than justice. Whichever view is correct, there is an important debate to be had, one that the Sistema sphere has largely avoided.

THE PROVISION AND STATUS OF TEACHING

One sphere in which social justice is sometimes conspicuously lacking is that of music teaching. Hourly teaching in satellite núcleos is poorly remunerated, low-status employment—the bottom of the Sistema ladder. This may partly explain why so much is done by students rather than experienced teachers. In Veracruz, it often entailed long bus journeys and antisocial hours. Many therefore regarded it as unattractive work and accorded it a low priority. I met a number of older students who taught in outlying núcleos, and while some were motivated and dedicated, many were less than keen on working in these schools. Such teachers quickly lost interest, leading to high turnover, frequent absences, and a lack of continuity. The first two times I tried to observe the núcleo at Santa Ana, a town near Veracruz, my visit was canceled at the last minute because no teachers turned up for work. On visits to two other núcleos, I arrived to find the coordinators panicking because no teachers had appeared.

One núcleo director admitted that it was difficult to schedule times for teachers to go to the núcleo, since many were university students with other commitments. The day I visited, only one of four teachers turned up on time; another arrived very late, and the other two never appeared. One, the cello teacher, had not been for weeks. As we were talking, a cello pupil wandered in and asked what was going on. The director replied honestly that the teacher had not come, she did not know why, and perhaps they would find a new teacher. "I'll never make any progress this way!" replied the pupil, wandering out again. The director acknowledged that irregular attendance by teachers had a dampening effect on the numbers and motivation of students.

At another núcleo, the same thing was occurring: work was progressing slowly because the teaching supply was irregular. In this case, teachers were reluctant to work at the núcleo because it was in a dangerous zone. On its launch, it was heralded as a shining example of El Sistema's commitment to the poor, but it went through periods of up to six months without teachers because they insisted on going by taxi for safety reasons, and there was no money available.

El Sistema's publicity makes much of the self-renewing process of feeding students back as teachers, but on the ground matters are more problematic, with gaps and shortages widespread. Numerous students recounted that their formative years had been marred by constant changes and absences of teachers. In Caracas, some teachers in the least prestigious núcleos are in fact students at the traditional conservatoires, much maligned though they may be by Abreu.

For all the claims that El Sistema is a social project first and foremost, the social end of the continuum—núcleo teaching—is low-paid, low-status, and often entrusted to the least experienced, while the project's stars work at the musical end of the spectrum, their focus being the showpiece orchestras. In Veracruz, front-line teaching was systemically neglected as older students were told to prioritize their orchestral commitments. The percussionist in *The Promise of Music* goes occasionally to teach at Los Chorros núcleo, but admits that he does not have much time because of his SBYO duties. He is prevented from doing social work by his musical commitments, reproducing the problems of irregular tuition that he suffered as a child.

One of the most persistent complaints concerned the treatment of teaching staff. Many teachers were paid by the hour, making for a frugal and uncertain existence. Patricia, a núcleo teacher, claimed that El Sistema's foundations were rotten because there was a lot of dissatisfaction among rank-and-file teachers. The pay was poor and often arrived late or not at all (as for many orchestral musicians). She had spent the previous three months trying to get her final payment for teaching at her old núcleo, without success. One teacher at Veracruz had not been paid for a year and was subsisting on a university grant.

The online forum described in the Introduction elicited numerous accusations of autocratic management, chaotic administration, and rude or discriminatory treatment by central administrators in Caracas. It also appeared that El Sistema's workers had few rights: there were complaints that FESNOJIV refused to pay national holidays, as stipulated under law, or social security for its hourly-paid staff, in contravention of the Venezuelan constitution. Several respondents called for a thorough audit in order to root out the employment abuses, nepotism, and corruption they claimed were rife. There was a notable level of animosity toward the project's leaders, who were portrayed as living regally off the sweat of downtrodden workers. Accounts of an institution where front-line workers were the lowest priority recalled accusations that swirled around Abreu's CONAC in the early 1990s.

Complaints about pay surfaced again in February and March 2013, when a group of provincial teachers made several public petitions for a raise on the pro-Sistema Facebook page "Yo soy 100% FESNOJIV." Arguing that salaries had been severely devalued by rampant inflation, they proclaimed: "we cannot go on like this, we demand to be listened to." They stated that "the top orchestras of El Sistema get a pay rise, but the teachers in the provinces were ignored last year," underlining that perceptions of unequal distribution of resources are a source of resentment. Numerous supportive comments indicated that the problems of poor pay, morale, and working conditions were felt across the country. One teacher stated that his pay barely covered his transport costs; like many others, he was working in "precarious conditions" as he received no medical insurance or social security.

In April 2013, an open letter to El Sistema's executive director, Eduardo Méndez, appeared on the site. Teachers proclaimed "we can no longer live on the same salary" and "what we are paid is totally unjust." They complained that there was money for the showcase orchestras and their foreign tours, but not for ordinary teachers (coincidentally, another post on the same day was headed "Dudamel and the Simón Bolívar provoke euphoria in São Paulo"). Again, responses followed, alleging "miserable" pay, lack of insurance and travel allowances, extreme inequalities within the program, shortages and "deplorable" conditions in núcleos, and irregularities in the distribution of funds. One student wrote that the low pay and lack of recognition were dissuading him from becoming a teacher himself.

An argument broke out between the provincial teachers and members of the SBYO, with the former complaining of discrimination and the latter accusing them of jealousy. One teacher wrote: "while the Bolívar [musicians] live like kings, the teachers who trained them live in misery." Another commented: "I admit that YES I'M JEALOUS...but not of the salary...I'm jealous that my pupils don't have facilities like the Center for Social Action and the boys have to use toilets that don't have doors...I'm jealous that in my núcleo we've never in 38 years had a piano like the ones in almost every room in the Center for Social Action...I'm extremely jealous when one of my pupils has to make a big sacrifice to buy a slice of fried banana in the rehearsal break (because he can't afford more) and I remember the buffets that the SBYO enjoys in the breaks of every rehearsal...." This exchange, like many others, undermined the idealization of El Sistema as "one big family" in which the success of the few is celebrated by the many.

In June, the Internet group called for a nationwide strike by Sistema teachers, claiming to be receiving private messages of support from across Venezuela. Among the demands were social security and the creation of a union "to protect Fundamusical's working class." One respondent complained that Dudamel and the SBYO were "putting on a front to the world that everything is wonderful here in El Sistema"; the reality was one of sacrifices, and pay "so miserable that it can't be called a salary." He went on: "Only those who travel overseas are paid well and they make it look like this is the land of Cinderella." Just days later, the page's administrators vanished from the site for good, leading to speculation that their access had been revoked.

Interviews and Internet debates suggest that El Sistema reproduces many long-standing problems of music education and classical music culture rather than challenging and transforming them. FESNOJIV's claim that its staff consists of "multidisciplinary teams that are highly motivated and identified with the institution" is far from reality on several counts. El Sistema has produced a large tier of casualized musical labor, echoing a problematic trend of contemporary capitalism, and while it claims to alleviate poverty and promote social justice, many of its own employees suffer economic hardship, lack basic workers' rights, and complain vociferously about the injustice of their situation.

VISITING A CARACAS NÚCLEO

One day I visited an ordinary núcleo in Caracas. The school's facilities were in poor condition, and visiting the CASM the following day, I was struck by the gulf between the project's shop window and its everyday realities. Many musicians in the provinces imagined that life was easier in the capital, but this school struggled to find local teachers and had to bring some in from outside the city for bimonthly visits. Instruments came in slowly after the núcleo's foundation and it was nearly two years before they had a full set; securing the last few from FESNOJIV had required sustained pressure.

The staff had done some publicity in the community but relied mainly on children and their parents taking the initiative to go to the núcleo. The teachers were keen to reach out to all children, but the intake was essentially self-selecting; the school simply did not have the personnel or resources to do much recruitment outside its walls. Some of the children came from deprived homes, but those who suffered more acute domestic problems often dropped out. They needed a parent or guardian to come in and sign for their instrument, which was a challenge for the most neglected children. The staff seemed concerned about the dropouts, but they could not do very much beyond encouraging the children to continue. An understaffed voluntary program was not in a position to rescue the neediest in the community in a consistent manner. The director was troubled by a certain sense of impotence with regard to social action, recalling students who had left despite his best efforts. He portrayed the núcleo as fighting a losing battle against the wider social context in which the children lived. Unsurprisingly, this kind of view does not make it into documentaries.

The staff at the núcleo seemed dynamic and clearly cared about the children. They had to work hard: FESNOJIV would not give them any support staff, so the director doubled as cleaner and instrument-mover. A bright, committed, and inspirational figure, he talked about correcting the mistakes of the past and improving El Sistema's methods. He had instituted some basic teaching of music history. He described playing through a piece with the orchestra, then stopping and talking to the children about its composer, context, and meaning, and when they played it again it was transformed. "It's not just about playing, playing, playing," he said. Such views are unorthodox in El Sistema and a departure from his own training in the program. His orchestra was being supplemented by children from another núcleo that was homeless at the time, and one of the visiting students told him, "I'm understanding music for the first time."

Nevertheless, the sectional rehearsals that I watched, led by other teachers, were less inspiring. Children sat in rows, playing in unison, faces fixed in concentration as they stared at the music and the teacher shouted "ONE, two, three, four." It was hardly a model of creativity or critically reflective musicianship, and a disjunction with the director's words was apparent. He was caught between larger forces: a minimalist approach from FESNOJIV, which left the núcleo struggling with insufficient resources and inadequate facilities, unable to reach out properly into the most disadvantaged parts of the community, and the somewhat leaden pedagogy that is commonplace in the program.

Patricia was a low-paid hourly teacher at a Caracas núcleo. It was located in a dangerous zone, so few teachers wanted to work there. No one pays attention to this núcleo, she said; Dudamel and foreign guests are steered well clear. The upside was a fair degree of freedom to teach what and when she wanted. Nevertheless, there were certain Sistema priorities that were fixed: one was the need to persuade most children to learn the violin, since orchestras need mainly violins; the other was the requirement to prepare displays. Strategy was thus driven ᴜy the needs of the orchestra and the program rather than the children.

Patricia filled in for the musical literacy teacher for a while and was surprised to find that the children had almost no reading skills. There were children who had been in the núcleo for five years who could not read music. She found it hard to persuade the children to put their instruments down even briefly to learn some literacy skills. She would ask them: "So what are you going to do the day that you don't have someone here to teach you how the music goes?" Learning by ear would be fine with traditional music, she said, but they were in a classical orchestral training program and encouraged to have professional aspirations.

As an illustration, she told me about an eighteen-year-old oboist in the núcleo who had been playing for five or six years and announced one day that he was aiming to join the TCYO. She offered to help him with the audition pieces, but was shocked to find that while he played a fair approximation to the music, his technique was very poor and he was not reading but rather playing by ear. She found it tragic that El Sistema encouraged this kind of delusion, fueling students' ambitions while failing to provide them with elementary tools. She broke the news that he needed to go back to square one. The student joined the conservatoire anyway, but his new teacher scolded him for every mistake, exposed him to public humiliation in group-learning situations, and eventually suspended him because he could not read music.

Patricia described a chaotic, overwhelming teaching environment at her núcleo. Many of the instruments were in poor shape or broken; every day there would be new children arriving who did not know anything, obliging her to go back to the beginning repeatedly; and she was in charge of eighty children, making groups too large to manage. Some of the children had pronounced learning difficulties and she felt they needed specialized attention and equipment. As an untrained music student, she simply was not equipped for this kind of challenge. The final straw, though, was the money. She would have loved to carry on teaching at the núcleo, where the children really needed her, but coming from a family of modest means, she could not afford to; the low pay made it unsustainable. She now worked in a private music school.

Patricia painted a picture of a núcleo that could not have been further away from Montalbán in terms of facilities, staffing, and attitudes, even though it was located close by. She dismissed the oft-cited story of Sistema teachers chasing up missing children at home (e.g., Booth 2008, 6). Nonsense, said Patricia: there are too many children, too many problems, and not enough staff, and the overworked and underpaid teachers have their own issues to worry about. It is hard enough to find teachers willing to do poorly paid and demanding work in dangerous places like this, she said, let alone go out on their own into the surrounding backstreets and alleys in their spare time.

OUTSIDERS INSIDE EL SISTEMA

I interviewed three young foreign musicians who had worked in different núcleos in El Sistema and whose views provided a valuable counterpoint to my own and those of my Venezuelan interlocutors. They spoke good Spanish, had joined up independently and chosen their own destinations, and had worked or played as ordinary members of the program. In contrast, many publicly circulating reports by foreigners are written by special guests of the program, some with limited Spanish, whose exposure to any individual núcleo is usually limited to days or weeks rather than the months that my interviewees spent in situ.

All three singled out orchestral rehearsals for criticism. Gustav had traveled halfway round the world to participate in the "Venezuelan musical miracle," but quit after several months in a Sistema orchestra. Rehearsals centered on constant repetition, omitted discussion of repertoire, and therefore lacked a clear sense of direction; as a result, the rate of improvement was slow, despite much longer rehearsals than he was used to back home, and the orchestra was shown up if it strayed from familiar territory. Alex described full rehearsals in his núcleo: "they would just play through and it would be terrible, and they would play through again and it would be terrible, and there was no close work. . . . Musically, it would just go nowhere—every rehearsal there would be no progress."

In the núcleo where Julia taught, the children's orchestra learnt by pure drilling. She observed a seminario, which consisted of three days of playing scales ten hours a day, yet without even teaching the children how scales worked in theory. The pace of learning was slow, as students were stretched beyond their limits technically yet many had little idea what was going on in the music or why they were playing it. She saw children's playing deteriorate as technique and reading were sacrificed to produce fast but superficial results.

Julia had originally been inspired by El Sistema's openness to all, but she soon came to realize that the weak were often weeded out. She also noticed that most children in the núcleo were middle class; poorer children lived further away and some could not afford to take the bus in every day. Alex concurred, estimating the proportion of students from impoverished circumstances in his núcleo at 10 percent. Despite this social makeup, Julia believed that some students were there mainly for the scholarship money.

Alex liked the daily interaction with the children at the núcleo where he taught, but, like Gustav, he decided to leave halfway through his planned stint: "I'm not enjoying it anymore. It's unbelievably disorganized and inefficient compared to my experiences of music schools back home. There is a lot of time wasting and laziness." His núcleo was "chaotic, to say the least." It never settled on a fixed timetable, and teachers' attendance was also patchy. "Management was terrible," leading to internal divisions among staff. Some employees were "really bitter about El Sistema," and grudges and accusations of favoritism were rife. "That was why I couldn't do it any more—it was too disorganized, and there was a lot of tension." Problems became so bad that the núcleo sometimes shut down altogether. Staff came and went without explanation. "One of the mottos of El Sistema is you'll never be sacked from El Sistema, you'll only be transferred."

Neither he nor many of his fellow teachers were paid during the months that he spent at the núcleo, even though they were working six or seven days a week. They had no contracts or formal employment rights. They had to apply to be paid—a difficult, opaque process in which many were unsuccessful. Staff turnover was unsurprisingly high.

There was an overriding emphasis on producing results. When it came to learning music, "there was a lot of pressure to get it done for the concert." Teachers also deliberately generated competition among the children: "The kids were encouraged to be like 'I'm going to beat you, I'm going to beat you.'" Yet as Alex asked rhetorically, "results for whom?" He was skeptical about the regular displays: "In order to keep the funding going, you have to keep the people who are paying you happy—it's logical, but it's really cynical."

There was no teacher training and discussion of teaching methods was almost discouraged, so "there's not that much fine musicianship going on in terms of teaching." One teacher received an official complaint for being too aggressive with the children. "She would go crazy, because she was a dramatic character, like a drama queen—it was in her nature—but I don't know if that would be allowed to happen in my country, for example, like screaming at your kids in every rehearsal." The teacher's defense was that as long as the children performed well, she should be allowed to do what she wanted. The núcleo's director "had all the rhetoric, he knows what to say...all the stuff you hear, like 'we're a community,' all that stuff, but that never actually happens...you can say that as much as you want, but if it's not applied, if it's not put into practice, then it's redundant."

Alex acknowledged that, despite all the problems, the children enjoyed being in the núcleo. Nevertheless, he qualified this statement: "when they're older and they look back they'll probably be a bit more skeptical about it." He was unconvinced by the claim that El Sistema was a social program, yet on a musical level, he regarded the standard as being lower than in his home country. With regard to attempts to translate El Sistema overseas, he stated: "I could never see it working in the *same* way El Sistema does, but it could work in a *better* way than El Sistema does."

CONCLUSION

Sean Gregory (2013), director of creative learning at London's Barbican Centre, enthused about a recent visit by Gustavo Dudamel, whom he saw as symbolizing a revolution in music education. At one pole he placed the U.S. education system, criticized for prioritizing repetition and rote learning; at the other, El Sistema. Gregory insisted that young people should be provided with opportunities

> "not just to learn the great works of the past but also to experiment and progress their musical skills across a wide range of styles and genres....In an era where our own education system seems to be increasingly focusing on classical work and rote learning, it is essential that culture gives young people opportunities to broaden their horizons and experiment with creativity, collaboration and composition....To do this we need to challenge ourselves constantly to ensure music and cultural education systems reflect the growing global nature of the arts.... We also need to recognize that artists and musicians are increasingly engaging with the worlds of digital technology and that boundaries between art forms are blurring."

He concludes: "it's essential that we not only give young people the ability to play the music of the past but also equip them with the skills to create the music of the future."

Ironically, El Sistema embodies the opposite of Gregory's vision, and has historically marginalized the skills and perspectives that he holds up as fundamental to creating the music of the future. El Sistema is being lauded around the world as a major new model for music education, yet in many ways it constitutes a step backward, a move away from the liberal tendencies in music education that have been taking root since the 1970s toward older educational practices. El Sistema is, in essence, a massification of old-fashioned "drills and skills" classical music education, and with little teacher training or encouragement to think deeply and innovatively, the kinds of progressive ideas and pedagogies proposed in recent decades by music education researchers and practitioners in the Global North have made little impact, and local counterparts have not been widely developed. This conservatism may be a positive feature for some, but those of more progressive tendencies who are interested in questions of social justice and arts education—and who, like Gregory, are attracted to El Sistema because of its promise of a revolution in artistic learning—may not be so thrilled.

Jorgensen (2003, 72) writes that over recent decades, "curricular thinkers have grappled with how to transform the learning process from a linear, static, subject-driven, goal-oriented, industrial model to a multifaceted, organic, experiential, process-oriented, postindustrial entity." Not in El Sistema. Such thinkers "have de-centered subject matter and re-centered the individual at the heart of the school." Again, not in El Sistema. While there has been a shift toward student-centered learning in education theory, which has critiqued the traditional teacher-student relationship as fostering monologue over dialogue, hierarchy over egalitarianism, passivity over independence, and convergent thinking over creativity, El Sistema is both teacher-centered and work-centered. The orchestral canon is the core of the Venezuelan program, and most individuals are treated as replaceable. One interviewee summed up El Sistema's pedagogy as telling students: "you're useless—and there's a better one coming through behind you."

The work of critical scholars of music education thus poses numerous challenges to the ideology and practices of El Sistema. Hebert believes that future historians will judge that "many leaders of our field supported an extraordinarily misguided agenda in diametric opposition to the scholarly discourse of music education." Given the scholarly critiques of large performance ensembles, high-level training of classical performers, and the lack of critical reflection, democracy, and pluralism in conventional music education, these words may have particular salience in the case of El Sistema.

Borzacchini (2010, 7, 90) hails Abreu as the "inventor of a new model of musical pedagogy" that leads to forming "happy, rounded people," but there are good reasons to question whether *tocar y luchar* warrants such a billing. Perhaps more illuminating is her comment that El Sistema's pedagogy "has achieved recognition from the complex industry and the international music business" (2010, 140), which has certainly benefited from this educational model. Venezuelan students, however, have missed out on a rounded music education that El Sistema, with its resources, could have provided if it had engaged with contemporary ideas. In the words of Jorgensen (2003, xii), "the narrow education advocated by those interested only in basal skills and the pursuit of purely instrumental ends shortchanges students by denying them a liberal education—a rich, holistic, balanced, intellectual, physical, emotional, spiritual, and cultural development that ought to be their birthright."

PART THREE

Social Education

CHAPTER 7
Social Action Through Music

When you train musicians you train better citizens.
　　　　　　　　　　　　　　　　　—José Antonio Abreu

Music instruction alone, without lessons in compassion, humility, self-restraint, and mutual respect...is no more likely to contribute to the development of good citizenship and humane values in children than is mere exposure to music likely to make them smarter.

　　　　—Paul G. Woodford, *Democracy and Music Education*

According to FESNOJIV's mission statement, the organization is "a social project." As a spokesman stated, "our first goal is not to create professional musicians. Our goal is to rescue the children."[1] Foreign supporters have adopted the idea that El Sistema is a social project first and musical project second (e.g., Booth 2008, 2). Nevertheless, such claims need to be scrutinized.

The democratization of high arts in the developed world has been driven in large part by the need to attract subsidies from government and business (Martorella 1983, 284–86). As it became harder to justify funding on cultural grounds alone, assertions were increasingly made that the arts served the community, alleviating social problems. In Venezuela, El Sistema would never have received so much support from the Chávez government and international institutions without embracing social goals. Such rhetoric may or may not reflect realities, but it is usually conceived instrumentally. Critical examination of the discourse and realities of social action through music is thus essential. This chapter is driven by two core questions: Was El Sistema conceived as a social project in 1975? And does it actually prioritize social action over musical goals today? It concludes with a broader discussion of classical music and social action.

Since I was not given access to FESNOJIV's archives, I was unable to carry out documentary research on the origins of the project's social discourse. Nevertheless, I spoke to a number of older musicians, including members of the original National Youth Orchestra, and their message was unanimous: in the early days, there was no talk of the social. For them, El Sistema started as and has always been a musical project, but social and political changes subsequently led to a shift in rhetoric.

Archival research might contradict musicians' memories. However, one piece of evidence that is publicly available, El Sistema's foundation document, provides modest support for their views.[2] The program's aim is defined narrowly as "the training of the country's human resources in the area of music." Its funding is justified by the statement "that the Venezuelan National Youth Orchestra has been one of the most important initiatives aimed at securing a significant future for Venezuelan musical youth." According to Article 1 of the foundation's constitution, "its objective will be to contribute to the training of human resources and the financing, direction, and evaluation of the process of training human resources that may be required in order to carry out the programs and activities developed by the Venezuelan National Youth Orchestra." El Sistema was thus born as a program to provide Venezuela with more young musicians and to offer them more and better opportunities—laudable aims, but there is nothing at the outset about social objectives.

"From the very beginning, the Sistema has been dedicated to realizing the simple but radical idea of its founder—that music can save lives, can rescue children, and can in fact be a potent vehicle for social reform and the fight against the perils of childhood poverty," writes Tunstall (2012, x). Yet this "unequivocal" social dimension makes no appearance in El Sistema's constitution. Similarly, Deutsche Grammophon's publicity about the project's origins claims: "It is all the vision of one man. José Antonio Abreu, qualified economist, organist and politician, resolved to do something to change social conditions in his country 30 years ago." This portrait of the heroic genius determined to change single-handedly his country's destiny has been highly successful in selling El Sistema internationally and garnering prizes for its leader, but its foundation in fact is questionable. These heroic scripts appear to have been written retrospectively.

On October 15, 1996, El Sistema's constitution was reformed.[3] The two most interesting aspects of the resulting document concern what does *not* appear in it. First, as previously mentioned, Abreu does not appear. Paradoxically, the founding director of FESNOJIV left no legal trace on its foundation. Second, there is no sign of a shift toward the social. El Sistema continues to have as its formal objective: "the training of human resources...that may be required in order to carry out the programs and activities developed by the orchestras"—in other words, meeting musical needs.

A second important change to the constitution occurred on March 1, 2011, with the change of FESNOJIV's name to Fundación Musical Simón Bolívar and its transfer to the Office of the President.[4] However, there is a tiny alteration in the wording about El Sistema, which had originally been "aimed at securing a significant future for Venezuelan musical youth." In 2011 two words—"Venezuelan musical"—are omitted, and the project is now described as "aimed at securing a significant future for children and young people." This removal of the word "musical" is clearly not accidental, for it gives the project description a more socially oriented ring. This change appears in 2011 but not 1996; a tiny piece of evidence, perhaps, but one that points to a shift in priorities between the late 1990s and 2011—as my interviewees suggested, during the Chávez period.

Three former state-level Sistema directors reported that they heard no talk of social action in the 1980s and much of the 1990s. There were no efforts to take the orchestra out to particular social groups; they worked with the students who presented themselves at the núcleo and aimed simply to train orchestral musicians. They, like almost all the older musicians I spoke to, placed the appearance of the social discourse as coinciding with the election of Chávez in 1998, although one claimed that Abreu had been much cannier than this: he suggested that Abreu had read events such as the Caracazo uprising (1989) and Chávez's failed coup (1992) as signs that social change was in the air, and had understood before Chávez came to power that the future of the project lay in stressing its social angle. In either case, these three senior informants claimed that El Sistema had taken a (largely discursive) social turn as a reaction to political changes in the 1990s.

A former top-level Sistema figure claimed that the idea of social action through music derived from a tour to Brazil in the mid-1990s, when Abreu and the orchestra visited a new foundation called "Ação Social Pela Música." (According to the Brazilian organization, the phrase was created and registered by its founder, David Machado, in 1994.) Abreu allegedly borrowed this name, which captured the populist direction in which the project was moving at that time. This informant claimed that Abreu was always looking for money and quickly realized that politicians were only interested in the political benefits they accrued by supporting music. "There's nothing that a populist politician likes more than the word 'social,'" he said.

Gloria Carnevali, the former cultural attaché at the Venezuelan Embassy in London, concurred that the social shift occurred in the 1990s. She contrasted the original program to its recent offshoot in Scotland: "El Sistema did not begin like Raploch. It was middle-class kids who went to music schools and had access to teachers privately."[5] Hollinger's (2006) informants, too, portrayed the first generation as made up primarily of young professional musicians or advanced music students. One had previously studied at the Paris Conservatoire. Their recollections suggest that the program's initial aim was to create orchestras stocked by Venezuelan musicians, rather than the Europeans who were the norm. One of her key interviewees stated that the focus on poverty grew over time as El Sistema sought funding and direction, rather than being there from the start. Further support for these views can be found in an early newspaper article on the National Youth Orchestra (Vestrini 1976). The orchestra's raison d'être is explicitly described as to provide opportunities for music students, who tended to give up or go abroad, and serve as an intermediary point between school and the music profession. There is no mention of social objectives; indeed, it states unequivocally "above everything comes the music."

The evidence thus points to relatively conventional thinking behind El Sistema's emergence. It is more recently, and predominantly in the discursive field, that signs of radicalism may be found. As Spich and Sylvester (1999, 31–32) discuss, symphony orchestras have always needed support from wider society, and have adopted various strategies over time to secure it. The authors indicate two future paths for orchestras: to change what they do, or to change how they present themselves. El Sistema has invested heavily in the latter option.

The new language that El Sistema learned is that of the "expediency of culture" (Yúdice 2003). The late twentieth century saw a move toward a utilitarian view of culture around the globe; increasingly, the prime way to convince government and business leaders to support cultural activity was to argue for its social and economic impact. For example, the rhetoric of social inclusion entered the arts world in the United Kingdom during the 1990s, as a response to the previous decade's decline in public funding and questioning of high culture's automatic right to subsidy (Belfiore 2002). Given many informants' opinions that El Sistema's social rhetoric was consolidated in the 1990s, the program's discursive shift appears to have been part of a wider international trend toward instrumental cultural policy, which was "originally a defensive strategy of survival, aimed at preserving existing levels of cultural expenditure. The hope was that, if the arts sector ... could speak the same language as the government, maybe it would have a better chance to be listened to" (2002, 6).

Major international institutions like the IDB and the World Bank started treating culture as a sphere for significant investment—an important detail, given that international development banks funded El Sistema to the tune of $500 million in the five years from 2008. Such organizations have large amounts of money to disburse, but only to organizations that speak the language of utilitarianism. Alongside the rise of Chávez, then, another force was increasingly coming to bear on El Sistema in the 1990s, reshaping its rhetorical direction, and these two currents converged in 1998—the year that Chávez's presidency and the IDB's support began.

Learning to speak a language that appealed to both Chávez and the IDB was a hugely successful strategy. At a time when orchestras around the world are facing cuts, El Sistema has secured ever larger state subsidies and development bank loans; the program's budget rose on average 24 percent per year from 2000 ("Program to Support" 2007, 4). The program's historical narrative may involve some mythologizing and redefining, but it has been spectacularly effective.

Nevertheless, the question of whether El Sistema was conceived as a social project or subsequently redefined as such for reasons of expediency is still important. The latter would be eminently understandable from the point of view of ensuring the project's survival and growth, but it would cast doubt on the idea that the program should serve as a model of social action through music for the rest of the world. Music educationalists who wanted to launch a socially oriented music program today might then decide to start from the latest thinking about music education and social justice, which points in a very different direction, rather than borrowing a preprofessional training program from 1970s Venezuela.

Clearly, the issue of results is also crucial. It is therefore worth noting the question marks over some of the claims made on behalf of the arts. In the late 1980s arts spending began to be promoted as a motor of urban renewal, but this "urban renaissance" failed to appear. This lack of evidence did not halt the increasing orientation of publicly funded arts programs toward addressing wider problems, though their focus shifted from the economic to the social realm in the 1990s. Again, however, convincing evidence that the arts produced significant and positive impacts was lacking. Belfiore (2002, 4–5) cites a literature review on the arts and social inclusion that concluded: "it remains a fact that relative to the volume of arts activity taking place in the country's poorest neighbourhoods, the evidence of the contribution it makes to neighbourhood renewal is paltry." In Chapter 11, I will argue that the effectiveness and efficiency of El Sistema, too, remain unproven.

In sum, the linking of the arts and social inclusion—in Venezuela as elsewhere—might be understood primarily as an instrumental response to changing political priorities, economic circumstances, and cultural beliefs in the 1990s. Furthermore, it took place before social impacts were even evaluated, much less demonstrated. A degree of caution about El Sistema's social claims would thus be justified.

THE SOCIAL TODAY

So much for the origins of the social in El Sistema; what about its realities today? Surprisingly, the social is often hard to pin down. The structure of Borzacchini's (2010) official history is telling. The preface lists recent highlights: the rise of Dudamel, recordings for big record labels, international tours, and international prizes. The main text starts with Abreu and the SBYO, followed by long lists of all the international concert halls the orchestra has played at and the famous soloists it has performed with, praise from numerous guest conductors, excerpts from music critics' responses in foreign newspapers, endorsements from big names in the arts world, and a double-page spread on Abreu's dozens of prizes. Rescuing poor children from the barrios has to wait until ninety pages in.

Even in the CASM, an enormously impressive venue, I found myself asking: what kind of social action is going on here? In theory, any Sistema orchestra or individual can (try to) book a rehearsal or practice room there, and I saw ordinary (if more advanced) children from núcleos who had gone there for a lesson or a masterclass. But it is, first and foremost, home to the program's elite orchestras and where its best young musicians go to be trained. Sitting in a Beethoven symphony concert by the SBYO in the CASM's world-class concert hall, observing the odd gray hair and balding pate on the stage, I was struck by the very traditional feel of this concert experience. Where was the social action that prompted the IDB to fund the construction of the hall to the tune of $50 million?

I observed concerts, rehearsals, lessons, and practicing in the first-class facilities, but for all the stunning architecture, it was hard to see how it differed from a traditional (if very upmarket) conservatoire-cum-concert-hall. Despite the name and the development bank funding, there was little sign of pedagogical innovation or radical departures from the norm. I picked up a publicity leaflet at the entrance, and read that the CASM was designed to be "an open university for specialized musical teaching, and a venue for orchestras and concerts, which will become the academic music centre *par excellence* in which masterclasses will be delivered by well-known teachers"—hardly a revolutionary vision.

Telegraph journalist Ivan Hewett (2012) had a similar sensation: "Wandering down the corridors, and peering at the pianists and brass ensembles rehearsing in the practice rooms, you might think you were in a normal conservatoire." El Sistema's executive director Eduardo Méndez put him right, however: "'We are a social agency first and foremost,' he says, 'and it's our job to provide services to lots of government agencies such as the Ministry of Prisons, various medical agencies, the Education Ministry.'" What Méndez says is true, yet also obfuscatory: El Sistema does not normally provide those services *at* the CASM. There is a certain irony in the fact that the Center for Social Action through Music is where most of the IDB's loans went, yet is also the Sistema site where social action through music is hardest to discern.

Shieh (2012, 1–2) described his first impression of El Sistema as "being underwhelmed.... It looks and feels, more or less, like music education in the United States multiplied on a grander scale." While he moved toward a more positive (if still mixed) assessment of the program, he concluded that it was, "very simply, a system of classical music training schools. Its teachers speak as if it is one. When I ask what the challenges are, they answer unequivocally in musical terms: the students are frustrated when starting a new instrument, they don't reach the level you want them to. When I ask about the program's successes, they name students who have gone on to play in major orchestras" (2012, 7).

I found the social similarly elusive in Veracruz. The young musicians I met there were focused on making music and, in numerous cases, preparing for life as a professional musician. They understood the social aspect primarily in the sense that their social lives revolved around the orchestra, since they spent most of their non-school or -university time there, and those who had more to say usually referred to what they had seen in a documentary or heard in a speech. Given also the origins of the National Youth Orchestra and El Sistema's original constitution, the insistence of foreign Sistema supporters that the program's goal has never been to create professional musicians rang hollow.

The most able children may be in the youth orchestra within a year or two of starting—and youth orchestras function more like professional orchestras than social projects. Promising musicians are fast-tracked into pseudo-professional or even professional roles, and may be playing with the paid regional youth orchestra or professional state symphony orchestra by their mid-teens. Many children may begin for fun and regard music as a hobby, but once they start attending five or six days a week, climbing the ranks, spending all their free time in the núcleo, and being paid, it easily transforms into a professional path. The most talented are encouraged to aspire to joining the CYO, TCYO, or SBYO, or a top professional orchestra, and Dudamel is the program's talisman. El Sistema dangles the SBYO in front of children to motivate them and keep the whole show in motion, said one musician; musical fame and fortune is the main driving force. The showcase orchestras select on the basis of musical ability, not social need. Social objectives are often rather hard to identify among all the (quasi-)professional musical ambitions and goals.

El Sistema does not directly teach or encourage reflection on social issues and values. According to Rodrigo Guerrero, the director of FESNOJIV's Office of International Relations, "the students are so excited by and dedicated to the musical fun and creation, they don't realize until they leave El Sistema that it is really a social development program more than a musical one" (Booth 2008, 11). The director of the Veracruz núcleo made the same point, and this was borne out in my experience: a number of students, even those in their late teens or early twenties, looked blank when asked about the meaning of the phrase "social action through music," yet this is not some obscure academic construction but El Sistema's supposed raison d'être and the justification for its huge IDB loans.

El Sistema's social action is supposed to be implicit and unconscious. On a day-to-day level, a núcleo is simply a music school, but one underpinned by a claim that playing orchestral music *automatically* produces positive social action. This idea has been challenged by critical music education scholars, as discussed previously, but it is also hard to square with responses from young musicians. Being unaware of social action through music is one thing, but I met a surprising amount of skepticism or disinterest, as Wald (2011) did in her study of Sistema-inspired programs in Buenos Aires. One student replied: "Isn't that the name of the HQ in Caracas?" He thought a bit and then went on: "in El Sistema they talk about social action but, I don't know, I don't see much of that." Almost all the students I spoke to believed the musical to be paramount. One member of the Veracruz youth orchestra dismissed the idea of El Sistema as a "school for social life," saying it did not really teach them anything—it was just about playing and playing. Another recalled a brief period a few years earlier when the orchestra had been obliged to put on "community concerts" in conjunction with the communal councils: "it was a pain," she said. "No one wanted to do them. Fortunately that didn't last very long."

El Sistema's supporters argue that students' lack of awareness of the social does not mean that it is of lesser importance, but the musical also predominates over the social in practice. For example, in Veracruz, orchestral performance was prioritized over teaching and given higher status. Julio, a percussionist, had been assigned teaching duties in a small town about two hours from the city. Six weeks after the start of the academic year, he still had not made his first visit to the núcleo, as he was too busy rehearsing with the youth orchestra. He spoke to the director and said that he would have to miss a few rehearsals, but the director said no: he would give Julio permission to miss teaching instead. Given that many of the region's teachers are drawn from the orchestras, it is hardly surprising that núcleo teaching is so patchy.

The núcleo in Veracruz houses both the Sistema teaching operation and the youth orchestra. In September 2010, when schools were suspended for three weeks due to forthcoming elections, the director organized intensive musical activities and rehearsals in the núcleo for the orchestra—but normal music lessons were suspended. When school is out for any reason, music classes stop as well; the orchestra, however, not only carries on but often redoubles its efforts. A teacher at the Veracruz núcleo claimed that the youth orchestra was the only thing that was taken seriously there; all the small children that one saw running around the núcleo and sitting in classrooms were the lowest priority. The ones who showed musical talent were extracted, given extra coaching, and inserted into the orchestra as soon as possible, he said; the rest got bored and left.

While many musicians told me they enjoyed teaching, it is also frequently presented as an obligation—"you can't play in the orchestra unless you give classes"—and may even be used a punishment for musicians who disappoint in auditions or commit a disciplinary breach. Children in El Sistema dream of making it to the SBYO and being a highly paid, globe-trotting performer; being a low-paid teacher in a núcleo is the bottom of the pile. El Sistema thus reproduces the standard hierarchy of practices and values of the classical music world, rather than adopting novel strategies that would grant social objectives a higher priority.

Consequently, skepticism about the program's social focus is widespread in Venezuela. "That's the idea that sells," commented one musician drily. A senior figure suggested that chamber music was a greater potential source of social action than orchestral music—but to a conductor like Abreu, it was of lesser musical interest, so it was given lower priority. One Veracruz musician argued that if El Sistema were really interested in social action, it would employ specialists in a range of areas rather than just instrumental teachers. A Sistema teacher with sixteen years' experience in Caracas núcleos concurred: if social change was the priority, he asked, why were there no psychologists or social workers involved in the day-to-day running of núcleos? (In contrast, Wald [2011] notes that health and social workers participate regularly in two Sistema-inspired programs in Argentina.) You cannot deal systematically with serious social or behavioral problems just by sticking a violin in a child's hands, he said, even though it will work occasionally if you try with enough children. He described two children with major behavioral problems at his núcleo, one of whom deliberately crashed two cymbals on the teacher's hand, leaving him in agony; these children needed specialist help, he said, not "Hymn to Joy."

Apparent social action sometimes turns out to be shallow or evanescent when examined up close. FESNOJIV's publicity arm, the Venezuelan press, and the film *Dudamel* all provided considerable coverage of a concert by the TCYO in the streets of the Caracas barrio of La Vega in 2009, attended by thousands of local residents. This event provided great copy, footage, and publicity shots, but as one of my interviewees pointed out, this was not community work, which requires long-term commitment: it was a day-trip by an elite orchestra from the CASM, and a publicity stunt designed to "demonstrate" El Sistema's work in the barrios. The concert provided a simulacrum of social action rather than the real thing; the hand of Abreu, the master of spectacle, could be felt behind the scenes. Borzacchini (2010, 115) quotes a La Vega resident: "Today there were no problems in the barrio...they cleared up the garbage, they painted the streets and there are lots of police and helicopters watching over La Vega. If only they would stay to combat the insecurity that always appears on these streets." The music did not improve the barrio in any lasting sense; rather, the neighborhood was cleaned up for a day, for the sake of the visiting musicians and the cameras, and then returned to business as usual.

In recent years, there has been a demonstrable emphasis on increasing social action, with an expanding special education program and a growing number of núcleos in poorer areas, special schools, and prisons. Nevertheless, it would be interesting, if accounts were publicly available, to compare the quantities devoted to these aspects of the project with those spent on the elite orchestras. In the absence of figures, one can only observe widespread complaints from El Sistema's own employees that it concentrates resources on its showpiece orchestras in Caracas while núcleos and teachers across the country suffer hardship, raising further doubts about its claim to prioritize the social over the musical.

If the SBYO gets top-of-the-range instruments and designer suits while provincial núcleos often lack basic equipment and their teachers go unpaid for months at a time, it would seem that the touring orchestra takes priority over children in provincial núcleos. If the SBYO musicians are paid several times as much as the teachers who trained them, it implies that Abreu considers good performing to be more important than good teaching. If El Sistema creates a pampered parallel universe for its top students, with seminarios in five-star hotels and masterclasses with the world's best musicians, while a single untrained teacher has to deal with eighty difficult children in a dangerous Caracas neighborhood, it would seem that musical results take priority over social action.

By examining where El Sistema concentrates its efforts, we see quite a different story from official narratives. Resources, both economic and human, are channeled toward the center and the top, jarring with the stated focus on the deprived and neglected. Rounded education and social action take a back seat to the formation of impressive orchestras and the presentation of spectacular displays.

In sum, the evidence suggests that El Sistema began as a conventional music education project for predominantly middle-class students, and its transformation into a revolutionary social program aimed at the poor has taken place in response to political pressure rather than stemming from a messianic founding vision. This conversion is exhibited to a large degree at the level of discourse; evidence for the prioritizing of social goals is patchy. In most núcleos, there is no concerted effort to discuss or deal with social issues; the students just learn music, success is conceived primarily in musical terms, and celebratory accounts tend to focus on musical achievements (e.g., Guarache Ocque 2012). The claim that this is not a music program but rather a social one should therefore be recognized as an instrumental rhetorical construct rather than a simple description of reality.

CLASSICAL MUSIC AND SOCIAL ACTION

Before examining El Sistema's supposed social action in detail, it is important to raise the general questions of how—and even whether—the arts (and specifically music) produce social effects, what those effects might be, and whether they should be invoked in justifications for arts education and funding. There is a huge body of research on the impact of musical learning on children's cognitive development, and much evidence of positive effects on the human brain and the acquisition of skills such as language, literacy, and numeracy (see

Hallam 2010 for a comprehensive overview). The issue of academic achievement has seen more debate, especially about the matter of correlation versus causation; children who learn music may be higher academic achievers because of their personality or upbringing rather than because of any direct influence of music ("Evaluation of Big Noise" 2011, 67–68). Winner and Cooper's (2000, 65) exhaustive study of nearly fifty years of published research in English concluded: "we have as yet no evidence that studying the arts has a causal effect on academic achievement." Additionally, Goldstein et al. (2013, 8) found no more than tentative evidence regarding the impact of arts education on behavioral and social skills. Nevertheless, most researchers have concluded that, in general terms, arts education and after-school programs are beneficial for children (e.g., Fiske 1999; Miller 2003; Vaughan, Harris, and Caldwell 2011).

Such studies are very valuable, but two questions deserve careful consideration: what *kind* of art or music is being evaluated, and whether the studies' conclusions are generalizable across other arts or forms of music. El Sistema's proponents often claim that a positive report on arts education demonstrates the effectiveness of their particular program. Yet can we assume that learning a variety of musics in a classroom setting is equivalent to learning a single kind of music outside school? Or that if learning to play guitar in a rock band or percussion in a small improvisation ensemble is good for children, then learning to play violin in a Sistema orchestra is equally good for them? The combination of classical music performance and positive social effects is not an obvious one. Among the principles that Nettl (1995, 42) identifies in classical music performance are conformity, rigid class structure, dictatorship, and overspecialization. Most arts education projects focus on creativity, flexibility, and problem solving, rather than the discipline and pursuit of excellence characteristic of classical music performers. Indeed, El Sistema embodies a move in the opposite direction to most progressive educational programs and academic studies in the developed world. For some four decades, music education literature has been pointing away from a focus on classical music and toward multiculturalism and diverse musical experiences, and the social science literature has been painting a somewhat bleak picture of classical music schools and professional orchestral life; yet Venezuela has gained global attention with a traditionalist project based on classical music performance and the unfashionable Enlightenment idea of the universality of European culture. In North America and the United Kingdom, arts education projects are often drops of liberal intent in a sea of cultural and educational conservatism; but El Sistema, under Chavism, is the reverse. Given the differences between musical cultures, contexts, activities, and their effects, there is a question mark over the extent to which conclusions from studies of arts education in North America, Europe, and Australasia may be applicable to El Sistema.

An important current in the sociology of music sees social action as inhering in the kinds of interactions or sociality that musical participation stimulates (e.g., Turino 2008; Born 2010). As Martin (1995, 194) argues, "experience of participating in a particular community will lead individuals to 'internalise' its values and conventions." From this perspective, broad claims about the social effects of the arts would be problematic. The nature of social action in a collective musical setting would depend on the type of ensemble, its internal dynamics, and the kinds of interactions or social relations that it modeled, and understanding social action would require careful attention to detail. The studies outlined in Chapter 5 suggest that a conventional orchestra constitutes a stratified, autocratic social microcosm, frequently riven with stress, boredom, frustration, and loss of individuality, with orchestral musicians likened to "rats in someone else's maze" (Levine and Levine 1996, 24). Faulkner's two studies (1973a; 1973b) point to the normality of conflictive relations between musicians and conductors, and competitive interactions among the musicians themselves. Control and competition were the two primary forms of relationship that he discovered. If the kind of social action produced by music depends on musicians' social interactions, a conventionally run symphony orchestra is hardly a promising place to look for progressive examples, and attempts to read social outcomes across from one kind of project to another may be flawed.

If social action is determined less by music than "musicking" (to use Christopher Small's term), even persuasive cases for the beneficial influence of classical music by Johnson (2002) and Kramer (2007) may be of limited use in analyzing El Sistema, since both focus primarily on this music's trandscendent effects on individual *listeners*. There may be significant differences, however, between listening to and playing, for example, a Mahler symphony. Orchestras are designed as instruments to elevate their audiences (and patrons), not their musicians, so while the emotional impact of concerts and recordings by the SBYO on listeners is incontrovertible, how do the liberatory effects of Mahler fare *within* the structure and value system of a symphony orchestra? How much transcendence goes on in the back desk of the second violins? Johnson and Kramer's arguments may tell us more about El Sistema's impact on its fans, supporters, and leaders than on its ordinary participants.

One of El Sistema's hallmarks, and a key to its success, has been Abreu's high-flown rhetoric about the power of music to change society. A microsocial approach is one way in which such assertions might be tested, but doubts have been raised from other perspectives, too, about some of the more expansive claims made on behalf of the arts. Carey (2010) responds to the question "do the arts make us better?" with a firm "no," arguing that "in place of answers what we have currently are lax and baseless assumptions and pious hopes" (2010, 134). Artists and patrons show no signs of being better human beings than ordinary folk. A century of experimental psychology shows that "there is no reason to expect that works of art will produce behavioural changes in their recipients" (101). Belfiore (2002) questions the effectiveness of the arts in ameliorating social and economic problems, and particularly in promoting social inclusion (El Sistema's watchword).

A high-profile doubter is, interestingly enough, Daniel Barenboim, who has placed himself in some refreshingly contrarian positions as a result. He declares: "The West-Eastern Divan Orchestra is of course incapable of bringing peace to the Middle East" (Cheah 2009, vii). His equally eminent project partner, Edward Said, agrees: "It doesn't pretend to be building bridges and all that hokey stuff" (Etherington 2007, 126); its goal is simply to awaken curiosity. For all that the WEDO and the SBYO are often mentioned in the same breath, they are separated by a fundamental (if rarely noted) difference in outlook, one that led to friction in 2010 when Barenboim was invited to Venezuela as a distinguished guest of El Sistema but ended up undercutting Abreu's utilitarian arguments on television (Padilla 2010a). Barenboim and Abreu express mutual admiration, but behind the fine words there is no disguising the fact that the former believes that "music cannot be used for anything" ("Barenboim Embelesado" 2010), while the latter's global success is built on the opposite idea. The WEDO's publicity gave a positive spin to the 2010 meeting: "The exchange between the orchestras was a true meeting of minds. Abreu applauded the WEDO's work to educate through music and noted the similarities between El Sistema and the WEDO's approach, pointing out that both projects aim to go beyond the aesthetic dimension of the music and use it as a tool for human development and peace. Maestro Barenboim could only return the compliment, stating that its music proved that El Sistema does not use music for social purpose, but rather gives back to music its authentic humanitarian dimension." Yet this report cannot cover up the gulf between the two positions and the fact that Barenboim "returned the compliment" in the sense of politely returning an unwanted gift.

Consequently, utilitarian arguments for the arts have been critiqued as scientifically weak, philosophically problematic, and politically risky. Winner and Cooper (2000, 66), after casting doubt on purported causal links between arts study and academic achievement, conclude that "advocates should refrain from making utilitarian arguments in favor of the arts. Such arguments betray a misunderstanding of the inherent value of the arts." Belfiore concurs and suggests that the arts play a dangerous game by arguing for their value on instrumental grounds without robust evidence of their efficacy; they are then vulnerable to being displaced by social programs with more demonstrable results. She concludes: "instrumental cultural policies are not sustainable in the long term, and…they ultimately may turn from 'policies of survival' to 'policies of 'extinction'" (2002, 22).

A highly unusual feature of El Sistema, and one that makes assessments of music's capacity for social action and comparisons with other arts education projects fraught with difficulties, is the fact that it pays scholarships—which may rival professional musical salaries—to more advanced students. El Sistema is somewhat shy on this point, which it does not broadcast widely. Booth (2008, 6) acknowledges the stipend, which he says "not only honors their accomplishments in a way that really matters, but places real value on the music making for the family, so they don't need to pull the child out of El Sistema to work." Booth's equivalency of "real value" and economic value is troubling, and indeed strange in such an idealistic observer. Furthermore, I suspect that the number of children at risk of being pulled out of El Sistema to work, and who avoid this fate thanks to their scholarship, is small. A group of Veracruz students who had spent between five and fifteen years in El Sistema debated this question, and between them, they could only think of one person who matched this category.

Uy (2012, 14) quotes a Sistema parent who stated that scholarships "are a motivation because they are like a prize for effort. For the children the money is a very large quantity, so it means a lot. Also, there are students with two or three brothers in the orchestra and so the *beca* would be multiplied by three, and this helps the family with its resources. So it is also a motivation for parents." The complex ethical issues around paying children "a very large quantity" to participate in a given program are not, however, explored, and important questions go unasked: Are there not significant risks if parents may be motivated by the financial inducements on offer? What might happen in a poor family if a child decided they hated the orchestra and wanted to leave? Is El Sistema fostering empowerment or dependency?

Casanova (2009), in contrast, is typically forthright: "Abreu's success with music schools comes down to being the only example in the world where children are paid a salary to go to school. That's right, they do not give scholarships, they pay salaries to underage children. That does not happen anywhere else in the world, because studying music comes from the heart not from being paid to do it; [elsewhere] they simply do not charge for studying." Musicians remembered that venerated music educators like Vicente Emilio Sojo and Emil Friedman, to whom Abreu is often contrasted, were implacably opposed to paying music students.

It might be assumed that young musicians themselves would be whole-heartedly in favor of pay, but one reported: "I remember when there wasn't money involved, people would help their stand-mate. Now it's different, now everyone is fighting for their rank." Another—from a low-income family—described money as an infection that distracted students from valuing music for its own sake, and claimed there were too many students motivated primarily by the money. The group of Veracruz students mentioned earlier agreed that their orchestra had taken a turn for the worse once it started paying scholarships, and the atmosphere had been better when people were just there for the music. There was also concern over the distribution and destination of scholarship money. One of the students said: "When they started paying the youth orchestra in Veracruz, there were kids as young as ten who started appearing with the latest BlackBerry, the coolest pair of trainers. Maybe there were a few kids out in the rural núcleos who were poor, but they weren't in the city orchestra so they weren't getting paid anyway."

Patricia, a conservatoire student, spent two years in a Sistema orchestra because she needed the money. She knew other conservatoire students who, like her, were unimpressed by El Sistema's methods and atmosphere but carried on playing for years in a núcleo orchestra just for the scholarship and the instrument—"tocar y cobrar" (to play and get paid). She also described a commonplace practice, especially among the violinists, of *meter paquete*, which essentially meant bluffing in order to keep getting paid. These violinists would work up a small section of music for auditions, but they could never play a whole piece, and they showed little real love for music.

Older musicians were more skeptical still. A Ministry of Culture official described the paying of scholarships as introducing a capitalist conception into the world of youth music, while a leading musician argued that El Sistema was producing materialistic rather than cultured citizens. A renowned conductor described El Sistema in terms of "the pursuit of easy results achieved through efforts stimulated by the abundance of resources and money," and stated that paying young musicians led to social problems: "many of those kids have become the main breadwinner in their household—but a breadwinner who manipulates, who controls the household, who controls their parents." Counteracting Abreu's spiritual discourse, he argued that being paid to play "doesn't nourish the soul."

Whether state and development bank social funds should be financing BlackBerrys and fashionable trainers for middle-class children is one issue here. Another is that any comprehensive, scientific evaluation of El Sistema's impact will have to address how to assess the specific benefits of music in a project in which students are (or can look forward to being) paid to participate. How does one separate out the effects of music from the effects of money? How much of the program's current growth is driven by this economic abundance? Could almost any activity become a successful social project under such conditions?

A good example of the potential confusion introduced by material incentives can be found in El Sistema's prison education program. I made two visits to a prison to observe the program in action and interview musicians, and most of my impressions were favorable: I was surprised by the positivity of the atmosphere and the warmth with which I was received, and I heard some moving words from prisoners about how discovering music had changed them personally. I have no doubt that these words were sincere, but I was disconcerted to find out that prisoners who participated in El Sistema were paid scholarships and given a six-month reduction in their sentence for each year they spent in the program. One of the prisoners who seemed genuinely attached to the musical activities confided that some of his fellow inmates were motivated more by these concrete benefits than a love of music. As a musician, I was delighted that these prisoners were being given musical opportunities; but the fact that they were being rewarded for taking part makes any assessment of the role and effectiveness of music much more complicated. Would the program function without incentives, with music alone? This is not the kind of question likely to worry Abreu, a pragmatist whose priority has long been visible results rather than the means used to achieve them, but those who seek to analyze or emulate his program need, perhaps, to worry a little more.

CONCLUSION

El Sistema's claims about social action through music need to be held up against notable skepticism on the part of former senior members of the program, bolstered by documentary evidence. They should also be examined against a backdrop of divided opinion over the nature and extent of classical music's effects, and greater consensus that social action is closely linked to the relationships and values that are modeled through music making. Even if the cognitive benefits and liberatory potential of music for the individual are taken as given, the kind of social environment in which music is learnt, or the social dynamics afforded by particular kinds of music making, will inflect outcomes. It seems reasonable to suggest that El Sistema, like any form of music making, produces social action; but the question is then, given what we know about orchestras, what *kind* of social action?

It is hard to find much support in the academic literature for the idea that simply playing good music automatically generates positive social effects; there is good reason, therefore, to approach sweeping claims about El Sistema and social action through music from a critical perspective. The social nature of the self means that if we are interested in music education from a social perspective, it is not enough to repeat claims such as "music makes you smarter" or assume a universality of effects; we must look beyond questions of individual psychology and attainment to consider social interactions, the structuring of groups, and the imparting of values in specific music education settings. Might the individual (personal development) and the social (interpersonal behavior) come into conflict under certain conditions? Might beneficial effects of learning music be reduced, canceled out, or even outweighed by simultaneous negative countereffects produced by certain kinds of learning environments and educational practices? These are issues that will be explored in the next three chapters.

CHAPTER 8

Social Inclusion and Discipline

As an educator, I was thinking more about discipline than about music.
—José Antonio Abreu

This isn't education, this is military training.
—Venezuelan university professor

El Sistema's funding and fame are built on a series of grandiose claims about its social effects. Given the lack of rigorous and reliable evaluations of the program (see Chapter 11), those claims are in urgent need of critical examination. They revolve around a number of key terms that recur frequently. The next three chapters explore these central ideas, considering how they are conceptualized, the ways in which they are or are not realized, and what kinds of social subjects are produced in the process. We may then have a clearer idea about the kinds of social action fostered by El Sistema and its self-characterization as a school for social life and a model for a better society.

The two most important words in the Sistema vocabulary, "inclusion" and "discipline," are the subject of this chapter. Placing competing understandings of social inclusion under the spotlight, it examines the inclusivity of the program's practices, El Sistema's relationship to the family and wider society, and the issue of cultural inclusion. In the second part, an outline of El Sistema's disciplinary attitudes and practices leads into a Foucauldian analysis of the program and the orchestra as archetypal disciplinary institutions.

SOCIAL INCLUSION

Social inclusion is El Sistema's primary raison d'être in the eyes of the Venezuelan state and the cornerstone of the program's fame and funding. Yet very little critical attention has been paid to this idea in its Venezuelan context; it is taken as self-evident that social inclusion is a laudable and achievable goal and that the orchestra promotes it. Both points are worth further examination, however.

Firstly, when assessing claims that El Sistema was conceived as a social inclusion project in the 1970s, it should be borne in mind that the discourse of social exclusion did not emerge until the mid-1980s (Boltanski and Chiapello 2005, 347), and the rhetoric of social inclusion first appeared in the arts world in the early 1990s (Belfiore 2002). Furthermore, as outlined in Chapter 7, claims concerning the arts as a motor of social inclusion should be understood as an instrumental response to changing political priorities and economic circumstances at this time, and they were made before social impacts were even evaluated, much less demonstrated. A certain skepticism is thus justified from the outset.

There have also been broader critiques of the concepts of social inclusion and exclusion and their attachment to culture (e.g., Logan n.d.). They have been accused of concealing or downplaying the determining role of economic factors; implicitly promoting middle-class culture and values; and encouraging homogeneity rather than diversity (Armstrong 2000). A key problem concerns "the underlying moral meta-narrative that shapes much social exclusion research, and which tends both to assume the goodness of inclusion and to proceed in terms of implicit normative assumptions about how social life should be organised. This often ignores the ways in which the terms of inclusion can be problematic, disempowering or inequitable" (Hickey and du Toit 2007, 3).

For leftist critics, the language of social exclusion effaces that of class, material inequality, and exploitation, and evidences a loss of critical focus (e.g., Boltanski and Chiapello 2005, 346–49). The Cultural Policy Collective argues that inclusion might appear a progressive ideal, but it serves as "a form of regulating the poor" rather than challenging inequality, and is "less . . . a mechanism of liberation than a top-down programme of social control" ("Beyond Social Inclusion" 2004). This report critiques social inclusion as a paternalistic, normative narrative: "Too many programmes are governed by a missionary ethos, projecting a set of hierarchically-defined cultural interests from the centre to the margins." Consequently, "social inclusion policy in the arts offers very little to progressive social change."

Brazilian anthropologist Hermano Vianna (2011, 247–48) makes a particularly apposite Latin Americanist critique: "When we speak of inclusion, we usually start from the assumption that the (included) center has something that is lacking to a periphery that begs inclusion. It is as if the periphery did not have culture, technology, or an economy. It is as if the periphery were to one day have, or hope to have, or be better off if it already had, something that the center already has—something to which the center could presumably lead the periphery, for the latter's own good." Yet Vianna argues that it is the periphery, more than the center, which is the source of rapid innovation in twenty-first-century Latin America, basing his argument on the cultural and economic vitality of popular music scenes on the outskirts of provincial Brazilian cities. He concludes that the periphery in fact constitutes the center of Brazilian musical life, and therefore "the very idea of inclusion—whether digital, cultural, or social—has to be rethought or discarded when confronted with this situation." Following Vianna, the top-down notion of social inclusion may have limited relevance to contemporary Latin America; indeed, a paternalistic social inclusion program based on the assumed superior value of the culture of the center may even constrict the continent's most dynamic forces. His argument that inclusion is increasingly working from the bottom up and the outside in poses significant questions for El Sistema, a program rooted in the culture of the Caracas elite of the 1970s. There are reasons, therefore, to treat the goal of social inclusion—and not just claims of its realization—with some caution.

Shifting our attention back more squarely to El Sistema, there are certainly some grounds for arguing that it is an inclusive organization, as the presence of disadvantaged children and special programs for disabled people and prisoners attest. In theory, at least, any child can sign up for the program. Nevertheless, there is an obvious contradiction in using an inherently exclusive organization—the symphony orchestra—as the basis for inclusivity. An inclusive arts education project would potentially provide everyone with a place, reflecting their particular skills and interests; but a conventional symphony orchestra excludes those who cannot meet its specific requirements. In focusing primarily on creating symphony orchestras, El Sistema exemplifies the approach critiqued by Bradley (2012, 414–45), according to which students' unique relationships with music are neglected "in favor of developing performing groups that by their nature exclude those students whose musical interests lie elsewhere." Bradley questions an "emphasis on developing 'talent' through performing ensembles and the attendant need to 'weed out the untalented' in the pursuit of 'musical excellence.'" El Sistema is focused on the search for and valorization of ability of a very particular kind, and thus has exclusivity in its genes.

"Weeding out" those who do not fit the profile of young, talented, and committed is an inherent part of preprofessional classical music training, yet many seem to overlook its role in Venezuela and the obvious challenge it poses to inclusivity. Such exclusivity is not a feature of all musical cultures (Turino 2008), but in classical music training, competition and selection at every level make for losers as well as winners. Like the WEDO, El Sistema's high-flown rhetoric is underpinned by "competitive professional exclusivity" (Beckles Willson 2009).

Ana, a teacher at Veracruz, explained how El Sistema weeded out students. To begin with, the Veracruz núcleo has entrance exams, and those who show more aptitude and better behavior are chosen; it is not, therefore, open to all, but rather excludes on the basis of two criteria from the very start. Then, of those who join, many fall by the wayside: "in the first years they put X [teacher] as a filter—saying to six-year-old kids that they're useless or shouting at them, 'sit up straight!' or 'you've got learning problems—you're a moron,' things like that—few kids can put up with that." The children are mainly middle class, and "a well-off kid isn't going to put up with this guy shouting at him. These kids aren't like their predecessors, who would sit there in silence—now they tell their parents 'this guy shouted at me' and the parents go and kick up a fuss and pull their kid out." As a result, "many kids leave in the early years. Those who manage to survive this make it into the orchestra, and the orchestra is constantly being renewed, new kids come in, from other cities or whatever, and the ones who are less skilled fall by the wayside—the staff humiliate them, shout at them." She went on: "and then there is the 'reduction'—'no, don't come to this rehearsal, you don't know the music, go away and practice it,' and before you know it the kid has gone three months without rehearsing and they say 'you haven't been for three months, you can't play in the orchestra, you're out,' but it's really that they can't be bothered to help them improve when they've got other kids coming through who can play better—why invest time in average students when there are new ones with more talent?"

The creation of the regional youth orchestra meant an influx of talented children from the small towns around Veracruz, which squeezed out the average students from the city: "They made them leave, one way or another—they pressured them." Ana described the orchestra as a Darwinian environment, in which the strong thrived and the weak were ground down. Humiliation was a daily occurrence and students either had to put up with it or leave. Ana described El Sistema's signature "stand-by-stand technique" as a "nightmare" and a deliberate attempt at weeding out the weaker players. It was in effect a public audition, and those who "failed" faced various possible sanctions (beyond embarrassment in front of a hundred of their peers), such as instantaneous expulsion from the rehearsal, the threat of exclusion from the forthcoming concert, or simply being told "you're useless, you're the worst in your section." The most humiliating, said Ana, was to be demoted on the spot—having to pick up one's music and move to a lower position in the orchestral hierarchy—and replaced by another (usually younger) student. Ana recalled crying or trying to suppress tears for the rest of the rehearsal. After enough public shaming, weaker students would often leave. Two music students who arrived at Veracruz from another city were subjected to the stand-by-stand technique at their first full rehearsal; they described the experience as a humiliating "initiation rite" that permanently soured their view of the conductor. Bradley (2012, 415) does not exaggerate, then, when she writes that weeding-out practices "often scar students' psyches."

One late-starter at Veracruz was dissuaded from continuing by a variety of such ritual humiliations. His teacher and the director both told him he was useless, and he was largely shunned by other students because of his low level in comparison to his age. He was included in the youth orchestra as *practicante* (practice-level), the lowest and worst-paid tier, which normally means attending rehearsals but not playing in concerts. The multiple levels of hierarchization in El Sistema (rank, pay, and duties) ensure that the weakest players are constantly reminded of their lowly station—an example of how the program practices exclusion within inclusion.

Ana went on to say that she understood El Sistema's approach up to a point, since when she was running a workshop, it was easier and more enjoyable if the standard was higher. "As a musician, one sometimes treats others badly—I've done it. You get exasperated with the kids and they cry and they don't want to come back—and it's much easier if they don't come back! What matters to you is that it sounds decent—it's that simple. I don't care who plays it, as long as it sounds decent." Ana was schooled in the Sistema way, and this ideology of the collective over the individual, the strong over the weak, the music over the musician, is passed down from generation to generation. Her words recall Freire's (2005, 45): "the oppressed, instead of striving for liberation, tend themselves to become oppressors, or 'sub-oppressors.' The very structure of their thought has been conditioned by the contradictions of the concrete, existential situation by which they were shaped."

Ana claimed that "at the moment here in Veracruz, those who play the best are those who have the most money." She argued that if a student had a better instrument, better strings, or better reeds, then they sounded better. They also had money to invest in traveling to Caracas for lessons and going on extra courses. As a result, "the orchestra has been filtered not just according to [playing] standard but also in that those who remain are the ones with more money." Most of the leading players in the regional youth orchestra owned their own instrument. A violinist confirmed that El Sistema's instruments are often of poor quality; they are fine for beginners, she said, but students who start taking music more seriously need something better, so she had bought her own instrument—not something that everyone had the economic resources to do so.

The better players are competing against each other for principals' chairs and membership of national orchestras, and those who can afford good instruments and accessories have an advantage. One of the positives of El Sistema, I was told, was that there was no social division between rich and poor; in a sequence intercut with Abreu's TED prize speech, a young musician claimed: "There is no difference between classes here, nor white or black, if you have money or not."[1] There is obviously musical stratification, though, and in Veracruz, economic differences made their way in through this back door.

GENDER

Another area in which El Sistema's inclusiveness needs to be examined is that of gender. The vast majority of the project's leaders have been men: Abreu, Igor

Lanz, Eduardo Méndez, Valdemar Rodríguez, Pedro Álvarez, Víctor Rojas, the list goes on. The same is true for conductors: Gustavo Dudamel, his forgotten predecessor Gustavo Medina, and his possible successors Diego Matheuz and Christian Vásquez. The directors of the Latin American Academies for orchestral instruments are almost all men. Musicians talk about Abreu's inner circle of students—those who receive individual conducting lessons and concentrated, personalized attention—as a male group. A website by Borzacchini and Sistema sponsor Bancaribe proclaims that the program "has formed an entire generation of orchestra conductors who are rising stars on international stages and also at home in Venezuela" (note the subsidiary status given to "at home"). It lists thirty-one up-and-coming conducting talents—not a single one of them female.[2]

Turning to El Sistema's two elite orchestras, the older "A" section of the SBYO is 69 percent male and 31 percent female, and the younger "B" section is 78 percent male and 22 percent female, with all the principals of the "B" orchestra except the flute being male, suggesting that the problem is getting worse over time.[3] A founder placed responsibility with Abreu's attitude toward women, but a current member of the SBYO had a different explanation: she claimed that women generally had to leave the orchestra when they had a child because the rehearsal schedule was too demanding and unpredictable for a mother with a baby. This would explain the nearly 4:1 ratio of men to women in the "B" section and would point to systemic discrimination. Whatever the cause, broader social inequities are being reproduced rather than countered. El Sistema confirms Jorgensen's (2003) picture of music institutions as marginalizing women's music-making and excluding them from positions of leadership. The ideal society that El Sistema models is unambiguously a patriarchy.

SOCIAL INCLUSION AS SOCIAL EXCLUSION

Left-wing critics have little truck with Abreu's claims of social inclusion, as evidenced by numerous posts on the blog *La Otra Cara del Sistema*. In his ironic dictionary of Sistema terms, Freddy Argimiro defines social inclusion as "the act and effect of musically uprooting Venezuelans so as then to 'include' them in El Sistema." In his eyes, El Sistema practices something more like cultural abduction, a view echoed by José Antonio Barrionuevo, who claims that children "are being kidnapped by El Sistema to play and struggle (*tocar y luchar*) against their own identity. They are torn away from their space, emptied of their knowledge." Diego Silva writes of the orchestras as disassociating children from their social contexts by feeding them a new value system that places their own culture on the bottom rung. A Ministry of Culture official described El Sistema as "declassifying" children—eliminating a sense of class consciousness—as it suspended them in limbo between the popular culture of their neighborhood and the high culture of classical music.

Lying behind such critiques is a belief that El Sistema is including children in its world but excluding them from theirs. The program is often described as a bubble, a parallel world, or a state within the state (e.g., Shieh 2012, 3), hinting at the shadows of division lurking behind the claims of inclusion. Indeed, there is often a marked separation between the núcleo and surrounding community. El Sistema treats the núcleo as a distinct social and cultural world where children are removed from their surrounding reality and remade. A leaflet at the CASM claimed: "Since 1975, El Sistema has represented the possibility of changing limited life chances and finding a door that opens onto a noble destiny, in which…dangerous surroundings and social problems are put aside." This view sets up an adversarial dynamic, since the community is treated as a problem to be escaped, rather than a partner from which something could be learned and to which something could be contributed. El Sistema also frequently uses the language of "rescue" (for example, in its mission statement). Karpman's (1968) "drama triangle" psychological model, mentioned in Chapter 4, explores how this construction implies a persecutor, a victim, and a rescuer, and El Sistema casts disadvantaged communities in the first role. This stigmatization bolsters El Sistema's status as rescuer but does little to promote social integration.

Aharonián (2004, 12) argues that "El Sistema's real aim can be deduced to be not the insertion of young people into real society but rather the resupply of El Sistema itself." In some ways, the program excludes young musicians from the "real" society outside it, above all through the time commitment that it requires. An ex-Sistema musician reported that every holiday or long weekend the núcleo would organize a seminario, workshop, or special concert. She attended a meeting at the Ministry of Education at which there was a proposal to create a núcleo in every Bolivarian school, so that children would go straight to orchestra after school. "When are these kids supposed to play," one participant asked, "or spend time with their family?"

One successful Sistema student spoke of her removal from the social world of school and friends; there was no hanging out in the park or going swimming after school. The núcleo and its surrounding society were two separate worlds that did not fit together, she declared. She recounted trying to bring her orchestra companions together with her university friends at social events, but the musicians would not mix with the nonmusicians. Indeed, it was hard to have a boyfriend outside the orchestra, she said, thanks to its all-consuming schedule and insular nature. Another musician enthused about gaining friendships through the orchestra, and then said: "well, I don't have any friends outside, because I haven't had time to develop any friendships outside music! In fact, all my friendships outside the orchestra have deteriorated [*laughs*]—they all hate me!" Although his comments were lighthearted, there is a serious point here, and these are not isolated cases (e.g., Shieh 2012, 2). Borzacchini (2010, 130) quotes a young horn-player who says that he rarely goes to parties with his school friends because he is always having to go to the núcleo, while Hewett (2012) met a cellist who claimed, "when I visit my old friends I don't feel comfortable anymore." Inclusion and exclusion are thus two sides of the same Sistema coin: as students are included in the orchestra, they may be distanced from the world around it.

These are not surprising findings. Half a century ago, Bensman (1967, 55–56) noted that classical musicians "tend to concentrate their social contacts on those who have chosen the same way of life. Many of them draw their friends almost exclusively from fellow professionals or devoted amateurs.... The musician, then, lives very much within the confines of his status community.... Relative isolation from the rest of the world combined with the relative density of social relationships within the musical community results in a rather inbred culture." The potential for exclusivity within communal experience was a concern for Sennett (1976), who argued that the formation of community around collective personality could lead to "the perversion of fraternity" as outsiders were shunned and class solidarity eroded. Anticipating El Sistema's "big family," he wrote: "Fraternity has become empathy for a select group of people allied with rejection of those not within the local circle. This rejection creates demands for autonomy from the outside world, for being left alone by it rather than demanding that the outside world itself change" (1976, 266).

Sistema supporters often regard the orchestra as providing a surrogate family for children who actually or effectively do not have one of their own, overlooking the fact that most children *do* have a family as well as the possible consequences of treating them as though they were orphans. With such a high level of time commitment to and identification with the "big family," what are the effects on real families? One Veracruz musician described El Sistema as more like family than family itself: she saw more of her musician friends than she did of her parents. The mother of a player from a satellite núcleo told me that her daughter had a tough routine, traveling a lot to Veracruz and getting home late in the evening, leaving little mother-daughter time. Sometimes her daughter did not get out of the evening rehearsal in Veracruz until after the last bus home and had to stay overnight in the city.

Carvajal and Melgarejo (2008) wax about the orchestra becoming "a second family, since on top of the daily general rehearsals, there are intensive seminarios in which students are confined [*internados*] in a place that is completely separate from their family units, enabling the strengthening of bonds of friendship and companionship between the training musicians and with their teachers." The verb *internar* is also used for asylums and other "total institutions," and the loosening of family bonds in order to create new allegiances is familiar from the history of British boarding schools (Monbiot 2013) and authoritarian political regimes.

Love (2006, 61) suggests that in El Sistema, "*Bildung* [education] reaches beyond state institutions deep into family structures; it supercedes parents' role in educating children and tries to reform those it presently deems unfit for citizenship." Love grasps the potentially conflictive or competitive relationship between El Sistema and the family, another way in which its inclusion rests on exclusion. Unlike many traditional musical cultures, in which family bonds are exceptionally important, El Sistema is unafraid to separate children from their families for long stretches of time and to act in loco parentis, and it has historically granted minimal value to domestic cultural activities. For such reasons, El Sistema's strongest critics regard it as including children in its world but excluding them from theirs. They describe a cult-like organization that removes children from their sociocultural context and reeducates (or indoctrinates) them. This is actually not far from how El Sistema itself conceives of its activities; the main difference, apart from the tone, lies in the value accorded to Venezuelan social realities.

CULTURAL INCLUSION AND INCLUSIVE CULTURE

Borzacchini (2010, 116) imagines a child growing up in humble surroundings, learning the violin, and ending up playing a Vivaldi concerto with the National Children's Orchestra: "That child from a modest home becomes a human being capable of fully entering society." The implication from El Sistema's official historian that, before learning classical violin, this poor child was not "a human being capable of fully entering society" is extraordinary, and highly revealing of El Sistema's paternalistic attitude to the poor, yet its seed can be seen in Abreu's much-quoted line: "From the minute a child is taught how to play an instrument, he is no longer poor. He becomes a child in progress, who will become a citizen" (Tunstall 2012, xii). Abreu has not only revived the ancient idea of music as a constitutive part of citizenship but seems incapable of imagining full citizenship without classical music.

In essence, El Sistema regards ordinary Venezuelan society as a hotbed of vice and a cultural desert from which children are best removed to the safety of a núcleo, where they can learn a new set of values—those of the European symphony orchestra. By describing itself as "rescuing children and young people from an empty, disorientated, and deviant youth," it implies that childhood without El Sistema equates to perdition. As Argimiro puts it ironically, "Poverty: state of ignorance, indifference, and material scarcity that is produced in humble people through their lack of contact with the National System of Orchestras." Compare this vision with progressive music education theory, as expressed by Abrahams (n.d., 2): "students have rich, significant and ongoing engagements with music outside of school." Consequently, the aim of music teachers is to "bridge the gap and integrate those two musical lives," rather than "rescue" students from one of them.

El Sistema's apparent inclusivity of the barrios rests on its prior designation of these zones as culturally and spiritually poor and thus in need of "salvation" through "art" (i.e., classical music). Over its history, it has shown a systemic lack of interest in everyday barrio culture, with its African and indigenous roots. As Wright (2010b) argues (see Chapter 6), exclusion takes cultural as well as social form—the marginalization or banishment of cultural images to which children are already attached. Wright's work suggests that El Sistema's cultural exclusion is an unpromising basis for social inclusion, raising doubts about how much inclusion really takes place when students' social and cultural concerns are left at the núcleo door.

Most would agree that Venezuela faces considerable social problems, but not all believe that the answer lies in "rescuing" children from their own culture. There are many musical projects in the Caracas barrios, such as schools run by Grupo Madera and the Escuelas Para las Artes y Tradiciones Urbanas (EPATU, Schools for Urban Arts and Traditions), which promote an active and critical engagement with Venezuelan cultural practices and social realities (see e.g., Fernandes 2010). Indeed, such projects may be notably more inclusive than the orchestral program. To take the example of EPATU, "conscious" hip hop makes for a promising basis for a social project because it encourages students to think about social issues (as they listen to and compose lyrics) and consists of four elements (rap, DJing, graffiti, and breakdance) from which they can choose. It thus provides a space for those with interest or skill in the musical, verbal, visual, physical, or technological sphere. Many young people will be able to iden-tify with at least one of these elements. Projects like EPATU have no Abreu be-hind them and therefore a fraction of El Sistema's funding and publicity, but they might be seen as representing more inclusive and socially focused initia-tives for the urban youth who are El Sistema's key constituency.

Looking beyond Venezuela, it is worth comparing El Sistema to the "radi-cally inclusive approach" of a free improvisation program that starts from the idea that all children are equally talented and that there is no wrong way to make music (Bramley 2012). Unlike a conventional orchestra, such impro-vised practice "fundamentally challenges exclusive and hierarchical systematic structures" (2010, 7). In Philpott and Wright's (2012, 455–56) vision of a so-cially inclusive music education program, there is no curriculum, learning is haphazard rather than sequential, and students identify their own needs and develop their personal projects. Starting from the desired outcome—social inclusion—may lead one far away from El Sistema's model.

DEFINING AND PROMOTING SOCIAL INCLUSION

At the heart of the debate lie competing understandings of social inclusion. In practice, El Sistema defines this term quite narrowly, as opening its doors to all and creating special programs for some marginalized social groups. A stronger conception of inclusivity, in which an equal role is sought for every individual, interest, and ability, is lacking. Contrast El Sistema with a study of youth music in the United Kingdom, which defines "social inclusion in terms of equal access to curriculum activities. Teachers saw new curriculum initiatives, such as the introduction of world musics and the increased use of technology in music, as going some way to achieving this notion of access" (Lamont et al. 2003, 233). This is a crucial point, echoing Wright's aforementioned argument: social inclusion is inextricably linked to issues such as curriculum and pedagogy, not simply physical access. Music educators need to "reach across the real and imagined borders of narrow and rigid concepts, classifications, theories, and paradigms to embrace a broad and inclusive view of diverse music educational perspectives and practices," writes Jorgensen (2003, 119). Yet even when such musical diversity is encouraged, inclusiveness is not automatic: "while outwardly espousing inclusiveness of many musics in the curriculum, music teachers of all stripes still practice the profession in exclusive ways" (2003, 79). There may then be systemic exclusion in the conventional practices of music education, despite overt commitment to inclusion and genuine efforts on the part of individuals. Inclusion is a complex topic, since activities themselves can be exclusive, even if they include marginalized social groups. Today, therefore, many argue that it takes much more than an open door to foster social inclusion.

Yerichuk (2014), for example, explores how progressive and inclusive ideals did not stop reformers in the field of community music from excluding certain races and ethnicities and subjugating particular musics and knowledges. Discussions about equity and social justice within community music have tended to revolve around ensuring access to currently existing musical structures or advocating for their replication; less attention has been paid to the actual practices that take place and the social relations they (re)produce. Consequently, assumptions that community music is automatically positive and assertions of social and musical inclusion, while widespread, are not necessarily well grounded.

Sistema Scotland has grasped such complexities more readily than its progenitor. "Big Noise understands that real inclusion is much more complicated than simply being open to everyone. True inclusion means putting in place the support, the informal and formal processes and the ways of working, including staff attitudes, to actively encourage and enable everyone who can take part and who wishes to take part, to do so" ("Evaluation of Big Noise" 2011, 11). For all Big Noise's reverence for its Venezuelan parent project, what we see here is actually a significant divergence.

In defining inclusivity in terms of access, El Sistema also ignores a fundamental tension between social and artistic goals that has been a feature of community-oriented music programs since the nineteenth century (Hollinger 2006, 24–30). N. J. Cords discusses this issue in her study of music in late-nineteenth- and early-twentieth-century settlement houses, institutions that served as a home for social reformers and a community center for neighborhood residents: "The two parts of this dualism were social music—the idea of music as a social-izing, democratizing force; and professional music—musical training for occu-pational use, such as teaching and performing. It was not that the two entities could not exist together in settlement music—they already did—but training students for professional music careers implied an exclusivity that was philo-sophically repugnant to many settlement music leaders" (quoted in Hollinger 2006, 29). The question of inclusivity and exclusivity thus revolves around mu-sical training per se, not simply access to it, and El Sistema has done little to re-solve this long-standing tension between social and professional goals by aiming at the wrong target.

By defining inclusivity in terms of access, El Sistema has ignored the prob-lems of exclusivity *within* its music training. The program's vast size appears to make its status as a promoter of social inclusion self-evident, yet behind the headline numbers lie social differentiation and a high dropout rate. Lying in plain view is a plethora of exclusions—of individuals lacking particular tal-ents, of nonsanctioned musical interests—and conceptual divisions between the orchestra, community, and family. El Sistema's claims to promote social inclusion are the key to its accumulation of unprecedented economic and po-litical power, but until the exclusivities of preprofessional classical music edu-cation are confronted and assumptions about the value of the system in which children are being included are scrutinized, social inclusion will remain a slogan to secure funding rather than a desirable and achievable goal.

DISCIPLINE

When I asked Sistema musicians what values were transmitted by the pro-gram, "discipline" was often the first word on their lips. It is a word closely associated with orchestras, regarded as a key attribute of a good ensemble. Nevertheless, El Sistema places an uncommon emphasis on this quality. Simon Rattle noted that "the players in the Venezuelan Youth Orchestra are incredibly disciplined" (Borzacchini 2010, 242–43), and this is no coincidence: Abreu not only considers the orchestra to be a school of social discipline, he has even stated that discipline was a higher priority for him than music.[4]

Borzacchini's list of El Sistema's values includes discipline, obeying rules, being silent and punctual, and behaving oneself (2010, 96–97). The reformed juvenile delinquent Lennar Acosta said of his own students: "All we ask of them is that they learn to be disciplined. To be respectful. And to be excellent" (Tunstall 2012, 29). FESNOJIV's website enthuses about "ardent devotion to the discovery, understanding, and command of music; giving oneself over to the work; a labor of love and the spirit, but also of moderation and strict intel-lectual control." This is an austere list for an extracurricular arts project, and one marked by a curious mix of domination and submission. The confluence of different strands of Abreu's formation—religious, corporate, and political—is again pronounced.

At times, the language of discipline spills over into that of the military. Lennar Acosta describes himself as "a soldier of El Sistema" (Borzacchini 2010, 119), and National Children's Orchestra seminarios are sometimes described as "boot camp." An informant told Hollinger (2006, 96): "The System is like a military or religious organization"—a fascinating remark considering that Abreu was educated by the Jesuits, a religious order that not only prioritizes discipline but whose foundational papal bull in 1540, "the *Regimini militantis ecclesiae*, made explicit the bellicose model at its foundation" (van Orden 2005, 228). Like the Jesuit order, El Sistema blends the religious and the militaristic in its language, symbolism, structure, and dynamics.

The military aspect to orchestras is widely recognized. Lubow (2007) noted of Dudamel's early podium experiences: "conducting a musical ensemble of that size is like commanding a regiment." Nettl (1995, 35) concurs, arguing that "the orchestra is also a kind of army and reflects a structure found in the military domain of culture." Spitzer and Zaslaw (2005) demonstrate that this relationship has a long history and is more than just metaphorical.

DISCIPLINE IN PRACTICE

In El Sistema, discipline is evident in the day-to-day business of orchestral rehearsing, in which one can see two contradictory dynamics at play. An orchestra is a vertical organization; but horizontal social relationships are created between members of the orchestra, above all in nonmusical moments during and around rehearsals. However, horizontal relationships (chatting, joking, making faces) upset the order and efficiency of the rehearsal, so a considerable amount of time is devoted to the conductor (and also his "centurions," the section leaders) imposing the vertical relationship over the horizontal. Discipline is not only conceived in nonmusical terms ("stop talking among yourselves"); there are also constant exhortations to watch the conductor, follow the beat, and play exactly what is written on the page. A "good" orchestra is one that plays in a disciplined manner, submitting itself fully to the orders of the conductor, the section leaders, and the written music. Imposing and absorbing discipline, then, are central elements of a youth orchestra rehearsal.

Discipline sometimes crosses over into something stronger, becoming a euphemism for despotism. One Sistema student said: "Discipline is positive—but there's no balance here. Here it's tyranny and bad language and repression and control." She recalled a two-week seminario during which the director succeeded in raising the youth orchestra's level quite noticeably by constant shouting and swearing at the students. In El Sistema, musical ends justify the means. Nevertheless, the orchestra was driven to complain formally because of the director's behavior, which included telling brass players they were *maricones* ("fags") if they played poorly.

Given the centrality of the orchestra in El Sistema, it is perhaps unsurprising that discipline spills over into other teaching situations. Booth's (2010) Sistema leitmotif is "loving children into wholeness"; many students, however, reported fierce teachers and an aggressive learning environment in which shouting was commonplace and hitting pupils not unknown. As an experienced violin student stated baldly: "here in El Sistema, anyone who doesn't shout isn't a teacher."

Héctor, a student, was assigned to a núcleo as a teacher. His first trip to the school was with his own teacher, only a few years older than him, who went along to show him the ropes. Héctor reported that his teacher acted like "a Hitler" and instructed him to be tough on the children. A young teacher dressed in jeans and t-shirt is therefore no guarantee of an easy ride. One musician argued that younger teachers imposed discipline simply because they had been taught in an authoritarian vein themselves; they were putting El Sistema's "teach as you were taught" philosophy into practice.

The reality is thus often quite far from Booth's idealized vision. He does acknowledge that "teachers can seem demanding, can drive rehearsals hard with little overt affectionate expression" (2010, 8), yet he seems too attached to his idea of El Sistema as love to absorb the reality he describes. Likewise, Wakin (2012) talks of children being "rehearsed to within an inch of their lives," without showing much sign of allowing the evidence to shake his faith.

Ana claimed that Sistema teachers standardly described their pupils as "useless." One of her teachers made her cry in every lesson, and would say things like "your chair has more musical talent than you do." Another teacher was so famous for verbally abusing his pupils that they created a Facebook group to post some of his choice phrases. Nevertheless, said Ana, these teachers have produced some amazing students. Like authoritarian classical music programs in other countries, El Sistema is effective at honing the talents of the elite, and may serve well the toughest and most able.

An older student, Rosa, told me about an episode when she was beginning to play French horn. There was an important concert coming up, and she was asked to play a difficult solo part, even though she was still a relative beginner, because she was the best student available. Her teacher started off patiently during the preparatory seminario, but as they got closer to the concert day, he became stricter and stricter. Eventually, the day before the concert, she cried out in exasperation, "I can't do it," and her teacher hit her. Every time she said, "I can't do it," he would hit her—and he added, "don't complain either," for good measure. She described this as "Nazi training."

Rosa recalled that it was commonplace for teachers at Veracruz to expel students from lessons for musical lapses. She had had one teacher who applied a "three strikes and you're out" rule: he would set her a long musical extract to learn from memory, and in the next lesson she would have three opportunities to play it perfectly. If she failed to do so, he would tell her to leave. Another teacher had been more capricious, repeatedly throwing her out simply for "not playing well enough" (even though Rosa was one of the better students in the núcleo). Eventually he refused to teach her any more, and she was left without a teacher for a considerable period. Even so, she became a good player and went on to play in a national-level orchestra; so does the end justify the means?

If El Sistema's capacity to produce good orchestral musicians is clear, what requires much more discussion are the psychological effects of such programs on students. The readiness with which high-level classical music training spills over into psychological abuse has recently attracted considerable attention in the United Kingdom.[5] In Venezuela, several interviewees raised concerns about the psychological mistreatment of children in the program. Ana described her Sistema orchestra as an environment in which emotional manipulation was much in evidence, as young musicians were continually being both built up and put down. The director would tell the orchestra that it was going to be as good as the Berlin Phil, yet the treatment in rehearsals was often abusive. Her analysis was that playing with children's self-esteem made it easier to manipulate them.

Ana's former stand-mate described El Sistema as demanding and hypercompetitive, and claimed she was subject to constant criticism and pressure. The director regularly told her and her companions that they were useless; she called this "negative reinforcement" and argued that a more constructive attitude would have been more effective and enjoyable. She was subjected to El Sistema's signature stand-by-stand technique. This practice was sometimes used as a punishment, for example, for talking in rehearsal, which sits oddly with the dominant discourses linking music with spirituality and love. She blamed these experiences for the fear of public speaking that she continued to suffer long after she had stopped playing. Her account of a culture of pressure, humiliation, and frequent tears was a long way from the rosy publicity of Deutsche Grammophon, which waxes about "an atmosphere of encouragement, affection, mutual support and sheer, unfettered joy in the music at hand."

DISCIPLINE IN THEORY

It is highly illuminating to consider orchestral discipline and militarism through the lens of Michel Foucault's famous study *Discipline and Punish* (1991). The orchestra may be seen as an archetypal "disciplinary institution," emerging as part of "the gradual extension of the mechanisms of discipline throughout the seventeenth and eighteenth centuries, their spread throughout the whole social body" (1991, 209). Foucault's arguments thus have great relevance to a study of an orchestral program.

Foucault examines methods for controlling and correcting the operations of the body, such as military training and dressage, to argue that "discipline produces subjected and practised bodies, 'docile' bodies. Discipline increases the forces of the body (in economic terms of utility) and diminishes these same forces (in political terms of obedience)" (138). As aptitude increases, then, so does subjection and docility. Foucault cites incredibly detailed eighteenth-century ordinances concerning military marching and firing a rifle, in which every micro-movement of the body is controlled: "The act is broken down into its elements; the position of the body, limbs, articulations is defined; to each movement are assigned a direction, an aptitude, a duration; their order of succession is prescribed. Time penetrates the body and with it all the meticulous controls of power" (151). He goes on: "Over the whole surface of contact between the body and the object it handles, power is introduced, fastening them to one another" (153), resulting in a coercive link between instrument and human.

This analysis has considerable relevance to the process of learning to play classical music, finding echoes in instrumental manuals and prescriptive scores. It points to a very different idea of music making than that of artistic expression, creativity, and freedom. In Foucauldian terms, the relationship between instrument and player, often expressed in terms of love, may be one of subjection or coercion.

Witness the National Plan for Teacher Training, written by members of El Sistema's Latin American Violin Academy (Profili 2011). Learning the violin is separated into four stages: imitation, precision, control, and automatizing.

Imitation: kids watch and imitate correct posture, instrument hold, 4/8ths per bow, first position, start with martelé, detache, spiccato, major scales (sol, la, re) and their relative minors, tuning (repeats by imitation), forte/piano, keeps time (60 quarter). Kids learn the note names by ear (Suzuki mother tongue).

Precision: kids have more scientific knowledge, understands/adopt correct posture by themselves, understands the correct way of holding the instrument and bow, 4 eights to a bow, first and 3rd position, detaché-martelé-spiccato-balsato, developing quality of sound, corrects intonation, keeps precise rhythm, piano, mezzos, forte, FF, tempo 90.

Control: controls body posture and instrument hold, eight 8th notes per bow, 1, 3, 5th position, detaché/martelé/spiccato/balsato, tunes correctly, sufficient sound quality, pianissimo-ff, control tempi when performing, beginning vibrato, tempo: 120.

Automatizing: correct body-instrument position, uses bow and instrument correctly, eight 8ths notes per bow, 1-7th position, uses vibrato and tempo with sensitivity.

Foucault's commentary on the eighteenth-century military ordinances, with their detailed prescriptions for position, movement, and time, can be mapped directly onto this twenty-first-century music instruction manual. For Foucault, a rifle becomes "a body-weapon, body-tool, body-machine complex"; the violinist learns "correct body-instrument position." Foucault talks of a "coercive link with the apparatus of production"; the violinist controls (or is controlled), automatizes (or is automatized)—tellingly, it is hard to know which, though perhaps the answer is both. DeNora (2000) provides a positive picture of music consumption as a "technology of the self," but learning to play classical music according to strict guidelines could be perceived as a more problematic "technology of self-improvement," setting up an ideal of perfection and a developmental path along which to strive that lead not to autonomy but to docility and constraint.[6]

MAPPING AND SURVEILLANCE

Foucault argues that "discipline is an art of rank" (146). Musical language is revealing: "progressing through the orchestral ranks," "rank-and-file players." Sistema students are ranked through audition and placed on one of five levels: principal, assistant, A, B, and C. Orchestras, too, are graded by letters of the alphabet, and these rankings determine status and pay. Ranking is not just abstract but also physical. In Jesuit colleges of the eighteenth century, it determined seating position as well as status. Foucault compares the educational space to "a learning machine, but also as a machine for supervising, hierarchizing, rewarding. Jean-Baptiste de La Salle dreamt of a classroom in which the spatial distribution might provide a whole series of distinctions at once: according to the pupils' progress, worth, character, application, cleanliness and parents' fortune. Thus, the classroom would form a single great table, with many different entries, under the scrupulously 'classificatory' eye of the master" (147). The control of space and position of individuals within it, the relationship between physical position and rank, the overseeing eye of a master/maestro—these are also characteristic of the orchestra, whose layout exemplifies many of Foucault's points: to a specialist, it is an instantly readable table and map.

Foucault identifies three techniques as central to disciplining: hierarchical observation, normalizing judgment, and the examination. The parallel between hierarchical observation and the physical layout of the orchestra is inescapable: "The perfect disciplinary apparatus would make it possible for a single gaze to see everything constantly. A central point would be both the source of light illuminating everything, and a locus of convergence for everything that must be known: a perfect eye that nothing would escape and a centre towards which all gazes would be turned" (173). This is discipline; punishment comes in the form of normalizing judgment. El Sistema's stand-by-stand technique is a way of putting the individual on display and comparing their efforts to the norm enshrined on the page. Here we see the penal mechanism that Foucault identifies at the heart of disciplinary systems: "the soldier commits an 'offence' whenever he does not reach the level required; a pupil's 'offence' is not only a minor infraction, but also an inability to carry out his tasks" (179). The third technique of discipline, examination, is evident in El Sistema's regular auditions, which determine ranking by status and pay. More advanced students are evaluated constantly: those in Veracruz went to Caracas twice a year for examinations, and were also inspected in situ by an evaluator from the capital. The three core disciplinary techniques are thus integral to El Sistema's practices.

One of the most intriguing aspects of Foucault's argument is his discussion of the military review as a new kind of ceremony of power. He reproduces a commemorative medal that shows Louis XIV taking his first military review in 1666; the soldiers "are frozen into a uniformly repeated attitude of ranks and lines" (188). This medal is of particular relevance because in 1661, the year that Louis XIV assumed the throne, Jean-Baptiste Lully became *surintendant de la musique*. Lully is credited with creating the prototype of the modern orchestra by imposing a new level of discipline on the French king's ensembles, the 24 Violons du Roi and La Petite Bande, and "it was the highly disciplined orchestral playing in Lully's operas that gave the impetus for creating orchestras throughout much of Europe" (Buelow 2004, 168; 1993, 21). The 24 Violons du Roi were supplemented by a military woodwind band, La Musique de la Grande Ecurie, which played at a variety of occasions including military reviews. Louis XIV was particularly interested in martial music, and his army created a system of musicalized military commands (Brenet 1917).

Beyond the military metaphors, then, there is a close historical relationship between the disciplined military review and the disciplined orchestral display, giving a new complexion to some of El Sistema's signatory features: visitors' review of the different ensembles that perform in a display of military precision at Montalbán; Chávez (a military man) and Abreu reviewing the various ensembles and spaces at the official opening of the CASM; Abreu's nightly review of the National Children's Orchestra during its intensive seminarios. With their colorful jackets (uniforms) and choreographed dancing and swaying (maneuvers), showcase orchestra concerts are a kind of review that is as much visual as sonic, and the logical conclusion of a program of intense disciplining of young bodies.

DISCIPLINARY INSTITUTIONS

The example that Foucault famously chooses to illustrate his argument is Jeremy Bentham's Panopticon. Many have noted the parallels between this semicircular penal structure and the orchestra, with the conductor's all-seeing eye (and all-hearing ear) as the center of all lines of sight (e.g., Bergeron 1992). One of the Panopticon's features is lateral invisibility, which reduces the possibilities for horizontal communication and social bonding and thereby promotes order. This is also, to a degree, true of the orchestra, in which there is less lateral visibility than in most smaller ensembles. At one rehearsal I attended, the conductor lost his temper several times because the children were looking sideways rather than at him, either while playing solos (and therefore losing the beat) or during rests (and then failing to come in). Maintaining the line of sight between conductor and musicians, and reducing horizontal dynamics, is essential to youth orchestral discipline.

Music is one of the techniques that have participated in the historical shift in prisons from punishing to correcting, reclaiming, and curing. Bergeron (1992, 3) discusses the use of concert bands in U.S. prisons and the belief that musical training leads to low rates of recidivism, and argues that "to consider the prisoners' rehabilitation within the penitentiary band is to discover something like the musical equivalent of Bentham's Panopticon." As they strive to become "good" ensemble players, the inmates "learn to conduct *themselves*, so to speak, according to the canons of performance they share…. [T]he band thus implicates the musician in a network where acts of mutual surveillance serve to maintain the musical standard" (1992, 4).

This extension from the visual to the aural is not just Bergeron's: Bentham tried to include acoustic surveillance in his architectural model, though he abandoned the idea. "The prison band, in fulfilling this project, becomes in effect the 'Panacouston' Bentham couldn't quite imagine" (9). In the light of El Sistema's reverence for the classical orchestral canon, it is illuminating to read Bergeron's suggestion that "it is not really the watchman in the prison's central tower (nor, by analogy, the conductor of the band or orchestra) that maintains order among those enclosed, but rather what such figures, seen or unseen, *stand for*: a 'higher' authority, a 'standard' of excellence, all ideals embodied in what we call the canon" (4). Her brief study reveals discipline as the thread running through the prison, large directed musical ensembles, and canonical repertoire.

El Sistema shows many parallels with the penitentiary program Bergeron describes, and indeed, it has found a ready home in Venezuelan prisons. Furthermore, Foucault identifies a network that spread out from prisons, "a great carceral continuum that diffused penitentiary techniques into the most innocent disciplines" (1991, 297), identifiable in institutions for abandoned or indigent children, orphanages, charitable societies, and moral improvement associations. Significantly, El Sistema has a presence in charitable schools and the Christian educational NGO Fe y Alegría. Its effortless expansion into the institutions of the "carceral continuum" points toward its disciplinary foundations. El Sistema, like the prisons Foucault discusses, talks the language of total reform of the individual, of correcting the sin of idleness through work. "By occupying the convict, one gives him habits of order and obedience; one makes the idler that he was diligent and active," stated Bérenger in 1836 (quoted in 1991, 242)—words that could have come from El Sistema, had "convict" been swapped for "child."

Foucault describes a Christian school that supervised parents as well as children (211). A child's absence or bad behavior was a pretext to visit and question their parents and neighbors. Foucault sees this as a form of disciplining the population at large, often by apparently benevolent religious and charity organizations. We may recall here Love's earlier comment that El Sistema "reaches beyond state institutions deep into family structures." When I visited Montalbán, teachers described the núcleo's involvement with the children's home and school life, demanding school reports, for example. In his TED prize speech, Abreu stated: "The child becomes a role model for both his parents, and this is very important for a poor child. Once the child discovers he is important for his family, he begins to seek new ways of improving himself and hopes better for himself and his community. Also, he hopes for social and economic improvements for his own family. All this makes up a constructive and ascending social dynamic."[7] This aspiration to discipline the wider population—from child to family to community, reaching not just the thousands of young people under its charge but Venezuelan society as a whole—perfectly exemplifies Foucault's argument, providing a close parallel with his conception of the ascending, capillary action of power.

Discipline is thus expansive—socially, spatially, and temporally. The eighteenth-century French general Joseph Servan "dreamt of a military machine that would cover the whole territory of the nation and in which each individual would be occupied without interruption.... Military life would begin in childhood, when young children would be taught the profession of arms in 'military manors'; it would end in these same manors when the veterans, right up to their last day, would teach the children.... Similarly, one uses the labour of children and of old people in the great workshops" (165). The comparison between child soldiers, child labor, and El Sistema's child prodigies is an uncomfortable one, but Foucault's example finds distinct echoes in Abreu's dream of expansion into every corner of Venezuela and his focus on reaching children at the youngest possible age, later to convert them into teachers.

PRODUCTIVITY AND ITS COSTS

Both the orchestra and El Sistema are clearly identifiable as disciplinary institutions, and Foucault's analysis underlines that discipline is not simply a matter of an authoritarian conductor imposing his will, but is also diffused throughout the structures, dynamics, and practices of these organizations. Strict training, judging, classifying, and reviewing are all part of the disciplining and subjection of the individual. Consequently, discipline functions largely in silence and may even have a friendly, photogenic face.

Furthermore, disciplinary forces may be couched in positive language. Power, in Foucauldian terms, is productive as well as repressive. Bentham writes of the benefits to be obtained from his Panopticon design: "Morals reformed—health preserved—industry invigorated—instruction diffused [etc.]" (207). Disciplinary institutions can be regarded as having productive effects, indeed they are designed precisely to this end. They produce results, capitalize time, and increase outputs and profits. Panopticism maximizes the effect of troops and the productivity of workers. The massive projection of military methods onto industrial organization (and musical organization, for that matter) sees results in terms of utility and efficiency. El Sistema, too, is highly effective when it comes to producing musical results. Eschewing creativity and flexibility, it teaches children to follow leaders and obey orders, socializing them in the way of soldiers and assembly-line workers. Consequently, it mobilizes people and equipment in huge numbers, generates strong emotional responses, and garners astonishing political and economic support.

One of Foucault's central points, however, is that such productivity and reforming zeal come with significant social costs. Panopticism is "a design of subtle coercion for a society to come" (209)—resonant words, given Abreu and Dudamel's claims that an orchestra is a model for a future society. Identifying the orchestra and El Sistema as disciplinary institutions is a crucial theoretical move because it points toward the control, constraint, subjection, punishment, stratification, and individuation that lie beneath the productive surface of the Venezuelan program, generating conformity and docility and promoting vertical dependency over horizontal solidarity. Such effects may also be grasped through ethnography and anonymous interviews, but Foucault's analysis provides them with an explanatory framework, allowing us to see them as systemic rather than isolated, and as predictable rather than surprising.

As James Johnson (1997, 571–72) explains: "Disciplinary mechanisms...do not just render social relations less symmetrical and reciprocal but, crucially, they do so by simultaneously disrupting the communicative relations that nourish social and political agency and replacing them with patterns of thoroughgoing objectification.... [D]isciplinary power is normatively objectionable precisely because it imposes unequal, asymmetrical, nonreciprocal relations and because, in so doing, it obliterates the sorts of extant communicative relations that, potentially at least, could promote social relations characterized by equality, symmetry and reciprocity." The price of El Sistema's disciplinary approach and impressive results may then be the very social values that it supposedly fosters.

The Venezuelan diplomat Francia Coromoto Malvar told the Quebec Music Educators Association that "the Venezuelan government values El Sistema for much more than its musical achievements—'the system' instills the values of liberty, democracy, solidarity, responsibility, equality, justice, and opportunity, equipping children to become agents of positive social change" ("Adopt or Adapt?" 2012). Yet, as Johnson suggests, disciplinary institutions and mechanisms in fact *counteract* most of these values, and actually curb rather than foster children's social and political agency, since, as Foucault (1991, 221) argues, "discipline is the unitary technique by which the body is reduced as a 'political' force at the least cost and maximized as a useful force." Foucault's suggestion is that intensive, specialized, and disciplined training of the body serves to produce docile rather than politically engaged citizens. This argument has great significance for El Sistema, a project embedded within and funded by a revolutionary government that has made considerable efforts to integrate ordinary citizens into political processes. It suggests that the government is devoting large resources to a project that may be counteracting its efforts at fostering political consciousness and agency.

The key question about a disciplinary system like El Sistema is not, then, whether it produces visible results, but at what cost. A huge children's orchestra playing Mahler 2 is certainly impressive, but it reveals the program's effectiveness as a system of production, not its ethical dimensions or social impact. Evaluating El Sistema through its choreographed displays is thus woefully inadequate, since it ignores the price of this spectacular façade—the imposition of "unequal, asymmetrical, non-reciprocal relations," and the enactment of "a design of subtle coercion for a society to come."

THE THIRD WAVE

Many of the benefits attributed to music programs were also generated in the short term by The Third Wave, an experiment in fascism carried out at a California high school in 1967 by a history teacher named Ron Jones. The experiment illustrated that discipline, motivation, and academic achievement can improve markedly under an autocratic system. In other words, these kinds of outcomes—exactly the same ones claimed for El Sistema—do not necessarily point to desirable educational or social processes.

Jones's (2008) account throws up some fascinating material. As we might expect, in the light of Foucault's argument, the authoritarian learning environment brought about some marked improvements in the classroom. However, it was productive of action rather than thinking, leading Jones to wonder: "Why did the students accept the authority I was imposing? Where is their curiosity or resistance to this marshal [sic] behavior?" Both teacher and students became swept up in the experiment: soon, "the whole class was standing and reciting. It was fun. The students began to look at each other and sense the power of belonging." The students not only enjoyed themselves but also became fiercely loyal to the program, in some cases actively enforcing its rules.

Despite the mock-fascist environment, no one wanted to drop out, and students joined voluntarily from other classes. "I had been pushing information at them in an extremely controlled setting but the fact that they found it comfortable and acceptable was startling." Jones, too, deemed the experience pleasurable: "I found it harder and harder to extract myself from the momentum and identity that the class was developing. I was following the group dictate as much as I was directing it." Jones had become part of the experiment: "The Third Wave had become the center of their existence. I was in pretty bad shape myself. I was now acting instinctively as a dictator."

There are many lessons that may be applicable to El Sistema. An authoritarian environment may generate authoritarian behavior even on the part of liberally inclined individuals. As Jones put it: "We get or take an ascribed role and then bend our life to fit the image." An orchestral program may thus become a production line of authoritarianism, as individuals step into roles in which they are expected (by orchestral tradition) to exercise power over others. It also illustrates how a disciplined environment may provoke participants to want *more* discipline rather than critique it. Indeed, most of my student interviewees regarded discipline positively, and a number wanted to see more of it in El Sistema. This is perhaps an unsurprising finding among advanced classical music students—few people ill-suited to or critical of discipline would continue for so long in an intensive classical music program, and positive reviews of orchestras often mention strict discipline—but Jones points to a wider phenomenon: discipline's production of disciplinary desire.

Most importantly, however, Jones illustrates the compatibility of authoritarianism and pleasure. The students not only embraced but developed fierce loyalty toward a system that reduced their freedom and autonomy. His account serves as a riposte to those who reject criticism of El Sistema with the words: "if it's so problematic, why do the children keep going back?" Of course, there are many possible answers to this question—some may be motivated by economic or parental pressures—but in many cases the answer may be "because they enjoy it." Following orders in pursuit of a common aim may be comfortable or even enjoyable for many individuals—perhaps more so than thinking. Just as Foucault portrays discipline as productive as well as coercive, Jones paints his experiment in mixed colors. However, given that most parents would probably not want their children to be educated in a fascist classroom, enjoyment in no way precludes or defuses ideological critique. Authoritarianism may be pleasurable as well as productive, but it is still ethically problematic.

CONCLUSION: SOCIAL INCLUSION, DISCIPLINE, AND CAPITALISM

On a final note, not only are El Sistema's claims to promote social inclusion multiply flawed, but its focus on this trope elides the crucial issue of equality (see also Logan n.d.). El Sistema produces social stratification and inequalities via the internal organization of the orchestra and also the structure of the program itself, implementing pay and status differentials between principals and *practicantes*, elite performers and núcleo teachers, yet those obvious effects are masked by talk of inclusion. The production of highly stratified social microcosms is a point of great significance for two reasons. First, more equal societies are associated with improved life chances (Wilkinson and Pickett 2010). Second, equality is considered a cornerstone of social justice. Since it is accompanied by the production of inequality, El Sistema's pursuit of social inclusion, even if taken at face value, is unlikely to foster a healthier or fairer society.

Borchert (2012) explores how El Sistema's concept of social inclusion merges with those of productivity, discipline, responsibility, respect, and punctuality. "Social inclusion" thus masks the production not only of inequality but also of disciplined subjects for capitalism (the same ideology that produced their exclusion in the first place). As David Holt, president of Modern Enterprise Ltd. and a sponsor of Sistema New Brunswick, puts it, "in the long-term *Sistema* will help create a better quality of workforce in our province" (quoted in 2012, 57). In Venezuela, needless to say, those who are unwilling or unable to submit to this socialization in capitalist values will generally be disincluded; El Sistema's miniature society has little space for the unruly or unproductive.

The dual process of including and disciplining children thus also involves stratifying them, reducing their political agency, and making them more productive. Rather than modeling a utopia—a fairer and healthier world—El Sistema produces a microcosm of capitalist society. It turns young people's free time to work rather than play and, in the case of the most talented, converts their efforts into profit for the global music industry. Discipline, for Foucault (1991, 219), is the expression of military and capitalist thinking; it is the perfect watchword, then, for Abreu, schooled in Jesuit theology and business administration. These twin ideologies, so deeply ensconced within El Sistema, provide the key to understanding social inclusion and discipline in the present context.

CHAPTER 9

Democracy, Teamwork, Competition, and Meritocracy

It's one big family...like the Sicilian mafia.
                    —Orchestral administrator

If a thousand must be sacrificed so that four make it, the sacrifice is well worth it.
                    —José Antonio Abreu

A team effort is a lot of people doing what I say.
                    —Michael Winner

One of the stranger claims made about El Sistema is that "the orchestra is a clear example of democratic functioning in a society" (Borzacchini 2010, 101). It is hard to see what kind of democracy is represented by an organization in which a single unelected leader exercises absolute power indefinitely. In earlier historical periods the orchestra signified, rather more accurately, "the wealth, power, and legitimacy of the ruler and the state" (Spitzer and Zaslaw 2005, 529)—in other words, absolutism.

As Channing (2003, 181) puts it simply, "orchestras are by their nature authoritarian—the conductor is the final arbiter." Osborne (1999, 72) identifies the growing autocracy of the conductor in the nineteenth century as "culturally isomorphic with the counter-revolutionary authoritarianism that evolved after the suppression of the 1848 revolts in central Europe." John Rawls could only link the symphony orchestra with liberal democracy by omitting the figure of the composer-conductor (Love 2006).

Cottrell (2004, 107) portrays the relationship between conductor and orchestral musician in an unflattering light. One of his interviewees claims: "You basically subjugate your whole person, all your ideas, your own personal ideas, you have to just completely throw them away. Just say, right, I don't matter. The guy on the box, on the podium, he's the guy that matters." Another states: "It's a little bit like being in a communist state really, being in an orchestra, in that you've got this Chairman Mao in front of you" (107).

Woodford (2005) underlines that the historical roots of large ensembles are found in autocratic institutions such as the military, Church, and aristocracy, and their "overemphasis on emotion, spectacle, ritual, or musical commodification may also contribute to the undermining of democratic culture by failing to adequately prepare children to intelligently participate in public musical life" (2005, 28–29). The contrasting of democracy and spectacle is telling. In a democratic culture, critical inquiry has a central place and "no one has a monopoly on truth and understanding" (35)—not views that find much space in the average orchestra. An intensive orchestral training program headed by two conductors is not, then, an obvious school for democracy.

Spich and Sylvester (1999, 24–25) argue that symphony organizations, too, tend to be autocratic in nature: "Symphony management style—and the resulting organizational culture—is often a carryover from the symphony tradition in which the conductor is the final and major authority figure, and deference to his or her interpretation of tradition is common. Thus authoritarianism and central control over all decisions has been the hallmark of symphony organization culture."

THE WEDO AND ORCHESTRAL POLITICS

A member of the WEDO explained that it would be impossible for the orchestra to print a statement of purpose in its concert programs: "how were you going to get over a hundred people from mutually hostile nations to agree on a single statement?" (Cheah 2009, 264). The orchestra can "agree on" a single musical statement, but not a sociopolitical one. Why? Because the first "agree on" means "obey," something that needs to be borne in mind when considering Abreu's much-quoted aphorism: "The orchestra is the only group that comes together with the sole purpose of agreement." The conventional orchestra is an effective instrument for the subjection of multiple viewpoints by the singular vision of its leader, but extramusical democracy is more elusive. Dudamel claims that the orchestra is an ideal community because "[w]hatever your differences are, you have to solve problems to make harmony" (Swed 2014). The WEDO exemplifies, however, the disjuncture between musical and social harmony in an orchestral setting—a disjuncture that undercuts the core Sistema claim that one produces the other.

As Riiser (2010) argues, for all the utopian discourse around the WEDO, the combination of the inherently hierarchical nature of the symphony orchestra and the leadership of a powerful, charismatic individual ensures that narratives emerging through the orchestra are dictated rather than negotiated. Barenboim's absolute power curtails the free debate necessary for democratic functioning: "Fear that they would not get a scholarship, not be invited to the next workshop, or more generally not be accepted as a musician by Barenboim, leads some orchestra members to self-censor themselves and their discussion comments in ways they think that Barenboim might approve" (2010, 31). Barenboim talks about democracy and self-expression, but closer examination reveals the orchestra as a tool for him to express his musical and political ideas.

Cheah's (2009) study of WEDO attempts to argue for a degree of social democracy in the orchestra, stating that anyone could stand up and confront Barenboim in rehearsals; but she admits that the musical hierarchy was strong, and her portrait of Barenboim as powerful, even god-like, "extremely didactic" (23), very demanding with musicians, and "the ultimate authority" (79) point to a fundamentally authoritarian system. As she admits, "Barenboim had the last word, of course" (68). Her portrait is revealing, even when slightly tongue in cheek. "There was . . . a dark side to the Maestro's attention to detail: once a principle had been demonstrated and established, it was practically a personal affront to him not to uphold it constantly. This could bring forth the evil cousin of Barenboim the patient pedagogue: Barenboim the ominous ogre" (115). (There are echoes here of Rivero's characterization of Abreu as "the philanthropic ogre.") Barenboim could be funny, but also angry, impatient, and relentlessly demanding. Cheah reveals a single, all-powerful, autocratic figure at the helm and a major cult of personality.

Particularly striking is Cheah's comment that "in rehearsal, the musicians are absolutely obedient and respectful of the most minor musical detail; outside of rehearsal and performance, they are irreverent" (118). This is a crucial observation: egalitarianism and democracy are not entirely absent in WEDO, but they are practiced largely in *nonmusical* situations such as mealtimes and breaks. It is precisely *during music making that authoritarianism is most pronounced*. El Sistema argues that the orchestra is a social microcosm that has the potential to reform an imperfect world; but Cheah shows that the outside world brings relief from the excesses generated through orchestral music making. A progressive vision would entail modeling the orchestra on everyday society, rather than the other way around.

AUTOCRACY IN EL SISTEMA

El Sistema, too, is dominated by a powerful, charismatic leader. It is a child of the Punto Fijo period, when Venezuela had "a model of illiberal democracy" (Buxton 2011, xv). Autocracy is found at the level of orchestral microcosm as well as organizational macrocosm—unsurprisingly, given Abreu's joint role as founding conductor and founding director. As a senior Sistema musician told Tunstall (2012, 65): "José Antonio was obsessed with working on the sheer beauty of the orchestra's sound. In rehearsals, he would say, 'I want this sound!' And they would play the same passage over and over and over, trying to get at what he wanted, until he would finally say, 'That's it! That's the sound!'" The idea that someone other than Abreu might have a say in the orchestra's sound seems not to occur to anyone, including Tunstall. The musicians' role is to realize their leader's vision, not express their own.

Higgins (2008) argues that Dudamel is forcing a rethinking of the hierarchies of the symphony orchestra. For all his charisma, however, he is no more upsetting the traditional hierarchy than a slave who became overseer was challenging the structures of colonialism. The power dynamic is the same; it is just played out with a winning smile. Dudamel openly admires the orchestra's autocratic system: "what a beautiful model for a society. Everyone together, listening to each other, with one goal" (Higgins 2011)—one decided, of course, by the conductor.

In Veracruz, the traditional hierarchy remained untouched, if anything exaggerated. In one rehearsal, a flautist who disagreed with the conductor was told that she was being disrespectful and that she "had to learn to respect," provoking her to walk out. The conductor explained later that there had to be "a single idea" (his, of course), and there was no room for competing visions. As a member of the orchestra said: "it has nothing to do with democracy— here no one gives their opinion."

For a while the director used to meet with the orchestra's section principals, one of them reported, but he really just informed them of what was going to happen, or guided them toward a predetermined decision. The meetings were not genuinely consultative, and the practice died out. When orchestra members started complaining about the lack of a finish time for evening rehearsals, they had to write a letter to the conductor, illustrating the lack of an existing space for discussion. Truly democratic functioning is a challenge for a large group, but consultation and the sense of having a voice are a major key to harmonious relations: "In most successful and happy orchestras, players are kept well informed of developments, both internally and externally.... Players' representatives or committees have real input into the vision, strategy and major decisions of these orchestras" (Gillinson and Vaughan 2003, 195). My informant's experience, however, was that conductors were rarely interested in listening to musicians' opinions, and that meetings were infrequent and entailed one-way communication. Consequently, most Sistema musicians preferred to work through private channels of communication with more senior figures, rather than engaging in public debate.

In Venezuela, classical musicians are socialized from a young age into the autocratic functioning of an orchestra, so many are either unaware of it or cannot imagine any other way of making music collectively. While most interviewees agreed that they had no power to take decisions or influence outcomes in the orchestra, they saw this as normal, natural, or even positive. If everyone had their say, stated one violinist, nothing would get done. Of his teacher, he said, "he chooses the repertoire and I play how he wants ... that's how it should be . . . you've got to agree somehow." Such reports contradict Uy's (2012) positive assessment of El Sistema, which is based on the notion that students are "dialoguing" extensively with their teachers.

As one of my interviewees pointed out, El Sistema has little time for grassroots, participatory democracy: it operates through direct dealings between high-level contacts, leaving most musicians out of the decision making. Compare the program to the Venezuelan community radio stations studied by Fernandes (2010, 182–85), in which spaces of deliberation are actively created and collective decision making encouraged. Fernandes portrays a culture of assemblies, consultation, debate, and public criticism—a far cry from life in the núcleo. This contrast is particularly important when considered in the broader context of Venezuelan politics. After Chávez's election in 1998, the Venezuelan constitution was changed to promote "participatory and protagonistic democracy" (López Maya and Lander 2011). This fundamental shift was seen as key to addressing deep-rooted problems of exclusion and social injustice: "now participation in all spheres of the state is regarded as a key educational practice for transforming fundamentally unequal social relations" (2011, 59). It is not just that El Sistema is organized undemocratically in the liberal sense; by ignoring the constitution's exhortation of "the participation of the people in the formation, execution and control of public administration" (59), its functioning, at the level of both organization and orchestra, runs squarely against the government's efforts to empower the grassroots and promote social justice by fostering direct democracy. Once again, the program appears as a state within (and in contradiction with) the state.

Orchestras and democracy are not necessarily in opposite corners. The Orpheus Chamber Orchestra made radical changes to traditional structures in order to "put power in the hands of the people doing the work" (Seifter 2001): "Unlike most orchestras, whose conductors wield full and unquestioned authority over the musicians playing under their baton, Orpheus musicians decide for themselves who will lead the group, how a piece of music will be played, who will be invited to join their ranks, and who will represent them on the board of trustees and within management." Orpheus members are expected to listen but also to talk: "No topic is considered out of bounds for the members of the group, and constructive criticism is always welcome. This freedom of expression is surprising when one realizes that orchestral musicians are trained from an early age specifically not to offer their opinions to the group and instead to defer to the direction of the conductor."

The Orpheus exemplifies a musical democracy rarely found in the orchestral world. It points up the authoritarianism of Borzacchini's (2010, 7) exhortation that in El Sistema, "everyone needs to be fully in tune in order to achieve unison," and her imagining of a future Venezuela that is "perfectly in tune, with all its citizens joined in a single direction" (2013, 213). Compare with Sennett's (2012, 14) more democratic vision: "sheer homogeneity is no recipe for making music together—or rather, a very dull recipe. Musical character appears instead through little dramas of deference and assertion; in chamber music, particularly, we need to hear individuals speaking in different voices which sometimes conflict."

HARMONY

El Sistema's use of musical metaphors, but particularly metaphors of harmony, is revealing. The rather sinister idea of tuning up children to achieve a single voice is hard to square with claims for democratic functioning, because democracies are not harmonious: they are diverse and discordant. Nor are liberatory, creative environments perfectly in tune; they make space for dissent and cultivate divergent thinking (Jorgensen 2004, 9–11). To imagine a harmonious society based on the orchestra is to imagine the presence of a script that must be followed and a leader with the power to correct or silence jarring notes. The dream of a society that sings in unison, perfectly in tune, evokes the (mono)culture of conformity typically found in cults (see Chapter 3).

Historically, images of a harmonious society have often revolved around strict control and an absolute ruler, imagined by the fifteenth-century urban theorist Rodrigo Sánchez de Arévalo as a prudent musician, loosening and tightening the strings of the civic instrument to create "perfect and sweet harmony and concord" (quoted in Baker 2010, 4). Jean Bodin, a French royal councilor who published *Six livres de la République* (1576), the first theory of absolute power, argued for princely sovereignty on the basis of harmonic principles (van Orden 2005, 68–76). He tried to prove that monarchy was the best form of "harmonicall [sic] governance," using harmony to rationalize the uneven distribution of power. Given its historical links to absolutist rule in Europe, it is unsurprising that harmony figured prominently in the colonization of the New World (Baker 2010). In Latin America, the language of harmony has masked the will to power since the sixteenth century, employed to naturalize elites' attempts to consolidate their position and discipline the masses.

Similar examples of the discourse of harmony cloaking the exercise of power may be drawn from many places and historical periods (e.g., Broyles 2012; Scott 2012, 54). One of the most striking passages in Foucault's *Discipline and Punish* is a quotation from T. N. Des Essarts's 1787 book about the Parisian police: "All the radiations of force and information that spread from the circumference culminate in the magistrate-general.... It is he who operates all the wheels that together produce *order and harmony*. The effects of his administration cannot be better compared than to the movement of the celestial bodies" (1991, 213, emphasis added). On the one hand, we have order and harmony, the music of the spheres; on the other hand, we have its origin— a centralized police force, "a single, strict, administrative machine" (213). The coercive aspect of harmony could hardly be clearer, leading the metaphors of El Sistema as a "big harmonious family" or a "harmonious society" to take on a different hue.

There are close echoes of Foucault's example in Rancière's argument that "[t]he essence of politics is *dissensus*," whereas consensus consists in "the reduction of politics to the police," resulting in "continual shrinkage of political space" (2010, 38, 42, 72). A discourse of social harmony is thus allied with the curbing of political agency discussed in Chapter 8. For Rancière, the logic of consensus underpins "hierarchical distributions where everyone's speech is determined in terms of their proper place and their activity in terms of its proper function" (2). It is not hard to see the orchestra in this autocratic formulation, and Rancière's analysis reveals its links to the discourse of harmony and the managerial state. The language of consensus—like that of harmony, *concertación*, and being "fully in tune"—articulates a desire for a rigid, hierarchical, and coercive social structure. For Rancière, consensus is antidemocratic, while dissensus and disruption are essential: "genuine political or artistic activities always involve forms of innovation that tear bodies from their assigned places" (1). The difficulty of imagining dissensus finding a home in El Sistema is highly revealing with regard to the program's position on the police/politics continuum.

Other scholars too, such as Rosalyn Deutsche, Ernesto Laclau, and Chantal Mouffe, have argued that antagonism and conflict are fundamental to a democratic public sphere: "a democratic society is one in which relations of conflict are sustained, not erased. Without antagonism there is only the imposed consensus of authoritarian order" (Bishop 2004, 65–66). In a similar vein, the "Holy Grail" for Sennett (2012) is not consensus but dialogic cooperation. Dialogic describes "a discussion which does not resolve itself by finding common ground" yet fosters understanding (2012, 19). Chamber music obliges cooperation, because there is no final authority, but does not depend on consensus, any more than good conversation depends on agreement. Sennett's interest in chamber music derives from its promotion of cooperation without consensus; he makes no mention of the orchestra, which often imposes consensus without cooperation.

Music education scholars are showing increasing interest in such ideas. Schmidt (2008) argues that music education must embrace dissensus, conflict, and disorder, which are not just inevitable but also productive and important. He notes that "the 'agreement' that enables discourse is often not so much a function of consensus as of the power held and wielded by those considered worthy: those whose voices count" (2008, 20–21)—an important point in light of Abreu's aphorism about the orchestra and agreement cited earlier. Wright (2014) draws on Biesta's "pedagogy of interruption" and Mouffe to argue for informal learning, since it produces gaps and disruptions that provide opportunities to rebalance teacher/student relationships and bolster student agency. As learning is "up for grabs" at such moments, disruptions have an important role to play in fostering democracy and inclusion in music education. This is the opposite of Borzacchini's vision of a nation in which "everyone needs to be fully in tune in order to achieve unison."

SYMBOLIC DEMOCRACY

Before leaving the issue of democracy, it is worth considering a deeper layer of political action. Lee (1998) sketches out a theory of symbolic democracy, which sees the symbolic order of society as a constitutive force that affects democratic organization. He regards this force as a form of political power that, since it is unequally distributed across the social order, is an undemocratic constraint on symbolic practices, and he thus seeks "the redistribution of symbolic power in *democratic* terms" (1998, 434). The core of Lee's argument is that "with regard to symbolic democracy, the goal of increased participation or inclusion centers on the potential for *active participation by the maximum number of interested citizens in the constitution of society's symbolic order*. In a culturally stratified social order, elite cultural producers and institutions commanding a felicitous mixture of symbolic authority and economic resources hold a disproportionate advantage in the creation and use of symbolic resources (meanings, categories, and knowledge) over less well-endowed individuals and institutions" (447, emphasis added). Crucially, Lee identifies inclusion as active participation in the *constitution* of society's symbolic order—not simply as active participation *tout court*, which may serve to reaffirm existing inequalities.

Lee continues: "The ultimate goal of affirmative recognition is to empower symbolically disadvantaged individuals...to exert symbolic power" (448). Empowering individuals means opening up the possibility of dissent, which is essential to democratic functioning: "*symbolic disobedience*, the disruption of established patterns of symbolic interaction, enables ordinary citizens to raise a critical perspective on the legitimacy of the symbolic order" (449). Lee proposes three criteria for judging the democratic, inclusive credentials of cultural creations: "the quality of the knowledge about the symbolic order that they bring into existence"; "their contribution to the de-hierarchization of existing symbolic categories"; and "the types of less coercive and less hierarchical symbolic interactions that they bring into the repertoire of symbolic practices" (450). Promoting symbolic democracy entails "enhancing the capacity of individuals and groups who are at risk to respond to this threat by creating and deploying their own self-representations and definitions" (451).

Lee's argument sheds important light on El Sistema's claims to inclusion and democracy. El Sistema does nothing to encourage those at risk to create and deploy *their own* self-representations and definitions; instead, it signs them up to elite representations and definitions. It has nothing to do with the right to cultural creation or challenging symbolic inequality; it reaffirms the symbolic order, simply allowing a few individuals to shift position within it while the structure remains the same. It does not promote de-hierarchization of existing symbolic categories or encourage less hierarchical symbolic interactions, since it focuses on conventional symphonic orchestral practice. Children play no part in the construction of the symbolic order, hence El Sistema does not fulfill Lee's definition of inclusion; and because "durable patterns of symbolic inequality are part and parcel of the unequal distribution of political and economic resources" (451), a program that maintains such symbolic inequality cannot be considered democratic.

The claim that El Sistema is advancing democracy is thus highly questionable. As Logan (n.d.) argues, the program "promotes the democratization of a ready-made culture, not cultural democracy." El Sistema is making autocracy available to many more people, and therefore realizing the oppressive rather than emancipatory potential of classical music.

THE COLLECTIVE VERSUS THE INDIVIDUAL

El Sistema's primary concern is the collective, not the individual. "Here, everything is communal, everything is about the team," asserts Higgins (2008) positively. A Veracruz violinist's tone was slightly different: "they obliged me to be in the orchestra. You know, they have to create masses...not an individual being, but a mass, a collective." Another student claimed that the program cares little about individuals, who are easily replaceable; "you may love El Sistema," he said rather poignantly, "but it doesn't love you." A third stated: "you have to be a small piece in order to make something big, a big machine...you have to function well so that the machine functions." An informant told Uy (2012, 18): "you are part of a machine, it is really sad, but this is what happens."

Young musicians see themselves as cogs in a vast mechanism; if it enables the machine to function better, a cog will be replaced. El Sistema trains children up to be interchangeable parts: as spokesman Rodrigo Guerrero told Tunstall (2012, 167), "a child who moves from one núcleo to another or from one city to another will be able to begin work seamlessly where he left off." This industrial image reveals a program driven not by progressive pedagogical principles but by the urge to ensure that the child, and above all the machine, keeps working smoothly.

Foucault (1991, 165) places the mechanization of education in historical context, describing the emergence from the seventeenth century of "the complex clockwork of the mutual improvement school" that "became a machine for learning." Disciplinary institutions more generally developed to produce "individuals mechanized according to the general norms of an industrial society"

(1991, 242). It is not just disciplinary education that is implicated; the orchestra, too, has a special place. Max Weber took the orchestra to epitomize the rationalization that he critiqued for bringing "disenchantment of the world" and reducing individuals to "a cog in a machine," trapped in a bureaucratic "iron cage."[1] His strikingly bleak depiction of El Sistema's central feature is echoed in reports from Venezuelan musicians.

Both the orchestra and El Sistema thus counteract the valuing of the individual that Julian Johnson (2002, 8–9) sees as an essential feature of classical music: "the rationalization of human life—both private and public—has severely threatened the idea of individuals' value by making them dispensable units in a quantitative system. The high value accorded to art, classical music included, derives from its opposition to the social devaluation of the particular and individual. In a social world in which individuals become increasingly interchangeable and dispensable, art dwells on the particular and finds in it something of absolute value." Yet Sistema participants perceived themselves precisely as "dispensable units," and Richard Hackman reveals that recognizing and valuing individuals is an endemic problem for orchestras more generally (Judy 1996, 8). A disciplinary orchestral training program forces on musicians the rationalization that the music itself potentially opposes.

Abreu's critics argue that he is not particularly interested in individuals unless they show great promise as conductors or mascots for the project. A founder described El Sistema as a personal army of musicians who can be wheeled out at Abreu's whim; these foot soldiers are not in themselves of great interest. What matters is that the visiting dignitaries are impressed and the funders open their wallets; who actually constitutes the orchestra, or the sacrifices they have to make, are of less importance. This is a project built in the image of a man who told a professional conductor: "if it is necessary to sacrifice a thousand so that four make it, the sacrifice is well worth it."

The emphasis on the orchestra over its individual members can be seen in the functioning of the National Children's Orchestra. This is not a permanent orchestra but rather one that comes together for irregular seminarios. Cara, a violinist who played in the orchestra for seven years, reported that it stopped meeting for a long period but that the members were not told anything—they simply were not contacted for two years. Luis, a member of the 2007 ensemble, described the orchestra coming together for ten days and playing under Simon Rattle. The seminario was a great success and the players' teachers told them that they would be going on tour to Germany, but that was the last that he heard. There were new auditions in 2010; a new orchestra was formed, and Luis was not in it. Andrés, a younger musician, was given a place in the same section from which Luis had been dropped. But Andrés had a similar experience: a few days of intensive seminario, a great performance, and then dropped without a word. Luis's sister auditioned, was accepted, and was then "deselected" before the seminario began, without a reason being given.

Of course, disappointment is part of life in a competitive world, and an elite orchestra inevitably discards many musicians in its selection processes, but these examples illustrate El Sistema's opaqueness. When musicians are needed, the phone rings from Caracas and the wheels are set in motion; one day the phone stops ringing and they hear no more. Hopes are raised and dashed, often without explanation. El Sistema holds up a dream to children that few will attain and even fewer will sustain. The showcase orchestras themselves continue onward and upward, reaping headlines around the world; but members may fall by the wayside, without even a phone call, much less words of encouragement or consolation. Booth (2008, 9), in his paean to El Sistema, writes of its "relentless, honed focus, on key goals.... [T]he focus has remained clear and unwavering, and they have refined, polished, refreshed, and deepened their practices to achieve those ends." Booth is right: El Sistema is driven by ends not means, giving it a ruthless edge that even his intended praise reflects.

A musician who had played in the National Children's Orchestra claimed that El Sistema encourages young musicians to devote their lives to their orchestra. It interferes with their education, leading some to have to repeat years at school or even drop out. What happens, she asked, to students who get injured or have to give up for whatever reason, yet have neglected their education? El Sistema's principal focus is collective orchestral performance rather than personal development. Systemically speaking, the orchestra and the music take precedence over the individual; the machine is more important than the cog.

A talented Veracruz clarinetist described how she had spent two weeks working every day to prepare a difficult solo part for a forthcoming concert. She arrived at the dress rehearsal to find an older musician from another city in her seat; the conductor had replaced her at the last minute, without telling her, in order to ensure the best possible performance. The music mattered more than the feelings of individual musicians. After this happened again, she left the youth orchestra, deeply dispirited by her lack of control over her musical life. If everything is about the team, what happens to the individual?

This issue is also evident in the question of instruments. One of El Sistema's selling points is that it provides instruments to students (though in practice there are sometimes shortages and the available instruments may be of insufficient quality for better players). The downside is that if a student stops playing in a Sistema orchestra—wishing to focus on other musical activities, say, or concentrate on their academic studies—that instrument may be taken away, with potentially disastrous consequences for the individual's musical career. The director of a non-Sistema music school asked incredulously how the program could encourage a young person to devote all their free time to music for a decade and then take their instrument away. Another director suggested that if the program insisted on paying students, their wages should go into a fund to buy them an instrument rather than be given to them in cash; that would eliminate the practice of *meter paquete*, or playing in a youth orchestra just for the money, and ensure the possibility of lifelong playing, rather than a musical career potentially delimited by Sistema participation.

TEAMWORK VERSUS INDIVIDUALISM

One of the most common assumptions underpinning justifications of El Sistema is that playing together in an orchestra fosters teamwork. This statement appears on the FESNOJIV website and in Cuesta's (2008) crucial report that underpinned a $150 million loan from the IDB (see Chapter 11). It is endlessly invoked by Sistema participants and supporters, but is it based on reflection and research, or on the internalization and repetition of commonplaces?

Studies of organizations illustrate that teamwork does not flow automatically from collective activities, hence the existence of team-building exercises (in sport or business). The literature on orchestras reveals that teamwork is in fact a significant problem in this particular sphere. Teamwork requires dialogue of a kind that is rarely found in orchestral settings. Paradoxically, an organization that prioritizes the collective at the expense of the individual is not necessarily one that fosters teamwork over individualism.

Criss (2010, 31), writing about music education, recognizes that team building is a crucial activity in a large ensemble setting: "Directors of performing ensembles sometimes mistakenly take for granted that students of their ensembles aim for a common goal and strive for effective teamwork to achieve maximum success in performance. Teachers of young performing arts students find that this is not necessarily so. Student performers need to be *taught* how to work together to achieve synergy." A group of people engaged in collective activity can learn to perform better and enjoy themselves more if they think of teamwork as something to be created through collective decision making. El Sistema, however, views teamwork as an automatic consequence of playing music together—and thus does nothing to foster it.

A project designed to promote teamwork would look very different from a Sistema starter orchestra: open-ended and creative rather than fixed and repetitive, involving interaction in order to solve problems rather than simply playing and moving in unison (e.g., Wolf 1999). Promoting teamwork means fostering discussion, evaluation, and negotiation, something that is much more likely to emerge from creative practices like collaborative composing, arranging, and improvising than from simply playing music together (Burnard and Younker 2010). One of the easiest ways to boost teamwork is to remove the teacher/conductor, which obliges musicians to negotiate rather than follow instructions (Green 2008, 133).

As for the symphony orchestra world, Faulkner (1973a, 336) describes it as "one of the most complex, competitive, and stratified organizational sets in existence." For all that activity is collective, thinking is individualist, since status is key. "Stratification within organizations enhances the importance of invidious comparisons among members" (1973a, 342). Professional mobility is important for orchestral musicians, given that room for personal and musical growth is often limited. Development or advancement is thus considered in personal terms, and may be at the expense of colleagues: Faulkner uses the telling phrase "colleague competitors," while a London-based professional orchestral musician stated simply that coworkers were friends and enemies at the same time. The collectivity afforded by communal music making can easily be undermined by the individualism of high-level classical music.

Hackman, well known for his detailed studies of orchestras, has also researched the issue of team effectiveness, and he repeatedly criticizes the symphony orchestra as an example of a poorly functioning team. He states: "There are two certain ways to make sure that team magic does *not* occur, both of which are seen far too often in work organizations. One...is to act like a maestro on the podium" (2002, 253). He also argues that while good teams respond quickly and flexibly to the unexpected, less effective teams "have more in common with a professional symphony orchestra, whose members' responsibilities do not extend beyond playing well what the score and the conductor dictate, than with a self-managing string quartet whose members have broad latitude for deciding both what and how they will play" (2002, 76). Sennett (2012), another keen observer of social interaction, echoes Hackman: when his discussion of cooperation and togetherness turns to music, he focuses on chamber music and to a lesser extent jazz—orchestras do not get a look in. Similarly, Cook's (2004) argument that classical music involves just as much improvisation and social interaction as jazz rests on the example of a string quartet; he has less to say about orchestras, in which, as he acknowledges, social interaction tends to be imagined by listeners more than experienced by musicians.

One of Hackman's (2002, 194) main examples of good teamwork is the Orpheus Chamber Orchestra: "Although that orchestra has no leader on the podium, it has much more *leadership* than do orchestras known for their famous conductors." Conventional symphony orchestras are held up as a negative contrast, accused of "leav[ing] enormous amounts of musical talent unused on the rehearsal stage and sufficing with less engagement and commitment from musicians than they could have" (2002, 122). If El Sistema is interested in promoting teamwork, it seems to have picked an unpromising model.

The Orpheus Chamber Orchestra and the Lahti Symphony Orchestra have recognized the inherent blockages to teamwork in orchestras. As Orpheus member Eric Bartlett notes, "in a conducted orchestra, you play a more passive role...you're not playing off your colleagues—you're playing off of that one person in front of the orchestra holding the baton" (Seifter 2001). The Orpheus has experimented to try to resolve this problem, and its stated goal to foster horizontal teamwork underlines that this dynamic is not standard in an orchestra but rather requires cultivation. Similarly, the Lahti Symphony Orchestra holds workshops centered on team building and problem solving; it seeks solutions through small group work and non-playing retreats. All the Lahti's talk of exploring and creating teamwork (Wagner and Ward 2002) confirms that this outcome does not happen automatically in an orchestral setting but rather takes concerted effort.

Conductor Benjamin Zander (2000, 69), too, has grappled with this issue. He notes: "An orchestra of a hundred musicians will invariably contain great artists," many with specialized knowledge or great insight, yet "verbal communication in an orchestral rehearsal is directed from the podium to the players and almost never the other way around." Recognizing that teamwork needed to be created through better interaction, he started putting blank sheets of paper on every stand so that players could give feedback. Other tricks include making eye contact with each individual who has made a suggestion at the relevant moment in the rehearsal, and asking a member of the orchestra chosen at random to step up to the podium and conduct while he listens.

The Lahti's conductor concurs with Zander and Hackman's claims about orchestras' wastage of their musicians' combined musical talent: "I have been so surprised how clever the people sitting in the orchestra are. There are a lot of good ideas. I have one brain. But the orchestra together has 70, or 90, brains. So it's not clever if one is using only his or her individual brain" (Wagner and Ward 2002, 49). What these figures are describing is distributed cognition and creativity—something that El Sistema shuns in favor of idolization of the brain of El Maestro.

While Zander has referred to Abreu as "one of the greatest visionaries of our time," his own vision of orchestral music making is strikingly more progressive. Zander's demystifying approach contrasts with Abreu's mystical discourse, exemplified by his TED prize speech: "In its essence, the orchestra and the choir are much more than artistic structures. They are examples and schools of social life, because to sing and to play together means to intimately coexist toward perfection and excellence, following a strict discipline of organization and coordination in order to seek the harmonic interdependence of voices and instruments. That's how they build a spirit of solidarity and fraternity among them."[2] This blurring of metaphor and reality is powerful and moving, but ultimately obfuscatory. The evidence suggests that musical harmony *can* build a spirit of solidarity and fraternity but, in the case of large ensembles in pursuit of excellence, usually does not unless particular, carefully considered efforts are made.

FRAGMENTATION

Abreu's evocation of "strict discipline" takes us back to Foucault, who focuses on the way that armies, factories, and schools individualize at the same time as they collectivize. A collective enterprise can thus have fragmentary social effects. Soldiers, workers, and pupils are observed, compared, assessed, and classified: "spread out in a perfectly legible way over the whole series of individual bodies, the work force may be analysed in individual units. At the emergence of large-scale industry, one finds, beneath the division of the production process, the individualizing fragmentation of labour power" (1991, 145). Discipline both joins individuals together and separates them by creating a cellular structure: "the crowd, a compact mass, a locus of multiple exchanges, individualities merging together, a collective effect, is abolished and replaced by a collection of separated individualities" (201). The effectiveness of the resulting collective effort is defined by quantity of output rather than quality of interpersonal relationships. Foucault's argument that discipline aims to neutralize "anything that may establish horizontal conjunctions" (219) is a direct challenge to Abreu's statement that it fosters solidarity and fraternity.

The orchestra, too, hides a current of "individualizing fragmentation" beneath its appearance as a communal endeavor, since its physical organization, hierarchical structure, and competitive relationships create a cellular structure rather than genuine teamwork. In El Sistema, musicians are auditioned and ranked, and those on the bottom rank (*practicante*) earn less and are usually omitted from important concerts and tours; they rehearse as part of the collective, but are simultaneously separated from the rest of the orchestra. This production of inequality has important consequences for teamwork, since, as Sennett (2012, 137) explores at some length, "inequality makes a profound difference in the lives of children, inhibiting their capacity to connect to and cooperate with one another." He argues: "children in relatively egalitarian societies are more likely to trust in one another and to cooperate; children in societies marked by great disparities are more likely to deal with others as adversaries" (2012, 190).

Furthermore, musicians in the Veracruz youth orchestra reported a tendency to mix socially with people of similar rank. Similarly, in a study of a civic orchestra in the United States, Malhotra (1981) found that social interactions tended to occur along (more than across) the status lines established by the orchestral hierarchy, and Faulkner (1973a, 342) concurs: "one's position in the [orchestral] set stands for where one is situated socially and musically." This is a highly significant finding: it suggests that the orchestra may indeed serve as a school for social life—schooling participants in social stratification and naturalizing status differences, and thus modeling fragmentation rather than collectivity. Certainly, the marked factionalism or tribalism of symphony orchestras—evident in musicians' stereotypes or negative beliefs about other instrumental sections—makes them unlikely symbols of social cohesion.

Teamwork would involve one individual's success depending on another's. In reality, since young musicians are competing against one another for rank, salary, and opportunities, success often depends on another's failure. Advancement

comes in the form of individual promotion, which neither depends on nor benefits the collective. *Pace* Higgins, I found a widespread culture of individualism,
one that sprang entirely logically from a competitive institutional culture. The
"salvation" that El Sistema supposedly provides, too, operates at the level of the
individual: the program selects the most talented children, removes them to a
state capital or central Caracas, and provides them with personal benefits. These
benefits supposedly radiate out into the child's community, but evidence for this
social equivalent of trickle-down economics is scarce. The success stories are
those who leave their communities, and who are therefore rarely at home. The
star player moves ahead; their núcleo's orchestra stays put, minus its best
musician.

The issue of teamwork illustrates the argument in Chapter 5 about orchestral metaphors and realities. Orchestral performances provide a *symbol* of
teamwork, and with the relationship between the two terms becoming natu-
ralized through repetition, many commentators have come to believe that
they actually *foster* teamwork. Scholarly studies, however, reveal quite a different picture. Furthermore, performances occupy only a small proportion of
Sistema orchestras' time relative to rehearsing, and as Weeks (1996) shows,
the principal dynamics of a youth orchestra rehearsal have little to do with
promoting teamwork.

Weeks characterizes rehearsals as "correction-sequences" in which playing
is constantly interrupted by a conductor who issues instructions, criticisms,
and desired modifications. Only the conductor is authorized to interrupt and
correct. Instructional techniques appear regressive when compared to other
educational methods: "'cluing' and other techniques aimed at eliciting answers
and encouraging self-correction from the students are virtually absent in
rehearsals" (1996, 252–53). In general, "the relation between the conductor
and the musicians appears at first sight to be far more authoritarian and uni-
lateral" (253) than in lessons; musicians can be interrupted at any time with
impunity, and negotiation over the playing of musical passages is almost absent. Negative evaluations are more frequent than positive ones, and a common technique is caricature, with the conductor singing back what has just
been played "in an exaggerated and faulted way, with a mocking tone, or done
in a hasty, offhand way" (274), before the "correct" interpretation is imposed.
The dynamics of this youth orchestra rehearsal chime with those I observed in
Venezuela and, when analyzed closely, involve bending the collective to the
conductor's will rather than promoting teamwork.

COMPETITION

"As Rattle also observes, you also immediately notice a different feeling among
these children from the competitive, individualistic atmosphere that prevails

if you are a young musician hot-housed in Britain. The culture here is one of mutual support." Higgins's (2008) statement is characteristic of idealizations of El Sistema, but it is inaccurate. Classical music is competitive around the globe: young musicians move in a world of auditions and examinations and competitions. Orchestras are hierarchical within themselves and between themselves. Even in the WEDO, according to Raymond Dean, "the real glue binding these young people together is ambition"; he rejects "stylising the orchestra as an exemplary space of reconciliation and understanding" (quoted in Wakeling 2010).

In the United States, the risk of unhealthy competition between young musicians leads the Atlanta Symphony Youth Orchestra to adopt special strategies, such as allocating string players' seating at the beginning of the year and prohibiting any changes (Kartomi 2007, 13). In Venezuela, however, El Sistema only heightens the competitiveness of youth classical music, by introducing or reinforcing pay and status differentials between ranks and orchestras. Being promoted from a regional to a national youth orchestra, for example, could mean a large increase in salary, a similar leap in status, and the chance to travel the world. Foreign observers play down competition and pressure, but on the basis of belief rather than any convincing evidence. Even Borzacchini (2010, 142) admits that every orchestra is a "battle ground and competition ground."

Competitiveness varies, but, like discipline, competition is systemic: what varies is how individuals react to it. In the woodwind and brass sections, players are often pitted against their neighbor or stand-mate as they compete for the principal's chair. A woodwind player in Veracruz who had left the youth orchestra was brought back at the last minute for a concert after two players had quarreled in a rehearsal over who was going to play the assistant principal role and had been expelled by the conductor. Another, weaker player was given a disrespectful nickname, and the better players tried to avoid sitting near her. The orchestra was described to me as a Darwinian environment, bolstering Green's (2002, 212) suggestion that institutions such as youth orchestras "seem to encourage attention to the relative skill or ineptitude of other students, rather than to any intrinsic enjoyment in making music." One musician claimed: "you don't want to be downtrodden, you want to tread down; you don't want to be ordered around, you want to order around."

Some within El Sistema regard competition as a stimulus to self-improvement, while others experience it as undermining the social bonding that collective activities may potentially stimulate. The phrase "healthy competition" came up in many of my interviews, but so did stories that exemplified *cuchillo* (literally, knife), Sistema shorthand for backstabbing. A founder claimed that competitiveness was increasing as the program expanded, leading to a steady loss of values. Several students stated that competitiveness was El Sistema's biggest weakness, and one acknowledged that it sometimes led to a hostile atmosphere in the núcleo; he regarded life as more competitive inside than outside El Sistema. He saw both sides of the coin: the stimulus to improve but also the negative treatment of others. It was a fine line, he said, and many of his companions were on the wrong side of it.

As a Veracruz violinist stated, "if a guy is better than me, I want to be better than him, so I put my back into practicing, practicing, practicing, and if I've really got the discipline, strength, and knowledge to practice and learn, say, a concerto better than him, then I overtake him—that's it." Such intense competition produces results, but how students aiming to "overtake" each other sits with cooperation and solidarity is another matter. Another student described the difference between good and bad competition: the former is trying to be better than someone else, the latter is trying to make someone else be worse than you. Trying to improve *together* did not come into the equation. A third student had a slightly different view: she claimed that students *did* help each other, "but never your competitors." A principal flautist might help an oboist, for example, but not another flautist who might have their eye on the principal's chair. "You might help someone in your section, but only if they were rubbish and would never get anywhere."

Whether or not we regard competition as a good thing, it sits uneasily with the rhetoric of social inclusion and solidarity. El Sistema's practices point less to social justice than to an ideology of social mobility, in which a few move upward without fundamentally disturbing the existing social hierarchy or patterns of exclusion, and private dreams of individual success trump public aspirations for a decent and fair society. As the CASM leaflet put it, El Sistema represents "a door that opens onto a noble destiny, in which . . . dangerous surroundings and social problems are put aside." The chosen few will pass through the door and receive impressive benefits; those who are weeded out will go back to their "dangerous surroundings and social problems," which are put aside rather than addressed.

MERITOCRACY AND *PALANCA*

It is often claimed that El Sistema is a model for society since it is a meritocracy. Those who reach the upper levels agree, of course, but those who do not—the majority—frequently argue that the driving force is not merit but *palanca* (literally "lever," figuratively "string-pulling"). El Sistema's ethos might seem to be the survival of the fittest, but for some, it is more a case of the survival of the best connected. Meritocracy is a touchy subject in Venezuela: constantly promised by social elites, constantly trumped by the "leverage" and politicking in which these elites excel. As the protest rockers Sentimiento Muerto sing in "Educación anterior": "no hay cosas imposibles sino hombres sin palanca" (there are no impossible things, just men without leverage).

Pulling strings is certainly not a Sistema invention—indeed, it is a basic mechanism of Venezuelan society—but it is not one that El Sistema overturns.

A former Sistema musician reported: "if you're a part of the director's little group, you're made." Unless you have exceptional talent, he said, "meritocracy doesn't exist." Decisions about who played the best parts, or even the application of attendance rules, came down to the director's needs and preferences. "That's why people leave, why they get fed up—you think, 'whatever I do, I'll never be able to get what I want, it'll always be what *he* says'—so fine, I'm out of here." The lack of meritocracy drained his desire to practice, since those who got ahead were those who flattered and bargained with the director. "Just like there's betrayal at work, there's betrayal in the orchestra. Just like there's palanca at work, there's palanca in the orchestra." I asked him what changes he would like to see. "It shouldn't depend on a single person and what that person thinks of you, but rather that if you work hard, and play better, you get the reward you deserve."

Everyone in El Sistema knows that if you are a relative or protégé of a *duro* (big cheese) you will get special treatment, claimed one musician, and he gave me three examples. The first involved a mediocre clarinetist who was promoted to the TCYO because his uncle was a senior Sistema figure. He was then handed over to El Sistema's top clarinet teacher until he became a decent player. The second example entailed a violinist in the regional youth orchestra who could barely play a C major scale, but whose father had installed the núcleo's air conditioning. The third concerned auditions for the youth orchestra; the results were made public and a particular girl's name did not appear. However, when the orchestra met for the first time, my interviewee was surprised to see the girl present. She was a relative of a duro. "Abreu called the director," she said simply. Of course, such judgments of skill are subjective; but the *belief* in the prevalence of palanca and special treatment stood out in many interviews and online discussions.

An audition system would seem to point toward meritocracy, but Sistema auditions function in idiosyncratic ways, and musicians who played in national-level orchestras struggled to explain how the audition system worked. Auditions take place sporadically and finding out about them sometimes requires inside information; they are often closed auditions to which individual musicians are invited, and they are not anonymous. In other words, a patron is a big advantage in finding out about auditions, being invited to them, and succeeding in them.

I spoke to a talented young percussionist in Veracruz who was thinking about going abroad because he felt that he had no options in Caracas. The SBYO had had two vacant percussion places but had organized a closed audition for three handpicked candidates, he said, so he had not even had a chance to present himself. A member of the TCYO explained various options for entering the orchestra: waiting for standard auditions (a very rare occurrence);

finding out on the grapevine about a vacancy and approaching the conductor directly for a personal audition; or by palanca. He had joined by using a friend, a member of the orchestra, as his "lever." Another musician claimed that five of the seven players of her instrument in the TCYO came from the same city—which happened to be where the section's instructor came from. That's how it works, she said: the ones who get to play aren't necessarily the best, but rather the best connected.

A high-level informant who knew exactly how SBYO auditions had worked in the past added substance to this generalized belief: "Abreu manipulated the membership of the orchestra behind the scenes. There was always an appearance of transparency around the auditions and the selection of the orchestra, but behind the scenes he interfered with the results and decided who got in and who did not. That created conflicts because it cast doubt over the credibility of the teachers." In theory a student who plays better than another will get ahead faster, he said, but in practice there is often a desired outcome with auditions, and this outcome is usually realized.[3]

National orchestra members also claimed that there were students in the second- and third-ranked orchestras (the TCYO and the CYO) who were just as good as those in the first-ranked (the SBYO), but that El Sistema wanted to keep them in their current place to raise the quality of those orchestras, so they had little chance of being promoted. A CYO violinist was given this explanation after being denied the chance to audition for the SBYO; he left the orchestra. The attitude that the orchestra takes precedence over the individual clearly contradicts the notion that individuals will rise according to their talents.

Alongside palanca, another commonplace term in El Sistema is *jalar bolas*: with power concentrated in the hands of a few individuals, "sucking up" is a key strategy for advancement. There are no transparent or consistent processes, a former SBYO member said: if you want to get ahead, you need palanca; if you want to get something done, you have to jalar bolas.

The frequent occurrence of the terms palanca and jalar bolas reflects an opaque institutional culture in which hidden channels of communication are often the most effective, leaving musicians sometimes struggling to understand how or why benefits are apportioned. Two former youth orchestra members mentioned cases in which young musicians had appeared one day with an expensive new instrument; in one case, the instrument had been handmade in Europe according to the player's precise hand measurements, at a cost that my informant estimated at five figures in dollars. An older Caracas musician recalled stories circulating about "Abreu's musicians"—members of the first National Youth Orchestra—being set up in apartments across the capital. Such claims were impossible for me to verify, but they are nevertheless revealing of an institution in which benefits are accrued in ways that mystify its own members, and the surest route to success is not so much talent as "leverage."

The operation of power within El Sistema is illuminated by its frequent description as "a big family" (Abreu has called it "a big family that is dedicated to harmony"). A member of the SBYO concurred: the orchestra is a closed group that is highly selective about whom it admits. She claimed that the orchestra is tough for new members, because it is run according to unwritten rules. It was thus the insularity and peculiarity of the family that she saw reflected in the SBYO. Mora-Brito (2011, 60) paints a similar picture, describing "a closed and inhospitable system for outsiders."

A former member who had been ousted from the orchestra claimed she was told by a superior that the SBYO was a big family that had grown up together, and she was not one of the family because she had been largely trained outside El Sistema. When she was fired, a senior administrator shouted at her that she had failed to abide by the rules of the orchestra. She replied that she had been given no rules, not even a contract; how could she abide by rules that she did not even know existed?

Another former member reflected on this insularity and exclusiveness: "They are really closed. They know that there would be upheavals in El Sistema if people found out how much they were really paid." He went on: "They exiled me when I left, once I decided to go and study rather than spend the rest of my life just playing. They treated me like I was a traitor." Such sharp divisions between orchestra and wider society cast doubt on the claim that beneficial effects radiate out from one to the other.

An experienced orchestral administrator said: "it's one big family...like the Sicilian mafia." His witticism points to two aspects of El Sistema's exercise of power: ruthlessness and nepotism. There are certain family clans within El Sistema. One director suggested that the first generation of Sistema musicians had been rewarded in part by making space for their children in the SBYO; another likened El Sistema to a family business, with Abreu's sister and brother-in-law occupying top positions and the organization's leaders acting like owners rather than state employees.

CONCLUSION

In the previous two chapters we have seen how key values that are often associated with the orchestra and cited in justifications of El Sistema are not usually fostered and at times even counteracted by the organizational dynamics of these institutions, in particular by their centralization, stratification, and focus on discipline. Strong goal orientation is another feature that can grate against constructive social action. As Weeks (1996, 276) suggests, even youth orchestra rehearsals revolve around the conductor preparing the musicians for a performance. Particularly when ambitious goals are set—one of El Sistema's hallmarks—and the orchestra has just a few rehearsals to prepare a difficult symphony, the pressure of dealing with formidable technical and musical challenges shapes the resulting social interactions. Fostering positive social dynamics may take a backseat as the conductor drives the orchestra toward its goal.

El Sistema's highly developed rhetoric obscures the gulf between orchestral metaphors and realities, seeking instead to draw correspondences between the two. Such a strategy has been highly effective, as El Sistema's fame and funding reveal, but the more complex and contradictory realities that it elides deserve to be examined carefully by anyone interested in designing the best possible project for social action through music and considering the role that the orchestra might play in it.

CHAPTER 10

Realities, Dreams, and Revolutions

The children who were participating in orchestras developed with a much more humane perception of their role within society. They had a completely different set of values.
—José Antonio Abreu

The saddest thing is that they believe they are changing the world when what they are doing is perpetuating the most backward thinking from Spain.
—Gabriel García Márquez, *The General in His Labyrinth*

Music, which in the eyes of some is just a luxury for the rich, is in fact a most useful help-meet for a life of laborious toil.
—Baron de Gérando, advocating for the inclusion of music education in French schools in 1819

This chapter concludes the critical examination of El Sistema's principal claims with regard to its social effects. It is often asserted that the program leads to improvements in personal conduct. The evidence is somewhat mixed, however, not least in the (until recently) unmentionable sphere of sex and music education, which is taken here as an example. The argument then shifts from the realm of earthy realities to that of aspirations and dreams, focusing on the issues of utopianism and preparing young people for the future. This discussion provides a foundation for a concluding assessment of claims that El Sistema constitutes a revolution in social, musical, and civic education.

"AN ORCHESTRA IS THE WORLD IN MINIATURE"

Andrés, a founder, recounted episodes from the National Youth Orchestra's earliest foreign tours. Recalling a trip to Scotland in 1976, he described going into a shop shortly after a group of his colleagues and finding the shopkeeper in tears, contemplating scattered, damaged, and stolen merchandise: "it looked as though a hurricane had passed through." A tour to Italy was a disaster, he said, as the musicians stole from hotels, shops, and even each other. They left hotel rooms in disarray and slashed tour bus seats with a knife. The Italian drivers were shocked by the behavior, which included a large fistfight between members of the orchestra.

Andrés was unsurprised by these events. Abreu gave no moral or social guidance, he claimed, but focused solely on rehearsing and performing; El Sistema trained young people as musicians but not as people. Andrés described the orchestra as Venezuelan society in miniature, with all its pros and cons: friendship and fun, but also disrespect for others and excessive alcohol, drugs, and sex. He eventually left, fed up with the negativity, internal discord, and rising competitiveness, and today he disdains the idea that El Sistema teaches positive values.

Stories about bad behavior on foreign tours continue to circulate, thirty-five years on. Members of the SBYO have a lot of disposable income and are treated like rock stars; unsurprisingly, a certain amount of rock star behavior occurs. Some members are no strangers to partying, at home as well as abroad. As one musician reported, "there are all these guys in Caracas, they have money and independence in their late teens, it's a dangerous combination. Then there are the girls, who keep getting pregnant really young. It's like they haven't heard of birth control in El Sistema." Musicians claimed that recreational drug use was not unusual within Sistema orchestras; in Veracruz, teachers as well as students indulged. A former member of the SBYO scoffed at the idea that it distanced young people from drugs, while a European musician who collaborated with the orchestra reported heavy drinking and drug use by the Venezuelan musicians. One Veracruz student commented, "I've been in El Sistema for 15 years and the only person I ever met who had been an addict got into drugs while he was in the orchestra."

Spending time with Sistema musicians in Venezuela, I saw little foundation for the idealized visions that predominate internationally. Their stories sounded much like standard orchestral gossip anywhere in the world. The orchestral profession in Europe and North America is known for the normality of drinking, drug use, and sexual liaisons—making the orchestra a strange focus for a moralistic, quasi-religious program like El Sistema—and Venezuela appeared to be no exception. Anecdotally, at least, there was no sign that Sistema orchestras were made up of model citizens.

A núcleo teacher described El Sistema as full of "anti-values" as well as values, resolving some problems only to create others: "it saves you from being a dangerous criminal, but it turns you into an unscrupulous person." A renowned conductor, pointing to payments to young musicians, stated: "being trained in a system like that corrupts you." A founder described the project as awash with money: in his teens, he earned double his father's salary. His father eventually pulled him out of the orchestra, describing it as unethical. These kinds of internal critiques are significant because El Sistema sets itself up as a moral authority and is held up as such globally.

FESNOJIV's management and administration are alleged to display the full range of human foibles, bearing out Jorgensen's (2003, 19) contention that, "because it is undertaken by human beings, music education is beset by systemic problems that afflict the wider society." One former Sistema musician argued that dishonesty was endemic in the program, manifested in false promises to motivate the musicians: "X used to lie a lot to the orchestra. For example, he would say to the orchestra that it had a tour in order to keep the kids in long seminarios, missing school, working them to the bone to push up the level of the orchestra, and at the last minute X would apologize saying that the tour had been cancelled, when in reality there had never been a tour in the first place."

The idea of the orchestra as an ideal society has sold exceptionally well to politicians and prize committees, but in private, Venezuelan musicians tend to see it as a concentrated version of everyday reality. As one Veracruz musician said, "what you see inside El Sistema is an urge to play and be famous— many of the vices of the outside world are alive and well on the inside." Another concluded, echoing Andrés, "an orchestra is the world in miniature: there you'll find drug addicts, homosexuals, loose boys and girls, rich kids, poor kids, the sick, the healthy, liars, good people, bad people—it's the universe in miniature."

SEX AND EL SISTEMA

Many stories that circulated privately concerned sex. This is hardly surprising given El Sistema's age profile and orchestras' reputation. Seminarios, which see large numbers of teenagers and young adults sent off on long residential courses, are notorious, and the reports that emerge sit uneasily with Abreu's austere, moralistic discourse.

Less predictable and more problematic than the frequent tales of promiscuity and infidelity was the relative normality of sexual relationships between teachers and pupils. On my first day in the Veracruz núcleo I had lunch with a teacher and his rather young-looking pupil/girlfriend; the next time I saw her she was wearing her school uniform. Rodolfo, a longtime Sistema musician, described a culture of permissiveness at all levels of the organization. He reported three cases of teachers being caught having sex with pupils in teaching rooms at a Sistema institution. He described this scenario as an institutional rather than individual problem, the result of a culture of turning a blind eye.

Eva, another Sistema musician, felt that there was a widespread problem around sex. She named five prominent Sistema teachers who were alleged to have a particular inclination toward their female pupils. One Veracruz teacher was renowned for working his way through female students during seminarios. Two núcleo directors had dated school-age members of their orchestras.

Relationships between teachers and pupils (some under eighteen) are conducted openly; they are not even viewed askance, much less the object of sanctions. This may be a consequence of blurring the line between youth and adult orchestras. Yet Eva was concerned that such relationships were clouded by institutionalized imbalances of power: students' career prospects are often in the hands of their teachers and directors, putting pressure on students to accept invitations or advances. Eva spoke from experience, having dated a teacher herself while a student.

The age of consent in Venezuela is sixteen, making most such relationships legal, but they would be illegal in some of the countries where El Sistema has been lauded and copied, and would be banned, taboo, or at least contentious in most countries because of the institutional connection and power imbalance between the parties. Sexual relations between teachers and students aged under eighteen have been illegal in the United Kingdom since 2001. Some music education institutions prohibit sexual relationships between faculty and students of whatever age, and the composer Michael Berkeley proposed a blanket ban on such relationships within U.K. music institutions (Higgins 2013).

Eva also reported an incident of group sex at a seminario, involving both teachers and students. Those responsible were caught and thrown out of the seminario, but they went back to their núcleos and carried on playing in their local orchestra and giving lessons to children. There are no criminal record checks on teachers, she claimed, and most sexual misdemeanors are brushed under the carpet.

Most disturbingly, a number of allegations of sexual abuse surfaced in my interviews. Two former Sistema students claimed to have been victims themselves, while a number of prominent individuals—including three founders, a senior journalist, and an institutional head—stated that they knew victims or had strong suspicions of abuse. Two teachers and two former students made similar claims. Several older musicians had heard rumors of abuse involving figures of authority, though most claimed to be unsure about their accuracy. One prominent Venezuelan musician said about allegations of sexual abuse: "I know some very serious individuals who claim this with certainty." He went on, however: "It is something so horrendous that I prefer to forget about it."

One ex-Sistema musician described the program as "like a chain of secrets and favors—like a secret society." She claimed that stories of sexual abuse were widespread and that other young musicians regarded the trading of sexual favors as an unremarkable, even humorous, subculture within the orchestra. She mentioned so-called niños bonitos (pretty boys) appearing with brand-new, expensive instruments: "you think, there's something more going on there than just talent."

One established musician with whom I discussed these issues emailed me a few days later: "Now that we are on this strange aspect of our subject matter, I am getting commentaries from almost everyone I talk to, with exactly the same script. Molesting attempts, then departed from Sistema, kept the secret for years." Four current or former Sistema musicians made allegations about the covering up of cases of sexual abuse. "These kinds of issues have always been managed with impressive stealth," confided a founder. "It's really difficult to prove the things that have happened because the network of complicity is very extensive." He named several of his contemporaries, now senior figures in El Sistema: "Among ourselves, when we were adolescents, I heard comments from them that suggest that some things happened that were at the very least incorrect."

There is no concrete evidence that these allegations or suspicions are true, for all that many come from seemingly reliable sources. It was impossible for me, a foreign musicologist, to assess their veracity, particularly since many related to events that had allegedly taken place years or decades earlier; but the regularity with which they surfaced in interviews, conversations, and Internet forums was striking. Whatever the reality, stories of sexual abuse circulate in and around El Sistema and form part of its belief system.

Nevertheless, my informants were unaware of any significant action being taken as a result. Allsup and Shieh (2012, 48) write: "At the heart of teaching others is the moral imperative to care. It is the imperative to perceive and act, and not look away." The starting point for social justice is noticing and responding to injustice, they argue. Such attitudes seem to have been somewhat thin on the ground in El Sistema. Yet they would appear to be vital to a project that claims to connect disadvantaged young people and classical music, since it could be argued that the kinds of practices and relationships commonly found in classical music education create the perfect conditions for sexual abuse—a point raised repeatedly during a scandal that erupted recently around U.K. music schools and colleges.

SEXUAL ABUSE AND CLASSICAL MUSIC SCHOOLS

In 2013 thirty-nine current and former teachers at Chetham's School of Music and the Royal Northern College of Music (RNCM) were investigated for alleged sexual abuse of pupils, with several other specialist music institutions also implicated (Pidd 2013). As former students began to speak out, it became increasingly clear that the problem had been endemic, especially in the 1970s and 1980s, though allegations spanned four decades. Former Chetham's pupil Ian Pace (2013) was among those calling for a full public inquiry given the number of stories circulating in the music profession yet the reluctance of victims to come forward "in a close-knit world of classical music in which careers are dependent upon the whims of a few powerful individuals."[1]

William Osborne, in a comment posted to *Slipped Disc* on February 17, 2013, pointed to the obstacles to uncovering this issue, helping to explain why decades may pass before such problems are properly investigated: "victims often do not find the understanding, confidence, and support to speak out until they are adults." One obstacle is a lack of support structures; another is denial. In the words of Michal Kaznowski (2013), cellist of the Maggini Quartet and former pupil at the Yehudi Menuhin School: "if you had confronted me aged 15 and asked me about the school I would have told you it was a wonderful place with huge opportunity....Almost nothing would have made me talk about the lessons and my humiliation and pain." If many victims simply could not articulate their experiences, those few who did found their complaints were generally swept under the rug. Even when problems were common knowledge and reported, allegations were extremely hard to prove. It was thus very rare that anyone spelt out the problem in public or took significant action to confront it.

There is increasing recognition today not just that sexual abuse has been a widespread and longstanding problem within classical music educational institutions, but also that there is a particular relationship between the abuse and the institutions. In other words, there is a systemic problem within classical music education, not simply a few rogue individuals or schools but a more generalized culture of abuse, manifested internationally. Tindall (2005) suggested that faculty-student sexual relations were part of the landscape of North American music schools in the 1970s and 1980s. Osborne provided a catalogue of more recent cases of sexual harassment and abuse from North American and European institutions and orchestras.[2] Robert Fitzpatrick (2013), former dean of the Curtis Institute of Music, went much further, describing physical, psychological, and sexual abuse as endemic in European and North American conservatoires since the nineteenth century, yet, "[l]ike the Catholic Church, music schools tended to sweep their dirty little secrets under the rug. Students were never willing to discuss the improper actions of their instructors because of fear of reprisal that could sink their career as a performer." Fitzpatrick's own institution had been nicknamed the "Coitus Institute" in the 1930s. Among the soul searching, there were suggestions that abuse of one kind or another was an inherent feature of learning classical music.[3]

Several prominent musicians spoke out about the risks of intense, power-laden, one-to-one teacher-student relationships in hothouse musical environments. Vicci Wardman, a former teacher at the RNCM, described this relationship (Pidd, Ibbotson, and Carroll 2013): "Its very nature is intimate, detailed and precise, and most often conducted behind closed doors....Tragically, that very structure can also be an invitation to the sort of predators who up to now have operated freely within musical institutions." Martin Roscoe, another former RNCM teacher, identified classical music schools as high-risk places, pointing to the combination of one-on-one lessons, the idolization of top players, teenagers "with hormones going berserk," and the music itself: "you are inevitably touching on the most passionate places of the soul with adolescents" (Higgins 2013b).

Researchers are beginning to respond to this issue and underline the need for serious examination. Gould (2009, 66) describes sexual harassment as "music education's unspoken 'dirty little secret,'" one that demands urgent attention. Bull (2012) confronts the

> "sexual economy" [that] shapes both the well-known phenomenon of sexual relationships between music teachers and students; and the now-emerging issue of child sexual exploitation and abuse that this relationship arguably facilitates, with its privacy, intimacy and entrenched power imbalances. It is well established (e.g., by Catherine Donovan, Liz Kelly, and many others) that power imbalances (for example, age differences) between adults are a predictor for abusive or sexually exploitative relationships. I would argue that the combination in classical music pedagogy of intense musical experiences, intimate one-to-one lessons, and the authority of the teacher or conductor, is a perfect recipe in which sexual exploitation or abuse can occur, and so examining structures of power and authority in classical music institutions and practices is an urgent point of investigation.

Given the systemic nature of this problem, it is important to know what child protection measures El Sistema has in place. I could not make an official inquiry without jeopardizing my research, but Sistema musicians in Veracruz were unaware of any specific institutional measures. Many Sistema teachers receive little training of any kind, let alone child protection training targeted at preventing abuse. Nevertheless, there is a growing consensus that clear institutional strategies are essential to combating this problem, so establishing a rigorous and widely known child protection policy would surely be a wise move. Fitzpatrick (2013) gives a detailed list of suggestions for avoiding and dealing with cases of abuse, and in comments on his post, Osborne provides examples of programs and training that have been implemented in some European and North American institutions, such as clear sexual harassment policies, specifically assigned staff, and online reporting of complaints. Such developments reflect a shift in attitudes since the 1970s and 1980s—a shift that still seems to be waiting to happen in El Sistema.

The reports that I heard in Venezuela raised a number of fundamental issues. El Sistema's disciplinary focus, production of power differences, male dominance, and opaque, autonomous institutional culture are ideologically problematic in themselves, but they also create the perfect conditions for abuse. The urgency of critiquing these dynamics is thus redoubled. As discussed in Chapter 3, progressive scholars of music education have been wary for some time about hallowed institutions such as specialist music schools, and their views have been borne out by recent events in the United Kingdom. Their argument that schools need to be put under the spotlight is irrefutable, and El Sistema is no exception, since reports of abuse (psychological as well as sexual) from Venezuela suggest that endemic, problematic features of classical music education are being reproduced rather than revolutionized in El Sistema.

The knottiest question of all, however, is whether intensive classical music education is the most suitable focus for a program centered on vulnerable children and youths. Power imbalances are at the core of sexual abuse, and they are as evident in El Sistema as in classical music institutions in other countries. Given the emerging evidence of an endemic culture of abuse in such institutions, putting vulnerable children in this situation looks like a high-risk strategy. Indeed, one ex-Sistema musician reported that his núcleo director tried to abuse him precisely when he, at that time a troubled adolescent with family and drug problems, went looking for help. Classical music education appears to be a problematic sphere, and adding at-risk youths may be creating a potentially volatile combination.

At present, the allegations and suspicions that circulate around El Sistema are no more than that. However, events in the United Kingdom illustrated that even world-renowned institutions had skeletons in their closets; that grave problems could take decades to become public knowledge; and that while these problems were discussed within musical circles, many students were nevertheless unaware of them. The fact that this problem has not emerged publicly in Venezuela does not therefore mean that it is insignificant there. Even stern, open critics of El Sistema told me that they would not touch the issue of sexual abuse, despite having heard about it, for the simple reason that conclusive evidence was too hard to come by. Also, the fear factor that Pace describes in the United Kingdom is even more pronounced in Venezuela: El Sistema's dominance of the national classical music scene means that any public allegation would be tantamount to professional suicide. It may take careful research, then, to determine whether the silence hides personal troubles that ought to be turned into a public issue.

PRAGMATISM VERSUS UTOPIANISM

If music learning and making often reveal, on close examination, the present world in miniature, they may also be oriented toward the future, driven by aspirations, ideals, and dreams of change. "Music-making...may be a parallel expression of the same concerns that structure social interaction, but it may also offer a different way of being and acting together, even serving as a catalyst for social change or an outlet for psychological needs that are not satisfied in other types of human interaction," writes Brinner (2009, 286). Fischlin and Heble's (2004, 11) conceptualization of improvised music illustrates the latter option: "musical practices in which improvisation is a defining characteristic *are* social practices, envisionings of possibilities excluded from conventional systems of thought and thus an important locus of resistance to orthodoxies." They regard improvisation as a critical and potentially utopian practice: "Encoded in the alternative relations that musical improvisation can summon forth lies the possibility that these alternatives are also, in some profound way, radically alternative of the social sphere to which they are addressed and in which they occur" (2004, 13).

Several questions then follow: Where does symphonic music fit into this picture? Should music education provide a pragmatic space (training for the real world) or a utopian one (the chance to experience alternatives)? Which side of the binary does El Sistema lean toward?

Jorgensen (2004, 8) argues for the utopian position: "music educators may...seek to prefigure in their studios, classrooms, and all the other places they teach, what society might become." Listening to Abreu and Barenboim, we might imagine that orchestral training fits this bill: the former claims that "El Sistema is a utopia with all the immense energy of utopia, with all the beauty and energy of utopia" ("Música, Armonía Cósmica" 2012), while the latter describes the orchestra with the same term because of its allegedly flat structure (Riiser 2010, 23). Such idealistic views seem to be limited mainly to conductors, however. Far from being flat, the symphony orchestra—like El Sistema—is an intensely hierarchical structure, and seen from the ranks, there is little utopian about it. One of Venezuela's top classical musicians compared different types of musical activity: orchestral playing was like going to work every morning and clocking in at the factory production line; it paid the bills, but it was in solo and chamber music that he found art and meaning. His comments are echoed in the words of a retired orchestral musician: "to the outsider it may look like a glamorous job, but it's not. It's a factory job with a little bit of art thrown in" (quoted in Langer, Russell, and Eisenkraft 2009, 126).

It may be useful to distinguish between utopias and dreams of order and harmony. As Foucault (1991, 169) explains: "Historians of ideas usually attribute the dream of a perfect society to the philosophers and jurists of the eighteenth century; but there was also a military dream of society; its fundamental reference was not to the state of nature, but to the meticulously subordinated cogs of a machine, not to the primal social contract, but to permanent coercions, not to fundamental rights, but to indefinitely progressive forms of training, not to the general will but to automatic docility." There can be little doubt which of these dreams is closer to Abreu's. Given that a hallmark of utopian imagination since the sixteenth century has been egalitarianism (Carey 2010, 103–4), to describe the military dream as utopian is highly debatable.

Born (2012, 269) notes that musical practice "may enact alternatives to or inversions of, and can be in contradiction with, wider hierarchical and stratified social relations. These are performed contradictions that contribute powerfully to the nature of socio-musical experience by offering a compensatory or utopian microsocial space." It could be argued that El Sistema offers alternatives to existing social relations—a poor child may rise up to become the leader of the orchestra—yet there is nothing utopian or egalitarian about the new micro-social space that is created, which simply replaces one set of hierarchical and stratified social relations with another. Elsewhere, Born (2010, 235) takes the example of the Dutch "Movement for the Renewal of Musical Practice" of the 1970s: "at stake was the idea of musical practice as a crucible in which could be incubated challenges—and a space of exception—to larger structures of social power." The traditionalism of musical practice in El Sistema, however, reveals that any challenge takes the form of reasserting the power structures of an earlier period in the face of a political process, Chavism, which—whatever one's view of its results—has pushed for change. El Sistema constitutes a conservative program within a progressive context, running counter to some of the more utopian aspirations of contemporary Venezuelan politics, such as egalitarianism, direct democracy, and empowering the grassroots. Its reproduction of historical structures and practices betrays a lack of serious efforts to construct a new kind of society for the future. Abreu may portray himself as a visionary and a utopian, but he is in fact a dyed-in-the-wool pragmatist whose gaze is turned firmly toward the past.

It is revealing to compare El Sistema with the Lahti Symphony Orchestra, whose conductor reports: "We have always made some time in the retreats for Utopia. We look at something that is out of reality—something we don't think is too practical. So think seriously about what you want to do, and in five years or so, those dreams are going to be what happens. When 70, or 90, brains are thinking what we need to be in five years, someone is going to have a great idea" (Wagner and Ward 2002, 49). The Lahti's utopia is thus collectively produced: "the workshops included all the musicians, the chief conductor, the orchestra manager, the office staff, and even the cleaning staff. What was unique was the institution's commitment to the empowerment of each member of the organization. As cellist Ilkka Uurtimo explained, 'This is like one team. All together with everyone supporting the same thing. Everyone is important; the goal is the same for everyone'" (2002, 50).

In contrast, the story of El Sistema is related as that of one man's vision; the collective features only as an army of willing servants, dedicated to realizing the dream of the visionary-in-chief—a dream that usually boils down to expansion rather than innovation. Tunstall (2012, 44–45) writes approvingly of her PR handler having "absorbed the vision and mission of Maestro Abreu" and notes that all the directors she met show "a clear and defining internal alignment with Abreu's principles and worldview." Booth (2008, 3) recounts: "At every núcleo, all the educators and staff can tell you exactly what the goals of El Sistema are—a stunningly unified vision and purpose…, from the national leaders to the local leaders to all the teachers to every janitor." This sounds almost identical to the Lahti, yet it is completely different—unity achieved through alignment with authority rather than discussion and consensus building. El Sistema is Abreu's dream, and his alone.

Utopias may also be projected through music itself. Julian Johnson (2002, 90) argues: "Art is fundamentally utopian: it embodies the human hope that the world and we who inhabit it might be remade." Yet the radical promise of the best classical music is mediated through institutions, and this mediation can transform it into conservatism (Born 1995). In Venezuela, classical music's utopian potential is often curbed by conservative structures, among them the global music industry with which Abreu is so keen to do business. For Adorno, utopianism was tied to *resistance* to the process of commodification; it was alien to the logic of the culture industry, with its celebrity conductors and star musicians (Gebesmair 2009, 470). Utopianism resided in "advanced" musical works, not crowd-pleasing spectacles, world tours, and the constant repetition of canonical repertoire.

Furthermore, Johnson suggests that revolutionary messages do not necessarily lie in full view on the music's surface but rather need to be apprehended. Accordingly, classical music requires education and study, not merely training or exposure, in order to yield up its utopian meanings. One has to understand the horizon of expectations of the time it was written and the ways that composers wrestle with ideas rather than simply reproducing them. *Meanings* as well as notes have to be struggled for, otherwise not only can radicalism in music be missed, but its opposite can actually be heard. Utopianism, like social inclusion, is thus tied to pedagogy, not simply access.

Classical music could play a role in ameliorating Venezuelan social realities, since it may potentially articulate critiques and dreams. However, its capacity to do so is much reduced by El Sistema's avoidance of non-mainstream repertoire and critical reflection. *Tocar y luchar* reduces classical music to its conservative stereotype by focusing on repetitive drilling in canonical works. As Beckles Willson (2009) suggests with regard to the WEDO, utopianism may therefore be mainly for export—projected overseas for foreign audiences.

EDUCATION FOR A POST-FORDIST AGE?

Utopianism versus pragmatism is one way of framing the issue of preparing children for the future. Another perspective draws on the work of Alvin and Heidi Toffler, discussed by Jorgensen (2003, 26), who see history in three huge waves: agricultural settlement, industrialization, and information explosion.

> The Tofflers characterize third-wave societies as culturally heterogeneous rather than homogeneous; "demassified" (in the sense of being able to customize production) rather than "massified" (or relying on mass production); ... information-based rather than based on traditional raw materials of land, labor, and capital; emphasizing intellectual rather than manual labor; and organized in "flat" rather than "pyramidal, monolithic and bureaucratic" institutions and structures. Against

the factory—the model for the industrial age, with its values of standardizing products, centralizing production, maximizing outputs, concentrating resources, and bureaucratizing organizations—is pitted the computer—the model for the information age.... [D]ecisions are taken at an organization's periphery and dispersed throughout it rather than undertaken by its top or central management.... Creative thinking and a high level of educational skill are required at every point in the organization and on the part of every individual within it.

If the previous section raised doubts about El Sistema's utopian credentials, the Tofflers' analysis makes attaching the pragmatic label equally problematic. El Sistema is clearly a classic second-wave organization, so pragmatists may question whether the program is preparing Venezuelan children for the future or for a world that no longer exists. Jorgensen notes that the old industrial paradigm is based on values like practicality, efficiency, and productivity, while the new informational paradigm stresses intuition, imagination, ingenuity, and problem solving. It is obvious which of these paradigms is reflected in the symphony orchestra. In the modern world, "multiple perspectives and individually tailored strategies are especially important; *lockstep, standardized* processes are outmoded; and new ways for working together with others must be forged" (2003, 73, emphasis added). Yet Swed (2012), a Sistema fan no less, notes that the Venezuelan program consists of "lock-step learning" via "endless daily rehearsals," and argues that "solidarity is enhanced through standardization. All núcleos follow the same teaching methods and teach the same standard repertory. That means that the more than 1 million kids who have gone through the núcleo process are all literally on the same page." The old industrial paradigm could not be more evident.

As Swed notes, "the fostering of individual creativity is simply not, for Abreu, a goal." This is surely unfortunate, considering that modern economies depend on creative thinking, which is a key ability for twenty-first-century workers (Cohen 2012, 152; Peters 2008). Projects that foster initiative and innovation may provide pathways to new employment opportunities in contexts where old ones are diminishing. In Latin American countries, where up to 80 percent of under-thirties work in the informal sector, creativity has arguably become *the* core capacity for young people and a signature quality of the most dynamic individuals (García Canclini 2012, 28–30; García Canclini and Urteaga 2012, 193). Whether seen from a utopian or pragmatic perspective, creativity is thus of central importance in education.

Berardi (2009, 21) and Wortman (2012, 69) trace an evolution from the industrial era, which required the disciplining of the body, to the rise of post-Fordism, in which creativity became the fundamental tool for the production of value. By emphasizing discipline over creativity, El Sistema looks to the past (Fordism) rather than the future of work. The future looks to be individuals who fill multiple roles and small, independent, flexible, innovative enterprises

(Luckman 2008, 190), not the pyramidal hierarchy, serried ranks, and hyper-specialization of El Sistema's vast music factory. Whatever one's view on the post-Fordist shift—and there are many reasons to be critical—Fordism is gone. It is therefore hard to see the logic in preparing children for a Fordist world, unless it is to provide a utopian space of exception; but the lack of un-ionization and collective bargaining shows up El Sistema as Fordism without its principal benefits.

"Where formerly workers could acquire a single set of skills and expect to progress upwards through a rigid organizational hierarchy, now they are re-quired to periodically re-skill as they move from institution to institution, from role to role. As the organization of work is decentralized, with lateral networks replacing pyramidal hierarchies, a premium is put on 'flexibility,'" writes Fisher (2009, 32) in his critical analysis of post-Fordism. Intensive or-chestral training hardly looks like ideal preparation for this new reality. Indeed, Tindall (2005, 259) notes that highly trained classical musicians often get stuck precisely because of their narrow range of skills and lack of flexi-bility. When the North American music profession went through a downturn in the mid-1990s, she realized that "[s]witching careers was tough. Performing musicians resembled tradesmen with limited obsolete skills rather than aca-demic intellects."

Estrada Rodríguez's (2012, 246) critique of the prioritization of training over education in Latin American music schools is highly relevant here: "The problem with technical training is its narrowness and its assumption that it can prescribe exactly what people will need to know and do in the future. The instructional practices in institutions devoted to training professional musi-cians often prepare them only for preconceived, immediate futures that are identical to the present. Such practices are incompatible with our rapidly changing times where diverse cultural realities are interacting to create fu-tures we cannot possibly predict. . . . Conventional, 'music stand' practices pre-pare Latin American musicians for a future based on other cultures' pasts." One of the three key sets of "skills for innovation" identified by Goldstein, Vincent-Lancrin, and Winner (2013, 4) is "skills in thinking and creativity (questioning ideas, finding problems, understanding the limits of knowledge, making connections, imagining)"—a major lacuna in the kind of technical training that Estrada Rodríguez describes.

With its pyramidal structure, centralization, standardization, and mass production approach, El Sistema is clearly a classic second-wave organization, one that prioritizes the manual labor of orchestral work—the "factory job" of the music profession—over developing creativity. It was born at the tail end of Fordism and has stuck to its course. Pragmatists as well as utopians might then ask how well El Sistema is preparing Venezuelan children for life in the twenty-first century and whether the conventional symphony orchestra is an appropriate educational tool for a third-wave world.

In his much watched and quoted TED talk, the educationalist Sir Ken Robinson argues that the modern public education system was a nineteenth-century invention that came into being to meet the needs of industrialism, and as such it constitutes a poor way to prepare children for life in the uncertain, rapidly changing twenty-first century.[4] Part of the nineteenth-century model is the stigmatization of mistakes, yet Robinson suggests that "if you're not prepared to be wrong, you'll never come up with anything original." He thus proposes a much more catholic approach to education: "Our education system has mined our minds in the way that we strip-mine the earth: for a particular commodity. And for the future, it won't serve us. We have to re-think the fundamental principles on which we're educating our children." He sums up this holistic, forward-looking view as a need to focus on, and use wisely, the gift of the human imagination: "the only way we'll do it is by seeing our creative capacities for the richness they are, and seeing our children for the hope that they are. And our task is to educate their whole being, so they can face this future."

El Sistema exemplifies the educational model that Robinson critiques. The Venezuelan program, too, is "trying to meet the future by doing what they did in the past," and its standardization and production line mentality are everything that he opposes.[5] In focusing on repetitive learning of canonic works, it grants minimal importance to creativity, his primary concern. Robinson identifies divergent thinking as an essential capacity for creativity, yet it is hard to think of a form of music making more dependent on convergent thinking than the symphony orchestra. He defines creativity as "the process of having original ideas" and "to see multiple answers, not one"—hardly priorities in an ordinary orchestra, where originality is identified with the conductor and multiple interpretations must be boiled down to a single one.

What is extraordinary here is not that El Sistema's underlying philosophy is strongly criticized by a leading progressive educationalist—such examples abound—but rather that these two radically opposed positions are presented as mutually supporting in the documentary *Dudamel: Let the Children Play*. Segments of a speech by Robinson are incorporated into the film and presented as though they provided an intellectual buttress for the program, whereas his complete argument actually does the very opposite. Robinson may be a proponent of the idea that the arts should be given much higher priority in education, but his overriding concern is fostering creativity, something that is sidelined by traditionalist schooling like El Sistema. The bizarre forced marriage between Robinson's radical ideas and El Sistema's conservative practices is a prime example of the muddying of the waters around the Venezuelan project by documentaries that are supposedly illuminating the subject.

A REVOLUTIONARY SOCIAL PROGRAM?

The identification of El Sistema as a second-wave organization, tied to the thinking and practices of the industrial age, raises questions about the validity of the label "revolutionary social program" that is regularly applied to it by journalists and supporters on both sides of the Atlantic. In what sense is it revolutionary? Where might we identify the radical changes that this word suggests?

One place to look would be in the actual practices of orchestras. El Sistema is very traditionalist, however, and there have been no attempts to reshape the orchestra for the twenty-first century or reconfigure its power relations. Far from questioning the figure of the conductor, El Sistema bolsters the cult, sanctifying Abreu and Dudamel and striving to produce the next generation of superstar maestros. El Sistema's pedagogy is also markedly traditionalist, and it, too, looks back to earlier periods in Western music history rather than representing a rupture.

For signs of revolution, perhaps we should look to the promotion of music education for the moral and spiritual improvement of disadvantaged children. There are clear problems here, however, since such a vision can be found fully formed in the nineteenth century when, for example, music education was promoted among the poor in Britain as part of a drive for moral and religious uplift. As George Hogarth wrote in his *Musical History* of 1835: "Wherever the working classes are taught to prefer the pleasures of the intellect, and even of taste, to the gratification of sense, a great and favourable change takes place in their character and manners." Evoking Handel and Haydn, he goes on: "Sentiments are awakened that make them love their families and their homes; their wages are not squandered in intemperance; and they become happier as well as better" (quoted in Smither 2000, 269–70).

The Platonic idea of music as moral influence, exemplified by John Turner's belief that the music education of the masses would "contribute largely to the rooting out of dissolute and debasing habits" (quoted in Rainbow 1967, 156–57), was widespread in nineteenth-century educational thinking. The Tonic Sol-fa Movement, displaying the characteristic paternalism of Victorian reform movements, saw the middle classes attempting to "elevate" the working classes while reproducing their own values (McGuire 2009); in its close association with missionary and temperance movements, Tonic Sol-fa anticipates El Sistema's spiritual discourse and evocations of "the horror of drugs." Moralism and reformism also underpinned the establishment of music education institutions in the United States in the nineteenth century (Cavicchi 2009). The great expansion of music education in the English-speaking world was thus permeated by its conception as an elevating moral mission targeted particularly at the working class.

Smither (2000, 269–70) suggests that one motivation behind such moves was the political protection of the wealthy upper middle classes. Music was seen as a way of keeping the workers out of taverns, hence increasing their productivity and decreasing their opportunities to discuss revolutionary ideas. McGuire (2009, 32) concurs, describing the British choral music boom of the nineteenth century as "meant to be both distracting to the working and middle classes (keeping them away from the pub and similarly dangerous leisure-time pursuits while reinforcing the class structure) and morally edifying." Carey (2010, 97) regards this ideology as generalized in the nineteenth century: "It was felt in particular that if the poor could be persuaded to take an interest in high art it would help them to transcend their material limitations, reconciling them to their lot, and rendering them less likely to covet or purloin or agitate for a share in the possessions of their superiors." (In Carey's reference to transcending material limitations through art, we see a precursor of Abreu's aphorism: "the huge spiritual world that music produces ends up overcoming material poverty.") For all its focus on the betterment of the poor, then, the drive for music education and expanded access to high culture was fundamentally conservative, aimed at countering revolutionary urges.

Gramit's (2002) study of music education in early nineteenth-century Germany both confirms the currency of the idea of social action through music at the time and underlines how educational reform resulted in the reaffirmation of traditional social structures. Popular enlightenment, as it was termed, "equip[ped] the populace to fulfill more adequately its established role in the social and economic order rather than challenge that order" (2002, 10). Discipline and obedience were central values in music education, ensuring that realities were "far removed from the cooperative utopia of the idealized choir" (117)—points as relevant to Venezuela today as to Germany two centuries ago.

Disciplined music education was seen as a route to forming productive subjects among the lower classes: Gramit quotes 1828 guidelines on singing instruction that aimed to teach people that "there is no pleasure without work, and that work itself must become pleasure for them" (118). He argues, citing other nineteenth-century sources, that "[a]s an art that developed the 'disposition for regularity, accuracy, order, and harmony' and provided a 'bond of sociability,' music could supply an ideal mode through which to socialize productive workers" (118). Thus, "music education meshed naturally with an economically oriented educational policy that sought to create a disciplined but docile labor pool" (118). As Gramit reveals, El Sistema's nineteenth-century precursors promoted efficient capitalism rather than revolution, just as its offshoots do today (Borchert 2012; Logan n.d.).

In his 1812 singing method, Hans Georg Nägeli imagined an ideal future society, "the age of music," which "begins only where higher art is practiced not just by representatives—where higher art has become the common possession of the people.... Take hosts of people; take them by the hundreds, the thousands; try to bring them into human interaction, and interaction in which every individual... receives and circulates enlightenment" (quoted in Gramit 2002, 105). As

Gramit notes, however, "if we contrast the utopian language of the vision with the concrete instructions of the opening lesson, we are brought abruptly back to the process through which these singers were to be cultivated" (105)—a process that included the denial of all prior musical experience and abstract aesthetic ideas, and one that Gramit sums up as "educational ground zero" (105) and "coercion, manipulation, and breaking down" (107). Nägeli's introduction displayed a highly developed and appealing rhetoric, addressed to well-educated adult readers, but the instructional text itself "provides a graphic demonstration of the distance between Nägeli's theoretical discourse and that which was to be imparted to children:... they were to receive no such courteous introduction" (100), but were rather to be instructed in obedience. Here, two centuries ago, we see music education combining a utopian macrovision for external consumption and disciplinary micropractices in the classroom, heralding future developments in Venezuela. Gramit's study serves as an important reminder of the potential gaps between utopian discourses and pedagogical realities.

El Sistema forms part of a long historical trajectory of music as social action programs with deep roots in nineteenth-century capitalist ideology; its attachment to the word "revolutionary" is thus highly inappropriate. In *Capital* Marx uses the figure of the conductor to explain the idea of a capitalist extracting surplus value and exploiting labor power; disciplined music education was intended to aid this process by instilling docility and efficiency in the labor force. Whether or not we agree with the idea that producing productive subjects for capitalism is a suitable aim for arts education, the Venezuelan program's revolutionary credentials are decidedly thin.

For all their obvious nineteenth-century antecedents—Abreu's philosophy also has clear roots in Romantic idealism (Pedroza 2014)—many of El Sistema's values stem from considerably earlier. In Chapter 3 I argued that many of the program's premises date back to the Spanish (musical) conquest of Latin America five centuries ago, when churchmen began to found schools that taught music as a core subject. Their aim was to instill in the indigenous population what the Spaniards called *policía*—a complex term that encompassed order, Christianity, and civilization (Baker 2010). Social elites have thus been trying to "civilize" or "improve" poor and/or darker-skinned children through education in European-style music for five hundred years in Latin America; far from a revolution, El Sistema is heir to a long-standing colonialist project. The history of social action through music is, if anything, more dubious in Latin America than in Europe.

I would argue that El Sistema has become so popular today precisely because it plays on orthodox, time-honored cultural assumptions like the universality of European art music and its civilizing effect on the masses, while also making appealing claims to novelty. The notion of European music as a positive influence on Latin America has been a recurring one since the early colonial period, reemerging after independence with the efforts of social elites to define themselves and their newly formed nations, and again in the context of mid-twentieth-century modernist developmentalism. Abreu has revitalized age-old ideas like the linking of music education and discipline—the seventeenth-century Andean chronicler Felipe Guaman Poma de Ayala shows a choirmaster standing over his young charges with a whip—and the duty of social elites to spread their supposedly superior tastes to the common people.

Felipe Guaman Poma de Ayala, 1613, folio 670, *Los maestros de coro y de escuela de este reino* (the choir- and school-masters of this kingdom).

When we strip away El Sistema's claims to be radically innovative, underneath we find something more akin to stasis or even regression to practices and ideologies of the past (Born 1995).

The Guardian is one regular purveyor of the "revolutionary social program" discourse. More revealing than most of its coverage, however, is an article—equally gushing—by Hewett (2010) in the conservative *Daily Telegraph*. For Hewett, El Sistema demonstrates, contrary to the belief of the "left-leaning social work establishment," that "democracy of access can go together with an elitism of outcome" and education need not be "child-centered." Within El Sistema, according to Hewett:

> The success of an individual belongs to everyone, whether it's the solo player who's cheered on by his mates in the orchestra, or the successful kid from the backstreets who's the hero of those same streets.
>
> And what fires up these children is that the adults lead from the front, presenting them with a vision of what adulthood is. As does the music; there is absolutely nothing "child-centred" about Beethoven.

Though his idealized vision of success and failure is misguided, this conservative commentator correctly identifies El Sistema as flying in the face of progressive ideas about education. He is absolutely right that it is not child-centered; in El Sistema, adults decide and issue orders, and children obey or leave. El Sistema's expansion is based on Abreu's idea that what works for one poor child should work for all poor children, which is much closer to Enlightenment universalism than to progressive modern notions of diversity and difference. Abreu's insistence that material poverty is in the mind and can be overcome by exposure to classical music (Hollinger 2006, 127–28) downplays both structural factors in impoverishment and the cultural value of other musics, two common progressive beliefs. At the heart of El Sistema's thinking lies the reactionary idea that free time is dangerous, idleness is a sin, and, without the program's intervention, everyday life is "empty, disorientated, and deviant." In contrast, for leftist French thinkers of the mid-twentieth century, everyday life and free time were spaces of hope and revolutionary potential, because they offered up the possibility of resistance and alternatives to institutionalization and capitalist modernization (Crary 2013, 68–70). The appeal of El Sistema to a conservative newspaper is thus eminently logical.

It is equally illuminating that the fiercest criticism of the project within Venezuela has come from the Left. Such critics recognize that the cultural values that El Sistema reproduces are those of the dominant conservative culture of Venezuela's Fourth Republic (in which Abreu served as minister), not of the Fifth Republic of Chávez. To regard El Sistema as a revolutionary social project is to overlook how deeply it is rooted in Abreu's education and training in the politics and economics of the Punto Fijo period. Overseas, too, the most coherent and penetrating critiques have come from leftist critics who recognize conservative ideologies behind the progressive language (e.g., Borchert 2012; Logan n.d.).

El Sistema's conservative realities are all the more apparent when held up against the challenges to classical music's institutions and ideologies in Europe discussed in Chapter 5. Kutschke's (2010) study of the 1970 Beethoven Bicentennial reveals playful, critical, anti-authoritarian approaches to the classical canon and its "sacred cow" in Germany. This deconstructive attitude contrasts dramatically with the traditional, reverential performances of Beethoven symphonies that I heard at the CASM in 2011, which seemed to date from forty years *earlier* than the German developments rather than forty years later, even though a Latin American youth-oriented social project would be precisely the place one might most expect to find irreverence and challenge.

Yet, as Yúdice (2003, 16) points out, the rise of the expediency of culture in the intervening four decades has greatly reduced the space for critical or playful approaches: "the 'bottom line' is that cultural institutions and funders are increasingly turning to the measurement of utility because there is no other accepted legitimation for social investment. In this context, the idea that the experience of *jouissance*, the unconcealment of truth, or deconstructive critique might be admissible criteria for investment in culture comes off as a conceit perhaps worthy of a Kafkaesque performance skit." Similarly, Cee (2013) argues that the rise of utilitarian justifications for music learning constituted a conservative shift after a more radical period (the late 1960s and 1970s), accompanying the rise to hegemony of neoliberalism. By playing the utilitarian game, the arts may retain or enlarge their place, but only by becoming techniques of government rather than revolution.

Comparison with European musical and educational revolutions around 1970 highlights the conservatism of the Venezuelan music scene under Abreu's baton. Reactionary, authoritarian aspects of classical music culture came under the spotlight in Europe, but such questioning left no mark on the emergence of El Sistema around the same time. Behind the rhetoric lies a program that has avoided making fundamental changes to classical music culture in favor of simply increasing its scope, and whose transformation—conservative to revolutionary, musical to social—has been largely discursive. Simon Rattle claims to have seen the future of classical music in Venezuela, but the future was what radical musicians in Europe were trying to do four decades ago; in reality what he saw was its past in disguise.

MUSIC EDUCATION AND CITIZENSHIP

Jorgensen (2003) argues that social change derives from *changing* music education, not making it more widely available. Hers is a much more radical vision than El Sistema's, focused on processes—liberation and utopianism at the microlevel of instruction—rather than products. To imagine how such a revolution in music education might look, we can turn to Keil's (n.d.) "Paideia Con Salsa," a radical, utopian vision of rounded cultural education and active citizenship based on Afro-Latin dance music—an abundant resource in Venezuela.

"Why Afro-Latin music-dance as the focal point for a restoration of Greek paideia?" asks Keil. It is central to twentieth-century music and familiar to children; it brings together Old and New Worlds; it speaks to social minorities, promoting inclusion; it involves a range of musical and motor skills; and "most important, it will encourage all students to create their own songs in various languages, choreograph their own dance variations, develop their own bands, stage, costume, and set their own music-dance-dramas." Keil argues for reconsideration of the Ancient Greek concept of ethos, or the power of music to shape character: "All the Afro-European syntheses contain utopian feelings about a better world tomorrow. They invite wholehearted participation rather than deepening alienation. They encourage improvisation on the basis of the ontological security that a living tradition provides. They require sensitivity to all other participants in a realm free of composers and conductors. They demand collective responsibility and individual expression simultaneously. Latin music-dance, because it is at the center of Afro-European hybrid vigor, is the proper vehicle for creating such an ethos."

Keil's vision of social action through music, which contrasts so notably with El Sistema's, revolves around the Ancient Greek concept of paideia, an all-round civic education that "has the overall aim of developing the capacity of all its members to participate in its reflective and deliberative activities, in other words, to educate citizens as citizens so that the public space could acquire a substantive content. In this sense, paideia involves the specific aims of civic schooling as well as personal training" (Fotopoulos 2005). What distinguished paideia from the learning of mechanical tasks (*banausos*) carried out by laborers and artisans—including professional musicians—was the centrality of participation in reflection and deliberation. Music learning might fall into either category, depending on whether it was part of broad, amateur, civic education or narrow, professional training. As Stamou (2002, 12) notes, Aristotle had little time for the pursuit of technical excellence in music instruction, regarding professional music making—virtuosic performance to entertain an audience—as having no place in general education.

"El Sistema develops citizens not musicians," claims a report by influential advocates in the United States.[6] Yet by omitting the crucial deliberative element that characterizes paideia, and providing just the technical training that Aristotle dismissed, El Sistema has clearly *not* revived the Ancient Greek idea of music as a constitutive part of citizenship. The Ancient Greeks would have regarded a program that prioritized the mechanical learning of musical skills over participation in deliberative activities as adhering to banausos rather than paideia and thus preparing young people to be musical laborers rather than rounded citizens. They would have seen El Sistema's core philosophy of musical training *as* civic education—"when you train musicians you train better citizens," as Abreu articulates it—as nonsensical, and the idea that one could receive a civic education without realizing it as equally absurd. As Fotopoulos (2005) argues, a democratic civic education would be nonhierarchical and encourage students to experience democracy through participation in assemblies and involvement in determining the educational process. By turning to the concept of paideia, we may glimpse what a true civic education might look like and perceive how far El Sistema falls short of this ideal.

To this day, a fundamental principle of citizenship is considered to be free and public debate or, more broadly speaking, political participation. Indeed, Bellamy (2008) writes of the irreducibly political nature of citizenship. By discouraging participation in political deliberation, both in its day-to-day educational practices and in the example set by its leaders, El Sistema fosters a neutered form of citizenship.

Furthermore, the frequent linking of music and citizenship in discussions of El Sistema ignores a fundamental contradiction between authoritarian, hierarchical institutions and democratic citizenship. As Scott (2012, 78) asks: "Is it reasonable to expect someone whose waking life is almost completely lived in subservience and who has acquired the habits of survival and self-preservation in such settings to suddenly become, in a town meeting, a courageous, independent-thinking, risk-taking model of individual sovereignty? How does one move directly from what is often a dictatorship at work to the practice of democratic citizenship in the civic sphere?" He raises the possibility that life within hierarchical institutions, far from fostering citizenship, actually "saps the vitality of civic dialogue" and "produce[s] a more passive subject who lacks the spontaneous capacity for mutuality" (2012, 80).

Such questions have been taken up by music education scholars such as Elliott (2012) and Woodford (2014), who focus on "artistic citizenship" and urge direct engagement with urgent social and political issues. Woodford, drawing on John Dewey, argues that avoiding such topics in the name of an illusory political neutrality simply fosters ignorance and susceptibility to manipulation among the populace, allowing an oligarchy to maintain control over society. Dewey felt strongly that teachers should encourage children to become historically and politically informed: "The hope was that this kind of education for children would in time raise the level of political discussion and debate while making political leaders and experts more democratically accountable to the public" (2012, 25). In reality, argues Woodford, music education "continues to be described as politically neutral while serving a capitalist agenda" (29), and rather than fostering democratic citizenship, it generally contributes to the indoctrination of the public, cultivating intellectual and political passivity via uncritical reverence for masters and masterworks and using music to overawe rather than enlighten.

There is thus a clear need to explore further not just issues of radicalism and conservatism but also their relation to the core issue of music education as civic education. Henry Giroux argues that "education can function either to create passive, risk-free citizens or to create a politicized citizenry educated to fight for various forms of public life informed by a concern for justice, happiness, and equality" (quoted in Mota and Figueiredo 2012, 188). There seems little doubt which kind of citizen is more likely to emerge from a conservative, authoritarian institution that avoids reflection and debate.

CONCLUSION

Let us conclude this section on social education by returning to the questions set out at its start about the relationships between the musical, the individual, and the social. El Sistema is based on the idea that playing in a symphony orchestra has beneficial effects on children. Historical and sociological studies, however, suggest that neither the musical sounds nor the microsocial structures and practices that enable their performance are necessarily seeds of goodness. El Sistema, like most orchestras, produces stratification and hierarchies; such a form of social organization might be productive in certain ways, but there is considerable evidence that highly stratified societies are unhappier and more prone to a range of social problems (e.g., Wilkinson and Pickett 2010; Brule and Veenhoven 2012). El Sistema's foundational premise appears flimsy, and thanks to the program's perpetuation of many conservative features of classical music education and culture, there are good reasons to suspect that many of its supposed social benefits are being realized only partially, if at all.

The musical, individual, and social aspects of El Sistema may work against each other rather than in harmony, maybe even cancelling each other out. In Chapter 9, we saw Julian Johnson's argument that classical music may resist the rationalization of human life clash with Max Weber's characterization of the orchestra as a symbol of that very rationalization, suggesting a clear tension between benefits and costs for orchestral musicians. Similarly, it is widely agreed that for arts education to be socially effective, it needs to be long-term—yet the longer children stay in El Sistema, the more likely they are to harbor professional ambitions, meaning that potential benefits may clash head-on with the sobering realities of orchestral music as a professional activity. The cognitive benefits of learning music are widely accepted, and yet, as Levine and Levine (1996) demonstrate, lack of control may lead orchestral musicians to experience high levels of stress, which may lead to a reduction in cognitive skills. The orchestral setting may therefore cancel out some of the benefits of music learning.

Let us imagine a young clarinettist called Pedro. Participating in El Sistema improves Pedro's cognitive ability and thus capacity for academic achievement.

It also provides him with a new and absorbing social environment. Nevertheless, it also uses up a lot of his time. As he advances, he starts having to travel to Caracas for lessons, which occupies two full days out of every fortnight. His time for academic study is thus reduced. During his trips to Caracas, he discovers that some of El Sistema's leading musicians have modest academic qualifications. Academic study seems less important than instrumental practice, particularly since Pedro's world is becoming increasingly competitive, with auditions for regional and national orchestras and assistant principal and principal chairs.

Pedro's friends are also his competitors: he has spent years playing next to Luisa, forming bonds of friendship, but only one of them can be principal and it is a post they both want. Not only are the principals paid more, but they also exercise authority over other members of the section. I met a real-life Pedro and Luisa who had fallen out after a decade of almost sibling-like relationship as a result of competing for the principal's chair. Pedro, who was older, had helped Luisa with her homework and shared his hobbies in the gaps between classes and rehearsals; but Luisa was promoted over him to principal—by *palanca* (influence), he claimed—and began to assert her authority over him. Here, the social benefits provided by El Sistema were subsequently eroded by its systemic inequalities, illustrating how orchestral dynamics can foster camaraderie but also weaken or break it.

Some relationships within orchestras hold friendship and competition in a workable balance; but in the final analysis, the vertical orchestral dynamics may trump horizontal social bonds, meaning that stories of betrayal and backstabbing are not uncommon. There are thus question marks over the relationship between the individual and the social in El Sistema. Music might make you smarter, but does mass orchestral practice make for a happier, healthier society?

El Sistema is a curious kind of social project: in its everyday practices, it makes minimal mention of the social. The pinnacles of achievement are musical, while "social work" activities, such as teaching small children in satellite núcleos, are granted little value. It is also curious that copious social funds are destined for a project in which social benefits, even according to official rhetoric, are only a byproduct. Why not create a project that foregrounds the social and makes advanced musical skills the contingent outcome?

An example of such a project can be found in the Scottish fiddle program described by Cope (1999), with its focus on acquiring traditional, amateur, socially relevant skills. There is a nice irony in the fact that this project was trialed very close to where the first Sistema Scotland núcleo was launched in the following decade with far more fanfare and funding. Classical music is money-intensive, and it is reasonable to ask whether similar or better results could be achieved with a less costly activity—or simply whether Cope's low-key program might have had more positive social effects per pound invested than a Sistema offshoot.

Returning to Venezuela, it is interesting to compare the hip hop–based EPATU schools with El Sistema ("Nacen las Primeras" 2010). EPATU's manifesto describes creativity as a bottom-up process and defines inclusive art as "that which stems from the people." The project aims to "generate spaces of reflection and debate…encouraging our people to research, debate, and take collective action." Its schools put aside time for political discussion; indeed, for many participants, "hip-hop and the political struggle are inextricably linked, and this is their chance to play a tangible part in building the better future they want to grow up in" (McIntyre and Navarrete 2012). Unlike El Sistema, then, EPATU is closely aligned with the Venezuelan constitution and its promotion of "participatory and protagonistic democracy." Where EPATU promotes engagement with social problems, El Sistema draws a veil over them; as Rafael Elster, the director of Sarría núcleo, puts it in the 2010 film *La Tierra de Las Mil Orquestas*, "[this is] a place where those bad things that happen to them outside—we don't talk about them." EPATU speaks of the fusion of indigenous and African elements with hip hop, giving a central place to local, national, and Afro-diasporic traditions. The final aim is "to achieve the collapse of the system that oppresses us." EPATU seeks social action through music, but the contrast with El Sistema—top-down, acritical, Eurocentric, and conservative—could hardly be clearer.

Similarly, Shieh (2012, 4) compares El Sistema to Tiuna el Fuerte, a project that I visited several times.

> Like El Sistema, Tiuna is an arts education space open to all youth, mostly in the afternoons after school. Unlike El Sistema, Tiuna's space is dramatically unstructured and grows out of student interest: students come at all times to hang out and attend concerts, to participate in classes such as hip-hop dance, community radio, and graffiti, and to develop political interventions across the city. The idea behind Tiuna is that it is a place where, in the words of one of its directors, Maria, "youth energy and resistance can be politicized and made constructive…where discourse can be created." It does not stand apart from the street, but builds from it and attempts to leverage student experiences towards a critical voice and awareness through artistic work. Interestingly, it is also the site of a failed orchestra program—the project never seemed to catch on, and youth attended sporadically.

It is indeed interesting that the orchestra, when offered alongside other alternatives, failed: it raises the question of whether El Sistema has triumphed because of the Venezuelan population's desire and love for orchestras, or because, in many places, it is the only decently funded option they have been offered.

Here at Tiuna, unlike in El Sistema, we find many strands of progressive educational thinking: student-led learning, diverse activities, a focus on creativity, and the development of critical awareness and agency. One project aims to foster social inclusion through withdrawing children from society, the other pursues social change through engaging them with local realities. One seeks to produce docile, disciplined subjects for capitalism, the other to produce critical, politicized subjects to resist it. The symphony orchestra is a rigidly stratified, authoritarian miniature society in which everyone plays a part assigned to them by someone else and no one speaks out of turn. El Sistema thus proposes a model of citizenship that, in contrast to EPATU or Tiuna el Fuerte, is unitary rather than pluralistic, obedient rather than critical, and politically passive rather than active. Which of these projects sound like a platform for revolutionary social action through music?

PART FOUR

Impact

CHAPTER 11

The Politics and Economics of Impact

Many more battles are won by marching in good order and making a good show than by blows of the sword and musket. This good order shows confidence, and it seems that it is enough to look brave, because most often our enemies do not wait for us to approach near enough to have to show whether we are in fact brave.
—Louis XIV

An experienced Venezuelan music educator accompanied a friend to witness a display at La Rinconada núcleo. "I was flabbergasted. I couldn't believe it. I think there may have been 700 people who participated in that show, for my friend and me....So what does the show consist of? We went into a classroom and some 5-year-old children came in and played the recorder and sang some lovely songs, there were some young teachers and perhaps 30 children. As soon as we left the classroom we were led into another one. But we realized that the previous children were not in a class, they were waiting for us. As soon as we went into the new classroom, those 30 kids ran off. And they do this every day! This is an amusement park!...We went to 7–10 classrooms one after the other, and then the orchestra. But you say to yourself, all these people are here just to amaze us. It's not as though we went to a school and saw children in their normal activities; rather, it was something put on specially to impress visitors....It's very impressive, but if you look at it with a critical eye...."

Why have so few people outside Venezuela noticed the problematic aspects of El Sistema? How has a project founded on backward-looking, widely critiqued ideologies and practices become a global model for music education today? There has certainly been a striking failure to scrutinize it rigorously, as discussed later in an analysis of the program's demonstrations and evaluations; but this failure begins with the program's own image management, which recalls early 1990s accounts of Abreu's predilection for show over substance and the inflation of his achievements by a compliant press.

In early 2012 El Sistema put on an "elaborately choreographed showcase" (Wakin 2012c) in Caracas for the visiting L.A. Philharmonic (and accompanying press). The project's signature features were prominently on display: gigantic orchestras (640 musicians in one of them); playing from memory; "Hallelujah Chorus"; the last movement of Tchaikovsky 4, played ridiculously fast and loud; a special needs choir; the colorful jackets. It is a well-honed formula of unrepentantly propagandistic tub-thumping, and, as usual, it worked. The American orchestra's president, Deborah Borda, responded: "We are simply overwhelmed. You have worked a miracle."

Abreu has been very astute in using the power of orchestral music to astound and influence listeners and suspend disbelief. El Sistema bypasses the brain and goes straight for the heart. This tactic was not dreamt up by Abreu, however, but was a fundamental aspect of the functioning of the "magical" Venezuelan state of the mid- to late twentieth century. Coronil (1997) characterizes the magical state as heir to the culture of the Baroque, drawing on the work of Wlad Godzich, who stated that in the Baroque period, "the audience does not participate, nor does it internalize the arguments: It is conquered, subjugated, carried by the persuasive flow of the rhetoric" (quoted in Coronil 1997, 4). The Venezuelan state, too, secured compliance through spectacular display, argues Coronil: it "'captivates minds' through highly rhetorical cultural forms which seek the public's compliance by leaving it, in Godzich's words, *boquabierto* (dumbfounded; literally, open-mouthed).... Typically, the Venezuelan state astonishes through the marvels of power rather than convinces through the power of reason...it casts its spell over audience and performers alike" (1997, 4). El Sistema thus emerges as congruent with Venezuelan political history of its time. Abreu, like his mentor CAP, is the personification of the magical state: the conductor waving his baton merging with the magician waving his wand. Most importantly, Coronil reveals spectacle to be more than mere decoration; it constitutes a technique of power. El Sistema's spectacular displays may thus be seen as a form of politics—a politics of impact.

The calculated effect of massed orchestral performance—casting a spell over the audience, leaving it open-mouthed—has been extremely important for the fortunes of El Sistema, which has consequently escaped close scrutiny. How can you ask rational questions when your eyes are full of tears after watching a special needs choir or an ocean of children playing Beethoven 9? Yet questions must be asked. For whose benefit are such disciplined, choreographed displays performed—the children's, the observers', or the organizers'? Are the children the project's ends, or rather its means? El Sistema molds masses of children into a vast, slick, effective machine—but a machine for what?

One answer is: for generating funds, popularity, and publicity. Showcases and displays keep foreign and domestic support rolling in. As one conductor put it, children playing "Ode to Joy" and "Hallelujah Chorus" not only stir the emotions but also persuade politicians to open their checkbooks. One might argue that this is an important goal. More problematic is when the children at Montalbán or La Rinconada become a means to obtain publicity and funding for El Sistema, rather than an end in themselves—when displays for outsiders substitute the business of learning. It is important to consider the implications of focusing an educational project so squarely on impressing observers. An ex-Sistema musician argued that the emphasis on displays led to pushing children too hard and too fast. Children should be learning music and values, he felt, not drilled intensively to astonish visitors. Education takes on an instrumental aspect in such circumstances, centering on money, power, and publicity rather than children and their explorations; wheeled out for a purpose, the young musicians become pawns in an adult game.

Others see El Sistema as a mechanism for self-promotion and the accretion of power—"a gigantic flattery machine designed to satisfy the interests of its founder," in the words of Abreu's former right-hand man, Gustavo Medina. Abreu's pursuit of his vision has certainly had gratifying side effects: he has become the most powerful figure in the Venezuelan cultural sphere; he has been lavishly rewarded by international prize committees; and he has seen his personal interest converted from a minority activity into Venezuela's major cultural investment. One of El Sistema's most notable products is Abreu's ever-growing influence and collection of prizes.

Above all, El Sistema is a machine for impact. In Venezuela, many musicians echoed the old criticisms of Abreu: El Sistema is all about show business; it is 50-percent music and 50-percent show; it creates "show musicians" (*músicos de espectáculo*); it is a media circus. Spectacle produces the impact on observers that enables all else: the national and international funding, the expansion at home and around the world, the global media fascination, and the political and music industry alliances. If, as Aharonián (2004, 12) suggests, El Sistema's real aim is the resupply of the program itself, it might be argued that El Sistema is a machine for reproducing and expanding itself.

Impact is carefully orchestrated through image management. A telling detail of concerts that I attended at the CASM was the presence of five cameramen and broadcast-standard cameras. While núcleos just a few miles away lacked basic necessities, El Sistema was ensuring professional-quality filming in its world-class headquarters. This prioritizing of self-representation and self-promotion constitutes a key institutional policy.

Image management focuses on three main tropes: youth, deprivation, and talent. Several musicians reported that, in the earlier phases, Abreu had micromanaged to the degree of dictating the facial hair of young men in the national orchestras, telling them not to grow beards or mustaches so they appeared younger. A former senior figure claimed that Abreu told teachers to get rid of girls who started to look like women "in order to protect the image of the children's orchestra. When they developed [physically] they were thrown out. There were many things like this that contradicted ethical and moral principles." Gustavo Medina publicly accused El Sistema of ordering videos of the National Children's Orchestra to be edited so that only the youngest members appeared. The impression of talent is fostered through selection and intensive drilling for public displays and master classes with illustrious foreign teachers; that of deprivation is largely left to foreign observers to embellish. The resulting appearance is impressive but, as a former SBYO musician put it, in reality "it's nothing like the picture they paint."

Perspicacious observers understand that there is a politics of impact at work and that it carries risks. On his blog on April 6, 2012, Govias noted "Abreu's 'Kool-Aid' approach to advocacy: putting the children front and center, serving up a metaphorical pitcher and inviting all to drink." He wrote about Sistema fans "drinking the Kool-Aid." The result? "Intellectual intoxication." El Sistema's politics of impact works like a drug, getting politicians and audiences high but loosening their grip on reality.

El Sistema's politics of impact is easy to discern, and the success of this approach is equally apparent. Critical observers note a twin process of manipulation: one directed internally, in the form of a chaotic, improvisational structure that keeps participants in a powerless position; the other directed externally, in the form of emotive spectacles for public consumption. Perhaps less obvious, and thus more urgent to examine, is how this politics of impact rests on the foundation of a closely allied politics of representation; how display comes to stand in for evidence; and how such priorities are reflected in the economic sphere.

REPRESENTATION

El Sistema's close control over representation is greatly bolstered by the acritical, even hagiographical, approach of those who document it. The most high-profile films (such as *Tocar y Luchar* and *Dudamel: Let the Children Play*) and books (by Borzacchini and Tunstall) have been produced in close collaboration with FESNOJIV. The films tug the heartstrings with carefully chosen stories of individual redemption intercut with stirring images of children playing moving music. *The Promise of Music* begins with images of Caracas barrios accompanied by the music of the SBYO—a visually and sonically striking opening, if one with scant relation to the reality of this privileged orchestra. Infomercials rather than documentaries, the films omit all mention of Abreu's former career or politics more generally; no difficult questions are posed; everyone gives the "correct" answer.

Among Sistema musicians, however, attitudes toward *Tocar y Luchar* were skeptical. Some described the barrio scenes as deceptive, because cases of "rescuing" children were the exception rather than the norm. Several condemned the film for its emotional manipulation. One informant stated that the film was no more than 30 percent true, concluding, "El Sistema disguises everything with *Tocar y Luchar*." Nevertheless, the film has had a big impact in Venezuela as well as abroad, and many younger musicians derived their vision of El Sistema's social action from it. There are close parallels with Wald's (2011) study of Sistema-inspired programs in Buenos Aires, in which participants tended to learn about grandiose social claims through the media and often disagreed with the ways their activities were presented.

A Sistema musician reacted to the film *La Tierra de las Mil Orquestas*, narrated by Placido Domingo. "It's awful," she said. Why? "Because it's a farce. It's sensationalist." She went on: "They say it's a social project, not a music school. That's ridiculous! They never even asked me how I was." Of the four characters introduced at the start, one is an orphan, another lives in the middle of the jungle, and a third is an ex-convict—all of them exceptional cases. "It really annoyed me. They show the worst of Venezuela to make El Sistema look good. It's a film to make Spaniards cry."

Turning to the books, Borzacchini's official history does not trace the program's development but rather includes information on the project's earliest days and then a series of short reflections on the past by a number of senior figures. Large parts of El Sistema's history thereby remain in darkness. A former senior Sistema figure asked me rhetorically: "Why has no book been written telling this 'epic' history? José Antonio [Abreu] doesn't like things to be written down because then it is hard to adjust to the political interests of the moment."

Borzacchini only mentions once, in passing, Abreu's years as minister of culture and president of CONAC. In her interview, she does not ask him a single question about this period, the height of his political career. The reason is not hard to deduce: Abreu was a right-hand man of CAP, a famously corrupt politician and sworn enemy of Chávez. Indeed, this key period is not discussed in any films or recent publications, which do not begin to match the probing by journalists two decades ago. Musicians and conductors who fall out with Abreu or decide to pursue their career overseas are expunged from the record; others who achieve international recognition are included, even if they received little of their education in El Sistema. Borzacchini continues this rewriting of history in a website linked to the book, claiming, for example, that a list of noted popular musicians received their entire training within El Sistema; the list includes Héctor Molina, who actually studied at the Universidad de los Andes music school; Luis Julio Toro, who has a degree from London's Royal College of Music; and Huáscar Barradas, whose CV includes studies at two conservatoires in New York and one in Frankfurt.[1]

Tunstall, the author of the principal English-language book on El Sistema, is a non-Spanish-speaker and true believer who relied heavily and uncritically on set-piece interviews with El Sistema's senior figures. Her book thus resembles an extended FESNOJIV press release. Indeed, Tunstall told the *Los*

Angeles Times that she wanted not just "to tell a compelling tale" of El Sistema but also "to proselytize on behalf of its mission" (Johnson 2012). She succeeded in these twin aims, if at the cost of critical inquiry, and like the films and Borzacchini's book, her study, rather than analyzing El Sistema's politics of impact, becomes another medium for its enactment.

The Venezuelan media has provided only occasional exceptions to this rule. Today, as two decades ago, Abreu's critics point to his unparalleled influence over the media, his network of personal contacts, and the consequent difficulty in publishing critiques of his project, resulting in wide and almost universally glowing press coverage (though cracks began to show during the social unrest in early 2014). Abreu was closely linked with the newspaper *El Nacional* in the 1990s; Borzacchini, a key ally, was head of the paper's culture section. While Borzacchini (2010, 51) alluded to Abreu's "valuing of what we as communicators could transmit in the interests of his orchestras and his musicians," Santodomingo and Rivero published claims of alleged payments to journalists during this period (see Chapter 1), and more recently Casanova (2009) wrote, "if someone does an audit they will find the names of several cultural journalists from high circulation newspapers who were and are on Abreu's payroll." Two of my informants claimed to have seen evidence of

Cartoon of Abreu that accompanied Roger Santodomingo's 1990 article. Illustration by Hugo Ramallo.

payments to journalists. Santodomingo's (1990) article was accompanied by a cartoon of Abreu conducting the media.

Less than positive coverage is not tolerated. Behind El Sistema's charitable surface lies a system of image control that would do a major corporation or political party proud. A prominent music educator recalled Abreu's "brutal" and "ugly" reaction to Gustavo Tambascio's critical article in 1979, and claimed that from that moment on, music critics started to be more careful: "no one says anything in the press—just positive things." Nevertheless, Javier Sansón published a satirical piece about El Sistema on February 15, 2005, in his column "Música de solfa" in *El Universal*; he was suspended shortly afterward. A journalist reported: "When X left his job as a music critic for *El Nacional*, he recommended me to Y [a member of the paper's culture team] to replace him, and in the interview, Y told me very clearly and upfront that if I were to become a music critic for *El Nacional* I would never, ever be able to say anything negative about El Sistema, not even in passing…about everything else, whatever I wanted."

CHRISTOPHER SMALL, OLIVIER URBAIN, AND EL SISTEMA

Rose-tinted representations of El Sistema are commonly found in the academic as well as journalistic field. Olivier Urbain provided a particularly illuminating example in a volume entitled *Music and Solidarity* (Laurence and Urbain 2011), to which the well-known musicologist Christopher Small contributed the prologue. The case of Urbain and Small demonstrates the ease with which understandings of El Sistema can become skewed and obvious contradictions overlooked, even in the hands of experienced scholars.

In his critique of classical music's industrial-capitalist apparatus, *Music/Society/Education* (1977), Small railed against the European canon and "the terrible ubiquity of masterpieces" (1977, 200), and promoted avant-garde and improvised music, which he saw as "attempting to restore lost communality to western music, to restore the importance of the creative process over that of the glossy finished product" (175). He criticized music education for focusing on preprofessional training and transmission of knowledge rather than children learning and experiencing for themselves. Small looked forward to a future society in which "hierarchical organizations are replaced by networks of co-operating individuals" (209) and creativity forms the center of music education: "The real power of art lies, not in listening to or looking at the finished work; it lies in the act of creation itself" (218). He saw the relationship between classical music and education as deeply problematic: "to confine our teaching, in this time of profound and turbulent change, solely to the traditional values of western music is to risk limiting the imagination of our charges to those modes of thinking which have brought our culture to its present disastrous condition. One must consider at least the possibility that there might be a conflict between the 'propagation' of

Mozart and Beethoven (and their latter-day successors) and the real interests (in both senses of the word) of our pupils" (220).

One might assume, therefore, that Small would have taken a dim view of El Sistema. And yet, shortly before his death, he contributed the prologue to the coedited volume in which Urbain praised El Sistema fulsomely. Had Small changed his tune?

Not at all. His prologue reaffirms many ideas from his earlier work. It is concerned overwhelmingly with popular and traditional musics; classical music gets brief and unflattering mentions, with Beethoven's Fifth Symphony characterized as functioning today as "a source of comfort and a vision of security to the middle classes" (Small 2011, ix). The work of the nineteenth-century masters "resembles those fascinating and often beautiful shapes in the cooled lava from volcanoes, giving testimony to the violence of past eruptions but no longer capable of reshaping the landscape" (2011, xii–xiii). This is a strange choice of prologue for a book in which Urbain, one of the editors, holds up classical music as a source of radical, large-scale change; indeed, one wonders whether the two authors actually read each other's contribution.

This awkward juxtaposition is highly illuminating, however, as it illustrates two common features of written representations of El Sistema. First, they are often ill-informed; and second, glaring contradictions are missed or ignored. The glue that holds together this shaky construction is a romanticization that has swamped rational analysis.

Urbain's sources are problematic: five newspaper articles and a speech by Abreu. He thus repeats many of the common myths and misconceptions: three hundred thousand children escape "the anonymity of a life of misery in the barrios" (2011, 19); most participants "come from the most vulnerable sectors of society, many of them from the slums surrounding Caracas" (2011, 26). He also reproduces well-worn slippages: "As Gustavo Dudamel and the Simon Bolivar Youth Orchestra became famous, it has made many people throughout the world aware of the existence of the barrios of Caracas, and of the fact that many more potential 'Dudamels' are living in appalling conditions.... This awareness is reinforced by the fact that most news about El Sistema mentions the origins of Dudamel and of the whole enterprise, describing the situation of the poor in Caracas" (27). Yet Dudamel was a middle-class boy from Barquisimeto.

Urbain can hardly be blamed for such misinformation, though it is risky to build an academic argument solely on newspaper articles and institutional propaganda. However, there is more: "Much has already been written about El Sistema, but in this chapter the achievements of this organization will be given a new 'twist': for I find it a source of revelation in terms of my own feelings of identification with and care for the children whose lives are transformed within the project.... What is it about El Sistema that touches me in such a way? Does it depend on my own conception of solidarity, or perhaps the extent to which I am 'ready' to be moved by what I know of this project?" (18).

Urbain does the reader a great service by this self-reflexivity, for it unveils the "twist" that occurs in almost *all* foreign attempts to grasp El Sistema. It is not just that "what he knows of this project" has already been constructed as a moving story, but also that he is "ready to be moved by it." Indeed, most foreign observers want to be moved by it, so they make various mental leaps and erasures to make it a personal "source of revelation" rather than an object of critical examination.

Urbain suggests that "this huge organization can be seen as testament to the possibility that people, all people, no matter how poor or hopeless, can be inspired by music and change their lives in radical ways for the better. The most spectacular example of this is that of Gustavo Dudamel, who started in the children's orchestra in his hometown in Venezuela, learned the violin and today conducts some of the world's greatest orchestras. The fact that Dudamel's life was transformed by music, as were those of thousands of children, enhances this author's feelings of solidarity with the rest of humanity" (19). Urbain's misleading implication is that Dudamel is an example of "people, all people, no matter or poor or hopeless," whose life was "transformed by music"—an odd way to describe a middle-class child born to musician parents. Dudamel's is a nice story, but hardly the revelatory example of social action through music that it becomes in Urbain's hands.

It would be wrong to mark down Urbain's study as particularly at fault; its idealization is typical of academic interventions on El Sistema, and it has particular value in uncovering the process by which most people outside Venezuela grasp the program. It is instructive to witness how Urbain's readiness to be moved shapes the construction of his image of El Sistema and elides the contradictions between the program and Small's views.

DEMONSTRATING EFFECTIVENESS

On February 8, 2011, an orchestra and choir of prison inmates, part of El Sistema's penitentiary music program, performed at the National Assembly. According to press reports, the performance "demonstrated the advances made in the matter of humanizing the prisons."[2] Later that year, Abreu lent his support to the government's presentation of its record to the UN's Human Rights Council. "'We will demonstrate that Venezuela is a country that has managed to undergo a profound revolution to construct socialism via the path of freedom of expression, the debate of ideas, education for life and for the freedom of our people,' affirmed the Minister for External Relations, Nicolás Maduro. These declarations were offered moments before attending the concert named 'So That Humanity May Be Human,' offered by the SBYO in Geneva" ("Maduro" 2011). The minister (and future president) also stated that the SBYO showed "a good part of the most beautiful essence of our people"

(Izarra 2011). If the February performance had "demonstrated" the humanization of Venezuela's prisons, the October concert demonstrated the humanization of all of Venezuela, and indeed of humanity itself.

Such visions rest on the idea that performances by large ensembles reveal the social and moral development of their musicians. The assumption that if music affects the listener, something profound must surely be taking place among and within the musicians, has a very long history. However, Julian Johnson (2002, 40–41) is skeptical: musicians, he writes, can move an audience to tears even when going through the motions. He warns that "when the emotional responses aroused by political orators have been taken as a measure of their truth, social disaster has usually ensued." His warning recalls the French philosopher Denis Diderot's "paradox of acting," according to which the greater the emotional impact, the more artifice involved in performance. Indeed, Diderot argued that the most effective actors had the least sensitive personalities and were in fact cold-blooded (Le Guin 2002, 228–30). There are reasons to be wary, then, of the idea that if an orchestra produces intense emotional responses in listeners, some kind of deep inner movement (or "humanization") must be taking place within the ensemble's participants.

According to the report on the prisoners' performance, "this program of music teaching was created with the aim of lowering the level of violence in prisons." Just four months later, Venezuela was gripped by a major outbreak of prison violence, which involved thousands of troops and left dozens dead and many more held hostage by heavily armed prisoners. Further outbreaks of violence in 2012 and 2013 led to many more deaths. It would be unfair to expect El Sistema to solve the problems of Venezuela's prisons, but there is a stark contrast between the "demonstration" of the program's effectiveness in the National Assembly and the much more sobering reality behind prison walls.

At a seminar in the United States, Bolivia Bottome, a senior Sistema figure, succinctly and openly explained the relationship between the program's politics of impact and its funding. Whereas the Americans were concerned with measurement, research, documentation, and evaluation, Bottome declared breezily: "In Venezuela, we don't show numbers—we do a lot of large showcase demonstrations to fundraise." These displays may therefore reveal more about music's persuasive power over *listeners* than about its effect on performers. Performance is a rhetorical mode, a casting of a spell, not a simple window onto underlying reality. Orchestral performances may conjure up a utopian fantasy for audiences (Beckles Willson 2009), but whether this fantasy demonstrates anything beyond its own persuasiveness is another matter. As Scott (2012, 138) notes, evoking the parades of North Korea's "Dear Leader," Kim Jong-Il: "The minutely coordinated movements of uniformed gymnasts, like those of a marching band in close-order drill, conveyed an image of synchronized power and, of course, of choreography scripted by a commanding but invisible orchestra conductor." He suspects that "such demonstrations are literally for 'show,' that they represent a substitute for more substantive change...designed in large part to mesmerize both rulers (self-hypnosis?) and a larger public with a Potemkin façade of centralized order" (2012, 140). If such performances demonstrate anything, then, it is above all the power of their choreographer and his efforts to mesmerize audiences. Rather than revealing deeper individual and social processes and thus providing a shortcut to evaluation, spectacular display may actually short-circuit the assessment process by seeking, in Baroque fashion, to leave listeners dumbfounded and unable to think rationally.

EVALUATING EFFECTIVENESS

Jonathan Govias stated on his blog on August 17, 2011: "Maestro Abreu's *ultima ratio regis* is not his eloquence or a raft of economic studies—it's the public showcase performances that his charges can, as a rule across the 240+ núcleos, execute on a moment's notice. The music speaks volumes too." Yet Govias's remarks beg many questions. What does the music speak of? Can a showcase performance substitute for rigorous studies? Is there no more robust evidence of El Sistema's social impact?

Sistema supporters often claim that widespread belief in the effectiveness of the program, particularly by illustrious figures, constitutes evidence of that effectiveness (see, for example, Marshall Marcus's blog post on July 18, 2012). Yet few of those VIPs have a deep knowledge of the program, most having been given short, stage-managed, red-carpet tours. A roll call of people who believe El Sistema to be a force for good is no more evidence for that conclusion than a list of fervent believers is evidence for the existence of God.

I discussed Simon Rattle's enthusiasm for El Sistema with a former member of the program. "Of course Simon is going to say that it's marvelous," he responded, "because that's what they show him. When Simon comes to conduct an orchestra, it has already spent two months working on the repertoire—of course it's going to be good....When musicians from the Berlin [Phil] come, they [the Sistema students] do audition after audition after audition, until the musicians, after going through four auditions, and two months of work...obviously that's what gets shown to the Berlin musicians. You've already got everything totally polished, you know everything by heart, you've played the same passage for 200 hours." What visiting VIPs see reveals little even about musical realities, much less about social impact.

Supporters' and even funders' convictions are not, then, evidence of the program's social effectiveness. As Harford (2012, 117–18) explains, "it can be surprisingly difficult to distinguish between what is working and what is not, and nowhere is this more true than in the area of economic development—and particularly, of development aid. This is partly because when the challenge is as big as the problem of poverty, our desire for simple stories seems to go into overdrive: we don't ask what works, we simply gravitate to what sounds miraculous.... Many apparent successes are not what they seem, and the people who fund them are often poorly placed to spot the failures." The line between success and failure can be subtle, and seeing that line can be hard for foreign funders and fans "who have nothing to guide them except a few well-chosen words and photographs" (2012, 120). Development schemes may obtain both institutional and celebrity backing and project an aura of success, but, when put to the test, turn out to be of limited value or even counterproductive.

Harford describes a school assistance program in Kenya (127–30). It gave out textbooks, which looked like a promising strategy on paper, but a randomized trial showed otherwise. It then tried donating flip charts—same result. Only a deworming program produced significant improvements. Harford concludes that "there is a strong incentive in development to focus on projects that look good and sound good" (130), but only randomized trials will tell if projects are useful, useless, or harmful. In the context of El Sistema, the crucial point is that *this is not a matter of common sense*: a project that strikes observers as patently beneficial may be no such thing.

Evaluating effectiveness requires defining the initial problem, and as Beckles Willson (2009) notes, there can be a certain circularity here. Projects like the WEDO and El Sistema define the problem in such a way that the orchestra looks like an effective solution. So for the WEDO, suffering in the Middle East boils down to feeling misunderstood by the Other, while Abreu defines poverty in cultural and spiritual terms. In his TED prize speech, he declared: "the most miserable and tragic thing about poverty is not the lack of bread or roof, but the feeling of being no one—the feeling of not being anyone, the lack of identification, the lack of public esteem." He went on: "Arnold Toynbee said that the world was suffering a huge spiritual crisis. Not an economic or social crisis, but a spiritual one. I believe that to confront such a crisis, only art and religion can give proper answers to humanity."[3] More recently, he stated: "the most terrible poverty is the lack of an identity" (Márquez 2013). In both projects, structural issues—broad social, economic, and political conditions—are downplayed or ignored in favor of problems that may potentially be solved by playing in or listening to an orchestra.

If Venezuela's problems are defined in terms of spiritual crisis and a lack of identity, then El Sistema might be said to offer a potential solution. If its problems are seen as social inequality and high crime, however, then its effectiveness appears to be more limited, since it produces stratification and its rapid expansion has been accompanied by sharply rising crime levels. Caracas has been described as "the deadliest city in the world" ("High Crime Rates" 2010). The U.S. Department of State regards Venezuela as more dangerous than Iraq, Afghanistan, and Somalia, a view backed up by figures from the Pan American Health Organization, which show the murder rate as having tripled under

Chávez, and the UN (Birns 2011; Dickey 2011). When Wakin (2012a) alluded to this issue, Abreu simply replied, "orchestras and choirs are incredibly effective instruments against violence." Utopian visions of orchestras like the SBYO and the WEDO are remarkably resilient in the face of evidence for their limited impact (Riiser 2010, 21).

EVALUATIONS OF EL SISTEMA

Considering the longevity, size, fame, and budget of the program, surprisingly little monitoring or evaluation of El Sistema has been undertaken. El Sistema increasingly talks up its utilitarian credentials, yet there are very few external evaluations and those that exist are not publicly available. The first was initiated when the program had been running for nearly twenty-five years (and long after its success had been hailed internationally). This is a stark contrast with Sistema Scotland, for example, which began in 2008, commissioned an evaluation in 2010, and had a report publicly available in 2011. The paucity of evaluations in Venezuela undoubtedly reflects their low priority in a culture in which numbers and measurements have less of a hold than in Europe or North America. Nevertheless, it is striking that after thirty-eight years, El Sistema had nothing equivalent to the report that Sistema Scotland produced within three years (though Logan [n.d.] is highly critical of this report). As a result, foreign observers have been proclaiming the program's success largely on the basis of personal impressions, FESNOJIV's glowing self-reports, and a few choice numbers from external reports filtered through other sources.

There are two principal external reports. The first was carried out by the Universidad de los Andes (ULA) in Mérida between 1999 and 2003.[4] This quantitative study purports to demonstrate the beneficial effects of El Sistema. Like many studies of music education programs, however, it shows correlation rather than causation, so it may simply indicate that motivated, socially adjusted children are more likely than others to join El Sistema and to prosper in a program whose values they already share. The results, while generally positive, do not therefore demonstrate El Sistema's effectiveness, and there are several further question marks over the report: as Hollinger notes (2006, 41–42), it has "a number of inherent design weaknesses" and resembles "less a scholarly endeavor than necessary documentation to advocate for The System."

I spoke to a senior member of the research team and gleaned some details. The project was commissioned by FESNOJIV, and the team was bound to keeping the results confidential. The results were presented to Abreu, in person and in private. This was as much an internal as an external evaluation, then. Sistema staff organized the interviews, which were not anonymized and usually took place in the núcleo itself—procedures that undoubtedly decreased the chances of critical responses. I watched video recordings of some of the interviews. The questions were fairly leading and opened up little possibility of a negative response. Conversations were largely superficial and formulaic. As with any large-scale interviewing project, there was minimal personal bond between interviewer and interviewee, and therefore little chance of glimpsing a hidden transcript.

The researchers' conclusions thus closely reflected El Sistema's own, and even adopted its proselytizing tone: "It may be stated without any doubt that El Sistema is a very effective form of social intervention for the development of the nation. For that reason, all efforts—economic, administrative, and personal—to achieve its expansion, strengthening and projection are fully justified. . . . Without any doubt, it may be declared that, in general terms, belonging to El Sistema represents a beneficial move for any child or young person who takes the initiative to sign up for it." Such unequivocal statements are easily contradicted by ethnographic research; questions thus arise about whether it was methodological flaws or political factors that led the researchers to overlook a host of relatively obvious problems.

Many studies of the effects of music on social and personal development depend on self-report, yet questionnaires and interviews are likely to be focused on individuals who identify significantly with the process of music learning. As Hallam (2010, 280) notes: "research has largely focused on those currently participating in active music making, not taking account of those who have not found it an enjoyable and rewarding experience." The risk of exaggerating benefits is therefore notable. Ethnography, in contrast, allows the researcher to take into account the dropouts and dissenters as well as the success stories, and to unearth critical views that might not be captured through other methods. Discontent with El Sistema is visible even on the Internet; why is it invisible in the ULA study? How useful is an evaluation that fails to convey any hint of systemic problems that are so widely discussed?

One area that remains murky after reading this report is the oft-cited connection between music learning and academic achievement. The IDB's first loan in 1998 included a vague suggestion of a correlation between performance in the orchestra system and in school, while in 2007, the bank stated more firmly: "The primary individual benefits attributed to the System include improvements in academic achievement" ("Program to Support" 2007, 1). Yet comprehensive studies by Winner and Cooper (2000) and Hallam (2010) did not corroborate claims of a causal effect of arts or music education on academic attainment. In fact, buried deep in the ULA report is evidence that longer-term Sistema participation had a small *negative* effect on school attendance and academic achievement, contradicting the report's own conclusion—that El Sistema is "without any doubt" beneficial for students—and undermining a common claim made for the program. Why was such an important finding silenced in the conclusion?

There is a certain logic to this discovery. A Veracruz student reported being continually taken out of school for orchestral commitments. He pooh-poohed the official Sistema line that it keeps a firm eye on children's school marks: he had seen no evidence of it actually happening outside show núcleos. A founder and former senior figure claimed: "There are many contradictions around the orchestra, concerning the institution's principles and what really happens . . . that the kids who are in the orchestra improve their school marks and that fewer drop out; they say that, yet there's no proof that it really works like that. What we saw was that it was difficult for the kids to keep up good marks at school because the orchestra demanded too much of their time for rehearsals. What happens is that it's a source of prestige, an opportunity (a series of benefits) that makes the parents and the schools proud, and they look the other way when the kids get bad marks. In the first and second generations of the SBYO the percentage of players who had graduated from high school was small. There's quite a contradiction there!"

The second report, by José Cuesta (2008), underpinned the IDB's Phase II loan proposal. Cuesta provides evidence of a link between participation in El Sistema and school performance, employment, and community participation. There is a question mark over Table 1 (2008, 2), which shows that 10 percent more of the control group were living in poverty than of the treatment group, which could offer one possible explanation for the remaining figures. There are also issues familiar from the ULA report: there is some evidence of correlation, but none of causation; and in his acknowledgments, Cuesta thanks Abreu and Igor Lanz (El Sistema's executive director) "for their involvement in specific parts of the analysis and comments to earlier versions. Without their work, commitment and suggestions this analysis would have not been possible." It thus appears that Abreu and Lanz may have had a hand in creating the report that was then used to justify the IDB's $150 million loan.

There are also serious issues around methodology, not least the very lack of discussion of methodological problems and caveats. For one, to call the Sistema participants a "treatment" group is problematic, since they are really a self-selected or "opt-in" group. This is not a randomized control trial. By and large, we might expect the opt-in group to be more disciplined, motivated, educated students; the correlation illustrated by Cuesta is therefore exactly what one would anticipate, and shows nothing about the effectiveness of El Sistema. His research is based on the strong (yet contentious) assumption that the only difference between control and treatment groups is participation in El Sistema, and not preexisting cognitive or social differences between children. As a result, there is a high risk of overestimating El Sistema's impact.

Despite its multiple problems, this report (filtered through the IDB's Phase II loan proposal) has become a cornerstone of arguments for El Sistema around the world. Its dubious cost-benefit calculation—estimated as a ratio of 1:1.68— has been widely repeated, even though there is a strong likelihood that the figure is exaggerated, given that positive outcomes may well be the result of preexisting social, economic, or cognitive advantages. This, of course, does not mean that El Sistema does not work—El Sistema *may* cause positive child development outcomes—but rather that the current "proofs" are unconvincing.

EVALUATIONS AND THE IDB

Despite hundreds of millions of dollars of investment over decades, robust evidence that El Sistema is effective in achieving its social goals is thus lacking. Future research may demonstrate the program's effectiveness; but to date, claims of extraordinary success have been founded less on evidence than on the impact of El Sistema's sheer size, age-old beliefs about the uplifting power of high art, and a sustained PR campaign by the program itself. A sign of this impressionistic approach can be seen in the failure to take account of El Sistema's dropout rate, a key statistic for evaluating such a program.

Little attention is paid to those who "fail" in El Sistema. All the interest is in the success stories. El Sistema does not seem to collect information on how many children fall by the wayside and what happens to them afterward. A Veracruz teacher claimed she had asked the director about following up with children who left and he had replied that he did not have time. Even the program's biggest supporters have been unable to elicit figures. Booth (2008, 4) notes that "a number of students leave around age 12 (percentages were not available...)." Borzacchini (2010, 101) asked Igor Lanz a straight question: "What is the percentage of children who leave the orchestras?" "One cannot talk about dropping out," replied Lanz evasively.

As a single researcher, I was therefore obliged to proceed anecdotally, and it seemed that the dropout rate was high. Various successful musicians told me that their siblings had dropped out after short periods, while a violist in a small núcleo told me that eight had started the instrument the previous year but now only two remained. Is this high dropout rate typical? There is no way of knowing, since "percentages are not available." As discussed in Chapter 4, a teacher at Veracruz reported a severe drop-off during the first year after enrollment. He gave two explanations: first, the disciplined regime did not suit many children; second, the núcleo's raison d'être (whether explicit or not) was to produce a decent youth orchestra, for which it needed perhaps between 100 and 150 students, and children who were seen as poor prospects for the orchestra were paid little attention or even encouraged to leave. A high dropout rate is a major source of anxiety for music educationalists in other countries, and it would seem problematic to describe El Sistema as a miraculous success story without having any statistics in this area.

Interestingly, the IDB itself has become somewhat skeptical. In 2011 a senior figure at the bank admitted to me that there was no empirical evidence for the program's impact.[5] She described the two principal studies as inconclusive and alluded to methodological problems: a striking opinion, given that justification of the Phase II loan of $150 million had rested on these two reports. Everyone feels the emotional power of seeing the children in action, she said, but the bank wants more robust evidence. Indeed, the IDB's project completion report on Phase I recommended that "a more systematic effort to identify and quantify social impacts was needed. This will allow for more accurate evaluation, as well as an *evidence-based strategy* for adjusting System interventions" (9, emphasis added). The key elements of the Phase II proposal were the construction of regional centers and monitoring and evaluation; vagueness about effects was thus officially acknowledged. Tellingly, external assessment was one of the planned organizational improvements that had been sacrificed in order to channel extra resources into the construction of the CASM during Phase I. It was not until mid-2011, however, that the IDB launched a thorough evaluation (full results were due in late 2013 but no announcement had been made as of mid-2014).

The impact evaluation proposal ("Sistema Nacional" 2011) makes for interesting reading. It states: "clear identification of the impacts of El Sistema is a fundamental prerequisite for justifying future support of the program" (2011, 2)—after thirteen years of funding and two major loans. It admits that the evaluation "would be the first rigorous evidence of the results of the program, and would allow the justification of future support from the Bank and other donors, as well as its possible replication in other countries in the region" (3)—long after the program has started to be replicated in many other countries. It acknowledges that Cuesta's cost-benefit analysis—a pillar of the Phase II loan— "was the result of various suppositions and not of a rigorous measurement of the impact of El Sistema on the beneficiaries of the program." Three years on, it seems that even the IDB did not find Cuesta's report entirely convincing.

Although the current evaluation will be the most thorough to date, there are some aspects that demand further attention. First, the evaluation involves randomly selected control and treatment groups, drawn from applicants to El Sistema: the treatment group consists of those accepted by the program in 2011, the control group of those rejected. The selection of these groups presupposes that children are *randomly* accepted or rejected by El Sistema according to capacity—in other words, that there are no a priori differences between the two groups. In Veracruz, however, the núcleo conducted entrance auditions and selected those who showed more musical talent. Thus an evaluation of the comparative development of control and treatment groups in Veracruz would entail comparing more and less musically talented children, which would render any judgment about El Sistema's impact meaningless. Furthermore, according to a teacher at Veracruz, children who showed signs of attention deficit or poor behavior in auditions were often rejected, since it was assumed that they would be harder to teach. The children who were accepted were those who *already* showed signs of talent and socialization into institutional norms. The IDB's evaluation method simply would not have worked in Veracruz.

Second, the evaluation is comparing a group that spends up to twenty hours a week on an organized activity with another group that may not be involved consistently in any alternative activity. Expected impacts include lower school dropout rate, reduction in risky behaviors, and reduction in unplanned pregnancies. One might expect a group of young people who did *any organized activity at all* for twenty hours a week to have better results on these indicators than a group who did nothing. The results might then tell us less about the power of orchestral music than about the power of keeping children busy. They might demonstrate that orchestral music is better than nothing, but not that it is a particularly efficient solution. More revealing would be to bring a third group into the study, one that did a different activity but with the same level of time commitment, coaching, and investment as the Sistema children, ideally with subjects randomly assigned between the two projects (Goldstein et al. 2013, 10). Comparing the results would give a clearer picture of the impact of El Sistema in particular, rather than organized activity in general.

At the core of El Sistema lies the contention that there is something special, even unique, about orchestral practice, and the IDB evaluation—at least as described in its proposal—will not demonstrate this. Even if the evaluation showed positive outcomes, these might simply reflect the amount of resources that have been invested in the program; the orchestra itself might play no part in them at all. Indeed, the scholarly literature implies that any positive outcomes of El Sistema might be *despite* rather than *because of* its focus on orchestral practice. One would expect an organization that spent hundreds of millions of dollars to achieve some notable outcomes; more important is assessing the relationship of investment to results and the role of El Sistema's distinctive features.

On a final note, a lot is riding on the current evaluation. Phase II of the IDB program is both delayed and underfunded. I was informed that work on the regional CASMs, due to have been completed by 2011, would not begin until 2012, and the IDB did not believe they would be finished by the end of Phase II in 2015 (indeed, there was still no sign in mid-2013 that work had begun). In all probability, more money is going to be needed in 2015 in order to complete the project. The evaluators will undoubtedly be very aware that a negative conclusion would leave seventeen years' support, several half-built facilities, and $160 million of funding hanging uncomfortably in midair.

As Sistema-inspired programs spread around the globe, interest in evaluation is increasing. Quantitative evaluations are an important step, and they may well demonstrate positive outcomes in certain spheres; but their results can never resolve all ethical issues and may not account for significant social and cultural complexities and noneconomic costs, particularly over the longer term. In Chapter 4, Scott claimed that "high-modernist designs for life and production tend to diminish the skills, agility, initiative, and morale of their intended beneficiaries" and "foster a less skilled, less innovative, less resourceful population." Are his concerns borne out in El Sistema? How might one find out? Impact on unplanned pregnancies or school dropout rates is easily measurable; impact on creativity, initiative, or resourcefulness is just as important but much harder to judge. The IDB's evaluation may be a step forward, but it will not settle many issues that concern observers and participants in Venezuela. Careful qualitative studies are thus essential as well.

Looking back over the IDB's two loan proposals of 1998 and 2007 raises some important questions. The first loan, of $16 million, was made on various conditions; the second loan proposal openly stated that many of these conditions had not been met, and the evaluations it used to demonstrate effectiveness were clearly inconclusive at best (and have been subsequently disowned). Why, then, was Phase II funded to the tune of $150 million? There is an echo here of Ferguson's (1994) argument that development projects routinely fail to meet their stated objectives, succeeding only in achieving the expansion of bureaucratic power. Furthermore, why was a rigorous evaluation exercise only planned for the tail end of Phase II? El Sistema is finally being asked to demonstrate its effectiveness *after* receiving that major loan, and in early 2011, the IDB was already talking about a Phase III loan in 2015, before evaluation had even begun.

Yúdice (2003, 15) argues that development banks need quantitative data to measure benefit, and that "measurement instruments have to go beyond intuitions and opinions." Yet this rule has been bent in the case of El Sistema: large sums have been devoted to a project with unproven outcomes and a poor record of achieving targets. The key to this paradox lies in the politics of impact, successfully pursued by the program, in place of offering data, to convince those responsible for key decisions. Like the Baroque audience, the IDB appears to have been "conquered, subjugated, carried by the persuasive flow of the rhetoric," as Abreu and his musicians cast their spell. There is no better symbol of Abreu's powers of persuasion and El Sistema's politics of impact than the $500 million in development bank loans paid out to the project between 2008 and 2013 on the basis of hopes and hunches.

THE ECONOMICS OF IMPACT

El Sistema is striking not just because of its use of spectacle to raise funds but also because of its use of funds to put on a spectacle. For an arts education project, it spends an impressive amount of money on being impressive. It is not cheap to create model núcleos and huge orchestras that tour the globe, and El Sistema often pays for the best that money can buy.

Abreu is widely acknowledged to be a master fund-raiser. One of his tactics has been to diversify and multiply the funding sources for the project to allow it to grow. El Sistema has gone on a pilgrimage through a number of government ministries, including Youth, Family, Social Work, Communes, the Vice Presidency, and the Office of the President. According to a musician who saw relevant documents, another strategy was to create a range of "independent" music associations, societies, and academies that applied under their own name for regional funding from CONAC's Dirección General Sectorial de Artes Auditivas, even though they in practice formed part of El Sistema. The CASM is the epitome of Abreu's financial inventiveness: a rather traditional conservatoire-cum-concert-hall for classical music, built largely with social funds provided by a development bank.

Many musicians claimed that El Sistema's signature features, such as the huge orchestras, colorful jackets, and populist repertoire, were signs of a project geared around constant fundraising. Investing in the spectacular end of the project has certainly been an effective strategy in terms of the overall sums raised; where problems arise is over the efficient use of resources and their trickle down to the base of the pyramid. The topic of lavish or even wasteful expenditure surfaced regularly in interviews as a source of concern. One Veracruz musician recalled being sent two return plane tickets to Caracas for a seminario that was organized, postponed, and then canceled. Since the tickets were never requested, he used them to go to the beach. Abreu had a reputation for financial extravagance and high spending on bureaucracy when he was minister of culture; cost efficiency does not seem to be one of his strengths.

Another recurrent issue is the concentration of spending at the top of the pyramid. At its summit, El Sistema is a luxury project, which uses the best instruments, teachers, hotels, buses, uniforms, and so on; no expense is spared for its elite musicians. A senior oboist reported that El Sistema had forty Lorée cor anglais on order, instruments that normally retail for around $10,000 each; he also claimed that members of the SBYO had made-to-measure French oboes with gold-plated keys—the most expensive instruments in the world. A teacher in Veracruz spoke to an instrument dealer who had sold five instruments to the TCYO in the space of two weeks, at a total cost of more than 50,000 euros, something that grated since there had been a shortage in Veracruz for years. Such sums are a significant outlay for a project that supposedly puts the social before the musical.

The expenditure on the SBYO, in particular, makes jaws drop in Venezuela. One cultural official recounted a dispute with Abreu many years before over the latter's decision to take more than two hundred people—twice the number actually needed—on an Asian tour. Today, that looks like small beer: Borzacchini (2010, 231) reports a party of more than 350 on foreign tours from 2007 to 2009, including, of course, "embedded" (and compliant) journalists. The number of nonmusicians must have been impressive. One musician recalled going to a seminario at a luxurious hotel on the island of Margarita, a top tourist destination; he estimated there were as many hangers-on as musicians. Another described a multiweek seminario in a five-star hotel, during which students were plied with huge luxury buffets three times a day and twenty-four-hour room service, and had bracelets that entitled them to unlimited alcoholic drinks.

In late 2012 the SBSO salary was reportedly around 20,000 bolívares—almost ten times that paid by the Veracruz Symphony, and four times the pay of a university dean whom I knew. In the age of Facebook, extravagant expenditure is no secret; I saw musicians' photos of top-of-the-range cars and lavish meals in expensive hotels. Those who work or study in ordinary núcleos, which are plagued by shortages, are often disturbed by the spending of eye-watering sums at the top of the organization. Claims of revolutionary social action ring somewhat hollow when funds are so manifestly concentrated on talented young adults—a musical elite—rather than vulnerable children.

The financial aspect of music education becomes particularly apparent with overseas tours. El Sistema sent 1,400 young musicians to the Salzburg Festival in 2013, and paid them 800 Euros each as well as covering all their costs. Musicians appeared on Facebook buying computer games and suitcases full of clothes, and there was a sudden glut of offers to exchange hard currency for bolívares. Venezuela has currency controls and thus a thriving gray market; Euros and dollars can sell for many times their official value. The TCYO's European tour in mid-2014 saw the young musicians paid 1,300 Euros each; they were also promised a bonus from concert ticket sales of 400 to 600 Euros, and were given 40 Euros a day for food (some ate at McDonald's every day in order to save extra money). Behind the talk of changing lives, a lot of money is circulating.

El Sistema does spend considerable sums of money further down the pyramid, but not necessarily on the most pressing necessities. For example, large amounts are paid out in non-means-tested scholarships. In Veracruz, there were plenty of teenagers who lived at home in comfortable circumstances and spent the money on fashionable clothes or a BlackBerry.

Lubow (2007) tells an illuminating anecdote about the construction of the CASM: "After attending concerts of Dudamel with the Youth Orchestra at the Lucerne Festival in Switzerland, which is one of the most impressive settings for music in the world, Abreu admired the granite entry floor of the concert hall. 'He went to the Ministry of Finance,' Antola [an IDB representative] says. 'He convinced them. There was not even enough granite in the country. They had to bring it back from Panama, where they had already sold it. He is like a serpent enchanter. You can't resist.'" Few would argue against the democratization of quality, but is a granite entry floor really a more pressing need than decent facilities for provincial núcleos? Christine Witkowski quoted Abreu's catchphrase "culture for the poor cannot be poor culture" on the *Key Changes* blog on March 1, 2010, and stated: "As Dr. Abreu put it, you need the best educators for the poorest children, the highest quality instruments for the poorest children, the most state-of-the-art building for the poorest children." Yet this inspiring rhetoric bears little relation to a reality in which the poorest children are much more likely to be found in underresourced and understaffed núcleos, and the primary beneficiaries of the granite entry floor, the best instruments, and the top teachers are adult members of the elite, touring orchestras.

One problem that El Sistema faces is ever-rising expenditure, not just because of expansion but also because it is training many more aspiring professional orchestral musicians than the country needs, and thus has to create paid work for some of them itself. In 2011 the SBYO became the SBSO, in a tacit recognition that it had stretched the definition of a "youth orchestra" to the limit, yet it continues as the flagship ensemble of El Sistema. Large sums are thus devoted to musicians who are neither young nor vulnerable. The program resolved the problem of what to do with these maturing musicians by adding them to the state payroll indefinitely. Will each new generation of Sistema stars become a new state-funded professional orchestra? Members of the TCYO told me this was indeed their vision, and FESNOJIV director Eduardo Méndez told Tunstall (2012, 125) the same thing. Méndez also declared that El Sistema was aiming to create a professional youth orchestra in every state capital—yet these cities already have a professional orchestra, in most cases attracting small audiences and struggling to survive. Does Venezuela actually need more subsidized professional orchestras? Who would their audience be? Is this really the best way to spend social development funds? Given the lack of demand, the only way out of the oversupply problem seems to be an ever-expanding budget—an unsustainable solution that feeds comparisons to a Ponzi scheme.

ACCOUNTING

El Sistema is legendary for its economic power, but also for the opacity of its financial affairs, just like CONAC was under Abreu. Several informants reported that there had been little transparent accounting or external monitoring of the program's financial practices, making the movements of money difficult to track. Attempts to investigate El Sistema bump up immediately against a lack of public records; its economic activities are thus as hard to assess as its social impact.

Even El Sistema's musicians are perplexed by the financial arrangements of their own institution, pointing to certain individuals' international movements and acquisition of expensive new instruments. As might be expected, the combination of opacity and plentiful funding spawns speculation, rumors, and accusations of irregularities, if with little concrete evidence to back them up. An Internet forum threw up dozens of allegations of corruption and mal-administration; though such claims are nearly impossible to verify, they illuminate perceptions of the program by its own participants.[6] More detailed reports came from former senior Sistema figures and journalists, who claimed that expenditure had not been properly supervised and did not obey normal accounting rules. Their reports suggested that El Sistema had inherited the lack of financial transparency characteristic of Venezuelan institutions of the Punto Fijo period.

Abreu's brilliance and experience as an economist have clearly worked in El Sistema's favor. A former government official claimed that Abreu, when minister, would instruct Congress's budget planning office to move money around in complicated operations; staff would be required to stay late into the night if necessary until these transfers were completed. A former CONAC employee confirmed that Abreu would do night watches at the budget commission. Abreu also has a reputation for creating illegible institutions. A former Ministry of Culture official described El Sistema as a financial "black hole," while Casanova (2009) claimed that Abreu left CONAC in a state of "inauditable financial chaos." He continued: "no one has carried out an external audit of the hundreds of billions of bolívares that the nation has given Abreu over the last 30 years."

The perception of financial irregularities in some areas of El Sistema is also reflected in the recollections of former cultural officials. One claimed that, many years ago, he saw evidence that plane tickets for a tour that showed the full price had actually been bought at a discount rate, suggesting that the travel costs charged to the funder may have been overblown. He believed that this explained why such large parties were sometimes taken on tours, since there was allegedly a profit that might be made on each ticket.

Similarly, a former Ministry of Culture official who knew El Sistema well claimed to have seen a variety of financial improprieties over the years. He named El Sistema employees who owned a luxury overseas home, charged several salaries simultaneously, and owned a company that provided services to El Sistema. He alleged that the provision of services was often not put out to tender but simply handed over to a favored company, and that commissions were sometimes pocketed as part of the bulk purchase of instruments.

A former Sistema figure, too, claimed that there had been financial irregularities in past decades. For example, he recalled instances where instruments were donated but government money was also allocated to buy the same instruments, and where expenses for foreign tours were provided twice, by the state and by a sponsor; the extra funds "evaporated," he claimed, or were spent on lavish gifts and treats. Other informants made similar allegations about expenditure that was double-funded.

None of my informants suggested that these strategies had benefited Abreu, who lives a simple, almost austere life. In recent years he has resided in his sister's house in a small room reminiscent of a monk's cell. It is the project and others further down the pyramid that have allegedly profited.

CONCLUSION

El Sistema has caught the world's imagination for two principal reasons: its unrivaled ability to put on a show, and its emphasis on rescuing disadvantaged children. Its success has depended on the generation and delivery of a highly appealing narrative, something hardly uncommon in the worlds of business and entertainment. Adding a dazzling spectacle to this heartwarming back-story, El Sistema has played the marketing and public relations game with great skill, resulting in innumerable endorsements from prestigious international organizations. Still, given the huge sums of money and attention being directed toward the project and the lack of evidence for its supposedly extraordinary transformative effects, it is legitimate—indeed urgent—to investigate the relationships between rhetoric, representation, and reality.

El Sistema has been a highly effective machine, but there is more evidence of its effectiveness in generating funds, publicity, and acclaim than in fulfilling its core mission. This disjuncture is encapsulated in its securing of $500 million in development bank funds without a rigorous, reliable evaluation. Historically, the project has not shown numbers or proof, but has relied instead on Abreu's charisma and influence; and more recently it has settled everything with some broad statements about social inclusion, some mystical lines about the power of music, and a massive performance of Beethoven 9 or Bernstein's "Mambo." To question this apparent success story is often treated as tasteless or even an offense against poor children; but it remains valid, indeed vital, to ask whether El Sistema actually works or simply appears to.

CHAPTER 12
Impact on Venezuelan Cultural Life

In Latin America the aspiration to overcome underdevelopment has often turned into an insidiously tragic means of continuing the conquest and colonization by its own hand, of recognizing itself in other histories, and therefore of misrecognizing the history that unfolds in its own land.
—Fernando Coronil, *The Magical State: Nature, Money, and Modernity in Venezuela*

The internationally renowned folk singer Cecilia Todd spoke out in the aftermath of Abreu's controversial meeting with Juanes and Miguel Bosé (see Chapter 1):

> [W]hat we are criticizing is not El Sistema in itself—it is, among other things, its Eurocentric orientation and its media manipulation of "social action." Girls and boys, when they take up the violin and are oriented towards the idea that higher values come from European music, start to disdain their own music as a natural response. They are implanted with the idea that everything that comes from overseas is better....
>
> If it is really about distancing girls and boys from drugs, why not do it with our own music, which is so wonderful? There is no reason to train our children just with Eurocentric music, the same that is played everywhere, nothing original. If we are going to give this opportunity to these girls and boys who want to get into music, they can easily study their instruments through Venezuelan music—here too there are composers from the eighteenth century, for example, and also contemporary composers of symphonic music whose works are played once and then forgotten. This is a very musical country: why take our children away from their roots? (Hernández 2013)

Todd is far from alone in suggesting that El Sistema has been a mixed blessing. Its spectacular growth—in 2005 FESNOJIV received 48 billion bolívares from the state, while CONAC disbursed 47 billion bolívares to 2,500 groups and organizations across all the arts (Duque 2006)—has converted it into a de facto national plan for culture and music education. Its impact on Venezuelan cultural life is thus undeniable, but due to its narrow focus, this impact has been highly uneven. This chapter approaches El Sistema from the perspective of two constituencies—popular and traditional musicians, and art music composers—that have historically been marginalized by the program's limited interest in Venezuelan music. It examines the new traditional music initiative Alma Llanera and the issue of repertoire, and assesses Todd's charge of Eurocentrism. Finally, Venezuelan cultural life is considered as an ecological system in which dramatic changes in one area may have an unbalancing effect on the whole.

POPULAR AND TRADITIONAL MUSIC

Todd's complaint that El Sistema is Eurocentric and neglects Venezuelan popular and traditional music is a common one. The program claims to "overcome the false distinction between popular and classical music," and on October 11, 2010, its website title read "Spreading Venezuelan Culture." Yet the site also describes how the original National Youth Orchestra permitted audiences "to enjoy the beauty of works by Tchaikovsky, Mozart, and Berlioz." Its first concert in 1975 consisted of Bach, Handel, Mozart, and Vivaldi (Hollinger 2006, 79). Thirty-six years later, the program at the CASM one busy weekend included three symphony concerts: the composers represented were Brahms, Prokofiev, Beethoven, Rachmaninoff, and Tchaikovsky. Now as then, Latin American and contemporary music were absent. La Rinconada núcleo has infant ensembles called Baby Mozart, Baby Haydn, Baby Corelli, and Baby Vivaldi: "these names are used not to indicate the music being played by the 'babies,' but to introduce the great composers into children's lives at a very early age" (Tunstall 2012, 157). Even though the infants sing popular songs, they are inculcated with the program's hierarchy of cultural values from the start.

Abreu told Lubow (2007): "As a musician, I had the ambition to see a poor child play Mozart. Why not? Why concentrate in one class the privilege of playing Mozart and Beethoven? The high musical culture of the world has to be a common culture, part of the education of everyone." In a television interview, he claimed: "El Sistema breaks the vicious cycle [of poverty] because a child with a violin starts to become spiritually rich: the CD he listens to, the book he reads, he sees words in German, the music opens doors to intellectual knowledge and then everything begins." He continued: "when he has three years of musical education behind him, he is playing Mozart, Haydn, he watches an opera: this child no longer accepts his poverty, he aspires to leave it behind and ends up defeating it." The cultural hierarchy is again unmistakable.

It is European classical music that can save Venezuelan children; Abreu makes no mention of Venezuela's existing common musical culture—Afro-Latin popular music.

Abreu's grandparents were Italian immigrants whose house was a shrine to European culture, and his favorite composers are all European (Borzacchini 2010, 51–52, 64). He is representative of the mid- to late-twentieth-century Venezuelan intellectual and cultural establishment, which generally took the centrality and superiority of European culture for granted (Mayhall 2005). Regarding European culture as universal and seeking to legitimate Venezuela by contributing to this tradition were the norm among the white Caracas elite, whose interests dominated cultural policy. The prime conclusion that Luis Alberto Machado took from his 1979 musical experiment with Abreu, the Pemón indigenous group, and the music of Haydn and Beethoven (see Chapter 3) was the proof that Venezuela was equal to any other country on earth, and he praised the headline in the previous day's edition of *El Universal* newspaper: "One Can Get from Santa Elena de Guairén to Salzburg in Two and a Half Months."[1] As Lombardi (1982, 253) wrote during this period: "The music and the plastic arts that flourish in Venezuela serve more to indicate the sophistication and competence of the Venezuelan elite than to illustrate the context of the country's past." With their focus on European symphonic music, Abreu and El Sistema reproduced the cultural ideology of Venezuela's elite in the mid-twentieth century, and prominent features of the program, including a preference for high over popular culture, foreign over local, are eminently familiar from cultural policy of that time.

Abreu has left his mark on his most famous disciple: in *The Promise of Music*, Dudamel declares that the world would be a better place if everyone had access to culture. Even though his father was a salsa musician, he uses the word "culture" to mean "high culture." Similarly, Abreu argues that "one of the most painful traits of poverty is not having access to art" (Borzacchini 2010, 113), a category from which he clearly excludes popular culture, and his claim that "for me, the most important priority was to give access to music to poor people" is highly revealing—as though poor people did not have music until El Sistema appeared. "I've sought to take music, which is usually a luxury item, and turn it into cultural patrimony accessible to all," says Abreu modestly, ignoring his country's huge range of popular musical traditions.[2] As Eatock (2010) noted: "When he says 'music,' it's sometimes hard to know whether he's talking about music in general or classical music in particular." The inference is clear: for Abreu, music is classical music, and anything else is barely on his radar. Such conflation of "music" and "Western art music" has been critiqued in European and North American music education for half a century.

El Sistema's attitude was encapsulated by Rafael Elster, director of Sarría núcleo, who appeared on a 60 *Minutes* documentary ("El Sistema" 2009): "What they have at home on the radio is popular music all the time. Their father, who drinks every day, gets drunk with that music. So you have to give them something different. And when they sit in one of these chairs in the orchestra, they think they're in another country, in another planet, and they start changing."

Unsurprisingly, then, El Sistema has granted little space to Venezuelan musical traditions over the last four decades. As it has grown exponentially, emblematic festivals of traditional Venezuelan music, such as La Siembra del Cuatro and the Festival de Violín de los Andes, have been left in limbo due to lack of funding. Accordingly, many traditional and popular musicians lament El Sistema's effect on Venezuelan cultural life. As one Veracruz musician put it, "the Europeanization that El Sistema is fostering is a knife to the heart of the cultivation of our native culture." Another questioned why "the state invests millions annually so that our academic musicians may fan out around the world holding up foreign music as a flag for Venezuelan talent, while our own [music] remains struggling for decent spaces and for a modicum of recognition for its creators."

Many in the Venezuelan arts world believe that El Sistema consumes a disproportionate amount of state funds and contradicts the government's broader cultural and political agenda. The criticisms of fifteen well-known figures were published on November 16, 2010, on the blog La Otra Cara del Sistema under the title "The Myth Crumbles." Todd again spoke for many the following year: "There is a monstrous imbalance between the economic support given to El Sistema and popular music. It's an absurdity. There are children in the highlands who play violin, and they have never in their lives held a cuatro and they don't want to play in the Paradura del Niño [traditional festival]. They only play what they're told by the orchestra; it's like putting a chip in their heads" (Hernández 2011).

In order to understand more fully such criticism from significant voices in the popular music sphere, it is necessary to go back to the 1970s. While Abreu's European symphonic music program was gestating, a number of young, leftist popular musicians—among them Todd and (most famously) Alí Primera—were encouraging resistance to the dominance of foreign cultural models (Marsh 2013). Their "New Song" (Nueva Canción) movement was the opposite of what El Sistema would be: rooted in the popular culture of the masses, voicing the discontent of the poor and powerless, critical of capitalism and show business, and rejecting foreign influence. Todd's irritation is thus rooted in an unresolved debate that stretches back decades, with leftist singer-songwriters in one corner and Venezuela's more conservative, Eurocentric elite in the other. Many New Song musicians were dismayed that Chávez, whose politics so closely matched theirs, chose to back the opposing camp, which also allowed the emergence of a narrative that portrayed Abreu as a leader of the forces of change in the 1970s, rather than a representative of the ideology that was under attack. For critics like Todd, El Sistema is emblematic of Venezuela's enduring Eurocentrism, and its power today is symptomatic of a frustrating lack of progress on this issue since their youth.

Most foreign observers have failed to grasp the marginalization of Venezuelan music and the extent of criticism from outside El Sistema, focused as they are on the program's public relations discourse. Yet we cannot understand El Sistema without taking account of such long-standing debates over the value of foreign and local music and the broader cultural history of which they form part. A European symphonic music program has particular resonances in a country in which the old cultural establishment—theoretically out of power since the election of Chávez—looked to the global North for direction and the local has historically been relegated to a secondary plane.

ALMA LLANERA AND OTHER SISTEMA INITIATIVES

If El Sistema's long-standing attitude toward Venezuelan music was clear, during my fieldwork change seemed to be in the air. On my visit to Montalbán I heard Venezuelan, Latin American, and popular music. A Latin-Caribbean band had recently been formed at the Sistema conservatoire, and 2011 saw two new ensembles—an Afro-Venezuelan orchestra and a Venezuelan music youth orchestra—and the announcement of a major new Sistema initiative, Alma Llanera, to create a national network of traditional Venezuelan orchestras.

In February 2011 the CASM was officially inaugurated with a carefully orchestrated televised event with Chávez present. First, an orchestra performed in the stunning new concert hall. Afterward, as Abreu and Chávez made their way out into the entrance area, a choir of special education students burst into song. Finally, the Guárico traditional music orchestra played on a special stage that folds out into the park beside the building.

The organization of space and sound was revealing: the symphony orchestra performing in the grand concert hall to an invited audience, the Venezuelan traditional music presented outside in the park to "the people." So much for "overcoming the false distinction between popular and classical music." Furthermore, the traditional music orchestra was given a prominence that belied its true insignificance alongside El Sistema's 400-odd symphony orchestras. The Guárico orchestra itself is revealing, since it entails the refiguring of Venezuelan music into an orchestral format, symbolizing the incorporation of Venezuelan music into El Sistema by making it conform to the standards of European classical music. Its repertoire would normally be played by a handful of closely interacting musicians; but here there were perhaps a hundred, lined up in rows, following the conductor, moving strictly in time— an intimate chamber ensemble converted into a large orchestral machine. The inauguration enacted a fictitious display of inclusivity for a political class suspicious of cultural elitism, but on El Sistema's terms and for El Sistema's ends.

Following Green (1988; 2003b), the issue here is one of ideology: not simply *whether* traditional music is included, but *how*. If it appears primarily in the form of orchestrations or starter instruments, its inclusion ends up simply affirming the underlying cultural assumptions about the innate superiority of classical music. The handful of popular music ensembles that appeared in 2010–11, far from undermining the idea that El Sistema favors classical music, actually underlined this reality, dwarfed as they were by classical orchestras. To hold up these ensembles as evidence of the program's catholic approach is to obfuscate rather than illuminate, for it elides how popular music has functioned since the 1970s as El Sistema's "constitutive outside," to borrow a term employed by Derrida, Butler, and Laclau. Beyond a small number of schools (in particular the Simón Bolívar conservatoire) that had broadened their curriculum somewhat since 2008, El Sistema's 1970s ethos was still predominant in 2010–11.

As Green argues, without a shift in ideology and pedagogy, diversification can actually strengthen the centrality of classical music. El Sistema, however, is still run by its founder, who standardly conflates "music" and "classical music," and who, for thirty-five years, was quite happy for Venezuelan traditional music to be limited to occasional orchestrated appearances as light relief from European music. Since 1975 he has idealized the symphony orchestra, which he regards as "universal" and "natural"—not a promising platform for cultural diversity—and the best motor of social action. His attitude toward popular music was consistent for decades, with a marked preference for high culture noted repeatedly during his ministerial years, suggesting that recent changes reflect not so much an ideological or pedagogical shift as a calculated strategy.

Knowledge of Abreu's past and his long-standing views explains why El Sistema's sudden rash of popular music activities was met with some skepticism in musical circles. He is famed among older Sistema musicians for his dislike of popular music. In the early days, if they wanted to play popular music, they had to do so in secret or they risked being expelled from the orchestra. Allen (2012, 123) claims that Abreu saw salsa as "emblematic of his country's ills of chaos, crime, and addiction." A popular musician wrote: "orchestral musicians (the majority of whom did not exactly come from 'the underclass') were forbidden from playing in salsa bands, moonlighting in the capital's nightlife, walking the streets. They had to do it on the sly. The majority of the trombonists and trumpeters of the Caracas salsa bands that I played in—that is, most of them—were from 'the youth orchestra,' in other words from El Sistema, and they tried to hide as best they could behind the bells of their instruments" (Padilla 2010b). Such musicians struggle to imagine that Abreu has changed his stripes in his seventies.

Abreu had been closely involved with a predecessor to Alma Llanera, the Orchestra of Latin American Instruments (ODILA), launched in 1982 for the bicentenary of Simón Bolívar's birth (Mendoza n.d.a). As soon as the bicentenary was over, however, the project was shelved, and nothing similar happened for the next twenty-five years. Why was a new flurry of popular music activity taking place after a quarter of a century of disinterest, people asked? Possible answers included FESNOJIV's transfer to the Office of the President—Chávez preferred traditional to classical music—and the looming of another important bicentenary in 2011, that of Venezuela's declaration of independence. Suspicions were voiced that Abreu was presenting a "popular" face to the president and the nation at a key historical juncture rather than undergoing a personal transformation.

David, a musician close to Alma Llanera, believed that the inherent contradictions of El Sistema—which represented the precise opposite of the Bolivarian government's declared focus on national, indigenous, and marginalized cultural forms—had come to Chávez's attention. He recounted: "Maestro Abreu started the Alma Llanera program to protect El Sistema. There have been many complaints from people close to the national government and to the cultural field, as well as from his usual critics, with regard to the scant attention paid by El Sistema to non-academic Venezuelan music. El Maestro knows that the current government has as one of its banners the promotion of Venezuelan cultural expressions, and that if he continues to ignore this he will lose cultural space and resources." David went on: "I see it as an obligatory antidote to the criticisms of those who have always been annoyed by El Sistema. I think that in its essence, it [El Sistema] will carry on the same, but with an extra layer of protection, one that Abreu has already broadcast in the media, saying: 'one should not talk about incorporation. Popular music has always been part of El Sistema,' something that is totally and demonstrably false." David mused: "I don't know whether in general terms traditional music, its institutions and musicians will benefit overall from Alma Llanera. What does seem clear to me is that El Sistema is going to achieve even greater hegemony, something which I'm not convinced is going to be the best thing for all these very different musicians in Venezuela." What made David's words particularly significant was not just that he was intimately acquainted with Alma Llanera, but that he was contemplating joining it: "I haven't been able to resist feeling attracted to it. The effectiveness of El Sistema appeals to me and makes me forget some of its monstrous aspects, such as its great inefficiency and its cruel exclusivity."

There had been a tide of criticism of El Sistema in 2010, but a number of critics fell silent the following year as well-paid jobs started to appear or to be promised in Alma Llanera. Others, however, continued to express strong reservations. There were fears that Alma Llanera would be a repeat of ODILA and that the flurry of visible activity would peter out once the bicentenary and 2012 elections were over. There were whispers of problems behind the façade. A well-known popular musician described Alma Llanera's showpiece ensemble,

Orquesta Cantaclaro, as a phantom project: launched with a great fanfare and then disbanded. A member of the ensemble confirmed that Abreu had personally torpedoed the orchestra the day after its inaugural concert: "the ensemble that was supposedly going to head the project is finished... you might say that we were used." The ensemble tried to start up again a year later, but Abreu intervened immediately to shut it down, leaving the players in little doubt that their Sistema careers were on the line. Two years later, I could find no references to the ensemble other than the rash of articles about its debut, quoting the enthusiastic speeches of the assembled dignitaries—Abreu included—who showered it with praise.

In 2012 there was another inaugural concert, this time of Alma Llanera itself, strategically timed for Independence Day (an echo of ODILA). Once again there were fine speeches, public commitments, and mutual congratulations. This time it seemed that something real was afoot: the National Assembly had granted 395 million bolívares specifically for the program, with the aim of creating 275 traditional music orchestras. Nevertheless, longtime Sistema watchers would need evidence of action before they were convinced. Some asked why this program had been entrusted to a classical musician famous for his dislike of popular music, rather than to the Ministry of Culture's National System of Popular Cultures or the existing network of traditional orchestras, the *orquestas típicas*.

An Alma Llanera press release ("Programa Alma Llanera" 2013) stated that El Sistema "is propelling the study of Venezuelan traditional instruments via its academic and philosophical model," meaning that "the teaching of these traditions will not be oral or empirical, but rather systematic." The form of musical transmission is thus being changed (or "systematized"), and much of the activity in early 2013 was taking place in a computer lab, where traditional music was being collected and transcribed. Borzacchini's account of Alma Llanera, too, details the transformation of an oral tradition as repertoire is "written down and adapted to the novel format of an orchestra"; local musical heritage is "rescued" through transcription and arrangement. Venezuelan music provides the "flavor," while academic training "imparts elegance and a high level of technique," she writes, articulating attitudes of an earlier era.[3] With traditional music as with children, then, El Sistema's "inclusion" is simultaneously a process of disciplining and normalization, and the underlying cultural hierarchy is abundantly evident in the belief that folkloric music is being improved in the process.

As Green (2003a, 269) warns: "It is one thing to bring a variety of musics into the classroom, but if the learning methods of the relevant musicians are ignored, a peculiar, classroom version of the music is likely to emerge, stripped of the very methods by which the music has always been created, and therefore bearing little resemblance to its existence in the world outside." Elsewhere, Green (2002; 2008) further critiques this tendency to accept popular music but sideline its learning practices, and argues that genuine engagement requires changes to pedagogy—a seemingly unlikely step if El Sistema is determined to impose its "academic and philosophical model." As noted in Chapter 5, a key benefit of a broad curriculum is the opportunity for students to experience different forms of sociomusical relations, something that is lost when "other" musics are "systematized." Diversifying the curriculum provides an opportunity to broaden minds and skills through exploring issues of transmission, formality/informality, and the priority granted to different musical activities, but if musical cultures are shoehorned into a single mold, that opportunity is likely to be missed.

In sum, there are signs of major changes afoot, and for all that Alma Llanera is a notably tardy response to progressive educational thinking—in the United States, cultural diversity in music education was heralded by the Tanglewood Symposium in 1967 and took off in the 1970s (Schippers and Campbell 2012)—it has tremendous potential. Nevertheless, changes have met with skepticism from long-term observers who see it as a classical musician's attempt to colonize the traditional musical sphere, and there are distinct signs of ideological continuity beneath the surface, which may lead diversification simply to reaffirm preexisting cultural hierarchies. It is also unclear at present whether changes are taking place at grassroots level across Venezuela or are concentrated on the creation of a few showcase ensembles to "demonstrate" diversity. The creation of Alma Llanera after decades of classical focus needs to be interrogated carefully in order to determine whether El Sistema is adapting to traditional music or vice versa.

COMPOSITION AND REPERTOIRE

As Cecilia Todd noted, it is not just Venezuelan popular and traditional music that has been marginalized by El Sistema; there is also minimal provision for new or recent repertoire by national art music composers—something that is almost a calling card of youth orchestras in other countries. The sidelining of contemporary music is matched by the neglect of older Venezuelan compositions, most of which languish unplayed in archives. Buenaventura (2010) asks why the program is not a showcase for Venezuelan composers: "does it not work as an excuse to tear off the colored jacket, in a 'fit of emotion,' and make the Europeans go crazy?"

The composer Emilio Mendoza titled an article "Composition in Venezuela: A Profession in Danger of Extinction?" (n.d.b). Venezuelan composers have been almost completely ignored by El Sistema, he argues. He sees the inclusion of the occasional Venezuelan warhorse among the canonical European repertoire as little more than a sop, and claims that cliché and self-exoticization have triumphed over more ambitious efforts to redefine musical expression.

El Sistema's reign has neither left a body of compositions nor fostered a generation of composers, and there are currently no composer-in-residence schemes in the program's hundreds of orchestras. Mendoza is astounded that a program of such resources could have completely omitted musical creation: "There are more orchestras than composers! No one criticizes, no one points out this terrible omission" (n.d.b., 15).

This situation is particularly ironic given that a major justification for launching El Sistema was to end the country's reliance on foreign orchestral musicians. Meléndez (2011) writes of the fecund school of nationalist composition from the time of Vicente Emilio Sojo, when orchestra members were mainly foreigners but there was national repertoire; now the problem has reversed. Musicians spoke of a huge catalogue of national compositions from the last three generations, most of which have never been performed twice and some of which have never even been premiered. Why was no Venezuelan composer commissioned to write music for the 2011 bicentenary celebrations, they asked? Where is the reflection of Venezuelan national particularities in the SBYO's showpieces like the Mexican "Danzón" and Bernstein's "Mambo"?

A new Sistema program, the National Composition Academy, was announced in 2009, but two years after its official launch, its purpose and activities remained a matter of conjecture. As with Alma Llanera, there was an information vacuum behind the headline. It was impossible to tell whether these initiatives would produce real change or echo the phantom cultural projects that were allegedly found under Abreu's stewardship of CONAC. Mendoza—a professor of composition at a leading university—claimed that his repeated inquiries had met with silence. He thus circulated publicly a list of basic questions about the program's budget, policy, commissioning, target audience, and so on. His frustration with El Sistema's silence is palpable: "is there a public call for proposals, or do we just wait to be called?...When is (or was) the announcement, and who decides the outcome, a committee or 'The Pope' [i.e., Abreu]?"

In 2012 a National Composition Competition was announced, with a sizeable prize. Víctor Rojas, a Sistema director, declared implausibly: "We are seeing the fruit of the education of composers that El Sistema has provided in recent decades." One composer responded privately: "Sounds great (all the lies), but a first prize of 80,000 BsF...it seems as though this huge amount could have the effect of wiping out all the years of inactivity towards creation...throw money at it! Very typical of Abreu and of Venezuela, with loads of money everything can be solved."

Close collaboration with composers has been a hallmark of youth orchestras in other countries such as Australia (Kartomi 2007b) and the United States (Bohlman and Bohlman 2007). Pear (2007, 88) notes that "an important element in the 'enculturation' of young musicians in a youth orchestra is the exposure to their own national music, and to music by living composers." He quotes a director who argued that contemporary music "provide[d] for them not merely new summits to climb, but more excitingly, new musical contradictions to resolve." Young Australian musicians were encouraged to question the music and even the composer when present; the focus was on adventure, play, and improvisation, with more responsibility landing on performers than in mainstream orchestral repertoire. Abreu claims to be fascinated by contemporary music and techniques (Borzacchini 2010, 64), yet he largely avoids them in his program.

Bergeron's (1992, 3) comments on the classical canon's close relationship to discipline (in the Foucauldian sense) illuminate El Sistema's conservative programming: the canon "implies a type of social control—a control that inevitably extends to larger social bodies as individual players learn not only to monitor themselves but to keep an eye (and an ear) on others. To play in tune, to uphold the canon, is ultimately to interiorize those values that would maintain, so to speak, social 'harmony.'" She goes on: "The canon, always in view, promotes decorum, ensures proper conduct. The individual within a field learns, by internalizing such standards, how not to transgress" (1992, 5). Conservatism of repertoire thus forms part of El Sistema's larger disciplinary project. It is no accident that the program has shunned the opportunity to train up a new generation of adventurous composers and performers. The WEDO displays the same trait, preferring "music designed to elicit tears of catharsis and get an audience to its feet" (Etherington 2007, 127) over musical forms that hold particular ideological force. In both cases, radical potential is blunted by artistic choices made more to please foreign audiences and record companies than to challenge and transform musicians.

A certain alienation from national and regional musical traditions was evident in mid-2011. In May I attended an event at the CASM billed as a "multicultural concert." The program was Mozart, Weber, Piazzolla, and Aldemaro Romero (a Venezuelan composer). Since Beethoven concerts at the same venue had not been given any special label, "multicultural" signaled the inclusion of music by Latin American composers—in a concert in Latin America. The SBYO then went off on a high-profile tour of the continent's leading concert halls to celebrate the bicentenary of Venezuela's declaration of independence. The cornerstone of its program to mark the throwing-off of European shackles? Mahler 7. The Afro-Venezuelan Orchestra and the Venezuelan Music Youth Orchestra stayed at home, performing in a Caracas school.

It is illuminating to compare the two major waves of recording activity by the SBYO. The first, between 1991 and 1997, produced nine CDs of Latin American and Spanish music for Dorian Recordings; the second, from 2005, has seen a series of CDs for Deutsche Grammophon focusing on Beethoven, Mahler, Tchaikovsky, and Stravinsky, plus one of Latin American compositions. Far from using its burgeoning fame as a springboard for New World composers, the SBYO has retrenched into the core repertoire, and the Latin CD's title—*Fiesta*—illustrates the trivialization of this repertoire. Venezuelan and Latin American pieces now tend to be slipped in as a final party-piece or encore, a kind of exotic icing on a European cake; thus the hierarchy of European and Latin, serious and light, is maintained. The second period coincides precisely with Dudamel's emergence as a darling of the international music industry. A diet of Beethoven and Bernstein has been invaluable to imprinting Dudamel's image on the consciousness of CD and ticket buyers around the world, but it has arguably blunted the critical and ethical force of the orchestra, which could have done much more to challenge its own players and boost Venezuelan creativity.

In ordinary Sistema núcleos, Venezuelan music is unquestionably in a subsidiary position, but it is not excluded altogether. "Popular" orchestral concerts are a regular occurrence, and they tend to focus on three kinds of repertoire: early to mid-twentieth-century nationalist music based on folk rhythms; arrangements of international popular music (The Beatles, Pink Floyd); and arrangements of film music. However, there is little room for the distinctive instruments, timbres, and techniques of national popular and traditional music. Núcleos embrace orchestrations of popular tunes more readily than popular music and musicians. Indeed, suspicion of actual popular music shines through in claims that it "is being enriched by the possibility of being orchestrated" (quoted in Aharonián 2004, 10) or, in Borzacchini's words, granted "elegance and a high level of technique." This paternalistic vision recalls Latin American nationalist art music of the early to mid-twentieth century (e.g., Moore 1997), and there are clear parallels with the scenario that Green (2003a) describes in European schools until the 1970s.

The conservatism in the field of repertoire and programming is also evident in the constitution of ensembles. Once again, it is instructive to compare El Sistema with progressive European developments in the 1970s. Holland "saw the flourishing of numerous small groups in the fields of contemporary music, early music, jazz, and improvisation. In conscious opposition to the perceived authoritarianism of the symphony orchestra, new ensembles...aspired to a more democratic model of musical practice" (Adlington 2007, 540). Small ensembles were viewed as offering more artistic and personal fulfillment to musicians than orchestras. Musicians attempted to provide more space for new initiatives, diverse programming, and cross-genre collaboration. El Sistema could have fostered similar kinds of artistic experimentation; yet ODILA, one of its few innovations, died on the vine, and there have been no subsequent attempts to reshape the orchestra for a contemporary Latin American context. Many have argued for the necessity of transforming orchestras to fit the twenty-first century, and as a heavily subsidized program focused on the young, El Sistema has had an unparalleled opportunity to revolutionize structures and repertoire. So far, it has passed up this opportunity, transforming the discourse about orchestras while keeping the ensemble and its music the same.

EUROCENTRISM AND CULTURAL SELF-COLONIZATION

Complaints from traditional musicians are commonplace, but I was struck when a prominent Sistema musician claimed that the program had had a negative effect on Venezuelan music. He described a recent visit to a rural area where there were no Sistema núcleos nearby. Wearing his Sistema hat, his first reaction had been that it would be very interesting to create a núcleo there; but he soon came to feel the opposite—that, unlike his home state, this was a zone where local traditions and cultural understandings were still strong, and the intrusion of El Sistema would be a disaster. This view of the program as a colonizing institution that was displacing Venezuelan culture came from one of El Sistema's best-known teachers in Veracruz.

El Sistema's growth has entailed large-scale, long-term investment in "universal" culture (i.e., European culture of the long nineteenth century). Embracing the universalizing discourse of the European Enlightenment aids the accumulation of economic and cultural capital (Martin 1995, 181), but it may also ring alarm bells in a postcolonial context, since it risks reproducing colonialist ideologies of the period, which privileged and normalized the experiences of Western masculine elites, downgraded indigenous and popular alternatives, and legitimated cultural imperialism. As Miller and Yúdice (2002, 118) note, "cultural policy in Spanish America and Brazil has been marked by conquest and colonization.... Some would argue that the colonialist legacy—especially the subordination of indigenous, African, and mixed-race peoples' popular culture, and non-European religious forms—has endured to this day." Cultural imperialism is thus still a live issue two centuries after independence, and one that is particularly pertinent to El Sistema, given the links frequently made between the orchestra's global expansion and colonialism or imperialism (e.g., Spich and Sylvester 1998, 23; Cottrell 2003, 251). However, this topic is ignored in the program's public discourse.

Venezuela is one of the South American countries with the least coherent sense of national identity, thanks to the large-scale influx of foreign culture that has been one of the consequences of its oil wealth. In the mid-twentieth century, "Venezuela was literally bulldozing its past and replacing it with North American mass culture—baseball, pizza, hamburger, commercials, skyscrapers, movies, and their cultural imports," while "advertising saturated the media with North American cultural norms" (Hellinger 1991, 79, 77). The IDB's 2007 proposal to expand El Sistema lacks any consideration of the possible *cultural* effects of such a move in a country that has already been heavily "de-nationalized." Its section on "risks" makes no mention of the potential hazard to Venezuelan musical culture from the displacement of traditional forms, skills, and creativity.

In his TED prize speech, Abreu argues that "the child becomes a role model for both his parents." He imagines a boy playing the violin at home while his father works on his carpentry, and a girl playing the clarinet while her mother does the housework. "The idea is that the families join with pride and joy in the activities of the orchestras and the choirs their children belong to." There is a curious reversal of the traditional form of transmission; now culture starts with children—the new role models—and makes its way up to their parents. There is no mention of children whose parents or relatives teach them to sing or play the cuatro at home; there are no musical adults in this picture. It is a vision of a Year Zero in which children lead their parents and traditional forms of musical transmission are erased.

The composer Diego Silva talked of a trinity of beauty queens, baseball, and orchestras—the three things for which Venezuela is most famous and of which it is most proud. Yet all are backed by foreign capital and shaped by foreign aesthetic codes. Alluding to Dudamel as well as baseball players, he claimed that Venezuelans idolize stars who leave for the United States and come back to Venezuela only for the occasional VIP visit. He contrasted Venezuela with Cuba, an island with a strong cultural identity and pride. No one in the outside world knows about Venezuelan culture, he argued, just about Venezuelans playing other people's games.

To describe El Sistema as Eurocentric is in some ways a truism, given its focus on the symphony orchestra and the European canon, but its Eurocentrism is more than just a question of paying homage to the European past: Europe is still seen as the center of the classical music universe today. El Sistema's aesthetic and professional norms are determined by Europe, with the Berlin Philharmonic the ultimate benchmark. Workshops and masterclasses with members of the Berlin Phil are considered the pinnacle of instruction. Two of the most-quoted highlights of El Sistema's history are Simon Rattle's visits to Caracas, and bass-player Edicson Ruiz's move to the Berlin Phil; the latter is the program's ultimate symbol of success as an orchestral player. Booth (2010, 2) writes of El Sistema as a direct challenge to Western musical traditions, yet few in Venezuela see it that way: the gold standard for performance and teaching is still European.

There are again parallels with the WEDO. Riiser (2010) entitles a section of her study "Becoming German," and notes that the WEDO's "shared human values" are really German values. The project speaks of strengthening music in the Middle East and yet actually serves to strengthen Europe as the center, offering a "highway to German national culture and identity mimesis" (2010, 35). There are echoes in Rattle's invitation to the Venezuelan National Children's Orchestra to move to Berlin and play with him every week (Aloy 2013). He may not have been completely serious, but many young

Venezuelan musicians dream of doing precisely that, and an increasing number are attempting to study in Europe.

The colonialist aspects of European(-style) music education have received recent critical attention from scholars. Bradley (2012) highlights the "epistemological colonialism" prevalent in conventional music education, which is shaped by the philosophies that underpinned European expansion, and identifies the continued valorization of the European over the indigenous as "colonial residue." Rosabal-Coto (2014) draws on seminal work by postcolonial theorists like Aníbal Quijano and Walter Mignolo, who explore the continued hold of the logic of domination termed "coloniality" in Latin America. Despite the achievement of formal independence two centuries ago, hierarchical Eurocentric systems have been perpetuated in many social and cultural domains, notes Rosabal-Coto, among them music education. Bates (2014, 313) critiques classical music programs—including El Sistema—in similar terms: "Modern music education in many places throughout the world remains predominantly an extension of Immanuel Kant's imperialist, Euro-centric cosmopolitanism, described by Eduardo Mendieta…as *arrogant* (it is the sole measure of universal morality), *insouciant* (it ignores its own negative effects on the world), *autarchic* (it fails to acknowledge excellence in *all* places and among *all* people), and *impatient* (it 'has established the goal, the means, and the time line'). The world, in other words, is progressing towards a glorious cosmopolitan future patterned after North American and European middle and upper-class, urbane cultural norms." Since such scholars locate colonialism *within* music education programs, self-colonization becomes possible; a foreign imposer is not required.

As discussed further in the final chapter, not just scholars but also musical and broader cultural programs in Latin America are increasingly grappling with such issues. They are seeking to go beyond the simple reproduction of European cultural norms and expectations of difference. This does not mean abandoning classical music, but rather thinking about what Latin American classical music might consist of beyond Bernstein and orchestrated folk tunes— an important conversation in which El Sistema barely participates.

Clearly, the propagation of classical music does not automatically equate to cultural colonialism. Nevertheless, there are numerous features of El Sistema that show close parallels with the "musical conquest" of Latin America in the colonial period. Whatever benefits it may produce, a program that places European classical music on the highest pedestal and relegates the indigenous and African to distant margins has obvious colonial precedents—particularly when it promotes such music as cultural salvation for the Other, whose life is otherwise "empty, disorientated, and deviant"—and it reproduces colonialist dynamics. The program's foundational premises demand greater interrogation than has currently taken place, since they are underpinned by and reaffirm unspoken and often unexamined assumptions and hierarchies of cultural value that hark back to earlier historical periods and relations of dependence.

One of the paradoxes of El Sistema is that it has stimulated a lot of musical activity and put Venezuela firmly on the global cultural map, and yet some experienced observers qualify its local impact in equivocal or negative terms. The explanation lies in their perception that exponential growth has led to a progressive unbalancing of Venezuelan cultural life, as the program has come to absorb a disproportionate amount of state funding and attention. Cultural life might be considered as an ecological system—one in which drastic changes in one area lead to knock-on effects in others, and effective management requires a balanced, holistic view.

Traditional musicians are prominent among those who feel marginalized, but there are classical musicians who make the same complaint: chamber music, early music, or new music projects, or indeed any project not patronized by Abreu, can struggle to get off the ground. A leading musician announced he was ready to leave Venezuela because he was so fed up with seeing his independent projects stalling. Composers often have to settle for not having their music performed, or for paying for the performance themselves. The point that non-Sistema musicians make is not simply that they are excluded: it is that there is hardly any money or institutional interest left over once El Sistema has taken its huge share of the pie.

One of the most dramatic examples of the negative impact of unbalanced cultural policy on Venezuelan classical music concerns Venezuela's conservatoires, above all the José Ángel Lamas (JAL) Conservatoire in Caracas. When I visited the JAL in 2011 I found a building filled with musical activity but clearly unfit for human habitation—indeed, it had been declared unsafe by the fire authorities. The roof was made of sheets of corrugated iron; walls and ceilings were propped up with internal scaffolding; the corridors filled with water when it rained. Simply walking through the building was a shocking experience, particularly when the rain hammered on the tin roof so hard that conversation and practice were almost impossible; it seemed that the building could collapse at any moment.

Even more shockingly, it had been in this state for nearly twenty years. An article appeared in the national press in 2010 about the deplorable conditions at the JAL (Hernández 2010), yet such articles had been appearing for two decades. Newspaper clippings from *El Nacional* and *El Mundo* dating from between 1994 and 1997 described the paralysis of restoration work for years at a time, the closure of the school for a year, student and staff protests (including a hunger strike), and endless appeals, debates, and letters to officials—all to no effect. In 1997 *El Mundo* described the school as "in a state of miserable abandonment," and little had changed since.

Most strikingly of all, the JAL is not only one of Venezuela's legendary musical institutions but also Abreu's alma mater. In 1991, when at the height of

The José Ángel Lamas Conservatoire. Photo by Geoffrey Baker.

his political power, Abreu visited the conservatoire and publicly took on responsibility for its restoration, promising that CONAC would pay (Corona 1991;
Arenas 1991). He did not go through with his promise, but he did find funds to
construct the state-of-the-art CASM less than two miles away.

I spoke to a number of former and current teachers and students at the
JAL, and they believed that the school's plight was no accident. Many of the
structural problems date from the early 1990s when María Guinand was director; a close ally of Abreu, she went on to become El Sistema's head of choirs.
Musicians believed Abreu had a vendetta against his alma mater; speculation
centered on an alleged argument with its director, Vicente Emilio Sojo, which
resulted in Abreu's expulsion from the conservatoire. These tales of decades-old

Music lesson at the José Ángel Lamas Conservatoire. Photo by Geoffrey Baker.

events are hard to confirm, but stories of a dispute between Sojo and Abreu circulate widely, and interviewees attached to the JAL viewed Abreu as having responded by taking revenge on the institution, in the process neutralizing competition to El Sistema.

Does the CASM deserve its privilege and the JAL its ruin? It is hard to see why, given that both institutions uphold traditionalist (if different) views of classical music education while opening their doors to students from a wide range of socioeconomic backgrounds. Rather, for many Venezuelan musicians the condition of the JAL symbolizes one of the hallmarks of El Sistema: success at the expense of other institutions and projects.

In promoting his own project, Abreu has suggested that other forms of classical music education are elitist and El Sistema is popularizing this sphere. One of his signature aphorisms appears on the FESNOJIV website: "In the past, the artistic mission was a matter by a minority for a minority; then it was by a minority for the majority; now, it is by the majority and for the majority." In his TED prize speech, he claimed: "Our ideal is of a country in which art is within the reach of every citizen so that we can no longer talk about art being the property of the elite, but the heritage of the people." Yet this is a rewriting of history. The JAL provides a free music education to children of all social classes; it has a number of children on free school meals.

Casanova (2009) took Abreu to task over such claims, referring to the latter's appearance on Chávez's television show *Aló Presidente* on September 2, 2007. "Abreu lied when he said to Chávez that 'until a few years ago artistic culture was the monopoly of the elite,' since our great plastic artists... were not people from rich or millionaire families, and they studied art in public, free art schools. Abreu lies when he says that 'music education has been restricted to a minority,' since our great composers and performers... were not from wealthy families, they were all individuals from modest families. Abreu lies when he says that music education was 'restricted to a minority' until Chávez and he arrived. That is false, because for more than 70 years before Chávez, all Venezuelans could study FREE in the various STATE CONSERVATOIRES like the Juan Manuel Olivares, Vicente Emilio Sojo, Juan José Landaeta, etc." Casanova goes on: "Now, those conservatoires that educated the great Venezuelan musicians are dying because Abreu got the governments of the Fourth Republic to give him a music institute... and the government gives him all the money he asks for while the state conservatoires are in a coma because of a lack of resources."

Even more striking is Pérez Rescaniere's (1998) argument about the neoliberalization of Venezuelan culture in the 1990s. The author describes the rise of a "neoliberal cultural elite" under the second government of CAP, in which Abreu, as minister and president of CONAC, was the leading cultural authority. Public subsidies for culture grew dramatically, yet the public saw diminishing returns in terms of access, with concert prices (for example) rising alarmingly. Pérez Rescaniere argues that since CONAC's budget rose while its offerings to the Venezuelan public declined, "during the ministry of J. A. Abreu there was an effective, concrete, and secret privatization of culture." During earlier periods, "the majority of those admitted to the music schools maintained by CONAC were people from modest circumstances; today it is perhaps only in that at the corner of Santa Capilla [i.e., the JAL] that one might find such people." This depiction of Abreu in his neoliberal pomp provides a stark contrast with his public persona today, at the elbow of Venezuela's socialist presidents, but the most crucial point is the suggestion that elitism in conservatoire music education was a *consequence* of Abreu's neoliberal cultural politics, rather than a preexisting condition that he set out to resolve. In the previous chapter it was suggested that El Sistema defines Venezuela's social problems in such a way that the orchestra looks like the perfect solution; Pérez Rescaniere goes further, accusing Abreu of actually creating the problem.

There is no shortage of praise for Abreu's single-minded advancement of El Sistema, but his monopolization of resources and apparent suspicion of pluralism have had a profound effect on other music institutions. A musician in a small town near Veracruz related how he had learnt to play in the 1950s in a music school linked to the municipal band. The ensemble had later disappeared through a lack of funding. Municipal bands used to be found in many towns across Venezuela, though the number is greatly reduced today. CONAC's budget in 1991, under Abreu, provided 130 *million* bolívares to youth orchestras and 300 *thousand* to provincial concert bands (López Mujica 1991). Venezuela was no land without music before El Sistema, but preexisting institutions have been starved of funds and in some cases taken over or put out of business as Abreu's project has gathered pace.

The praise for Abreu is thus balanced by criticism. Álvarez Pifano (2014) characterizes El Sistema as a "funnel" that channeled resources into orchestral performance, leaving other musical activities to struggle alone: "everything for Abreu, nothing for the rest." Countering the revisionist history of El Sistema, he claims: "Venezuelan children learnt to play and sing in the thousands of music schools and academies and the few conservatoires that we have always had, until El Sistema took over all the economic resources for its own ends (in particular, expensive foreign trips, luxury hotels and the maintenance of a parasitic and sycophantic bureaucracy, as well as an army of journalists willing to write eulogies, and big-money contracts for famous musicians who sing the System's praises), which has left Venezuela's schools virtually destitute and musicians who do not form part of it in poverty."

Founder members of El Sistema described how the program's growing economic muscle had converted it into a colonizing institution. One recounted his experience teaching at a non-Sistema music school in a cultural center on the outskirts of Caracas. When a Sistema núcleo was created in the community, it was housed in the same building. At first, there was a whole range of arts on offer, but now the núcleo and music school were the only ones left. He believed it was only a matter of time before the núcleo had the whole center to itself. The municipal music school was being edged out partly because of its financial disadvantage (it could not offer free instruments or pay students) and partly because El Sistema's public profile was so much higher. Despite being a Sistema founder, my informant was distinctly uneasy about the program's takeover of Venezuelan music education. A year later, another teacher at the same municipal school wrote to me that "this place originally made for diverse cultural activities has been taken over completely" by El Sistema and the school was closing down after thirty years. The conversion of this cultural center from a place where people of all ages could go to learn arts of all kinds, into one where only children went to learn symphonic music, seemed like a microcosm of the impact of El Sistema on Venezuelan cultural life.

SUPPLY AND DEMAND

Another example of a failure to take an ecological approach can be seen in El Sistema's overexpansion, leading it to produce an oversupply of musicians. El Sistema is a preprofessional orchestral training program, and given its size, even if only a tiny percentage of students come out wanting to be a professional orchestral musician, the number of aspirants will be impressive; and yet, demand for orchestral musicians and for classical music in general is relatively low. There simply are not enough good or decently paid adult orchestras in Venezuela to provide for all the young talents that El Sistema produces. While El Sistema's numbers climb sharply, the economic foundations of the provincial symphony orchestras have become increasingly shaky: many are already suffering from lack of investment and some are in a precarious position, so most are unable to provide a decent living for the new generation of aspirants. Thinking in ecological terms, massive investment in training makes little sense without serious consideration of subsequent employment.

Similar problems are evident in the sphere of audiences. With its multiple subsidies, El Sistema has not been obliged to think about audience development. The result, in provincial cities at least, is that audiences at symphony concerts are often smaller than the orchestra itself, and consist primarily of the musicians' friends and relatives.

There is, then, a growing imbalance between El Sistema's funding and the place of classical music in Venezuela. The program's apparent successes may therefore be hiding structural problems. For example, El Sistema is creating a large body of adolescents who are devoting all their energies to orchestral music in return for a scholarship, a quasi-professional arrangement that is unsustainable for both individuals and the collective. At some point, the state either has to take that salary away, leaving the individual without a job or broad skill set, or provide long-term employment, at considerable cost and with dubious justification given the low demand.

The gulf between supply and demand worried a number of prominent musicians. A leading flautist reported that there were literally hundreds of decent players recently emerged from El Sistema or in the latter stages of their training: what were all these players going to do? El Sistema had not been an *organic* musical development, he said: it had produced an oversupply of unrealistically ambitious young musicians, distorting the country's musical life.

A leading Sistema teacher in Veracruz contrasted the public optimism around the project with what he described as its hidden tragedy: children are led to believe that they will be able to join the SBYO, travel the world, and become a star, but for most this will not be the case, yet no one tells them they do not have the talent. Children grow up in El Sistema dreaming of greatness, but the vast majority will end up as low-paid musicians in struggling provincial orchestras and/or teachers of elementary students, or simply give up music altogether. If El Sistema imparted a rounded education, there would be less of an issue, but training children primarily to be orchestral musicians is setting up thousands for disappointment. One founder gave up teaching altogether because he became so dispirited at receiving a stream of young musicians who had been filled with false hopes of greatness. Another founder expressed his sadness at seeing former SBYO colleagues; some were working as mariachi musicians (a low-status occupation), while one was running an accessory stand in a shopping mall. A few are chosen to be the face of the circus, he said, and the rest are left to struggle on in obscurity or leave and do something else.

MORE ORCHESTRAS THAN GERMANY AND AUSTRIA COMBINED

A number of Venezuelan musicians saw El Sistema as bloated, unbalanced, and overly dependent on the charismatic Abreu and unconditional government support. Consequently, they believed that sooner or later an implosion was coming. Such an argument finds support in Spich and Sylvester's study of "The Jurassic Symphony" (1998), which could be taken to question El Sistema's policy of limitless expansion. They adopt an ecology model of arts organizations, arguing that "saving actions" by symphony organizations have led to an "unnaturally" large number of orchestras, "more than the 'carrying capacity' that a 'natural' market environment could bear." They predict a "natural adjustment process" to "bring back a more 'natural balance' with the conditions of the environment."

Does Venezuela, too, have an "unnaturally" large number of orchestras? Can its orchestral scene continue expanding, or will it eventually face a "natural adjustment process"? A publicity campaign in 2011 with Coca-Cola proclaimed that Venezuela had more orchestras than Germany and Austria combined (and thus three times as many orchestras per head of population).

Do Venezuelans really love classical music three times as much as the Germans and Austrians, or is this figure actually a warning signal of ecological imbalance? Caracas, a city with a small classical music audience, has half a dozen professional orchestras without even counting El Sistema's ensembles. Most of the provincial symphony orchestras were created to provide work for ex–youth orchestra musicians—to solve a problem of supply rather than demand. Has El Sistema really faced up to the broader cultural forces that are threatening orchestras around the world, or is it simply using its economic muscle to inflate the orchestral scene beyond sustainable limits?

Herndon's (1988) study of the Oakland Symphony unearthed a "cognitive disjuncture" between how city residents talked about the orchestra and what they actually did. Residents had fine words to say about the orchestra's importance to the city, but when it collapsed, their half-hearted efforts to salvage it revealed a poor fit with the cultural context and a low degree of concrete engagement and support. "The symphony orchestra was viewed as good and necessary, but this sentiment was unsupported and iconic," Herndon concludes; "community response has been much more symbolic than real" (1998, 144). Once again, a gulf appears between rhetoric and realities in the orchestral world.

Audience demand and the movement of money may be more revealing than rhetoric, as Herndon suggests. Behind the impressive surface, provincial Venezuelan symphony orchestras have struggled in recent years; uplifting speeches at national level are not always matched by the disbursement of funds by local politicians or significant audience support. When one orchestra was suspended due to lack of funds, the musicians themselves—not the community—stepped in to save it, by carrying on playing for free. The lack of a firm cultural foundation means that adult orchestras, in particular, may be susceptible to a "natural adjustment process," with obvious consequences for El Sistema's production line of aspiring orchestral musicians.

VALORIZING YOUTH AND PROFESSIONALISM

Other ecological imbalances can be found within El Sistema itself. One is generational: the creation of a musical system which overvalorizes youth. Trainee musicians often have more opportunities than the trained. In Veracruz, there were teenagers in the regional youth orchestra who were earning more than adults in the symphony orchestra. Members of the SBYO were often paid several times more than their teachers. Classical music career paths in Venezuela often resemble those of professional sportspeople, with a sharp rise in the teens and a slow decline from the late twenties. The difference is that musicians' skills and knowledge continue to improve after thirty, yet, except for an elite few, their status and even pay often decline. Musicians in their thirties may feel that their best days (in career terms) are already behind them. I met a lot of grumbling middle-aged musicians, who asked: How can a teenaged youth-orchestra member earn more than the concertmaster of a professional orchestra? How can a conservatoire student—a mid-desk orchestral violinist—earn more than its director?

Cara, a member of the SBYO, agreed that El Sistema's dependence on the image of youth was hard on older musicians. She described resentment among the "A" section of the SBYO that the "B" section—less experienced, and in some cases the pupils of the "A" players—received most of the tours, fame, and perks. But she noted that the "B" section looked at the "A" and saw their possible future. Would they find themselves washed up in an orchestra no one was interested in anymore? Would they have a short top-level career followed by a long decline? Shortly afterward the SBYO became the SBSO, pointing to plans for the "B" orchestra to keep its place on the world's concert stages rather than follow the "A" into obscurity.

A particularly interesting area to observe the impact of El Sistema on Venezuela's musical ecology is that of amateur adult music-making. Green (2003a, 263) notes the paradox that the expansion of formal music education in the West has gone in tandem with the decline of everyday music-making among adults. Though much more research is required, it seemed that El Sistema was having a similar impact in Venezuela, and for similar reasons—namely that classical music skills have limited use outside the institutional sphere. The young adult Sistema graduates whom I met fell neatly into two categories: those who played in a paid orchestra, and those who had given up playing altogether. A Sistema musician agreed that there was almost no middle ground: the program provides preprofessional training, and at the end most students either become a professional orchestral musician or give up. "Are you a musician?" I asked one young man I met. "An ex-musician," he replied. He had studied in El Sistema for some years, but he left when he began university, as the time commitment was too great to combine with his studies. "The orchestra is everything, you know, and once you leave, you've got nothing."

Being an orchestral musician involves a major time commitment in Venezuela, with rehearsals taking place almost daily; one cannot play in an orchestra once a week for fun. By resolutely professionalizing and monopolizing musical practice, El Sistema leaves virtually no amateur classical scene to speak of. Booth's (1999) elegy to amateuring in the United States serves only to highlight its absence in Venezuelan classical music.

CONCLUSION

Even El Sistema's critics like Cecilia Todd would not argue with the project's starting point—creating youth orchestras and supplying adult orchestras with local musicians. But its uncontrolled growth, disproportionate funding, and narrow focus are a different matter. Mendoza (n.d.b) provides a rare public critique of "orchestral practice amplified to a degree unprecedented in the history of music," as El Sistema "overflowed its initial borders as a personal project and took on the role, because of its size, resources, and longevity, of a national music plan." However, his criticisms were echoed in private by senior figures in the music world. One described Abreu's monopolization of funds as potentially jeopardizing all other musical institutions and projects in Venezuela. Another asked whether it was healthy for one man's personal interests and idiosyncrasies to have such a profound sway over a nation's cultural policy. A third lamented the loss of diversity in the Venezuelan musical scene: imagine, he said, if the minister of agriculture announced that subsidies were only going to be made available to farmers who sowed potatoes, since that was what the minister liked to eat for his dinner.

Returning to Scott's *Seeing Like a State* provides a useful frame for considering the ecology of Venezuelan cultural life. Scott addresses the long-term ecological damage caused by scientific forestry and monocropping. Boosting production in the short term often brings unexpected and unwelcome side effects in other areas. If many monocropping schemes eventually miscarry, polycropping—even though it may *look* more disordered—brings many benefits: it is more stable, sustainable, adaptable, and resilient. Scott draws on Jane Jacobs's work to make the link between the natural and social worlds: "The case of polyculture also raises an issue relevant to both agricultural practice and social structure . . . *the resilience and durability of diversity*" (1998, 281). Jacobs saw complex neighborhoods and mixed-use spaces as fostering a positive human ecology, and Scott makes an overarching argument for cross-use and diversity as promoting resilience and sustainability.

I would argue that we can read across from the natural and social spheres to the cultural, and that the advantages of polyculture over monoculture may be just as applicable to the musical realm as to the agricultural. For most of its history, El Sistema has been engaged in the cultural equivalent of monocropping, with impressive results in one area but problematic side effects on the broader cultural ecology. Alma Llanera may constitute an opportunity to reverse the damage and promote polyculture, though the devil is in the details; but until this project develops and is rigorously evaluated, there are reasons to be concerned about the long-term impact of El Sistema on the diversity and resilience of Venezuelan music.

CHAPTER 13

Advances, Alternatives, and the Future

If they want to copy El Sistema in Scotland, they need to shout at the kids and tell them they're useless.

—Sistema musician

In March 2013 there were three stories on display on the Facebook page "Yo soy 100% FESNOJIV." Abreu had just won yet another international prize; a group of provincial teachers had posted several petitions complaining about their low pay and demanding a raise; and a press release described how Alma Llanera was imposing El Sistema's "academic and philosophical model" on traditional music. The three stories exemplified El Sistema's strengths, weaknesses, and ambiguities, and raised the question of what El Sistema would be without its founder.

What does the future hold for El Sistema and classical music in Venezuela? This question was on many musicians' lips in 2011. El Sistema was expanding nationally and internationally, Abreu and Dudamel's fame continued to grow, yet concerns were voiced in private. One took me back to my earlier research in Cuba, where the recurring question was "what happens when Fidel dies?" El Sistema is another system presided over by a charismatic and autocratic but aging figure whose reluctance to plan for succession has created uncertainty over its future. Indeed, the same question arose when Chávez, another caudillo, was diagnosed with cancer in 2011. Abreu is a great leader, I was told repeatedly, but no one else in the project could step into his shoes. The fact that El Sistema was created in his image makes the issue of succession complicated: Gustavo Medina suggested in 1999 that the project might be storing up a problem, and he was ousted for his pains. The directors below Abreu are regarded as executors of his orders, lacking his charisma, political connections, and economic skills. Promoting unconditional supporters has simplified the exercise of power, but critics (and even some supporters) regard the program's dependence on Abreu as a ticking time bomb.

Spich and Sylvester (1998, 25) note that the survival of symphony orchestra organizations "has always depended on how well they represented the ethos of their times, how legitimate their claims to being a valued tradition stayed, how well they kept their eye on the fickleness and 'nowness' of audience taste, and their ability to make constant and effective claims to a flow of resources." While El Sistema shifted its discourse in the 1990s to boost its legitimacy and match the prevailing ethos, and has astutely judged audience taste overseas, it has relied on Abreu's personal capacities to make constant claims to resources at national and international levels. Should Abreu die or fall out of favor, the sustainability of El Sistema might be in doubt.

Two founders and two current SBYO members believed that El Sistema would eventually come tumbling down. One of the former described the program as a house of cards that could collapse at any moment. If there were something of substance within it, he said, the musicians would still be able to go out and conquer the world, but he feared the worst. Mendoza (n.d.b, 16–17), too, argued that despite all the investment and publicity, El Sistema could end up being ephemeral, having sacrificed a long-term legacy for short-term impact. The founder added that Abreu had steamrollered too many people during his thirty-six years in charge, and his enemies would not stay quiet forever. Similarly, a prominent figure in the Caracas musical world claimed that numerous skeletons in El Sistema's closet would eventually come to light, and the program would collapse under the weight of its own scandals.

Equally, El Sistema could become a victim of its own success. The period since 2008 has been marked by massive expansion, and there is a risk is that it may be growing beyond its capacity to deliver. Will it be able to provide a high-quality music education to a million children? Is this a sustainable picture, particularly once Abreu is gone? The combination of ambitious expansion and dependence on an aging leader is a potentially unstable one.

In *The Breakdown of Nations*, Kohr (1986, xxiii) argued that "wherever something is wrong, something is too big." He was concerned by whether systems functioned at "the human scale." Large systems of any kind tended toward oppression, in his eyes; "the problem is not the thing that is big, but bigness itself" (1986, 79). Bigness easily becomes the focus of attention and the justification for accumulating more power, giving growth a cancerous quality that converts it into a prelude to collapse. Kohr argued that the only way to limit the abuse of power was to limit the amount of power that any organization had, which meant dividing up rather than expanding.

Turino (2008) has made similar points with regard to music, drawing on comparisons with local food and environmental movements to argue for the virtues of a diversity of small-scale cultural activities. He critiques massive size as "part of the problem, not part of the solution" (2008, 228), since it is often accompanied by competition, hierarchy, and specialization, and tends to strengthen capitalist values. If greater evolutionary potential may be identified with a diversified gene pool, cultural potential lies in a diverse culture pool; hence, "an expansion of the number of smaller cultural formations is a more practical and positive goal" (228).

There is also the issue of overproduction of musicians, a significant problem in the Global North as well. What is Venezuela going to do with twice or four times the current number of aspiring professional classical musicians? Manuel Hernández Silva's bitter attack on Abreu focuses mainly on the uncertain future for the thousands of students whom El Sistema is inspiring with dreams of becoming top professional musicians, while failing to provide the majority of them with the tools or opportunities to do so.[1] A founder argued that Abreu was creating a personal musical army, and he predicted the decimation of Venezuela's classical music profession when the general was gone. Another senior musician, too, believed the edifice would collapse upon Abreu's death, but she saw this more serenely as "things returning to their rightful place"— an echo of Spich and Sylvester's "natural adjustment process." Even today, while the great benefactor is still in power, the situation of Venezuelan orchestras is not entirely rosy. The current struggles of the professional orchestral scene may suggest that it is already starting to shrink because neither politicians nor the public are willing to pay for it.

The year 2011 saw El Sistema change its official name to Fundación Musical Simón Bolívar and move to the Office of the President. There was much private speculation about the meaning of these transformations: Was Chávez bringing Abreu to heel? Was he preparing wholesale changes for El Sistema, though obliged to keep the "sacred cow" in place? Or was Abreu moving closer to the political summit? Another 2011 development, Alma Llanera, was interpreted both as the beginning of the end of Abreu's conception of El Sistema and as his attempt to colonize new areas of Venezuela's musical life. Was it a tactic, a smokescreen, a response to pressure, or the start of a revolution in Venezuelan popular music? Answers are still scarce at the time of writing, but the questions and debate within Venezuelan musical circles were themselves highly revealing.

EL SISTEMA OVERSEAS

Given El Sistema's size and ambitions, a detailed analysis of the program is a vital project in itself. Yet the fact that by late 2012 the Venezuelan program was being held up as a model in some fifty countries in six continents, with more than seventy projects inspired by El Sistema in North America alone, makes this analysis more urgent still.[2] Signs of interest and enthusiasm abounded—umbrella organizations like El Sistema USA and Sistema Europe had sprung up, and symposia were being organized with increasing regularity in North America—yet knowledge of the Venezuelan program was often rather patchy. Opinions were overly dependent on foreign newspaper articles and websites, and even those who traveled to Venezuela were often hampered by time limitations, a lack of fluent Spanish, or the choreographing of their visit. Sistema spokespeople and foreign observers engaged in a circular process of mutual reinforcement of beliefs; the result was that, with few exceptions, foreign visions of El Sistema that were expressed publicly simply mirrored the official narrative. The Sistema sphere became an international echo chamber in which myths, beliefs, propaganda, and unsubstantiated assertions came to be seen as facts.

There were a few dissenting voices: both those that saw the hyping of all things Venezuelan as disrespectful or prejudicial to existing local initiatives, and those that questioned the idea that El Sistema was proposing something genuinely new (e.g., Stevens 2012; *On an Overgrown Path*, October 19, 2010). Booth (2010, 2–3) judges the latter as a failure to grasp the importance of apparently minor differences and therefore the meaning of El Sistema. Yet the differences he identifies—"sustaining the dynamic tension between polarities," or "the power of beauty"—are sufficiently abstract that they depend on belief rather than providing a solid basis for it.

There are, of course, ways in which El Sistema is unique. As a politician and economist, Abreu was ideally placed to secure unprecedented levels of funding and support, yet without having to fulfill rigorous requirements to account for expenditure or prove results. With its salaries, international tours, top-of-the-range instruments, workshops with the world's leading teachers, and lengthy seminarios in five-star hotels, El Sistema bears little resemblance to youth music in other countries. But is it realistic to look to the program as a model to follow?

A senior Venezuelan music educator noted two key factors in El Sistema's success: first, it emerged at a time when Venezuela was awash with money due to high oil prices; second, Abreu knew the state's budgeting processes firsthand and had many political contacts. Abreu's project was a typical youth orchestra at the start, but he had the resources and contacts to bring in a prominent figure like Mexican composer Carlos Chávez to work with the young musicians: "since it had much more money than any other orchestra, it had more options." My informant commented on El Sistema's seminarios in plush facilities: the young musicians "didn't go to school, they didn't do anything else, they were just stuck there, enslaved, from first thing in the morning 'til last thing at night. Of course, after two months, it sounds good. In what other country could they do that? The expense of having 200 people in that kind of place—that's oil money for you." Creating an orchestra like the SBYO required not just "slave labor" but also high salaries, expensive instruments, and first-class accommodation. He concluded: "it's primitive, and it's unrepeatable, because it's extremely expensive...it's paid for by oil."

A Venezuelan university professor concurred: "The model is not adaptable to any other country, since you need stupid politicians who are easily persuaded, and tons of money to maintain orchestras with hundreds of kids paid like adult production-line workers, all under the vertical management of a political and financial genius. It is neither a musical nor a social model, it is a political and financial scheme, which in my opinion is impossible to duplicate."

The near impossibility of copying El Sistema does not necessarily condemn overseas projects to second-class status. They are built as much on El Sistema's illusions as its realities, and may therefore end up (and may already be) improving on the original. For example, they are taking the idea of social action through music more seriously than in Venezuela itself. Many ideals and practices to which El Sistema pays lip service are seemingly being realized more fully in spinoff projects overseas.

By 2012 such projects appeared to be increasingly in favor of an "adapt rather than adopt" approach, identifying themselves as "Sistema-inspired" and thereby opening up possibilities for positive transformation. One of the biggest changes in translation is a shift toward greater targeting. The overseas projects are almost all focused explicitly on disadvantaged communities and social groups, something that is encountered more sporadically in Venezuela. Overseas, there is great concern with reaching out to the neediest children; in Venezuela, a more passive approach to social inclusion means that the neediest may never get anywhere near the núcleo. It seems that the conservative Venezuelan project has fallen onto more progressive educational soil overseas, and this may be a promising combination.

One of the key areas in which Sistema spinoffs are *not* copying Venezuela is that of evaluation. In Europe and North America, funding bodies insist on demonstrable results, so many organizations have committed to monitoring and evaluation from the start, and Sistema Scotland already has an external report available ("Evaluation of Big Noise" 2011), with more such documents appearing with increasing regularity. Monitoring and evaluation alone may be enough to ensure that the copies are more effective than the original.

The Sistema Scotland report presents a mixed picture. In comparison with Venezuela, it reveals a project with a more nuanced and proactive approach to fostering social inclusion and community relations, and a greater valuing of teachers (hiring highly qualified staff and providing them with training and support). Yet the project still seems in thrall to the orchestra and classical music, and shows a dismissive attitude toward popular and traditional music on the "frequent questions" section of its website. Sistema Scotland also seems to have borrowed El Sistema's tendency toward monopolization of cultural resources at the expense of other projects. Allan et al.'s (2010) research points to other continuities between Venezuelan and Scottish projects, such as a faith-based approach that reduces productive ambiguity, reflection, and critique, and a streak of paternalism and exclusion behind the trumpeting of social inclusion. The impressive drive and focused mission that propel the project forward appear to have some problematic undercurrents.

A North American music educationalist who led a Sistema-inspired project painted a similarly mixed picture by email. Despite passionate commitment to the project, he was struggling with a range of problems:

> (1) Even though our current teaching location is 2 blocks from a housing project, all of our students are coming from far enough away that their parents have to drive them. While this automatically creates parental engagement—a real key to success—we'd like to find a way to reach truly disadvantaged children—and those whose parents don't care, for whatever reason. (2) Many of our most disadvantaged students have poor attendance directly related to their parents' issues. Single moms. Multiple jobs. Transportation challenges. Lack of commitment and/or understanding of why attendance is critical. (3) Many of the same students have learning issues. They might have a diagnosed disability or it might be related to stress, much as Paul Tough describes in his book, *How Children Succeed*. We teach in group classes and don't have the kind of resources we need to deal with these children on an individual basis.
>
> Right now, we are talking about having to drop a couple of families because their attendance is so poor that when they do show, the children are so far behind they are lost and embarrassed in their class. We are all torn. The children can really benefit on many levels from participating, but the individual attention required takes away from the other students who have been coming. How can we help a child who is rarely there?

This honest account reveals problems in the Sistema model, such as reaching the most disadvantaged children when it is offered as an out-of-school program. The intensity and requirement for frequent attendance put great demands on families, and the most disadvantaged are the most likely to fall by the wayside. The problems described here were mentioned repeatedly in Venezuela. Nevertheless, this individual's self-critical insight and freedom from institutional dictates offer hope that overseas programs may be able to address such problems.

The evidence for Sistema-inspired projects is thus mixed. On his blog on September 26, 2012, Marshall Marcus describes overseas projects as "sometimes a pale emulation of what has happened in Venezuela," but there are reasons to believe the opposite. In some regards, their belief in El Sistema's myths is a source of strength, as they place social action at the center of their mission. That said, programs are being created on the assumption that El Sistema is as effective as claimed, which is unproven; their foundations may then be faulty. Much may depend, ultimately, on whether projects overseas are inspired to emulate El Sistema or to explore deeply the issue of social action through music, even if the latter means radically changing or abandoning the original model.

ALTERNATIVES

El Sistema's achievements are impressive. It has created many orchestras, provided work for many musicians, and opened up classical music to many more people. The creation of an extensively funded, nationwide music program has rightly attracted much attention, and its longevity is little short of extraordinary. However, many Venezuelan musicians have mixed feelings, and El Sistema's signature practices have problematic features that have been widely discussed in the scholarly literature. It is therefore worth imagining what El Sistema could look like in the future: a system in which children learnt a range of musical and social skills, created and questioned as well as executed and followed orders, and were educated as well as trained. What could El Sistema achieve if the energy and resources that go into the elite end—the showcase orchestras and buildings, the international tours, the star conductors—were devoted instead to devising and implementing a truly revolutionary, grassroots sociomusical program?

"Social action through music" is an important idea that deserves careful consideration. In critiquing El Sistema, it is not my intention to devalue this idea, but rather to suggest that with it now firmly on the broader agenda, it is time to look at improvements and alternatives that may realize El Sistema's stated aims more fully. What would be the implications of focusing the project on its official mission statement, which describes pursuing social action through collective musical practice, rather than its similar yet distinct goal of sowing Venezuela with orchestras? Is playing in a conventional orchestra the best musical means to promote social justice? Does it bring as many social benefits as other musical or music-related activities? Could better outcomes be achieved for less investment if the orchestra were decentered and the project opened up fully to other kinds of ensembles?

Bringing together music education and social change is too important for the conversation to be dominated by a single, problematic model. Thinking more deeply about social action through music means looking more carefully for alternative realizations of this idea to see if they offer a more positive example than El Sistema. Are there other projects—smaller, less heralded—that are more closely attuned to contemporary ideas about social justice? What could El Sistema learn from them?

An essential step is the recognition that El Sistema is, in its original form, a conservative or even regressive program. It need not remain that way, but it is a model that must be critiqued and transformed if it is to have progressive effects. To start from the belief that it is miraculous, radical, and revolutionary is to risk simply perpetuating its regressive aspects and distracting attention from more forward-thinking projects and ideas.

My ideal Sistema will not be everyone's. There has been a recent wave of enthusiasm in the United Kingdom for drilling, martial values, and boot camp methods in education, one that swelled after the London riots in August 2011. There was a right-wing backlash against progressive educational ideas, with public figures from David Cameron to teacher Katharine Birbalsingh flying the flag for discipline (Addley 2012). Traditionalists may therefore find much to cheer in El Sistema, the brainchild of an archconservative. What is noteworthy is that, having been given a Left-ish spin to allow it to thrive under Chávez, El Sistema is now generally couched in the terms of, and championed by, the cultural Left in the United Kingdom, which has projected its desires onto the program and now seems happy to overlook the authoritarian, disciplinary realities of orchestras and high-level training in the performing arts. Thus, many progressive educationalists and musicians, swayed by El Sistema's rhetoric, have been cheering too, perhaps unaware that the object of their desires embodies an ideology and practices to which they would probably be opposed. It is therefore worth pointing briefly to some alternatives that respond more closely to such desires.

ADVANCES IN THE SISTEMA MODEL

Encouraging signs may be found in Medellín, Colombia, in the city's Red de Escuelas de Música, a network of twenty-seven music schools in poor neighborhoods, which I visited briefly in 2012. While there are similarities with the Venezuelan program, it is not a Sistema acolyte. Staff explicitly contrasted their music schools, which provide a rounded music education and emphasize diversity and creativity, with Venezuela's núcleos, with their narrower remit as orchestral training centers. In 2005 the Medellín program dropped the reference to symphonic music from its name, and now includes Latin jazz and tango in its curriculum. It has organized collaborations with prominent hip hop, rock, tango, and fusion ensembles, and in 2010 it had a composer in residence who wrote Colombian-flavored music for the schools. When I visited, it was looking at opening a school dedicated to traditional stringed instruments and investigating ways to insert composition into the curriculum.

The network forms part of the University of Antioquia and receives funding from the local mayor's office. This has various consequences: first, the program has to respond to the dean of the university and the mayor, and as such is no state within the state. There appears to be a balance of independence and accountability. Second, many students go on to get a degree from the university, and almost all the school directors and the majority of teachers are university graduates. There is an emphasis, then, on gaining a professional qualification. Third, given its university connections, there is none of the anti-intellectualism of El Sistema. The program's director has a background in research, as well as in traditional Colombian music and other arts, which no doubt contributes to its more eclectic vision.

While this picture should unquestionably be tested by detailed research, the Medellín project seems to be looking for collaborations and improvements. El Sistema pays lip service to these aims, but underneath it has been resistant to change. The Medellín project started out as purely classical but has broadened its remit. A capacity to change is perhaps the most positive point to take from the Colombian example.

Another interesting project with certain similarities to the Sistema model can be found in Brazil. Andrés, a musician who had worked in both the Brazilian project and El Sistema, described the former as "an example of El Sistema that works so well, so much better than anything I saw in Venezuela." During his time in El Sistema he had come across few genuinely poor children, but he estimated that 75 percent of the children in the Brazilian project fell into this category. The organizers went into the favelas (shantytowns) looking for recruits and handing out leaflets. Where the Venezuelans' approach was largely passive, in Brazil he saw something akin to affirmative action: the organizers took concrete steps to encourage the most disadvantaged children to join.

The project "just worked a lot more efficiently" in Brazil: activities were structured better, there was more attention to the individual, and the children learned faster. Learning was helped by the fact that "the level of music theory was much, much better," as it was given more emphasis. Discipline was a feature, but it was focused on the organization's management and processes rather than the children. "The director in [the Venezuelan núcleo] was really authoritarian, but this [Brazilian project] was just a completely different way of doing things."

Democracy was more in evidence in Brazil: "there was a lot of emphasis on the kids thinking of ideas to do—it wasn't all on the directors, it was very much a group effort." Unlike in El Sistema, the posts of núcleo director and principal conductor were separate, and the director sat on a board with several colleagues, thereby avoiding the concentration of power in a single individual. Andrés saw this democratic structure as more than just window dressing: he sat in on a meeting where the other board members disagreed with the director, and they had their way. Rehearsals, too, were more democratic than in Venezuela, with the students given a voice. There was no fixed seating in the string sections of the orchestra, meaning more social mixing and less internal hierarchy.

When the project ran into funding problems, the students were encouraged to look for solutions, think up strategies for approaching local politicians, and put those strategies into practice. The project's senior orchestra met to discuss its options, and rather than leading the meeting, the director listened to the students' suggestions and encouraged them to act on them. In the end, the campaign was led by a seventeen-year-old orchestra member. This is what training for democratic citizenship might look like.

"I was really excited to see this passion that you hear about El Sistema before going, and now, seeing the difference, I definitely didn't see that in Venezuela, but here, in this project, they were absolutely passionate." Apart from the occasional monitor, participants were not paid, so involvement was not motivated by money. "It was so good to see—it was exactly what El Sistema preaches and exactly what I'd heard about before I went—and seeing it actually work was amazing."

It should be underlined, however, that this is one individual's response to a single project in a country that has many El Sistema–inspired programs, some of which have met with criticism from Brazilian music educators. One described El Sistema as a justification or "certification" of European cultural colonization. Concerns have also been voiced about Sistema offshoots' potential to monopolize funding and thereby displace existing musical projects, as has happened in Venezuela, and about a lack of consultation with those responsible for educating music teachers, who fear devaluation of their profession. The signs of improvement in the Sistema model may then be counteracted by the maintenance of problematic ideologies and practices imported from Venezuela.

Clearly, much more research is required in this area. The Colombian and Brazilian schools suggest that the Sistema model could be adapted and improved for the twenty-first century. A Sistema for the future could retain its focus on social inclusion and its commitment to offering classical music, but also recognize the importance to this mission of *cultural* inclusion, rounded education, and democratic functioning. Nevertheless, it would still need to address the thorny question of whether it is El Sistema's practice or ideology that is faulty. Evidence from Brazil and Colombia implies that the program can be practiced better, but the question remains: Is renovation a worthwhile investment of energy and resources, or is the whole edifice ideologically unsound?

PROGRESSIVE EDUCATION IN LATIN AMERICA

It is also worth considering alternative educational ideologies that could form the basis of a more progressive music education system, one that might have little to do with Abreu's model. Since the 1960s, and particularly since the publication of Freire's *Pedagogy of the Oppressed* in 1970, an emancipatory educational current has been developing in Latin America and elsewhere, one that emphasizes critical reflection on social and political issues, students' active participation in the co-creation of knowledge, and horizontal, dialogic conversations between teachers and students. It recognizes that social inclusion must take place at the level of pedagogy and curriculum as well as simple participation. Where El Sistema, like most conventional classical music education methods, transmits values such as discipline, efficiency, and hierarchy, there are alternative educational projects that focus less on training than on stimulating creativity and innovation. These educational alternatives are related to broader progressive social movements in Latin America, with their focus on grassroots rather than top-down action, horizontal rather than vertical structures, and self-sufficiency rather than dependence. Such ideas would constitute a logical foundation for progressive music education in Latin America.

I had the opportunity to observe some progressive educational programs during my visit to Medellín. The city saw some of the worst urban violence in the hemisphere during the latter part of the twentieth century, but subsequently invested heavily in forward-thinking cultural and educational projects. I visited and learned about hip hop schools and library educational projects in the city's toughest barrios. One element these initiatives had in common was *formación desde lo popular*—education based on popular culture and knowledge, which entails an emphasis on horizontal, nonhierarchical relationships and on using experience and skills already present in the community. These projects reject the idea of the all-knowing state that appears in a poor barrio and tells people what and how to learn. They promote independence of thought and action, self-management, and learning how to survive without state subsidy.

In a hip hop school run by Crew Peligrosos, I heard much of the same discourse as in El Sistema—a big family, learning to be a better person, learning to respect and cooperate with others. But there were marked differences: the variety of activities on offer, due to the presence of hip hop's four elements (rap, DJing, breakdance, and graffiti); the relatively egalitarian structure (they talked about "sharing" rather than "teaching"—indeed, they did not use the words "teacher" or "pupil"); and the valorization of improvisation. The hierarchy that I observed was one of skill more than power. A leader at another of the city's hip hop schools described classes in which students wrote a rap song together on a contemporary social or political issue. I recalled Sistema classes that consisted solely of playing scales in unison. Nevertheless, a classical music school is an easier sell to politicians and the middle class than a hip hop school; the deeply rooted idea of classical music as elevating deprived youth is appealing to people who may regard hip hop as part of the problem rather than the solution.

I also visited a digital urban cartography project, which was literally mapping the barrios that did not appear in detail on any official map. They were attempting to make their own aerial photography equipment. They started with a goal—to photograph their barrio from the air—and then built, scrounged, and hacked the necessary equipment. The "teacher" was part of the team; the problem was one they all had to solve together. Such projects emphasize agency, creative capacity, and above all plurality; they enable new forms of citizenship that include critical positions directed at resisting hegemonic forms of power and changing society, rather than simply slotting into a social structure ready-made by others (Rueda, Ramírez, and Fonseca n.d.). How could a music education project strive to offer a comparable experience, I wondered?

To see a project based on progressive ideals and contemporary music education research, we might turn to Costa Rica, which implemented a new general music curriculum in secondary public schools in 2009 (Rosabal-Coto 2010). Over the previous century, state initiatives had revolved around European music and nationalist derivatives thereof, silencing the indigenous and African population, as part of the construction of a myth of the nation as racially and culturally homogeneous (Rosabal-Coto n.d.). The 2009 curriculum reform, however, sought to overturn this pattern of colonialism and exclusion. Just as important as the full inclusion of many national and regional genres, and the concomitant acknowledgment of Costa Rica as a multiethnic and multicultural country, was the adoption of a critical, empowering, emancipatory music curriculum. According to its vision, "knowledge is constructed by the students themselves through research, active engagement, reflection and criticism, and close interaction with their community. It aims at educating citizens who are not only socially aware, and [i.e., but also] able to make responsible individual and collective choices and engage in healthy social relationships" (n.d., 21).

The curriculum is not content- but place-oriented. It is extraordinarily broad, encompassing not just a wide range of musics but also history, new technologies, creation (composing, arranging, and improvising), event organization, interaction with the community, and "exploring issues critical to adolescence." Students are encouraged to forge connections with other curricular subjects and develop respect for diversity. It is a student-centered program; the teacher is conceived of as a mediator, not a guru. "Students can engage in exploring, understanding, performing, creating *their* music, the musics in the community, as well as past and present musics of society at large.... It is expected that the implementation of this curriculum will promote awareness on a multiplicity of musics and identities, and that such awareness will be developed by the students themselves, as protagonists of the educational processes, rather than by vertical imposition" (21–22).

The emphasis on reflection and dialogue is particularly noteworthy: "Critical reflection about performances and interactions are crucial during and after these practices. Students are guided in exploring, expressing, and sharing their reactions, perceptions, sensations, and emotions in regard to sounds and musics listened or danced to, performed, composed, or researched.... The intent is that *talking about musical engagements becomes a tool of social action*" (69–70, emphasis added).

The broad idea of music education as a route to transformation of the self and society is familiar from El Sistema, but the Costa Rican version is utterly different in its detail: here, critical engagement is the key to change, and students are encouraged to be politically active. The Costa Rican program embodies many tenets of contemporary progressive educational theory: children should play a significant part in shaping activities; they should be encouraged to question and think for themselves; the curriculum should be flexibly designed; traditional and popular musics of different cultures should be included on an equal footing with classical music; room should be made for improvisation, composition, listening, and new technologies; leadership should be rethought and teamwork built proactively. This example shows the confluence of various currents—Latin American critical pedagogy of the 1970s onward, more recent research on education and social justice, the region's new social movements—into a coherent, contemporary vision of Latin American music education and social action through music. When held up against it, El Sistema's ideology and practices look both conservative and outdated, yet it is the Venezuelan and not the Costa Rican example that is being lauded and copied around the world.

Martín Giraldo, a Colombian digital activist, made two key points in comparing classical music schools and progressive educational projects. First, it is essential for culture to have, at least potentially, a critical function in Latin America, where social and political processes are so flawed; and classical music schools focusing on the orchestra and the canon reduce this critical function. Second, a big strength of Latin Americans is their capacity to improvise, one that puts them in good stead for the new society and economy of the twenty-first century; but classical music schools focus on inculcating norms and provide no space for improvisation. He described them as putting Latin Americans in a European box and curtailing one of their most important abilities.

Wherever one stands on the issue of progressive education in Latin America, there are clear reasons to argue that El Sistema does not fall under this umbrella. The Latin American projects described here may not be the perfect educational answer; they, too, deserve careful scrutiny and may reveal flaws. But they provide alternatives to the symphony orchestra as a model for music education and for a future society, and they deserve to be considered seriously by those with progressive leanings.

BRAZIL'S PONTOS DE CULTURA

Much can be learned by comparing El Sistema to a contemporary cultural program in Brazil, analyzed in detail by Célio Turino (2011). *Pontos de Cultura* are "culture hotspots" funded by the Brazilian government but largely left to choose and run their own activities. The Ministry of Culture does not determine how funds should be used; each Ponto develops its program according to its own needs and desires. Money may be spent on facilities, equipment, teaching, or cultural production. Pontos may focus on theater, dance, music, audiovisual production, or other activities. Cultural forms may come from the street or the academy, be experimental or traditional, and reflect the perspectives of the young or the old, the center or the periphery, and different ethnic groups. One active, diverse Ponto is run by young people themselves.

Large-scale, top-down schemes to take culture to the masses tend to curb their autonomy and capacity for leadership, and hence commonly lead to dependence. Turino sums up the program's theory in a simple equation: empowerment + agency = breaking relations of dependence (2011, 69). Presenting the elite as the fount of knowledge and good taste and thus qualified to choose for the majority, argues Turino, is a means of reproducing the existing class structure. The Pontos de Cultura, in contrast, aim at breaking down social and political hierarchies and emancipating ordinary people. They constitute a new critical response to Brazil's historical inequities at the hands of an elite that looked overseas for direction: "'Good things come from abroad!' was the message transmitted by having their clothes ironed in France or, in the present day, using their Rolex watches" (128)—a luxury product, it will be recalled, advertised by Dudamel.

A new cultural development paradigm is thus emerging in Brazil: ordinary people no longer have to wait for the master (*el maestro*) to tell them what to do. The central logic of Pontos de Cultura is to believe in Brazilian people and culture as they currently are, and hence to boost what already exists, rather than treat them as defective and in need of correction. Pontos de Cultura is not about the government providing culture, a service, or a program: "its focus is not on lack, on the absence of goods and services, but rather on the potential and capacity to act on the part of individuals and groups" (67). It is a decentralized project that promotes autonomy and pares the paternalist role of the state back to a minimum. Costa (2012, 33) describes the program's mission as working "on the nation's cultural body, massaging vital nodes that are temporarily numb or forgotten."

Pontos de Cultura forms part of the broader program Cultura Viva, which focuses on widening access, but "not to culture, since culture is inherent in human action and everyone does it, but rather to organized cultural goods— performance venues, recording studios, courses, and regular artistic programming—since the majority of the population is divorced from these resources.... [W]e tried to boost what already exists, striking agreements and making alliances with dynamic cultural agents who are already active in their communities" (Turino 2011, 130).

Turino's book is subtitled "Brazil from the Bottom Up," and it presents a vision of a changing world: "A bottom-up state presupposes a change in mentalities and values. It is necessary to overcome the temptation to plan in offices, ignoring what is really going on, and the uncontrolled desire of the governing class and cultural managers to take on the role of founders or demiurges" (130). This new world is not controlled by a singular, paternalistic guiding vision or a charismatic, omnipotent conductor. Disadvantaged social groups are no longer obliged to speak in another's voice or serve an institutional ideology dictated from above. This is a new, and arguably revolutionary, conception of cultural policy, one implemented from the grassroots.

The contrast with El Sistema is abundantly clear. El Sistema sees popular zones as cultural deserts that it must fill and a poor child as requiring its assistance to become "a human being capable of fully entering society," in Borzacchini's words. Pontos de Cultura, in contrast, believes that Brazilian communities are already culturally rich and simply need more resources. For decades, El Sistema has promoted "a single solution...applicable independently of local realities and needs" (130), believing the symphony orchestra to be the answer to every problem. Pontos de Cultura has no program, no institutional hierarchy of cultural value, and can thus take on a huge variety of forms. It promotes individuals' capacity to think and act autonomously—a central tenet of progressive educational theory (Green 2008, 103; Allsup, Westerlund, and Shieh 2012, 470), yet one of little interest to El Sistema.

Perhaps Turino's vision of Pontos de Cultura is an idealization. Nevertheless, the theory that it articulates comes from a very different (and much more radical) place than El Sistema—from twenty-first-century South America rather than the Europe of the past. As George Yúdice notes, Brazil has recently challenged the paradigm of Latin American cultural industries and institutions, which have historically followed a Eurocentric model that is somewhat out of touch with their surrounding cultural reality.[3] "Other countries still have the beaux arts museum, the national theatre of dance, the opera, in which almost all funding goes...when you have a society that's vibrant with all kinds of things." Pontos de Cultura, however, marked "a huge advance, in fact [they] advanced beyond what you could find in Europe or the United States." It is Pontos de Cultura, not El Sistema, that is at the cutting edge of culture and social development in Latin America. The top-down Eurocentric model is expensive and thus starts to break down during times of austerity; the bottom-up Brazilian one is less dependent on continuous government funding and therefore more resilient. If El Sistema is difficult to copy, given its reliance on oil revenue and huge loans, Pontos de Cultura is eminently replicable and has been adopted in neighboring Argentina and Peru without any need for dilution.

Pontos de Cultura draws on the ideology of new social movements and their rejection of the patriarchal, hierarchical, centralized dynamics manifested by older forms of state intervention and epitomized by the Venezuelan program. Today, progressive cultural momentum in Latin America is with initiatives like Pontos de Cultura and Cultura Viva Comunitaria, a continent-wide movement for grassroots, community-organized cultural programs.[4] Such initiatives embrace horizontalism, decentralization, and cultural diversity, empower ordinary citizens to think and decide as well as participate, and demonstrate the radicalism that El Sistema promises but fails to deliver.

ALTERNATIVES IN EUROPE AND NORTH AMERICA

In going beyond El Sistema's drawbacks to think about what might work better, but also what *is* working better, we can find valuable examples in Europe and North America. As Service (2010) writes evenhandedly, "El Sistema is wonderful, but the huge publicity its British manifestations garner must not blind us to the work that is already happening on our doorstep." Stevens (2012) found it "intensely frustrating that in their eagerness to praise Venezuelan music education so many commentators disregard or even seem ignorant of the UK's distinguished reputation in this field."

The National Youth Orchestra of Great Britain does not have the SBYO's profile or drawing power, but its range of repertoire and educational activities is broader, and the special place that it reserves for contemporary music and working with composers marks it out as more adventurous. Its program in August 2012 consisted of Varèse, Messiaen, a premiere by Nico Muhly, and an encore of Anna Meredith's *HandsFree*, "in which instruments are abandoned and the body—clapping, stomping, hissing, clicking—becomes music" (Maddocks 2012). The SBSO had been through London a few weeks earlier with Beethoven (twice), Strauss, Britten, and a rare premiere, by Esteban Benzecry, which stuck closely to the musical language of Bartók, Stravinsky, and Prokofiev (Ashley 2012).

Having traveled halfway around the world, enthused by the idea that social action through music might be found in far-off Venezuela, I now ask myself whether it might not be just as evident in, say, Sheila Nelson's (1985) string project in the London borough of Tower Hamlets. London's Animate Orchestra seems much more open-minded and daring than its Sistema counterparts. It "offers young musicians…opportunities to play together and create their own music in a 'Young Person's Orchestra for the 21st Century,'…while bringing their own ideas to how orchestras of the future might look and sound."[5] It welcomes players of any instrument and level of experience and from any cultural background, including those with skills in music technology and DJing. The Guildhall's non-formal Connect ensembles are similarly forward-looking: "Non-formal ensembles are usually open to anyone, regardless of their ability, and do not require participants to have learnt how to read music before taking part. What have become known as 'creative' music ensembles also do not perform the traditional repertoire, since almost all of the music is improvised or composed from scratch" (Renshaw 2005, 5). In contrast to El Sistema's reverential and reproductive approach to classical music, the BBC's Ten Pieces project focuses on creativity, encouraging schoolchildren to deconstruct and reconstruct classical repertoire and "develop their own creative responses to the pieces through music, dance or digital art."[6]

Cope's Scottish fiddle project has been dwarfed by the subsequent fanfare around Sistema Scotland, but its ideology and methods are closer to progressive visions of music education. One notable aspect is its emphasis on the local, which meshes closely with contemporary environmental concerns—for example, sourcing food locally and reducing international travel—and contrasts with the Venezuelan show orchestras' continual tours around the globe in groups several hundred strong. Bates (2014) makes a strong defense of staying home in the context of music education, arguing that a focus on overseas travel feeds environmental degradation, heightens social inequality, and devalues the local.

One of the most radical and promising music education initiatives is Musical Futures, which began in the United Kingdom in 2003 and is spreading internationally.[7] Musical Futures builds on Green's (2002; 2008) work on informal learning and its application to the classroom. Its central element is copying recordings by ear, and it integrates listening, improvising, and composing into the learning process, which is holistic and student-led (rather than sequential or drill-based) and promotes student choice of instruments and repertoire. Green (2008, 119–80) applies this informal learning pedagogy to ensemble playing and classical music, revealing that there is no inevitable bond between El Sistema's curriculum, collective ethos, and conservative pedagogy. Other researchers have applied Green's informal learning methods to large school ensembles and confirmed their positive impact on both autonomy and cooperation (e.g., Abrahams n.d.; Davis 2011). Informal learning programs point an important way forward for music education.

El Sistema requires an extraordinary and continuous outlay of money on infrastructure and instruments, primarily for the program's elite students, and would fall apart without the continuous injection of huge funds. It also creates dependency through its educational practices and monopolization of funding. Musical Futures represents a radical alternative: a genuinely new pedagogy, and a grassroots movement led by teachers and students rather than a central institution. With minimal funding required, it is not only much cheaper but also more self-sufficient and sustainable than El Sistema.

The National Foundation for Youth Music, too, is attempting to rethink approaches to mass music education in the United Kingdom (Lonie 2014). It questions the notion that music education equates to teaching children to play (primarily classical) instruments and critiques the pyramidal progression model associated with classical music training, envisaging instead a range of possible trajectories and outcomes for children who learn music (aside from becoming a professional instrumentalist or singer and/or a music teacher).

Committed to diversity and cultural democracy, it provides classical music with a significant but not dominant role (around a quarter of provision), and emphasis is placed on engaging with young people's existing interests, giving them decision-making power, and fostering their agency. The notion of inclusion is central, but in this case supported by current research, which means that it is defined as valuing multiple ways of musical knowing, involving participants in the construction of knowledge and methods, and promoting lifelong learning, rather than simply opening the door to all. Recognizing the hierarchization and exclusion prevalent in much conventional music education, the project asks: "Can an orchestra ever be inclusive?"

The United States, too, has its homegrown success stories. The Metropolitan Opera Guild's "Creating Original Opera" program has received glowing reports (e.g., Wolf 1999; Kratus 2007) and illustrates that an imaginatively designed classical music project can foster a wide range of skills. By encouraging children to write the music and make the sets, rather than just rehearse and perform, the project puts the focus on collaborative discussions, creation, and problem solving. Kratus (2007, 46–47) also reports on the very different Vermont MIDI Project, which "uses the Internet to connect student composers in general music classes with professional composers and with collegiate music education and composition majors.... Here, younger and older musicians form a virtual community of composers, making use of technology to bring people together and promoting the creativity of individuals." The musical genre in question is less important than the ideology and methodology behind its teaching. Also, these programs are not trying to turn out opera directors or composers, though it is possible they might do so. El Sistema says the same—and yet its calling card is its professional or quasi-professional ensembles.

The cognitive psychologist Gary Marcus (2012, 77) visited a class in computer music production at a performing arts school. He was amazed at the differences with his own high school experience: "No lecturer standing at the front of the room, but something more akin to a writers' or artists' workshop. Students worked individually or in pairs on compositions while [the teacher] circulated throughout the room, critiquing their compositions and making suggestions.... Instead of being asked to regurgitate some set of memorized facts for a final exam, the kids in [this] class build their own projects. And instead of competing, they were collaborating." Marcus concluded: "it is hard to know exactly what shape music education will take twenty-five years from now, but [this] classroom struck me as an excellent model." With such programs developing, is El Sistema really the future of music education?

Such innovation is not a recent development in the United States, which, like the United Kingdom, has a long tradition of progressive thinking and action in the realm of music education. The American Association of Creative Musicians (AACM), a 1960s collective of black musicians, "developed a pedagogical practice that insisted on the individual agency of musicians and students to create their 'own' sound, different from that of the traditions around them. For these musicians and the school they created, composition and improvisation are taught as inseparable from political and economic response.... The AACM, with its insistence on the nonneutrality of the musical act, was able to leverage the teaching of improvisation toward the development of political agency and a critical understanding of commercialism" (Allsup and Shieh 2012, 50–51). Far more progressive visions than El Sistema's had taken root in the United States before the Venezuelan program was even born.

Around the world, music educators are experimenting with a bewildering variety of new instrumental ensembles in search of greater inclusivity and creativity: hybrid groups mixing instruments, genres, and cultures, even using garbage or cell phones (Webb and Seddon 2012). Spillane (2009) presents an Australian school music project that offers aspects of El Sistema with fewer negatives and more positives. Children make their own musical instruments and then play in an ensemble; the homemade instruments are simple to make and play, boosting inclusivity. The aim is to involve every child, and the ensemble is not stratified according to talent. The children also created a radio show in conjunction with the ensemble, and they write and direct the music programs. Such a project is not going to get a contract with Askonas Holt or Deutsche Grammophon, but it gives children a proactive, creative role.

On a more personal level, I recalled the musical activities that I grew up around, like the amateur ensembles that my mother played in when I was a child, involving gregarious gatherings in our living room. I found it sad that after so much investment in music, Venezuela lacks a vibrant amateur classical scene and is instead teeming with ex-musicians. Small (1998, 208) writes: "The big challenge to music educators today seems to me to be not how to produce more skilled professional musicians but how to provide that kind of social context for informal as well as formal musical interaction that leads to real development and to the musicalizing of the society as a whole." This is a challenge that El Sistema, with its professionalizing focus, has failed to meet. One of the United Kingdom's great strengths is its amateur music-making (Finnegan 1989), which, with its friendly, fun atmosphere, may foster more social action than El Sistema's more goal-oriented approach. As Ward (2006) notes, however, the political ideology that most closely approximates to music making in a British town—varied, fluid, creative, pluralist—is anarchism, so it is hardly a surprise that Abreu shows little interest in amateur activities.

EL SISTEMA AS MODEL, INSPIRATION, AND RESEARCH TOPIC

There are numerous question marks over the desirability of taking El Sistema as model or inspiration. It may be that projects inspired by El Sistema's discourse will be more successful than those that attempt to use it as an actual model.

Nevertheless, the idea that intensive orchestral practice constitutes a suitable focus for music education and a motor of social action demands further scrutiny: even Andrés, so enamored of the Brazilian Sistema-inspired project, admitted that "I still don't think it's great to sit in orchestras for six hours when you're twelve."

In Venezuela, I encountered doubts about the desirability of internationalizing the Sistema franchise. Several top-level musicians felt that Europe had nothing to learn from Venezuela about classical music education, and they were skeptical about European flirtations with a poorly understood experiment. One, a leading Sistema teacher himself, praised the breadth of options available in the United Kingdom; he was less enthusiastic about Venezuela's more monolithic approach to music education. Another suggested that Venezuela did not provide the breadth of education that aspiring musicians needed, unlike a European conservatoire. She noted the irony of Europe and North America's obsession with El Sistema while so many advanced Venezuelan students were trying to go to study overseas.

Musicians' testimonies raise important doubts about core claims regarding orchestral practice and social action, and in a number of scholarly analyses, the orchestra is held up as the *negative* pole in a comparison: the opposite of empathy or teamwork or creativity, and a poor second (in social terms) to chamber music, jazz, or popular music. It has been presented as an example of rationalization and disenchantment (Weber), led by an exploitative capitalist (Marx). It is little short of extraordinary that a positive message about the orchestra has nevertheless taken root—testimony to the effectiveness of El Sistema's PR campaign and a collective failure to scrutinize it.

Where El Sistema has undeniably been successful is at the level of arts administration. It has been exceptionally effective in securing economic and political support for high culture, a holy grail in the arts world. By focusing on the promise of social inclusion, it has enabled the Venezuelan orchestral scene to grow exponentially at a time when orchestras around the world are feeling the chill wind of budget cuts. El Sistema has provided a beacon for orchestra executives and music education leaders in other countries.

Abreu's moment has come partly because of global cultural and economic changes. He is a master of securing subsidy for culture from noncultural sources, vital in the age of austerity; and he is a master of spectacle, which is central to the music industry in the era of declining record sales. The SBYO, which draws on social funds and packs concert halls, epitomizes Abreu's skills, which are more valuable today than ever. As much as the quality of the music making, it is these features that have made cultural leaders sit up and take notice.

Perhaps the principal and lasting value of El Sistema, however, is putting the idea of social action through music on the international public agenda. The program has a great capacity to publicize and inspire, resulting in much more interest around the world in the theme of music education and social change than there was before 2007.

El Sistema has opened up an extraordinary space for music education. Although it has long been more suited to the nineteenth than the twenty-first century, its recent openings to activities beyond symphonic performance may point to a sea change after decades of relative stasis. Many of these initiatives are still too new to be properly evaluated, but even if they do represent a genuine shift, those interested in El Sistema would still do well to reflect on what came before.

With the Venezuelan program apparently in flux and Sistema-inspired projects springing up around the world, the potential and need for further research is enormous. While the evangelical tone around many Sistema-inspired events makes critical reflection harder, encouraging signs emerged from the 2012 International Society for Music Education conference, which included a Special Interest Group on El Sistema. Several projects were presented, most notably from Costa Rica, Portugal, and the United States, and while various connections to El Sistema were traced, most notable were the differences and diversions, whether explicit or implicit, from the Venezuelan path. The Costa Rican program, in particular, defined itself against, rather than as part of, El Sistema. Signs of a move away from an overly reverent attitude were also evident in the increasing emphasis on evaluative research projects. While advocacy was still a feature, key issues like pedagogy and social inclusion were addressed critically, and the need for more rigorous research was recognized. There were still problems on display—most glaringly, the reliance on media representations of El Sistema, which were treated like research findings. Surprisingly, rigorous study of the Venezuelan program seemed like a lesser priority than analyzing its offshoots. Nevertheless, at the time of writing, moves are being taken in the right direction.

The growth of such spaces for deliberation is very important, given that honest public debate in Venezuela is unthinkable at present. One of the most encouraging impacts of El Sistema overseas is in providing new impetus and points of entry to a growing conversation about music education and social justice. This dialogue—paradoxically—can barely be heard in Venezuela, where it is overshadowed by a PR monologue.

One thing is certain: debate about El Sistema is on its way. Abreu, the master rhetorician and conductor of the media, created the perfect story, one that has had the world in thrall for years. But problems lie just beneath the surface; skeletons are rattling in the closet; and experts cannot continue forever to confuse propaganda and fact, or to ignore the gulf between progressive theory and conservative practices. Political developments in Venezuela in 2014 opened up Abreu and Dudamel to critical scrutiny overseas as well as at home. As ever more people take an interest in El Sistema, it is only a matter of time before the cracks in the rhetorical edifice start to show clearly enough for real discussion to begin.

NOTES

INTRODUCTION

1. http://fundamusical.org.ve. The acronym FESNOJIV was used between 1996 and 2011, when it changed its name to Fundación Musical Simón Bolívar. FESNOJIV was the term in use during my fieldwork, and I will use it throughout to avoid confusion.
2. The figures vary considerably among sources—see Chapter 4.
3. It is commonly supposed that all tuition is free, but this was not the case in two large núcleos that I studied. Students were expected to pay an annual inscription fee and a monthly subscription, though the poorest students could apply for an exemption.
4. http://elsistemausa.org/el-sistema/venezuela/.
5. http://www.artsjournal.com/slippeddisc/2011/05/85000-tickets-sold-in-the-first-afternoon.html.
6. http://www.laphil.com/pdfs/education/2010_symposium/symposium_social_outcomes.pdf. This document has since been taken down.
7. As this book was going to press, Creech et al. (2013) published an extensive bibliography on El Sistema, though focusing mainly on Sistema-inspired programs in other countries.
8. Silva has published numerous posts on blogs such as *Aporrea* and *La Otra Cara del Sistema*; Mendoza's articles are available at http://prof.usb.ve/emendoza/emilio-web/articulos_tema/articulos_frame.html.
9. For more on this debate, see http://geoffbakermusic.wordpress.com/el-sistema-the-system/el-sistema-blog/.
10. The webpage http://www.aldeaeducativa.com/aldea/Articulo.asp?Which1=908, titled "Premio Nobel Alternativo para José Antonio Abreu," consulted on March 6, 2011, has since been taken down.

CHAPTER 1

1. Oscar Ramos, "La trilogía." I was given a photocopy of this article with no publication details. It seems to date from around 1993–94.
2. http://saber.ucab.edu.ve/bitstream/handle/123456789/39033/sicr269919730725.pdf?sequence=2.
3. http://www.wikileaks.org/plusd/cables/1973CARACA03028_b.html.
4. I also spoke to a former CONAC employee who had worked under Abreu and confirmed many of these articles' details.
5. A list of some fifty articles can be found at http://laotracaradelsistema.blogspot.com.ar/2013/04/expediente-del-caso-abreu-juanes-bose.html.

6. Wakin (2012b) is a rare exception.
7. ODILA will be discussed further in subsequent chapters.
8. http://www.eltiempo.com/archivo/documento/MAM-50214.
9. http://www.state.gov/documents/organization/147999.pdf.

CHAPTER 2

1. Several open letters circulated on this issue; some were published by the blogs *La Otra Cara del Sistema* and *Aporrea*, for example: http://www.aporrea.org/medios/a90250.html.
2. http://www.artsjournal.com/slippeddisc/2013/09/big-pay-rise-for-dude-and-debs.html.
3. http://nyo.org.uk/pages/44.
4. http://fundamusical.org.ve/c ategory/el-sistema/impacto-social/#.U7p-Jl5P_IA.
5. As an illustration, see the presentation of the SBYO's recordings "Fiesta" and "Beethoven 5 & 7" by Deutsche Grammophon.

CHAPTER 3

1. I refer here to an advanced draft of this forthcoming article.
2. http://dspace.ucab.edu.ve/jspui/bitstream/123456789/39147/2/sicr636319790921.pdf.
3. Oficina Subalterna del Primer Circuito de Registro del Departamento Libertador, Nro. 44, Tomo 11, Prot. 1.

CHAPTER 4

1. http://www.ioe.ac.uk/64635.html.
2. http://www.calperfs.berkeley.edu/performances/2012-13/special-events/simon-bolivar-symphony-orchestra-of-venezuela.php.
3. http://www.ucab.edu.ve/tl_files/sala_de_prensa/recursos/ucabista/jul99/p36.htm.

CHAPTER 6

1. http://www.deutschegrammophon.com/es/cat/single?PRODUCT_NR=4776228.
2. This appraisal appeared in a circular email.
3. The incorporation of composition in the Sistema-inspired Youth Orchestra Los Angeles suggests that this deficiency of the original model has been recognized in the United States.
4. A "program of academic education for young teachers and conductors" was created in 2010 (http://fundamusical.org.ve/educacion/programa-de-formacion-academica-para-jovenes-docentes-y-directores/#.U70W9F5P_IA), suggesting that El Sistema might have finally embraced the concept of teacher training, but I heard no mention of the program in my interviews in 2010 or 2011.

CHAPTER 7

1. http://www.deutschegrammophon.com/cat/single/?PRODUCT_NR=4776228.
2. Decree 3093, dated February 20, 1979, published in the Gaceta Oficial de la República de Venezuela.
3. Oficina Subalterna del Primer Circuito de Registro del Departamento Libertador, Nro. 44, Tomo 11, Prot. 1.
4. Decree 8078, published in the Gaceta Oficial de la República de Venezuela.
5. http://www.wcom.org.uk/template.php?whichPage=newsdetails&News_ID=248.

CHAPTER 8

1. http://www.ted.com/talks/jose_abreu_on_kids_transformed_by_music.html.
2. http://musicabancaribe.com/Publicaciones/Libro_digital/VenezuelaEnElCielo/EN/index.php.
3. Statistics gleaned from Borzacchini 2010, 192–93.
4. http://elsistemausa.ning.com/forum/topics/dr-jose-antonio-abreu-talks-el-sistema.
5. For example, this debate was played out extensively on Norman Lebrecht's blog *Slipped Disc* in 2013.
6. See http://www.philosophyblog.com.au/cressida-heyes-on-embodied-freedoms-and-foucault/.
7. http://www.ted.com/talks/jose_abreu_on_kids_transformed_by_music.html.

CHAPTER 9

1. http://plato.stanford.edu/entries/weber/.
2. http://www.ted.com/talks/jose_abreu_on_kids_transformed_by_music.html.
3. For another account of manipulation and intrigue around auditions, see Sanoja 2013.

CHAPTER 10

1. Cases of alleged sexual abuse continue to come to light as this book goes to press. Ian Pace posted a detailed account of reported cases from 1990 to 2012 on his blog (ianpace.wordpress.com) on December 30, 2013.
2. http://www.osborne-conant.org/harrassment.htm.
3. E.g., BBC Radio 3, "Music Matters," March 9, 2013.
4. http://www.ted.com/talks/ken_robinson_says_schools_kill_creativity.html.
5. See Robinson's RSA Animate: http://www.youtube.com/watch?v=zDZFcDGpL4U.
6. http://ericbooth.net/the-fundamentals-of-el-sistema/.

CHAPTER 11

1. http://musicabancaribe.com/Publicaciones/Libro_digital/VenezuelaEnElCielo/EN/index.php.
2. Report published on the Ministry of Interior Relations and Justice website (http://www.mpprij.gob.ve/) on February 9, 2011.
3. http://www.ted.com/talks/jose_abreu_on_kids_transformed_by_music.html.
4. I obtained a PowerPoint copy from the university. Creech et al. (2013) include the original reports as Esqueda Torres 2001, 2002, and 2004.
5. While Creech et al. (2013) note the existence of other reports on El Sistema by Guevara, Rojas, and Sanjuán, these studies appear not to be regarded by the IDB as robust evidence of the program's efficacy.
6. The webpage, http://www.aldeaeducativa.com/aldea/Articulo.asp?Which1=908, consulted on March 6, 2011, has since been taken down.

CHAPTER 12

1. http://dspace.ucab.edu.ve/jspui/bitstream/123456789/39147/2/sicr636319790921.pdf.
2. http://www.guardian.co.uk/music/2012/may/20/worlds-youngest-conductor-venezuela-orchestra.
3. http://musicabancaribe.com/Publicaciones/Libro_digital/VenezuelaEnElCielo/EN/index.php.

CHAPTER 13

1. http://enfermedadelalma.blogspot.co.uk/2011/02/es-hora-de-quitar-disfraces. html.
2. *The Ensemble*, a Sistema newsletter, August 2012.
3. https://www.youtube.com/watch?v=KvTRQ7qDZgM.
4. http://culturavivacomunitaria.org/cv/.
5. http://animateorchestra.org.uk.
6. http://www.bbc.co.uk/programmes/articles/4KCVB2XVgPQ0JwnqLGJl8y0/ about-bbc-ten-pieces.
7. https://www.musicalfutures.org/.

BIBLIOGRAPHY

Abrahams, Frank. n.d. "Going Green: The Application of Informal Music Learning Strategies in High School Choral and Instrumental Ensembles." http://www.rider.edu/sites/default/files/docs/wcc_wccp_abrahams_goinggreen.pdf.

"Abreu: Vaya Nuestra Gratitud y Votos Por la Recuperación del Presidente." 2013. *El Nacional*, January 10. http://www.el-nacional.com/escenas/Abreu-Vaya-gratitud -recuperacion-Presidente_0_115791054.html.

Adams, Maurianne. 1997. "Pedagogical Frameworks for Social Justice Education." In *Teaching for Diversity and Social Justice: A Sourcebook*, edited by Maurianne Adams, Lee Anne Bell, and Pat Griffin, 30–43. London: Routledge.

Addley, Esther. 2012. "Government's New, Old-Fashioned Schools Agenda." *The Guardian*, April 20. http://www.theguardian.com/education/2012/apr/20/ government-old-fashioned-schools-agenda.

Adlington, Robert. 2007. "Organizing Labor: Composers, Performers, and 'the Renewal of Musical Practice' in the Netherlands, 1969–72." *Musical Quarterly* 90 (3–4): 539–77.

"Adopt or Adapt? El Sistema as an Inspiration for Music Education in Canada." 2012. *Quebec Music Educators Association*. October 20. http://www.qmea-aemq.org/news/ adopt-or-adapt-el-sistema-as-an-inspiration-for-music-education-in-canada/.

Aharonián, Coriún. 2004. "A Propósito del Sistema Nacional de Orquestas Juveniles e Infantiles: Música y Políticas Educacionales," November 26. www.voltairenet. org/article122990.html.

Allan, Julie, Nikki Moran, Celia Duffy, and Gica Loening. 2010. "Knowledge Exchange with Sistema Scotland." *Journal of Education Policy* 25 (3): 335–47.

Allen, Candace. 2012. *Soul Music: Taking the Pulse of Race and Music*. London: Gibson Square.

Allmendinger, Jutta, Richard Hackman, and Erin V. Lehman. 1996. "Life and Work in Symphony Orchestras." *Musical Quarterly* 80 (2): 194–219.

Allsup, Randall Everett, and Eric Shieh. 2012. "Social Justice and Music Education: The Call for a Public Pedagogy." *Music Educators Journal* 98 (4): 47–51.

Allsup, Randall Everett. 2007. "Editorial." *Music Education Research* 9 (2): 167–68.

Allsup, Randall Everett, Heidi Westerlund, and Eric Shieh. 2012. "Youth Culture and Secondary Education." In *The Oxford Handbook of Music Education*, edited by Gary E. McPherson and Graham F. Welch, 1: 460–75. New York: Oxford University Press.

Aloy, Patricia. 2013. "Simon Rattle: 'El Sistema Sigue Siendo El Modelo de Educación Más Inspirador Que He Conocido.'" *Venezuela Sinfónica*. August 9. http://www .venezuelasinfonica.com/noticias/internacional-noticias/simon -rattle-el-sistema-sigue-siendo-el-modelo-de-educacion-mas-inspirador-que-he- conocido.

Álvarez Pifano, Hugo. 2014. "José Antonio Abreu, El Dueño de La Gallina de Los Huevos de Oro." *Literanova*. http://www.literanova.net/blog5.php/jose-antonio-abreu-el-dueno.

Arenas, Zayira. 1991. "Conac Asumió La Remodelación de La 'José Angel Lamas.'" *El Nacional*, January 10.

Armstrong, Paul. 2000. "Include Me Out: Critique and Contradiction in Thinking about Social Exclusion and Lifelong Learning." http://www.leeds.ac.uk/educol/documents/00001431.htm.

Arroyo Gil, Diego. 2014. "El Ejemplo del Maestro Abreu." *El Nacional*, February 20. http://www.el-nacional.com/opinion/ejemplo-maestro-Abreu_0_358164295.html.

"Artistas Venezolanos Repudian Visita de Bosé y Juanes." 2013. *Patria Grande*. January 18. http://www.patriagrande.com.ve/temas/cultura/artistas-venezolanos-repudian-visita-de-bose-y-juanes-comunicado/.

Arvelo, Alberto. 2006. *Tocar y Luchar*. Film.

Arvelo, Alberto. 2010. *Dudamel: Let the Children Play*. Film.

Ashley, Tim. 2012. "Simón Bolívar Symphony Orchestra/Dudamel—Review." *The Guardian*, June 27. http://www.guardian.co.uk/music/2012/jun/27/simon-bolivar-symphony-orchestra-dudamel-review.

Baker, Geoffrey. 2007. "The 'Ethnic Villancico' and Racial Politics in Seventeenth-Century Mexico." In *Devotional Music in the Iberian World, 1450–1800*, edited by Tess Knighton and Alvaro Torrente, 399–408. Aldershot: Ashgate.

Baker, Geoffrey. 2008a. *Imposing Harmony: Music and Society in Colonial Cuzco*. Durham: Duke University Press.

Baker, Geoffrey. 2008b. "Latin American Baroque: Performance as a Post-Colonial Act?" *Early Music* 36 (3): 441–48.

Baker, Geoffrey. 2010. "The Resounding City." In *Music and Urban Society in Colonial Latin America*, edited by Geoffrey Baker and Tess Knighton, 1–20. Cambridge: Cambridge University Press.

Baker, Geoffrey. 2011. *Buena Vista in the Club: Rap, Reggaetón, and Revolution in Havana*. Durham: Duke University Press.

"Barenboim Embelesado." 2010. *Chávez: Corazón de Mi Patria*. http://blog.chavez.org.ve/temas/noticias/barenboim-embelesado.

Barrett, Frank J. 1998. "Creativity and Improvisation in Jazz and Organizations: Implications for Organizational Learning." *Organization Science* 9 (5): 605–22.

Bates, Vincent C. 2014. "Rethinking Cosmopolitanism in Music Education." *Action, Criticism, and Theory for Music Education* 13 (1): 310–27.

Beckles Willson, Rachel. 2009. "Whose Utopia? Perspectives on the West-Eastern Divan Orchestra." *Music and Politics* 3 (2). http://www.music.ucsb.edu/projects/musicandpolitics/archive/2009-2/beckles_willson.html.

Belfiore, Eleonora. 2002. "Art as a Means of Alleviating Social Exclusion: Does It Really Work? A Critique of Instrumental Cultural Policies and Social Impact Studies in the UK." *International Journal of Cultural Policy* 8 (1): 91–106.

Bell, Lee Anne. 1997. "Theoretical Foundations for Social Justice Education." In *Teaching for Diversity and Social Justice: A Sourcebook*, edited by Maurianne Adams, Lee Anne Bell, and Pat Griffin, 3–15. London: Routledge.

Bellamy, Richard. 2008. *Citizenship: A Very Short Introduction*. Oxford: Oxford University Press.

Berardi, Franco "Bifo." 2009. *The Soul at Work: From Alienation to Autonomy*. Translated by Francesca Cadel and Giuseppina Mecchia. Los Angeles: Semiotext(e).

Bergeron, Katherine. 1992. "Prologue: Disciplining Music." In *Disciplining Music: Musicology and Its Canons*, edited by Katherine Bergeron and Philip V. Bohlman, 1–9. Chicago: University of Chicago Press.

Bergh, Arild, and John Sloboda. 2010. "Music and Art in Conflict Transformation: A Review." *Music and Arts in Action* 2 (2): 2–18.

Beyond Social Inclusion Towards Cultural Democracy. 2004. Scotland: Cultural Policy Collective. http://www.variant.org.uk/20texts/CultDemo.txt.

Birns, Larry. 2011. "The Ramos Kidnapping and Violence in Latin America." *Council on Hemispheric Affairs*. November 16. http://www.coha.org/the-ramos-kidnapping -and-violence-in-latin-america/.

Bishop, Claire. 2004. "Antagonism and Relational Aesthetics." *October* 110: 51–79.

Bohlman, Andrea F., and Philip V. Bohlman. 2007. "The Family Symphony Orchestra: Growing Up Making Music." *Australasian Music Research* 9: 131–43.

Bohlman, Philip V. 2008. "Other Ethnomusicologies, Another Musicology: The Serious Play of Disciplinary Alterity." In *The New (Ethno)musicologies*, edited by Henry Stobart, 95–114. Plymouth: Scarecrow Press.

Boltanski, Luc, and Eve Chiapello. 2005. *The New Spirit of Capitalism*. London: Verso.

Booth, Eric. 2008. "Thoughts on Seeing El Sistema." http://www.americanorchestras. org/images/stories/lld_pdf/elsistema_Booth.pdf.

Booth, Eric. 2010. "El Sistema's Open Secrets." http://convention.artsusa.org/sites/ default/files/pdfs/Elsistemasecrets.pdf.

Booth, Wayne C. 1999. *For the Love of It: Amateuring and Its Rivals*. Chicago: University of Chicago Press.

Borchert, Gustavo. 2012. "Sistema Scotland: A Critical Inquiry into the Implementation of the El Sistema Model in Raploch." MMus, University of Glasgow.

Born, Georgina. 1995. *Rationalizing Culture: IRCAM, Boulez, and the Institutionalization of the Musical Avant-Garde*. Berkeley: University of California Press.

Born, Georgina. 2010. "For a Relational Musicology: Music and Interdisciplinarity, Beyond the Practice Turn." *Journal of the Royal Musical Association* 135 (2): 205–43.

Born, Georgina. 2012. "Music and the Social." In *The Cultural Study of Music: A Critical Introduction*, edited by Martin Clayton, Trevor Herbert, and Richard Middleton, 261–74. 2d ed. New York: Routledge.

Borzacchini, Chefi. 2010. *Venezuela en el Cielo de Los Escenarios*. Caracas: Fundación Bancaribe.

Boston, Rob. 2006. "Breaking the Opus Dei Code." *Catholics for Choice*. http://www.catho- licsforchoice.org/news/inthenews/2006/200605cs_breakingtheopusdeicode.asp.

Boulton, María Teresa. 1992. "¿Un Ministerio de La Cultura?" *El Nacional*, September 17.

Bowman, Wayne D. 2009. "No One True Way: Music Education Without Redemptive Truth." In *Music Education for Changing Times: Guiding Visions for Practice*, edited by Thomas A. Regelski and J. Terry Gates, 3–15. Dordrecht: Springer.

Bradley, Deborah. 2012. "Good for What, Good for Whom?: Decolonizing Music Education Philosophies." In *The Oxford Handbook of Philosophy in Music Education*, edited by Wayne D. Bowman and Ana Lucia Frega, 409–33. Oxford: Oxford University Press.

Bramley, Charlie. 2012. "The Free-Improvised Creative Space: An Experimental Revision of Musical and Creative Development." http://www.inter-disciplinary. net/at-the-interface/wp-content/uploads/2012/05/bramleycepaper.pdf.

"Brasilia Fundará 300 Orquestas Con La Asesoría Filosófica y Pedagógica de El Sistema." 2013. *Panorama*. April 10. http://www.panorama.com.ve/portal/app/push/noti- cia61814.php.

Brenet, Michel. 1917. "French Military Music in the Reign of Louis XIV." *Musical Quarterly* 3 (3): 340–57.

Brinner, Benjamin. 2009. *Playing Across the Divide: Israeli-Palestinian Musical Encounters*. Oxford: Oxford University Press.

Broyles, Michael. 2012. "The American Symphony Orchestra as Political Metaphor." Paper delivered at American Musicological Society Conference, New Orleans, November 3.

Brule, Gaël, and Ruut Veenhoven. 2012. "Why Are Latin Europeans Less Happy? The Impact of Hierarchy." In *Polyphonic Anthropology: Theoretical and Empirical Cross-Cultural Fieldwork*, edited by Massimo Canevacci. Reijka: Intech Open Access Publisher.

Buelow, George J., ed. 1993. *The Late Baroque Era*. London: Macmillan.

Buelow, George J. 2004. *A History of Baroque Music*. Bloomington: Indiana University Press.

Buenaventura, Oswaldo. 2010. "Otro Espaldarazo Del Gobierno a Las Corporaciones Musicales de Abreu." *La Otra Cara Del Sistema*. http://laotracaradelsistema.blogspot.com.ar/2010/06/otro-espaldarazo-del-gobierno-las.html.

Bull, Anna. 2012. "Book Review: Musicians from a Different Shore—Mari Yoshihara." *Talking Ethnomusicology*. http://talkingethnomusicology.wordpress.com/2012/10/30/book-review-musicians-from-a-different-shore-mari-yoshihara.

Burnard, Pamela. 2012. *Musical Creativities in Practice*. Oxford: Oxford University Press.

Burnard, Pamela, and Betty Anne Younker. 2010. "Towards a Broader Conception of Creativity in the Music Classroom: A Case for Using Engeström's Activity Theory as a Basis for Researching and Characterizing Group Music-Making Practices." In *Sociology and Music Education*, edited by Ruth Wright, 165–91. Aldershot: Ashgate.

Butterworth, James. 2014. "Andean Divas: Emotion, Ethics and Intimate Spectacle in Peruvian Huayno Music." PhD, Royal Holloway, University of London.

Buxton, Julia. 2011. "Foreward: Venezuela's Bolivarian Democracy." In *Venezuela's Bolivarian Democracy: Participation, Politics, and Culture under Chávez*, edited by David Smilde and Daniel Hellinger, ix–xxii. Durham: Duke University Press.

Cábez, Félix. 2010. *La Tierra de Las Mil Orquestas*. Film.

Campbell, Patricia Shehan. 2004. *Teaching Music Globally*. New York: Oxford University Press.

Carballo, Ana Estefanía. 2014. "The Opportunity of Latin American Development Thinking." *Alternautas*. May 22. http://www.alternautas.net/blog/2014/5/2/on-the-opportunity-of-latin-american-thinking.

Carey, John. 2010. *What Good Are the Arts?* New York: Oxford University Press.

Carlson, Alexandra. 2012. "The Story of Carora: The Origins of El Sistema." Unpublished manuscript.

"Carta Abierta a José Antonio Abreu." 2014. *El Universal*, February 13. http://www.eluniversal.com/arte-y-entretenimiento/140213/carta-abierta-a-jose-antonio-abreu.

Carvajal, Beatriz Carolina, and Indira Melgarejo. 2008. "El Sistema Nacional de Orquestas Juveniles e Infantiles de Venezuela. La Escuela Que Aprende." *Revista Estudios Digital* 1.

Casanova, Eduardo. 2007. "Abreu Siempre En Domingo." *Literanova*. http://www.literanova.net/blog5.php/abreu_siempre_en_domingo.

Casanova, Eduardo. 2009. "El Dictador Ya Tiene Su Músico y Su Director de Orquesta." *Libertad, Preciado Tesoro*. March 2. http://libertadpreciadotesoro.blogspot.com.ar/2009/03/el-dictador-ya-tiene-su-musico-y-su.html.

Cavicchi, Daniel. 2009. "My Music, Their Music, and the Irrelevance of Music Education." In *Music Education for Changing Times: Guiding Visions for Practice*, edited by Thomas A. Regelski and J. Terry Gates, 97–107. Dordrecht: Springer.

Cee, Vincent. 2013. "The End(s) of Advocacy: Responding to Our Own Mandates Instead of Creating New Leadership." *Action, Criticism & Theory for Music Education* 12 (1): 64–81.

Chang, Jennifer. 2007. "Orchestrating an 'Affluence of Spirit': Addressing Self-Esteem in Impoverished Venezuelan Children Through Music Education." BA, Harvard College.

Chang, Ying. n.d. "Beatbugs and Hyperinstruments—A New Toy Symphony." *Classical Source*. http://www.classicalsource.com/db_control/db_features.php?id=744.

Channing, Simon. 2003. "Training the Orchestral Musician." In *The Cambridge Companion to the Orchestra*, edited by Colin Lawson, 180–93. Cambridge: Cambridge University Press.

Cheah, Elena. 2009. *An Orchestra Beyond Borders: Voices of the West-Eastern Divan Orchestra*. London: Verso.

Clasen, Sharon. 2003. "How Opus Dei Is Cult-Like." *Opus Dei Awareness Network*. http://www.odan.org/tw_how_opus_dei_is_cult_like.htm.

Cohen, Nick. 2012. *You Can't Read This Book: Censorship in an Age of Freedom*. London: Fourth Estate.

"Concertación." 1989. *SIC*, no. 511: 2–3.

Cook, Nicholas. 2003. "Writing on Music or Axes to Grind: Road Rage and Musical Community." *Music Education Research* 5 (3): 249–61.

Cook, Nicholas. 2007. "Making Music Together, or Improvisation and Its Others." In *Music, Performance, Meaning: Selected Essays*, 321–41. Aldershot: Ashgate.

Cope, Peter. 1998. "Knowledge, Meaning and Ability in Musical Instrument Teaching and Learning." *British Journal of Music Education* 15 (3): 263–70.

Cope, Peter. 1999. "Community-Based Traditional Fiddling as a Basis for Increasing Participation in Instrument Playing." *Music Education Research* 1 (1): 61–75.

Cope, Peter, and Hugh Smith. 1997. "Cultural Context in Musical Instrument Learning." *British Journal of Music Education* 14 (3): 283–89.

Corona, Efrain. 1991. "Abreu: 'Las Escuelas de Música Serán Fortalecidas.'" *El Diario de Caracas*, January 8.

Coronil, Fernando. 1997. *The Magical State: Nature, Money, and Modernity in Venezuela*. Chicago: University of Chicago Press.

Costa, Eliane. 2012. "Políticas Públicas en Cultura para el Escenario de Las Redes: La Experiencia Brasileña, Sobre la Perspectiva de la Ecología Digital." In *En la Ruta Digital: Cultura, Convergencia Tecnológica y Acceso*, 32–40. Buenos Aires: Secretaría de Cultura de la Presidencia de la Nación.

Cottrell, Stephen. 2003. "The Future of the Orchestra." In *The Cambridge Companion to the Orchestra*, edited by Colin Lawson, 251–64. Cambridge: Cambridge University Press.

Cottrell, Stephen. 2004. *Professional Music-Making in London: Ethnography and Experience*. Aldershot: Ashgate.

Cottrell, Stephen. 2014. "Orchestras and Musical Terribilism." Paper delivered at "Classical Music as Contemporary Socio-Cultural Practice: Critical Perspectives," King's College, London, May 23.

Couch, Stephen R. 1983. "Patronage and Organizational Structure in Symphony Orchestras in London and New York." In *Performers and Performances: The Social Organization of Artistic Work*, edited by Jack B. Kamerman and Rosanne Martorella, 109–21. South Hadley, MA: Bergin and Garvey.

Crary, Jonathan. 2013. *24/7: Late Capitalism and the Ends of Sleep*. London: Verso.

"Crisis en Orquestas de Abreu." 1999. *El Mundo*, December 3.

Criss, Ellen. 2010. "Teamwork in the Music Room." *Music Educators Journal* 97: 30–36.

Cross, Ian, Felicity Laurence, and Tal-Chen Rabinowitch. 2012. "Empathy and Creativity in Group Musical Practices: Towards a Concept of Empathic Creativity." In *The Oxford Handbook of Music Education*, edited by Gary E. McPherson and Graham F. Welch, 2: 337–53. New York: Oxford University Press.

Cuesta, José. 2008. "Music to My Ears: The (Many) Socio-Economic Benefits of Music Training Programs." Unpublished report.

Daisey, Mike. 2011. "Against Nostalgia." *New York Times*, October 6. http://www.nytimes.com/2011/10/06/opinion/jobs-looked-to-the-future.html.

Davis, Sharon G. 2011. "Fostering a 'Musical Say': Identity, Expression, and Decision Making in a US School Ensemble." In *Learning, Teaching, and Musical Identity: Voices across Cultures*, edited by Lucy Green, 267–80. Bloomington: Indiana University Press.

DeNora, Tia. 2000. *Music in Everyday Life*. Cambridge: Cambridge University Press.

DeNora, Tia. 2003. *After Adorno: Rethinking Music Sociology*. Cambridge: Cambridge University Press.

Detels, Claire. 2002. "Softening the Boundaries of Music in General Education." *Action, Criticism & Theory for Music Education* 1 (1): 2–44.

Deveney, Catherine. 2013. "Three Months On, a Cardinal Is Banished but His Church Is Still in Denial." *The Guardian*, May 18.

Dickey, Keven. 2011. "Hugo Chávez and the Future of Venezuela." *Council on Hemispheric Affairs*. December 4. http://www.coha.org/hugo-chavez-and-the-future-of-venezuela/.

Duchen, Jessica. 2011. "Miracle Maestro: Gustavo Dudamel Brings Music from Venezuela's Slums to the Proms." *The Independent*, August 5. http://www.independent.co.uk/arts-entertainment/classical/features/miracle-maestro-gustavo-dudamel-brings-music-from-venezuelas-slums-to-the-proms-2331731.html.

Duque, José Roberto. 2006. "Tocar, Luchar y Andar Mamando." *Aporrea*. June 9. http://www.aporrea.org/tiburon/a22561.html.

Eagleton, Terry. 2007. *The Meaning of Life*. Oxford: Oxford University Press.

Eatock, Colin. 2010. "From Venezuela to the World: Exporting El Sistema." http://www.colineatock.com/el-sistema.html.

"El Sistema de Orquestas Recibirá 210 Millones Dólares." 2012. *El Universal*, November 22. http://www.eluniversal.com/arte-y-entretenimiento/121122/el-sistema-de-orquestas-recibira-210-millones-dolares.

"El Sistema: Changing Lives Through Music." 2009. *CBS News*. February 11. http://www.cbsnews.com/8301-18560_162-4009335.html?pageNum=2.

Elliott, David J. 2012. "Another Perspective: Music Education as/for Artistic Citizenship." *Music Educators Journal* 99 (1): 21–27.

Escobar, Arturo. 1995. *Encountering Development: The Making and Unmaking of the Third World*. Princeton: Princeton University Press.

Estrada Rodríguez, Luis Alfonso. 2012. "Education in Latin American Music Schools: A Philosophical Perspective." In *The Oxford Handbook of Philosophy in Music Education*, edited by Wayne D. Bowman and Ana Lucia Frega, 231–48. Oxford: Oxford University Press.

Etherington, Ben. 2007. "Instrumentalising Musical Ethics: Edward Said and the West-Eastern Divan Orchestra." *Australasian Music Research* 9: 121–29.

"Evaluation of Big Noise, Sistema Scotland." 2011. Scottish Government Social Research. www.scotland.gov.uk/socialresearch.

Faulkner, Robert. 1973a. "Career Concerns and Mobility Motivations of Orchestra Musicians." *Sociological Quarterly* 14 (3): 334–49.

Faulkner, Robert. 1973b. "Orchestra Interaction: Some Features of Communication and Authority in an Artistic Organization." *Sociological Quarterly* 14 (2): 147–57.

Ferguson, James. 1994. *The Anti-Politics Machine: Development, De-Politicization and Bureaucratic Power in Lesotho*. Cambridge: Cambridge University Press.

Fernandes, Sujatha. 2010. *Who Can Stop the Drums? Urban Social Movements in Chavez's Venezuela*. Durham: Duke University Press.

Finnegan, Ruth. 1989. *The Hidden Musicians: Music-Making in an English Town*. Cambridge: Cambridge University Press.

Fischlin, Daniel, and Ajay Heble. 2004. "The Other Side of Nowhere: Jazz, Improvisation, and Communities in Dialogue." In *The Other Side of Nowhere: Jazz, Improvisation, and Communities in Dialogue*, edited by Daniel Fischlin and Ajay Heble, 1–42. Middletown, CT: Wesleyan University Press.

Fisher, Mark. 2009. *Capitalist Realism: Is There No Alternative?* Ropley: O Books.

Fiske, Edward B., ed. 1999. *Champions of Change: The Impact of the Arts on Learning*. Washington, DC: Arts Education Partnership; President's Committee on the Arts and the Humanities.

Fitzpatrick, Robert. 2013. "A Betrayal of Trust." *Slipped Disc*. http://www.artsjournal. com/slippeddisc/2013/02/when-curtis-was-known-as-the-coitus-institute.html.

Ford, Charles C. 1995. "Free Collective Improvisation in Higher Education." *British Journal of Music Education* 12 (2): 103–12.

Fotopoulos, Takis. 2005. "From (Mis)education to Paideia." *International Journal of Inclusive Democracy* 2 (1). http://www.inclusivedemocracy.org/journal/vol2/vol2_ no1_miseducation_paideia_takis.htm.

Foucault, Michel. 1991. *Discipline and Punish: The Birth of the Prison*. London: Penguin.

Frei, Marco. 2011. "Wie Viel System Steckt Im System? Venezuela Und Das Soziale Musikprojekt «El Sistema»." *Neue Zürcher Zeitung*, November 21. http://www.nzz .ch/aktuell/feuilleton/uebersicht/wie-viel-system-steckt-im-system-1.13372944.

Freire, Paulo. 1974. *Education for Critical Consciousness*. London: Sheed and Ward.

Freire, Paulo. 2005. *Pedagogy of the Oppressed*. Translated by Myra Bergman Ramos. 30th anniversary ed. New York: Continuum.

García Canclini, Néstor. 2012. "Introducción. Creatividad y Jóvenes: Prácticas Emergentes." In *Cultura y Desarrollo: Una Vision Crítica Desde los Jóvenes*, edited by Néstor García Canclini and Maritza Urteaga, 19–36. Buenos Aires: Paidós.

García Canclini, Néstor, and Maritza Urteaga. 2012. "Epílogo. Estrategias Creativas: Entre Precariedad y Redes." In *Cultura y Desarrollo: Una Vision Crítica Desde los Jóvenes*, edited by Néstor García Canclini and Maritza Urteaga, 189–206. Buenos Aires: Paidós.

Gates, J. Terry. 2009. "Introduction: Grounding Music Education in Changing Times." In *Music Education for Changing Times: Guiding Visions for Practice*, edited by Thomas A. Regelski and J. Terry Gates, xix–xxx. Dordrecht: Springer.

Gebesmair, Andreas. 2009. "The Transnational Music Industry." In *The Ashgate Research Companion to Popular Musicology*, edited by Derek B. Scott, 467–83. Aldershot: Ashgate.

Gent, Paul. 2007. "BBC Proms Review: Was This the Greatest Prom of All Time?" *The Telegraph*, August 23. http://www.telegraph.co.uk/culture/music/3667396/BBC -Proms-review-Was-this-the-greatest-Prom-of-all-time.html.

Gillinson, Clive, and Jonathan Vaughan. 2003. "The Life of an Orchestral Musician." In *The Cambridge Companion to the Orchestra*, edited by Colin Lawson, 194–202. Cambridge: Cambridge University Press.

Goldstein, Thalia R., Stéphan Vincent-Lancrin, and Ellen Winner. 2013. *Art for Art's Sake? Educational Research and Innovation*. OECD Publishing. http://www.oecd-ilibrary.org/education/art-for-art-s-sake_9789264180789-en.

Goodman, Joshua. 2014. "Gustavo Dudamel Blasted by Critics for Not Speaking Out Against Nicolas Maduro." *The Huffington Post*. http://www.huffingtonpost. com/2014/02/14/gustavo-dudamel-critics_n_4791126.html.

Gould, Elizabeth. 2009. "Disorientations of Desire: Music Education Queer." In *Music Education for Changing Times: Guiding Visions for Practice*, edited by Thomas A. Regelski and J. Terry Gates, 59–71. Dordrecht: Springer.

Gould, Helen, and Mary Marsh. 2004. *Culture: Hidden Development*. London: Creative Exchange.

Govias, Jonathan. 2011. "The Five Fundamentals of El Sistema." *Canadian Music Educator*, 21–23.

Gramit, David. 2002. *Cultivating Music: The Aspirations, Interests, and Limits of German Musical Culture, 1770–1848*. Berkeley: University of California Press.

Green, Lucy. 1988. *Music on Deaf Ears: Musical Meaning, Ideology and Education*. Manchester: Manchester University Press.

Green, Lucy. 2002. *How Popular Musicians Learn: A Way Ahead for Music Education*. Aldershot: Ashgate.

Green, Lucy. 2003a. "Music Education, Cultural Capital, and Social Group Identity." In *The Cultural Study of Music: A Critical Introduction*, edited by Martin Clayton, Trevor Herbert, and Richard Middleton, 263–74. London: Routledge.

Green, Lucy. 2003b. "Why 'Ideology' Is Still Relevant to Music Education Theory." *Action, Criticism and Theory for Music Education* 2 (2): 3–21.

Green, Lucy. 2008. *Music, Informal Learning, and the School: A New Classroom Pedagogy*. Aldershot: Ashgate.

Gregory, Sean. 2013. "Music Education Must Keep on Moving." *The Guardian*, April 10. http://www.guardian.co.uk/culture-professionals-network/culture-professionals-blog/2013/apr/10/music-education-dudamel-future-play.

Guanipa, Rómulo Antonio. 2013. "Sistema Nacional de Orquestas y Coros Juveniles e Infantiles de Venezuela...¿Con Qué Se Come Eso?" *Aporrea*. January 25. http://www.aporrea.org/actualidad/a158181.html.

Guarache Ocque, Gerardo. 2012. "2012 Otro Año de Expansión para El Sistema." *El Nacional*, December 29. http://www.el-nacional.com/escenas/ano-expansion-Sistema_0_107992036.html.

Hackman, Richard. 2002. *Leading Teams: Setting the Stage for Great Performances*. Boston: Harvard Business School Press.

Hackman, Richard. 2005. "Rethinking Team Leadership or Team Leaders Are Not Music Directors." In *New Directions in the Psychology of Leadership*, edited by David Messick and Roderick Kramer, 115–42. Mahwah, NJ: Lawrence Erlbaum.

Hallam, Susan. "The Power of Music: Its Impact on the Intellectual, Social and Personal Development of Children and Young People." *International Journal of Music Education* 28 (3): 269–89.

Hammond, John L. 2012. "The Rise of 'Horizontalism' in the Americas." *NACLA Report on the Americas* 45 (4): 79–82.

Hardiman, Rita, and Bailey W. Jackson. 1997. "Conceptual Foundations for Social Justice Courses." In *Teaching for Diversity and Social Justice: A Sourcebook*, edited by Maurianne Adams, Lee Anne Bell, and Pat Griffin, 16–29. London: Routledge.

Harford, Tim. 2012. *Adapt: Why Success Always Starts with Failure*. London: Abacus.

Harper-Scott, J. P. E. 2013. "Daniel Barenboim and Music's Emancipatory Symbolic Violence." http://www.jpehs.co.uk/2013/07/29/daniel-barenboim-and-musics-emancipatory-symbolic-violence/.

Hebert, David G. 2009. "Musicianship, Musical Identity, and Meaning as Embodied Practice." In *Music Education for Changing Times: Guiding Visions for Practice*, edited by Thomas A. Regelski and J. Terry Gates, 39–55. Dordrecht: Springer.

Hebert, David G. 2010. "Ethnicity and Music Education: Sociological Dimensions." In *Sociology and Music Education*, edited by Ruth Wright, 93–114. Aldershot: Ashgate.

Hellinger, Daniel. 1991. *Venezuela: Tarnished Democracy*. Boulder: Westview Press.

Hernández, Clodovaldo. 2011. "'La Música Popular Merece Tanto Apoyo Como El Sistema de Orquestas.'" *Ciudad CCS*. December 12. http://www.ciudadccs.info/?p=240320.

Hernández, Clodovaldo. 2013. "'Hay Que Defender Nuestra Cultura Por Encima de Todo.'" *Ciudad CCS*. February 2. http://www.ciudadccs.info/?p=381929&cpage=1.

Hernández, Jorge. 2010. "Escuela de Música José Ángel Lamas Lleva 20 Años Dañada." *El Universal*, July 19. http://www.eluniversal.com/2010/07/19/ccs_art_escuela-de-musica-jo_1977073.shtml.

Herndon, Marcia. 1988. "Cultural Engagement: The Case of the Oakland Symphony Orchestra." *Yearbook for Traditional Music* 20: 134–45.

Herrera, Earle. 1994. "Los Humillados del Conac." *El Globo*, January 26.

Hewett, Ivan. 2010. "The Teresa Carreño Youth Orchestra Sweep Cynics Aside." *The Telegraph*, October 11. http://www.telegraph.co.uk/culture/music/classicalmusic/8050907/The-Teresa-Carreno-Youth-Orchestra-sweep-cynics-aside.html.

Hewett, Ivan. 2012. "El Sistema and Gustavo Dudamel: Rescuing Children with Music." *The Telegraph*, June 21. http://www.telegraph.co.uk/culture/music/classicalmusic/9319931/El-Sistema-and-Gustavo-Dudamel-rescuing-children-with-music.html.

Hewett, Ivan. 2014. "El Sistema Must Make a Stand in Venezuela." *The Telegraph*, February 24. http://www.telegraph.co.uk/culture/10658402/El-Sistema-must-make-a-stand-in-Venezuela.html.

Hickey, Sam, and Andries du Toit. 2007. "Adverse Incorporation, Social Exclusion and Chronic Poverty." Working Paper 81. Manchester: Chronic Poverty Research Centre, University of Manchester. http://www.chronicpoverty.org/uploads/publication_files/WP81_Hickey_duToit.pdf.

Higgins, Charlotte. 2008. "Bravo, Gustavo." *The Guardian*, August 14. http://www.guardian.co.uk/commentisfree/2008/aug/14/classicalmusicandopera.edinburghfestival.

Higgins, Charlotte. 2011. "Gustavo Dudamel Electrifies Young London Musicians." *The Guardian*, January 28. http://www.guardian.co.uk/music/2011/jan/28/gustavo-dudamel-rehearsal-london-young-musicians.

Higgins, Charlotte. 2013a. "After Michael Brewer: The RNCM Teacher's Story." *The Guardian*, February 13. http://www.guardian.co.uk/uk/2013/feb/13/michael-brewer-rncm-teachers-story-martin-roscoe.

Higgins, Charlotte. 2013b. "Call for Blanket Ban on Teacher-Student Sex." *The Guardian*, March 1. http://www.guardian.co.uk/education/2013/mar/01/blanket-ban-teacher-student-sex.

"High Crime Rates Make Venezuela One of the Most Violent Countries." 2010. *El Universal*, August 27. http://www.eluniversal.com/2010/08/27/en_ing_esp_high-crime-rates-mak_27A4390815.shtml.

Hollinger, Diana. 2006. "Instrument of Social Reform: A Case Study of the Venezuelan System of Youth Orchestras." DMA, Arizona State University.

Izarra, Sandra. 2011. "Nicolás Maduro: 'Venimos a Defender la Verdad de Una Venezuela Que Está Renaciendo.'" *Correo Del Orinoco*, October 5. http://www.correodelorinoco.gob.ve/nacionales/nicolas-maduro-venimos-a-defender-verdad-una-venezuela-que-esta-renaciendo/.

Johnson, James. 1997. "Communication, Criticism, and the Postmodern Consensus: An Unfashionable Interpretation of Michel Foucault." *Political Theory* 25 (4): 559–83.

Johnson, Julian. 2002. *Who Needs Classical Music? Cultural Choice and Musical Value.* Oxford: Oxford University Press.

Johnson, Reed. 2012. "Tricia Tunstall on 'Changing Lives' and a Transformative Sistema." *Los Angeles Times*, February 1. http://articles.latimes.com/2012/feb/01/entertainment/la-et-tricia-tunstall-book-20120201.

Johnson, Roger. 2009. "Critically Reflective Musicianship." In *Music Education for Changing Times: Guiding Visions for Practice*, edited by Thomas A. Regelski and J. Terry Gates, 17–26. Dordrecht: Springer.

Jones, Ron. 2008. "The Third Wave, 1967: An Account—Ron Jones." *Libcom.org*. October 14. http://libcom.org/history/the-third-wave-1967-account-ron-jones.

Jorgensen, Estelle R. 1997. *In Search of Music Education.* Champaign: University of Illinois Press.

Jorgensen, Estelle R. 2002. "The Aims of Music Education: A Preliminary Excursion." *Journal of Aesthetic Education* 36 (1): 31–49.

Jorgensen, Estelle R. 2003. *Transforming Music Education.* Bloomington: Indiana University Press.

Jorgensen, Estelle R. 2004. "Pax Americana and the World of Music Education." *Journal of Aesthetic Education* 38 (3): 1–18.

Judy, Paul R. 1996. "Life and Work in Symphony Orchestras: An Interview with J. Richard Hackman." *Harmony* 2 (April): 1–13.

Kamerman, Jack B., and Rosanne Martorella, eds. 1983. *Performers and Performances: The Social Organization of Artistic Work.* South Hadley, MA: Bergin and Garvey.

Karl, Terry Lynn. 1997. *The Paradox of Plenty: Oil Booms and Petro-States.* Berkeley: University of California Press.

Karpman, Stephen. 1968. "Fairy Tales and Script Drama Analysis." *Transactional Analysis Bulletin* 7 (26): 39–43.

Kartomi, Margaret. 2007a. "The Australian Youth Orchestra Inc.: Its Identity as a National Icon and Expansion of Its Performance and Educational Programs." *Australasian Music Research* 9: 27–53.

Kartomi, Margaret. 2007b. "Youth Orchestras in the Global Scene." *Australasian Music Research* 9: 1–26.

Kartomi, Margaret. 2012. "Youth Orchestras." In *The Oxford Handbook of Music Education*, edited by Gary E. McPherson and Graham F. Welch, 1: 860–77. New York: Oxford University Press.

Kaznowski, Michal. 2013. "It Wasn't Just Chetham's. Abuse Was Going on at Yehudi Menuhin School and Elsewhere." *Slipped Disc.* http://www.artsjournal.com/slippeddisc/2013/02/it-wasnt-just-chetams-abuse-was-going-on-at-yehudi-menuhin-school-and-elsewhere.html.

Keil, Charlie. n.d. "Paideia Con Salsa: Ancient Greek Education for Active Citizenship and the Role of Afro-Latin Dance-Music in Our Schools." *MUSE.* http://www.musekids.org/consalsa.html.

Kingsbury, Henry. 1988. *Music, Talent, and Performance: A Conservatory Cultural System.* Philadelphia: Temple University Press.

Kohr, Leopold. 1986. *The Breakdown of Nations.* London: Routledge.

Koutsoupidou, Theano, and David J. Hargreaves. 2009. "An Experimental Study of the Effects of Improvisation on the Development of Children's Creative Thinking in Music." *Psychology of Music* 37 (3): 251–78.

Kramer, Lawrence. 2007. *Why Classical Music Still Matters.* Berkeley: University of California Press.

Kratus, John. 2007. "Music Education at the Tipping Point." *Music Educators Journal* (November): 42–48.

Kutschke, Beate, 2011. "The Celebration of Beethoven's Bicentennial in 1970: The Antiauthoritarian Movement and Its Impact on Radical Avant-Garde and Postmodern Music in West Germany." *Musical Quarterly* 93 (3–4): 560–615.

Labonville, Marie Elizabeth. 2007. *Juan Bautista Plaza and Musical Nationalism in Venezuela*. Bloomington: Indiana University Press.

Lamont, Alexandra, David J. Hargreaves, Nigel A. Marshall, and Mark Tarrant. 2003. "Young People's Music in and out of School." *British Journal of Music Education* 20 (3): 229–41.

Lander, Edgardo. 2006. *Neoliberalismo, Sociedad Civil y Democracia: Ensayos Sobre América Latina y Venezuela*. Caracas: Universidad Central de Venezuela.

Langer, Ellen, Timothy Russel, and Noah Eisenkraft. 2009. "Orchestral Performance and the Footprint of Mindfulness." *Psychology of Music* 37 (2): 125–36.

Laurence, Felicity. 2008. "Music and Empathy." In *Music and Conflict Transformation: Harmonies and Dissonances in Geopolitics*, edited by Olivier Urbain, 13–25. London: I. B Tauris.

Laurence, Felicity. 2010. "Listening to Children: Voice, Agency and Ownership in School Musicking." In *Sociology and Music Education*, edited by Ruth Wright, 243–62. Aldershot: Ashgate.

Laurence, Felicity, and Olivier Urbain, ed. 2011. *Music and Solidarity*. Somerset, NJ; London: Transaction.

Le Guin, Elisabeth. 2002. "'One Says That One Weeps, but One Does Not Weep': Sensible, Grotesque, and Mechanical Embodiments in Boccherini's Chamber Music." *Journal of the American Musicological Society* 55 (2): 207–54.

Lee, Chris. 2012. "Bravo, Gustavo! How Maestro Dudamel Is Saving Classical Music." *Newsweek*, February 6. http://www.thedailybeast.com/newsweek/2012/02/05/bravo-gustavo-how-maestro-dudamel-is-saving-classical-music.html.

Lee, Orville. 1998. "Culture and Democratic Theory: Toward a Theory of Symbolic Democracy." *Constellations* 5 (4): 433–55.

Levin, Jordan. 2013. "UM's Shelly Berg Leads Music Education in Groundbreaking Direction." *Miami Herald*, September 28. http://www.miamiherald.com/2013/09/27/3654891/ums-shelly-berg-leads-music-education.html.

Levine, Seymour, and Robert Levine. 1996. "Why They're Not Smiling: Stress and Discontent in the Orchestra Workplace." *Harmony* 2: 15–25.

Logan, Owen. n.d. "Doing Well in the Eyes of Capital: Cultural Transformation from Venezuela to Scotland." Unpublished manuscript.

Lombardi, John V. 1982. *Venezuela: The Search for Order, The Dream of Progress*. New York: Oxford University Press.

Lonie, Douglas. 2014. "Strings Attached? Inclusive Ensembles and Non-orchestral Progression." Paper delivered at "Classical Music as Contemporary Socio-cultural Practice: Critical Perspectives," King's College, London, May 23.

López Maya, Margarita, and Luis E. Lander. 2011. "Participatory Democracy in Venezuela: Origins, Ideas, and Implementation." In *Venezuela's Bolivarian Democracy: Participation, Politics, and Culture under Chávez*, edited by David Smilde and Daniel Hellinger, 58–79. Durham: Duke University Press.

López Mujica, Joaquín. 1991. "Música, Descontrol y Conac." *El Diario de Caracas*, May 29.

López Mujica, Joaquín. 1992a. "¿Jerarquía o Burocracia?" *El Diario de Caracas*, July 29.

López Mujica, Joaquín. 1992b. "¿Complicidad?" *El Diario de Caracas*, October 2.

López Mujica, Joaquín. 1993. "Eurocentrismo Musical." *El Diario de Caracas*, April 13.

López Mujica, Joaquín. 2003. "El Discreto 'Encanto' de La Oligarquía Cultural." November. http://debatecultural.org/Nacionales/JoaquinLopezMujica1.htm.

Love, Nancy S. 2006. *Musical Democracy*. Albany: State University of New York Press.

Lubow, Arthur. 2007. "Conductor of the People." *New York Times*, October 28. http://www.nytimes.com/2007/10/28/magazine/28dudamel-t.html?pagewanted=all.

Luckman, Susan. 2008. "'Unalienated Labour' and Creative Industries: Situating Micro-Entrepreneurial Dance Music Subcultures in the New Economy." In *Sonic Synergies: Music, Technology, Community, Identity*, edited by Gerry Bloustein, Margaret Peters, and Susan Luckman, 185–94. Aldershot: Ashgate.

Maddocks, Fiona. 2012. "National Youth Orchestra; BBC Proms—Review." *The Observer*, August 5. http://www.guardian.co.uk/music/2012/aug/05/national-youth-orchestra-proms-review.

"Maduro: Venimos a Defender La Verdad de Una Venezuela En Renacimiento." 2011. *PSUV*. October 6. http://www.psuv.org.ve/temas/noticias/maduro-venezuela-renacimiento/#.UY_jCI5wa20.

Maidana, Humberto. 2012. "La Orquesta de La Transformación." *La Vanguardia*. November 12. http://www.vanguardiaps.com.ar/los-ninos-musicos-del-luduena-una-experiencia-transformadora/.

Malhotra, Valerie Ann. 1981. "The Social Accomplishment of Music in a Symphony Orchestra: A Phenomenological Analysis." *Qualitative Sociology* 4 (2): 102–25.

Mantilla, Ruiz. 2011. "Sembrar Música y Acción Social; Talento y Compromiso." *El País*, June. http://enpositivo.com/2011/06/sembrar-musica-y-accion-social/.

Marcus, Gary. 2012. *Guitar Zero: The New Musician and the Science of Learning*. London: Penguin.

Márquez, Humberto. 2013. "Music as Social Inclusion Shines in Salzburg." *Inter Press Service*. August 9. http://www.ipsnews.net/2013/08/music-as-social-inclusion-shines-in-salzburg/.

Marsh, Hazel. 2013. "Popular Music and Politics in Venezuela in the Chavez Period: The Case of Ali Primera's Canción Necesaria." PhD, University of East Anglia.

Martin, James. 1995. "Opus Dei in the United States." *America: The National Catholic Review*, February 25. http://americamagazine.org/opus-dei.

Martin, Peter J. 1995. *Sounds and Society: Themes in the Sociology of Music*. Manchester: Manchester University Press.

Martorella, Rosanne. 1983. "Art and Public Policy: Ideologies for Aesthetic Welfare." In *Performers and Performances: The Social Organization of Artistic Work*, edited by Jack B. Kamerman and Rosanne Martorella, 281–88. South Hadley, MA: Bergin and Garvey.

Marx, Karl. 1887. *Capital: A Critique of Political Economy*. http://www.marxists.org/archive/marx/works/1867-c1/index.htm.

Mattioli, Alberto. 2009. "Claudio Abbado 'La Musica Costa? Facciamone Di Più.'" *La Stampa*, April 27. http://www1.lastampa.it/redazione/cmsSezioni/spettacoli/200904articoli/43178girata.asp.

MayDay Group. 2009. "Action for Change in Music Education." In *Music Education for Changing Times: Guiding Visions for Practice*, edited by Thomas A. Regelski and J. Terry Gates, xxxii–xxxvii. Dordrecht: Springer.

Mayhall, M. 2005. "Modernist but Not Exceptional: The Debate over Modern Art and National Identity in 1950s Venezuela." *Latin American Perspectives* 32 (2): 124–46.

McGuire, Charles Edward. 2009. *Music and Victorian Philanthropy: The Tonic Sol-Fa Movement*. Cambridge, UK: Cambridge University Press.

McIntyre, Jody, and Pablo Navarrete. 2012. "Venezuela's Hip-Hop Revolutionaries." *Red Pepper*. March. http://www.redpepper.org.uk/venezuela-hip-hop-revolutionaries/.

McPherson, Gary E., and Graham F. Welch, eds. 2012. *The Oxford Handbook of Music Education*. 2 vols. Oxford Handbooks. New York: Oxford University Press.

Meléndez, Marcos. 2011. "Orquestas Juveniles ¿Un Logro de La Revolución?" *La Otra Cara Del Sistema*. http://laotracaradelsistema.blogspot.com.ar/2011/03/orquestas-juveniles-un-logro-de-la.html.

Mendoza, Emilio. n.d.a. "La Utilización de Instrumentos Étnicos En La Composición Del Arte Musical En Venezuela En La Segunda Mitad Del Siglo XX (1965–1999)." http://prof.usb.ve/emendoza/emilioweb/articulos/instrum_etnicos.pdf.

Mendoza, Emilio. n.d.b. "La Composición En Venezuela: ¿Profesión En Peligro de Extinción?" http://prof.usb.ve/emendoza/emilioweb/escritos/E.M_Composicion_en_Ven_ver.completa.pdf.

Midgette, Anne. 2010. "Gustavo Dudamel Can't Conduct Himself as the Savior of Classical Music." *Washington Post*, May 28. http://www.washingtonpost.com/wp-dyn/content/article/2010/05/27/AR2010052705091.html.

Miller, Beth. 2003. "Critical Hours: Afterschool Programs and Educational Success." Nellie Mae Education Foundation.

Miller, Paddy. n.d. "Orchestrating the Organization—Leadership and Team Work." *Business Management*. http://www.busmanagement.com/article/Orchestrating-the-organization--leadership-and-team-work/.

Miller, Toby. 2002. *Cultural Policy*. London: Sage Publications.

Mills, C. Wright. 2000. *The Sociological Imagination*. New York: Oxford University Press.

Monbiot, George. 2013. "When the Rich Are Born to Rule, the Results Can Be Fatal." *The Guardian*, January 28. http://www.guardian.co.uk/commentisfree/2013/jan/28/rich-born-to-rule-fatal.

Moore, Robin. 1997. *Nationalizing Blackness: Afrocubanismo and Artistic Revolution in Havana, 1920–1940*. Pittsburgh: University of Pittsburgh Press.

Mora-Brito, Daniel. 2011. "Between Social Harmony and Political Dissonance: The Institutional and Policy-Based Intricacies of the Venezuelan System of Children and Youth Orchestras." MA, University of Texas at Austin.

Morrison, Steven J., and Steven M. Demorest. 2012. "Once from the Top: Reframing the Role of the Conductor in Ensemble Teaching." In *The Oxford Handbook of Music Education*, edited by Gary E. McPherson and Graham F. Welch, 1: 826–43. New York: Oxford University Press.

Mota, Graça, and Sergio Figueiredo. 2012. "Initiating Music Programs in New Contexts: In Search of a Democratic Music Education." In *The Oxford Handbook of Music Education*, edited by Gary E. McPherson and Graham F. Welch, 1: 187–204. New York: Oxford University Press.

"Música, Armonía Cósmica." 2012. *TalCualDigital*. March 11. http://www.talcualdigital.com/Nota/visor.aspx?id=67400.

"Nacen las Primeras Escuelas Latinoamericanas de Hip Hop." 2010. *Corneta*. January 14. http://www.corneta.org/no_80/epatu_escuela_de_hip_hop.html.

Nelson, Sheila M. 1985. "The Tower Hamlets Project." *British Journal of Music Education* 2 (1): 69–93.

Nettl, Bruno. 1995. *Heartland Excursions: Ethnomusicological Reflections on Schools of Music*. Urbana/Chicago: University of Illinois Press.

Ng, David. 2009. "Some Dudamel Product Placement." *Los Angeles Times*, October 3. http://latimesblogs.latimes.com/culturemonster/2009/10/some-dudamel-product-placement.html.

Nichols, Greg. 2012. "Library Parks Foster Community in Colombia." *Pacific Standard*, February 28. http://www.psmag.com/culture/library-parks-bring-community-to-colombia-39915/.

O'Toole, Patricia. 1994. "I Sing in a Choir but I Have 'No Voice!'" *Quarterly Journal of Music Teaching and Learning* 4–5 (4, 1): 65–77.

Ocando, Casto. 2009. "Lorenzo Mendoza: Un Compromiso Con Venezuela." *El Nuevo Herald*, October 31. http://www.elnuevoherald.com/2009/10/31/v-fullstory /578147/lorenzo-mendoza-un-compromiso.html.

Odena, Oscar. 2012. "Creativity in the Secondary Music Classroom." In *The Oxford Handbook of Music Education*, edited by Gary E. McPherson and Graham F. Welch, 1: 512–28. New York: Oxford University Press.

Osborne, William. 1999. "Symphony Orchestras and Artist-Prophets: Cultural Isomorphism and the Allocation of Power in Music." *Leonardo Music Journal* 9: 69–75.

Pace, Ian. 2013. "Petition for an Inquiry into Sexual and Psychological Abuse at Chetham's School of Music and Other Specialist Institutions." *Desiring Progress*. http://ianpace.wordpress.com/2013/02/16/petition-for-an-inquiry-into -sexual-and-psychological-abuse-at-chethams-school-of-music-and-other-spe- cialist-institutions/.

Padilla, Xavier. 2010a. "Abreu-Dudamel, o La Vieja Hipocresía de Un «sistema»." *La Otra Cara Del Sistema*. http://laotracaradelsistema.blogspot.com.ar/2010/03/ abreu-dudamel-o-la-vieja-hipocresia-de_25.html.

Padilla, Xavier. 2010b. "Barenboim Echó Por Tierra El Discurso de Abreu." *Aporrea*. August 13. http://www.aporrea.org/actualidad/a105932.html.

Pear, David. 2007. "Youth Orchestras and Repertoire: Towards an Australian Case Study." *Australasian Music Research* 9: 79–93.

Pedroza, Ludim. n.d. "Of Orchestras, Mythos, and the Idealization of Symphonic Practice: The Orquesta Sinfónica de Venezuela in the (Collateral) History of El Sistema." Unpublished manuscript.

Pedroza, Ludim. 2014. "Music as Life-Saving Project: Venezuela's El Sistema in American Neo-Idealistic Imagination." *College Music Symposium 54*.

Pérez Rescaniere, Gerónimo. 1998. "CONAC: Exclusiones y Neoliberalismo." *Últimas Noticias*, May 28.

Peters, Margaret. 2008. "Risky Economies: Community-Based Organizations and the Music-Making Practices of Marginalized Youth." In *Sonic Synergies: Music, Technology, Community, Identity*, edited by Gerry Bloustein, Margaret Peters, and Susan Luckman, 169–84. Aldershot: Ashgate.

Philpott, Chris. 2010. "The Sociological Critique of Curriculum Music in England: Is Radical Change Really Possible?" In *Sociology and Music Education*, edited by Ruth Wright, 81–92. Aldershot: Ashgate.

Philpott, Chris, and Ruth Wright. 2012. "Teaching, Learning, and Curriculum Content." In *The Oxford Handbook of Music Education*, edited by Gary E. McPherson and Graham F. Welch, 1: 441–59. New York: Oxford University Press.

Pidd, Helen. 2013. "39 Manchester Music School Teachers Face Inquiry." *The Guardian*, May 7. http://www.guardian.co.uk/uk/2013/may/07/manchester-music-schools -teachers-investigation.

Pidd, Helen, Philippa Ibbotson, and Rory Carroll. 2013. "Pupils Accuse Third Teacher of Abuse at Top Music School." *The Guardian*, February 10. http://www.guardian. co.uk/uk/2013/feb/10/pupils-accuse-third-teacher-abuse-school.

"Postulan Al Maestro José Antonio Abreu Para Que Reciba el Premio Nobel de la Paz 2012." 2012. *Mérida Digital*. January 20. http://wwwmeridadigital.blogspot.co. uk/2012/01/postulan-al-maestro-jose-antonio-abreu.html.

Price, David. 2010. "How Not to Capture Learning." *Etc: Education Blog; Technology Blog; Culture Blog*. http://davidpricesblog.blogspot.com.ar/2010/08/how-not- to-capture-learning.html.

"Program to Support the Centro de Acción Social Por La Música." 1997. VE-0105. Inter-American Development Bank. http://idbdocs.iadb.org/wsdocs/getdocument.aspx?docnum=465688.

"Program to Support the Centro de Acción Social Por La Música, Phase II." 2007. VE-L1017. Inter-American Development Bank. http://idbdocs.iadb.org/wsdocs/getdocument.aspx?docnum=1002635.

"Programa Alma Llanera Multiplica Enseñanza de la Música Tradicional Venezolana." 2013. *FESNOJIV*. http://www.fesnojiv.gob.ve/es/prensaexterna/1620-programa-alma-llanera-multiplica-ensenanza-de-la-musica-tradicional-venezolana.html.

Purvis, June. 2013. "Illegitimate Grievances." *Times Higher Education*, January 31.

Quintana Castillo, Manuel. 1994. "¿Que Todo Siga Igual, También Con Caldera?" *El Nacional*, January 17.

Rainbow, Bernarr. 1967. *The Land Without Music: Musical Education in England 1800–1860 and Its Continental Antecedents*. London: Novello.

Ramnarine, Tina K. 2008. "Beyond the Academy." In *The New (Ethno)musicologies*, edited by Henry Stobart, 83–94. Plymouth: Scarecrow Press.

Ramnarine, Tina K. 2011. "The Orchestration of Civil Society: Community and Conscience in Symphony Orchestras." *Ethnomusicology Forum* 20 (3): 327–51.

Rancière, Jacques. 2010. *Dissensus: On Politics and Aesthetics*. Edited and translated by Steven Corcoran. London: Continuum.

Regelski, Thomas A., and J. Terry Gates, eds. 2009. *Music Education for Changing Times: Guiding Visions for Practice*. Dordrecht: Springer.

Reimer, Bennett. 2007. "Roots of Inequity and Injustice: The Challenges for Music Education." *Music Education Research* 9 (2): 191–204.

Renshaw, Peter. 2005. "Simply Connect: 'Next Practice' in Group Music Making and Musical Leadership." Paul Hamlyn Foundation.

"Report on the Eighth General Increase in the Resources of the Inter-American Development Bank." 1994. AB-1704. Inter-American Development Bank. http://idbdocs.iadb.org/wsdocs/getdocument.aspx?docnum=2080953.

Richardson, Carol P. 2007. "Engaging the World: Music Education and the Big Ideas." *Music Education Research* 9 (2): 205–14.

Riiser, Solveig. 2010. "National Identity and the West-Eastern Divan Orchestra." *Music and Arts in Action* 2 (2): 19–37.

Rivero, Rafael. 1994. "El Ogro Filantrópico." *Exceso*, March.

Roach, Kate. 2011. "Social Scientists Explain Many Things—but Can They Explain Themselves?" *The Guardian*, February 3. http://www.guardian.co.uk/commentisfree/2011/feb/03/social-sciences-david-willetts.

Rohter, Larry. 2001. "Marcos Pérez Jiménez, 87, Venezuela Ruler." *New York Times*, September 22. http://www.nytimes.com/2001/09/22/world/marcos-perez-jimenez-87-venezuela-ruler.html.

Rosabal-Coto, Guillermo. 2010. "Music Education for Social Change in the Secondary Schools of Costa Rica." *Action, Criticism and Theory for Music Education* 9 (3): 55–81.

Rosabal-Coto, Guillermo. 2014. "'I Did It My Way!' A Case Study of Resistance to Coloniality in Music Learning and Socialization." *Action, Criticism, and Theory for Music Education* 13 (1): 155–87.

Rosabal-Coto, Guillermo. n.d. "Costa Rica." Unpublished manuscript.

Rueda, Rocío, Lina Ramírez, and Andrés Fonseca, eds. n.d. *Ciberciudadanías, Cultura Política y Creatividad Social*. http://www.mediafire.com/download/g0wctdufr-z0ufee/LibroCiberculturas+versiónfinal.pdf.

Sánchez Lansch, Enrique. 2008. *The Promise of Music*. Film.

Sanoja, Alida. 2013. "Con Pérez Pirela y Marcos Meléndez: '¡El Imperio, ¡perdón!: José Antonio Contraataca!'" *Aporrea*. January 25. http://www.aporrea.org/actuali-dad/a158184.html.

Santodomingo, Roger. 1990. "Conac: Tocata y Fuga—Abreu y Su Partida Secreta." *Viernes*, September 21.

Schippers, Huib, and Patricia Shehan Campbell. 2012. "Cultural Diversity: Beyond 'Songs from Every Land.'" In *The Oxford Handbook of Music Education*, edited by Gary E. McPherson and Graham F. Welch, 1: 87–104. New York: Oxford University Press.

Schmidt, Patrick. 2008. "Democracy and Dissensus: Constructing Conflict in Music Education." *Action, Criticism, and Theory for Music Education* 7 (1): 10–28.

Scott, James C. 1998. *Seeing Like a State: How Certain Schemes to Improve the Human Condition Have Failed*. New Haven: Yale University Press.

Scott, James C. 2012. *Two Cheers for Anarchism: Six Easy Pieces on Autonomy, Dignity, and Meaningful Work and Play*. Princeton: Princeton University Press.

Seifter, Harvey. 2001. "The Conductor-Less Orchestra." *Leader to Leader* 21: 38–44.

Sennett, Richard. 1976. *The Fall of Public Man*. London: Penguin.

Sennett, Richard. 2012. *Together: The Rituals, Pleasures and Politics of Cooperation*. London: Penguin.

Service, Tom. 2010. "El Sistema: A Big Noise about Nothing?" *The Guardian*, June 22. http://www.guardian.co.uk/music/tomserviceblog/2010/jun/22/el-sistema-big-noise-music.

Shieh, Eric. 2012. "'Our Grain of Sand': Notes on Venezuela's El Sistema." Unpublished manuscript.

Sica, Alan. 2004. *Max Weber and the New Century*. New Brunswick: Transaction Publishers.

Silva, Leonardo. 2013. "Genio al Servicio del Mal." *Informe21.com*. http://informe21.com/informe-21/genio-al-servicio-del-mal.

"Sistema Nacional de Orquestas Juveniles e Infantiles. Evaluación de Impactos." 2011. http://idbdocs.iadb.org/wsdocs/getdocument.aspx?docnum=36583351.

Skyllstad, Kjell. 2008. "Managing Conflicts Through Music: Educational Perspectives." In *Music and Conflict Transformation: Harmonies and Dissonances in Geopolitics*, edited by Olivier Urbain, 172–84. London: I. B. Tauris in association with the Toda Institute for Global Peace and Policy Research.

Small, Christopher. 1977. *Music/Society/Education*. London: John Calder.

Small, Christopher. 1998. *Musicking: The Meanings of Performing and Listening*. Middletown, CT: Wesleyan University Press.

Small, Christopher. 2011. "Prologue: Misunderstanding and Reunderstanding." In *Music and Solidarity*, edited by Felicity Laurence and Olivier Urbain, vii–xviii. New Brunswick: Transaction Publishers.

Smither, Howard E. 2000. *A History of the Oratorio, Volume 4: The Oratorio in the Nineteenth and Twentieth Centuries*. Chapel Hill: University of North Carolina Press.

Spich, Robert S., and Robert M. Sylvester. 1998. "The Jurassic Symphony: An Analytic Essay on the Prospects of Symphony Survival." *Harmony* 6: 1–27.

Spich, Robert S. 1999. "The Jurassic Symphony: Part Two—Taking on the Dinosaur: Strategic Options for Symphony Organizations." *Harmony* 8: 15–43.

Spillane, Danny. 2009. "Boys in a Small Rural School: Developing a Culture of Confidence and Success." In *Male Voices: Stories of Boys Learning Through Making Music*, edited by Scott D. Harrison, 124–34. Victoria: ACER Press.

Spitzer, John, and Neal Zaslaw. 2005. *The Birth of the Orchestra: History of an Institution, 1650–1815*. Oxford: Oxford University Press.

Stamou, L. 2002. "Plato and Aristotle on Music and Music Education: Lessons from Ancient Greece." *International Journal of Music Education* 39 (1): 3–16.

Sundaram, Ravi. 2005. "Developmentalism Redux?" In *Incommunicado Reader*, edited by Geert Lovink and Soenke Zehle, 115–21. Amsterdam: Institute of Network Cultures.

Stevens, Clare. 2012. "Beyond Sistema." *Classical Music*. July 28.

Swed, Mark. 2012. "Critic's Notebook: El Sistema for All, U.S. Kids Too." *Los Angeles Times*, February 26. http://articles.latimes.com/2012/feb/26/entertainment/la-ca-caracas-notebook-20120226.

Swed, Mark. 2014. "Furor Follows L.A. Phil's Gustavo Dudamel." *Los Angeles Times*, February 19. http://www.latimes.com/entertainment/arts/culture/la-et-cm-dudamel-venezuela-20140219-story.html#page=1.

Teachout, David J. 2012. "The Preparation of Music Teacher Educators: A Critical Link." In *The Oxford Handbook of Music Education*, edited by Gary E. McPherson and Graham F. Welch, 2: 685–88. New York: Oxford University Press.

Tindall, Blair. 2005. *Mozart in the Jungle: Sex, Drugs and Classical Music*. New York: Grove Press.

Tinker Salas, Miguel. 2009. *The Enduring Legacy: Oil, Culture, and Society in Venezuela*. Durham: Duke University Press.

Toronyi-Lalic, Igor. 2012a. "Simón Bolívar Symphony Orchestra, Dudamel, Royal Festival Hall." *The Arts Desk*. June 27. http://www.theartsdesk.com/classical-music/simón-bol%C3%ADvar-symphony-orchestra-dudamel-royal-festival-hall.

Toronyi-Lalic, Igor. 2012b. "Sceptic's Sistema." *Classical Music*, June 30.

Tourish, Dennis, and Naheed Vatcha. 2005. "Charismatic Leadership and Corporate Cultism at Enron: The Elimination of Dissent, the Promotion of Conformity and Organizational Collapse." *Leadership* 1 (4): 455–80.

Tourish, Dennis. 2011. "Leadership and Cults." In *The Sage Handbook of Leadership*, edited by Alan Bryman, David Collinson, Keith Grint, Brad Jackson, and Mary Uhl-Bien, 215–28. London: Sage Publications.

Tunstall, Tricia. 2012. *Changing Lives: Gustavo Dudamel, El Sistema, and the Transformative Power of Music*. New York: W. W. Norton.

Turino, Célio. 2011. *Punto de Cultura: El Brasil de Abajo Hacia Arriba*. Medellín: Tragaluz.

Turino, Thomas. 2008. *Music as Social Life: The Politics of Participation*. Chicago: University of Chicago Press.

Urbain, Olivier, ed. 2008. *Music and Conflict Transformation: Harmonies and Dissonances in Geopolitics*. London: I. B. Tauris in association with the Toda Institute for Global Peace and Policy Research.

Urbain, Olivier. 2011. "Inspiring Musical Movements and Global Solidarity: Playing for Change, Min-On and El Sistema." In *Music and Solidarity*, edited by Felicity Laurence and Olivier Urbain, 17–29. New Brunswick: Transaction Publishers.

Uy, Michael. 2012. "Venezuela's National Music Education Program El Sistema: Its Interactions with Society and Its Participants' Engagement in Praxis." *Music and Arts in Action* 4 (1): 5–21.

Van Orden, Kate. 2005. *Music, Discipline, and Arms in Early Modern France*. Chicago: University of Chicago Press.

Vaughan, Tanya, Jessica Harris, and Brian J. Caldwell. 2011. "Bridging the Gap in School Achievement Through the Arts." Abbotsford, Victoria: The Song Room.

Vestrini, Miyó. 1976. "Tocar y Luchar: Una Gran Consigna para Una Gran Orquesta." *El Nacional*, February 2.

Vianna, Hermano. 2011. "Technobrega, Forró, Lambadão: The Parallel Music of Brazil." In *Brazilian Popular Music and Citizenship*, edited by Idelber Avelar and Christopher Dunn, 240–49. Durham: Duke University Press.

Wagner, Robert J., and Tina Ward. 2002. "Explorations of Teamwork: The Lahti Symphony Orchestra." *Harmony* 15: 47–53.

Wakeling, Kate. 2010. "Said, Barenboim and the West-East Divan Orchestra." *Jewish Quarterly*, November. http://jewishquarterly.org/2010/11/said-barenboim-and -the-west-east-divan-orchestra/.

Wakin, Daniel J. 2012a. "Caracas Diary: Dudamel, Abreu and a Multitude of Young Musicians." *Los Angeles Times*, February 17. http://latimesblogs.latimes.com/ culturemonster/2012/02/caracas-diary-dudamel-abreu.html.

Wakin, Daniel J. 2012b. "Music Meets Chávez Politics, and Critics Frown." *New York Times*, February 17. http://www.nytimes.com/2012/02/18/arts/music/venezu- elans-criticize-hugo-chavezs-support-of-el-sistema.html.

Wakin, Daniel J. 2012c. "Venerated High Priest and Humble Servant of Music Education." *New York Times*, March 1. http://www.nytimes.com/2012/03/04/ arts/music/jose-antonio-abreu-leads-el-sistema-in-venezuela.html.

Wald, Gabriela. 2011. "Los Usos de los Programas Sociales y Culturales: El Caso de Dos Orquestas Juveniles de la Ciudad de Buenos Aires." *Questión: Revista Especializada En Periodismo y Comunicación* 1 (29): 1–13.

Ward, Colin. 2006. "Anarchy in Milton Keynes." *Libcom.org*. April 29. http://libcom. org/library/anarchy-milton-keynes-music-colin-ward.

Webb, Michael, and Frederick A. Seddon. 2012. "Musical Instrument Learning, Music Ensembles, and Musicianship in a Global and Digital Age." In *The Oxford Handbook of Music Education*, edited by Gary E. McPherson and Graham F. Welch, 1: 752–68. New York: Oxford University Press.

Weeks, Peter. 1996. "A Rehearsal of a Beethoven Passage: An Analysis of Correction Talk." *Research on Language and Social Interaction* 29 (3): 247–90.

Wilkinson, Richard, and Kate Pickett. 2010. *The Spirit Level: Why Equality Is Better for Everyone*. London: Penguin.

Wiltermuth, Scott S., and Chip Heath. 2009. "Synchrony and Cooperation." *Psychological Science* 20 (1): 1–5.

Winner, Ellen, and Monica Cooper. 2000. "Mute Those Claims: No Evidence (Yet) for a Causal Link Between Arts Study and Academic Achievement." *Journal of Aesthetic Education* 34 (3–4): 11–75.

Witkowski, Christine. 2010. "8–15 Year Olds Take on the Titan." *Key Changes*. http:// cwabreufellows.wordpress.com/2010/04/29/8-15-year-olds-takes-on-the-titan/.

Wolf, Dennie Palmer. 1999. "Why the Arts Matter in Education: Or Just What Do Children Learn When They Create an Opera." In *Champions of Change*, edited by Edward B. Fiske, 91–98. Washington, DC: Arts Education Partnership; President's Committee on the Arts and the Humanities.

Woodford, Paul G. 2005. *Democracy and Music Education: Liberalism, Ethics, and the Politics of Practice*. Bloomington: Indiana University Press.

Woodford, Paul G. 2014. "The Eclipse of the Public: A Response to David Elliott's 'Music Education as/for Artistic Citizenship.'" *Philosophy of Music Education Review* 22 (1): 22–37.

Wortman, Ana. 2012. "Tiempo Futuro, Tiempo Pasado, Tiempo Presente. Metáforas de Viejas y Nuevas Desigualdades." In *Mi Buenos Aires Querido: Entre la Democratización Cultural y la Desigualdad Educativa*, edited by Ana Wortman, 59–83. Buenos Aires: Prometeo Libros.

Wright, Ruth, ed. 2010a. *Sociology and Music Education*. Aldershot: Ashgate.

Wright, Ruth. 2010b. "Democracy, Social Exclusion and Music Education: Possibilities for Change." In *Sociology and Music Education*, edited by Ruth Wright, 263–81. Aldershot: Ashgate.

Wright, Ruth. 2014. "The Fourth Sociology and Music Education: Towards a Sociology of Integration." *Action, Criticism, and Theory for Music Education* 13 (1): 12–39.

Yerichuk, Deanna. 2014. "'Socialized Music': Historical Formations of Community Music Through Social Rationales." *Action, Criticism, and Theory for Music Education* 13 (1): 126–54.

Younker, Betty Anne, and Maud Hickey. 2007. "Examining the Profession Through the Lens of Social Justice: Two Music Educators' Stories and Their Stark Realizations." *Music Education Research* 9 (2): 215–27.

Yúdice, George. 2003. *The Expediency of Culture: Uses of Culture in the Global Era*. Durham: Duke University Press.

Zander, Benjamin, and Rosamund Stone Zander. 2000. *The Art of Possibility*. Boston: Harvard Business School Press.

INDEX

ethnographic issues and observations, 5,
    10–11, 17, 19, 199, 266
euphemisms, unpacking, 121–125
Europe
    alternative projects, 317–320
    European musicians in Venezuela, 166
    musical and educational revolutions, 244
    protest concerts, 39
    Sistema Europe, 305
    See also particular countries by name
Eurocentrism/Western cultural superiority,
    14, 29, 35, 59, 60, 62, 63, 67, 115, 118,
    150, 278–291
    developmentalism, 98–107
    Enlightenment values, 121–122, 173, 243, 289
    impact of, 278–291
    industrial-capitalist apparatus, 259–260
    pedagogy and curriculum, 135–139
    Spanish conquest, 241–242
evangelizing/proselytizing, 8, 12, 67–68, 258,
    266, 322
exaggeration in number of participants, 92–93
excellence, definition of, 128–129
exclusivity, 13, 63
    See also social inclusion
"exotic," 60, 285, 288
expansion of El Sistema
    policy of limitless expansion, 298–299
    supply and demand, 297–298
    sustainability of, 302–303
experimental music, 64, 65, 147, 315
exploration within in pedagogical practice, 125
expulsion of musicians, 182, 192–193, 219, 282
external evaluations of El Sistema, 265–268
extravagant spending, 54, 272–273, 275, 296,
    305–306

Facebook comments, 38, 54, 77, 94, 152, 192,
    273, 302
failure, idealized vision of, 243
family relationships
    domestic problems in homes of students, 154
    importance of family bonds to El Sistema,
        186–187
    intensity of program, effect on poor
        families, 307
    role in educating children, 186–187
    See also parental participation and support
fatigue of players, 55–56, 134, 136
favoritism. *See* patronage and favoritism
Fe y Alegría, 197
feminist issues. *See* gender issues
FESNOJIV. *See* Fundación del Estado para el
    Sistema Nacional de Orquestas
    Juveniles e Infantiles de Venezuela

fiddle-playing in Scotland, 131, 248, 318
Fiesta CD, 288
Fifth Republic of Venezuela, 243
    See also Chávez, Hugo
finances. *See* budgets and funding
financial pyramid scheme, 31, 44
folk music, 59, 65, 137, 277, 284, 288, 291
    See also Afro-Latin music and culture
food stamps, 119
Fordism, 236–237
foreign attempts to grasp El Sistema, 261
foreign conductors and visitors, 1–2, 4, 134,
    140, 143, 156–158, 168, 175, 212,
    235, 256, 263
foreign franchising/overseas programs, 5, 14,
    270–271, 304–308, 321–322
foreign perceptions, public relations, 8–9, 50–52
foreign tours, 59–60, 78, 121, 167, 275
    audience taste, 303
    bad behavior on, 225–226
    dishonesty about, 227
    environmental degradation, social inequality,
        and devaluation of local, 318
    grassroots alternative programs, 308–309
    the Proms, 1, 3, 9, 52, 137
"Forging the Future," 97
form *vs.* substance, 253
    See also spectacle
Foucault, Michel and Foucauldian theory, 76,
    105, 127, 179, 193–202, 208, 209,
    211, 216, 217, 233, 287
Foundation for the National System of Youth
    and Children's Orchestras. *See*
    Fundación del Estado para el Sistema
    Nacional de Orquestas Juveniles e
    Infantiles de Venezuela
"the founders," 19, 20
Fourth Republic of Venezuela, 243, 295
fragmentation within collective enterprises,
    216–218
France, 32, 165, 196, 208, 253
franchise of El Sistema, 5, 321–322
fraternalism and solidarity, 112, 124, 186,
    216–217
free concerts, 59, 121
free time, 197–198, 243
freedom, principles of, 63, 112–113, 115
    emancipatory educational programs, 311–314
    liberatory pedagogy, 125, 144–145
    oppressed becoming oppressors, 183
Fundación del Estado para el Sistema
    Nacional de Orquestas Juveniles e
    Infantiles de Venezuela
    archives, 6, 164
    El Sistema becoming FESNOJIV, 72

Los maestros de coro y de escuela de este reino, 242
mafia metaphor, 7, 90, 203
management style. *See* business model of
    El Sistema
Manchester's Hallé Orchestra, 126, 130
manipulation, 256–257
marginalization, 13
    competing understandings of social
        inclusion, 188–190
    innovation, margins as source of, 180
    See also social inclusion
mariachi musicians, 298
martial music, 196
master/apprentice model, 148
MayDay Group, 63
Medellín, 83, 309–310, 312
media, 14–19, 31–33, 45, 56, 253
    covert control of information, 28
    critical scrutiny in international media, 39
    payments to journalists, 258–259
    "unthinking whitewashing" by, 15
    See also public relations; social media
Medina, Gustavo, 33–34, 48, 71, 75, 255,
    256, 302
mediocre, definition of, 128–129
memorization of repertoire, 140
meritocracies, 203–204, 217, 220–223
methodology
    quantitative evaluations of El Sistema's
        impact, 270–271
    research methodology, 19–21, 46
Metropolitan Opera, 319
middle-class participants, 93–98, 156, 172
    "downwardly mobile middle class," 95
middle-class values. *See* social inclusion
militarism, 119, 179, 191, 193–196
    boot camp training, 134, 191, 309
    child soldiers, child labor, and child
        prodigies, 198
    dressage, 58, 194
    spectacle of, 262–263
    utopian dream, 233
"mindful music-making," 142–145
Minister for External Relations, 261
Ministry of Culture, 71, 177
Ministry of Education, 71, 147
"minoritarian" group formations, 131–132
miracle
    use of word, 89–90
    the "Venezuelan musical miracle," 8–10, 156
missionary ethos, 66–68, 180, 191, 195
mistakes
    vs. groupthink, 87
    stigmatization of, 238
model, El Sistema as, 16, 91, 106, 138, 305, 320

modernist ideology, 98–104
    See also developmentalism
molestation, 227–228
money as motivator, 176
    tocar y cobrar, 54, 58, 177
monologue *vs.* dialogue, 159
Montalbán, 1, 2, 8, 58, 84, 92–93, 137, 255
moral values
    dishonesty endemic in program, 227
    learning, 245
    learning civility and moral character,
        148–149, 245
    Platonic idea of music as moral influence, 239
    See also ethical values
moralism, 239–240
movement as component of El Sistema's
        identity, 57–58
"Movement for the Renewal of Musical
        Practice," 234
Movimiento Desarrollista, 31
multiculturism, 138, 173, 287, 313
    See also social inclusion
El Mundo, 33, 292
municipal/local music programs, 119–121,
        189–190, 296, 297, 303
Music and Solidarity, 259
music centers. *See* núcleos
Music Education Research, 148
music history and theory, 145–147, 154
music schools. *See* núcleos
Music/Society/Education, 259
music teaching program and philosophy,
        133–159
    music first, 139–141
    orchestral practice as focus, 111–132
    rehearsal schedule, 133–135
    rote learning, 133, 135, 136
    seminarios, 134, 172, 186, 191, 196, 212,
        227, 305
    set works *vs.* technical training, 139–141
    specificity and narrow range of skills,
        140–141
    See also pedagogical practice
"Música de solfa," 259
"musical conquest" of Latin America, 291
Musical Futures program, 318
musical genres other than classical, 79–80
Musical History, 239
musical instruments. *See* instruments
musical literacy, 12, 155, 284
musicianship
    defining, 148
    músicos (musicians) *vs.* *tocadores* (players),
        145–147
"musicking" *vs.* music, 174